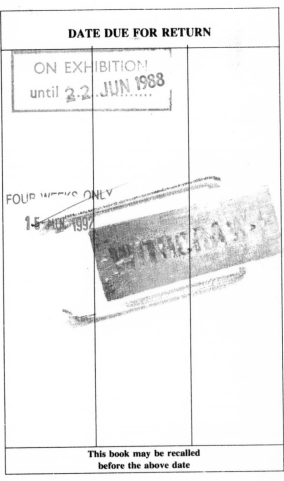

CAMBRIDGE STUDIES IN LINGUISTICS

General Editors: B.COMRIE, C.J.FILLMORE, R.LASS, R.B.LE PAGE,
J.LYONS, P.H.MATTHEWS, F.R.PALMER, R.POSNER, S.ROMAINE,
N.V.SMITH, J.L.M. TRIM, A.ZWICKY

Principles of dependency phonology

In this series

21 A. RADFORD: *Italian syntax: transformational and relational grammar*
22 DIETER WUNDERLICH: *Foundations of linguistics**
23 DAVID W. LIGHTFOOT: *Principles of diachronic syntax**
24 ANNETTE KARMILOFF-SMITH: *A functional approach to child language**
25 PER LINELL: *Psychological reality in phonology*
26 CHRISTINE TANZ: *Studies in the acquisition of deictic terms*
28 TORBEN THRANE: *Referential–semantic analysis*
29 TAMSIN DONALDSON: *Ngiyambaa*
30 KRISTJÁN ÁRNASON: *Quantity in historical phonology*
31 JOHN LAVER: *The phonetic description of voice quality*
32 PETER AUSTIN: *A grammar of Diyari, South Australia*
33 ALICE C. HARRIS: *Georgian syntax*
34 SUZANNE ROMAINE: *Socio-historical linguistics*
35 MARTIN ATKINSON: *Explanations in the study of child language development**
36 SUZANNE FLEISCHMAN: *The future in thought and language*
37 JENNY CHESHIRE: *Variation in an English dialect*
38 WILLIAM A. FOLEY and ROBERT D. VAN VALIN JR: *Functional syntax and universal grammar**
39 MICHAEL A. COVINGTON: *Syntactic theory in the High Middle Ages*
40 KENNETH J. SAFIR: *Syntactic chains*
41 J. MILLER: *Semantics and syntax*
42 H. C. BUNT: *Mass terms and model-theoretic semantics*
43 HEINZ J. GIEGERICH: *Metrical phonology and phonological structure*
44 JOHN HAIMAN: *Natural syntax*
45 BARBARA M. HORVATH: *Variation in Australian English: the sociolects of Sydney*
46 GRANT GOODALL: *Parallel structures in syntax*
47 JOHN M. ANDERSON and COLIN J. EWEN: *Principles of dependency phonology*
48 BARBARA A. FOX: *Discourse structure and anaphora*

Supplementary Volumes
BRIAN D. JOSEPH: *The synchrony and diachrony of the Balkan infinitive*
ANNETTE SCHMIDT: *Young people's Dyirbal: an example of language death from Australia*
JOHN HARRIS: *Phonological variation and change: studies in Hiberno-English*
TERENCE MCKAY: *Infinitival complements in German*
STELLA MARIS BORTONI-RICARDO: *The urbanization of rural dialect speakers*

*Issued in hard covers and as a paperback. Earlier series titles not listed may also be available.

PRINCIPLES
OF DEPENDENCY
PHONOLOGY

JOHN M. ANDERSON
University of Edinburgh

and

COLIN J. EWEN
University of Leiden

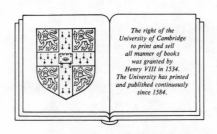

The right of the
University of Cambridge
to print and sell
all manner of books
was granted by
Henry VIII in 1534.
The University has printed
and published continuously
since 1584.

CAMBRIDGE UNIVERSITY PRESS

CAMBRIDGE   NEW YORK   NEW ROCHELLE

MELBOURNE   SYDNEY

Published by the Press Syndicate of the University of Cambridge
The Pitt Building, Trumpington Street, Cambridge CB2 1RP
32 East 57th Street, New York, NY 10022, USA
10 Stamford Road, Oakleigh, Melbourne 3166, Australia

First published 1987

Printed in Great Britain at the University Press, Cambridge

British Library cataloguing in publication data
Anderson, John M. (John Mathieson)
Principles of dependency phonology. –
(Cambridge studies in linguistics; 47)
1. Grammar, Comparative and general –
Phonology 2. Dependency grammar
I. Title   II. Ewen, Colin J.
414   P217.3

Library of Congress cataloguing in publication data
Anderson, John M. (John Mathieson), 1941–
Principles of dependency phonology.
(Cambridge studies in linguistics; 47)
Bibliography.
Includes index.
1. Grammar, Comparative and general – Phonology.
2. Dependency grammar. I. Ewen, Colin J.
II. Title. III. Series.
P217.A57   1987   414   86–24417

ISBN 0 521 32313 4

321771

EA

Contents

		page
Preface		ix
Introduction		1
PART I	PHONOLOGICAL STRUCTURE	5
1	**The structure of phonological segments**	7
1.1	Some basic assumptions	7
1.2	Non-componentiality	9
1.3	Minimal componentiality	11
1.3.1	*Binary features*	11
1.3.2	*Markedness and naturalness*	14
1.3.3	*Rule naturalness*	17
1.3.4	*Phonological scales*	19
1.4	Scalar features: an alternative minimal theory	24
1.5	Vowel components	28
1.6	Multi-gestural representations	34
1.6.1	*Arguments for greater componentiality*	37
1.6.2	*Phonetic evidence for greater componentiality*	39
2	**The structure of phonological sequences**	41
2.1	Non-constituentiality	41
2.1.1	*Introduction*	41
2.1.2	*The status of syllabicity*	42
2.1.3	*Recurrence, markedness and constituentiality*	45
2.2	The syllable as a constituent	50
2.2.1	*The syllable as a domain for sequential conditions*	50
2.2.2	*The syllable as a domain for phonological processes*	53
2.3	Syllable boundaries	58
2.3.1	*Principles of syllabification*	59
2.3.2	*Syllabification and morphology*	61
2.3.3	*Ambisyllabicity and the foot*	64
2.3.4	*Middle English Open Syllable Lengthening*	66
2.4	The basic domain of syllabification	69
2.4.1	*Words, formatives and morphemes*	69
2.4.2	*Beyond the word*	70

v

2.5	Syllabification and stress placement	72
2.5.1	*The Main Stress Rule, weak clusters and syllabification*	72
2.5.2	*Evidence for pre-stress-assignment ambisyllabicity*	75
2.6	Preliminary remarks on the foot and the tone group	78
2.7	The nature of syllabicity, stressedness and tonicity: an informal outline	80
2.7.1	*The headedness of phonological constructions*	80
2.7.2	*The binary character of phonological constructions*	82
3	**Dependency structures in phonology**	85
3.1	Dependency and syntax	85
3.1.1	*Constituency and precedence*	85
3.1.2	*The notion 'head of a construction'*	86
3.1.3	*The dependency relation*	88
3.1.4	*Dependency trees*	90
3.1.5	*VP and subjunctions*	91
3.2	The dependency structure of phonological sequences: a first approximation	96
3.2.1	*Syllabicity, stressedness and tonicity*	96
3.2.2	*Prominence, sonority and syllable structure*	97
3.2.3	*The configurational expression of phrasal categories and of relative prominence*	100
3.2.4	*Complex feet and complex rhymes*	102
3.2.5	*Layering of feet and tone groups*	103
3.3	Word structure *vs.* utterance structure	104
3.4	Remarks on the assignment of word structure	107
3.4.1	*Syllable-formation*	107
3.4.2	*Foot-formation*	110
3.4.3	*Group-formation*	116
3.4.4	*Iteration and cyclicity*	120
3.5	Word–utterance associations	122
3.6	Dependency within the segment	125
3.6.1	*Preponderance and dependency*	126
3.6.2	*Preponderance and prominence*	129
3.6.3	*Intrasegmental adjunctions: consonantal*	129
3.6.4	*Intrasegmental adjunctions: 'short' diphthongs*	134
3.7	Conclusion	136
	Overview of Part I	137
PART II	PHONOLOGICAL GESTURES AND THEIR STRUCTURE	139
	Introduction	141
II.1	Articulation *vs.* phonation	142
II.2	Phonation *vs.* initiation	145
II.3	The representation of the segment	148

4 The categorial gesture: phonation 151
4.1 The phonatory components 151
4.1.1 *Natural classes in the phonatory sub-gesture* 158
4.1.2 */r/-types* 159
4.1.3 *Lateral consonants* 162
4.1.4 *Sibilants* vs. *other fricatives* 164
4.2 Phonological complexity in the phonatory sub-gesture 166
4.3 Hierarchies in the phonatory sub-gesture 171
4.4 Lenition processes 175
4.5 Syllable structure 177
4.5.1 *Strength hierarchies and syllable structure* 177
4.5.2 *Distinctive feature hierarchies and syllable structure* 178
4.5.3 *Dependency phonology and syllable structure* 180
4.6 Neutralisation and Old English [v] 182

5 The categorial gesture: initiation 185
5.1 Glottal stricture 187
5.1.1 *The dependency representation of glottal stricture* 188
5.1.2 *Glottal stops* 190
5.2 Voiceless sonorants 191
5.3 Aspiration 193
5.4 |O|-languages 195
5.5 Airstream mechanisms 199
5.5.1 *Pulmonic airstream mechanisms* 200
5.5.2 *Glottalic airstream mechanisms* 200
5.5.3 *Velaric airstream mechanisms* 203

6 The articulatory gesture 206
6.1 Vowels: the basic vocalic components 206
6.1.1 |i| *and* |u| 212
6.1.2 |a| 214
6.1.3 *Old Norse vowel mutation* 215
6.2 Central vowels 218
6.3 Back unrounded vowels 220
6.4 Vowels: a minimal phonemic set 224
6.5 Place of articulation: feature systems 228
6.6 Gravity, linguality and apicality 233
6.6.1 *Gravity* 233
6.6.2 *Linguality* 235
6.6.3 *Apicality* 235
6.7 The dependency representation of place 236
6.7.1 *Apicals and laminals* 238
6.7.2 *Dentals and alveolars* 240
6.7.3 *Uvulars and pharyngeals* 242
6.7.4 *Laterals* 245
6.8 Secondary and double articulation 246

6.8.1   *Secondary articulation*   246
6.8.2   *Double articulation*   248
6.9   The oro-nasal sub-gesture   250

PART III   OVERVIEW   253

7   Dimensions of phonological representation   255
7.1   Intragestural relationships   255
7.2   Gestures and the segment   258
7.3   Complex segments and intrasegmental adjunction   263
7.3.1   *Complex segments*   263
7.3.2   *Long vowels and diphthongs*   266
7.4   Intergestural relationships   268
7.5   The tonological gesture   270
7.6   Associations between gestures and segments   274
7.7   Afterthoughts on lexical *vs.* utterance structure   279

8   Conclusions and consequences   281
8.1   Structural analogy   283
8.2   Realisation and neutralisation   288
8.3   Epilogue on concreteness   291

        References   297
        Index   307

Preface

Books which, like the present one, set out to provide a detailed account of a particular current approach to some general area of study, in this case phonological representation, can, in a sense, never be 'timely' overall. The framework under discussion is in a continuous state of development, both in terms of its own internal evolution as it interacts which an expanding range of phenomena for which it has to provide descriptions, and with respect to how it is defined in relation to rival and complementary approaches to what can be taken, pre-theoretically, to be the same (or a similar) domain, themselves also subject to constant revision. In addition, despite authorial attempts at consistency, the time which is required for the development of an extended presentation of this sort almost inevitably leaves marks of the work's history, in the form, for instance, of sections associated with different stages in its evolution. These remarks are not intended as any sort of *apologia* for the present work specifically; as we have indicated, it seems to us that the 'timing' problem faces any such undertaking. However, they may throw some light on the form taken by the following discussion.

In particular, we have concentrated on the explication of notions which have remained central to the framework of dependency phonology since its inception in the work of Anderson & Jones in the early 1970s, such as the single-valued feature, or component, hypothesis, and of course the relevance of the dependency relations to different domains, both segmental and suprasegmental. At the risk of replicating arguments available elsewhere, and in some cases scarcely fashionable, we have tried not to take too much for granted in our exposition of these central concepts. On the other hand, we have not attempted to provide histories of the development of particular ideas, except where this throws light on a central or currently relevant argument. The volume does offer, however, the most fully developed theory of phonological representation based on

these central properties, together with (in the final chapter) a consideration of some consequences for other aspects of phonology.

The non-linear framework of representation presented in *Sound pattern
of English* (Chomsky & Halle 1968) is taken as providing a well-defined
basis for analytic comparison with respect to the central properties of
dependency phonology. The last few years have also seen the emergence of
alternative conceptions of phonological structure which also deny the
'minimalism' of Chomsky & Halle's model. They involve proposals
concerning either segmental or suprasegmental structure or both, specifically within frameworks generally labelled 'autosegmental', 'metrical',
'particle' or 'natural'. We have attempted in the course of the book to
relate our work to these alternatives; however, such comparisons are
limited to general properties (such as the characterisation of 'prominence')
rather than the detailed analysis of particular phenomena. We are
reassured in pursuing our own work by the recognition of 'convergence'
from different theoretical standpoints on a number of structural principles
akin to those proposed in what follows (cf., for example, Anderson, Ewen
& Staun 1985; Goldsmith 1985).

Various more or less fragmentary introductions to the dependency
model have appeared elsewhere: e.g. Anderson & Jones (1974, 1977);
Anderson & Ewen (1980b); Anderson, Ewen & Staun (1985). The most
extended presentation, particularly of material relevant to Part II of this
book, is in Ewen's thesis (1980a). A range of work of this period, by the
present authors and others, appears in the Ludwigsburg collection
(Anderson & Ewen 1980a). More recent contributions to dependency and
related theories are collected in Durand (1986a).

The evolution of this book over the last few years has benefited from the
reactions of a range of people to preliminary versions of parts of it, as well
as to other writings on and oral presentations of aspects of dependency
phonology. We should particularly like to mention Henning Andersen,
Fran Colman, Mike Davenport, Ailie Donald, Jacques Durand, Heinz
Giegerich, Inger Henriksen, Harry van der Hulst, Charles Jones, Ken
Lodge, Cathair Ó Dochartaigh, Jørgen Staun, Menekse Suphi, Martine
Veenhof, Nigel Vincent, and an anonymous Cambridge University Press
reviewer. Frits Beukema, Roger Lass and Martina Noteboom deserve
especial thanks for reading and commenting on the entire manuscript.
Finally, thanks to Penny Carter for patiently and good-humouredly
steering this work through its final stages.

Introduction

In the pages that follow we set out some of the motivations for a view of phonological structure which is in certain respects somewhat novel, particularly in the context of major theoretical developments in the last two decades. Specifically, we shall outline a conception of phonological representation which involves an enrichment of, and a greater variety in, the structural relations that can hold between the atoms of a phonological structure. This enrichment, we shall argue, will enable us both to delimit more narrowly the class of possible phonological regularities and to characterise the relative 'markedness' (or potentiality for recurrence) of such regularities.

Our major concern, therefore, will be to pursue the consequences for phonological notation of the observed recurrence of certain groupings of elements and of certain relationships or rules in the phonologies of different languages – on the assumption that the existence of just such recurrences should be predictable from the character of the notation. These recurrences and the characterising notation are assumed to have a natural – i.e. phonetic – basis; thus, as well as optimising the expression of recurrent regularities, the structures allowed for by the phonological notation should, at the very least, not be incompatible with what can be established concerning the nature of the speaker/hearer's production and perception. We hope that, as our understanding sharpens, the relationship between notation and production/perception will be made more determinate. At present we lack both adequate knowledge of the range of recurrent phonological regularities and sufficient criteria for selecting between competing phonetic frameworks. The elaboration of a well-defined phonological notation should stimulate progress in both these areas, and their eventual reconciliation.

It is our contention (following particularly Anderson & Jones 1974a, 1977) that conceptions of phonological structure which were prevalent until recently, e.g. those adopted by most varieties of 'generative

1

phonology', fail to incorporate structural properties crucial to the explication of a wide range of phonological phenomena. These deficiencies involve both the internal structure of segments and sequential structure, i.e. the relations holding between segments in sequence. In Part I of this book (chapters 1–3) we attempt to establish that this is indeed so, and we delineate a phonological notation which possesses the appropriate structural properties. The precise character of these representations, in particular those characterising the internal structure of segments, will be investigated in greater detail in Part II (chapters 4–6). In Part III (chapters 7–8) we explore some further consequences of the model developed in Parts I and II.

There is nowadays a widespread recognition of the need to introduce into phonological representation units larger than the segment, such as the syllable, foot, etc. There is an almost equally great diversity of views on how to represent these notions (e.g. Fudge 1969; Hooper 1972; Fujimura 1975; Kahn 1976), although two (partly related) systems of notation have become particularly influential in the last few years: those of METRICAL PHONOLOGY (e.g. Liberman & Prince 1977; Kiparsky 1981; Prince 1983; Hayes 1984; Giegerich 1985), and AUTOSEGMENTAL PHONOLOGY (Goldsmith 1976, 1979, 1985; Clements & Keyser 1983; Clements 1985) (for an outline of the two approaches see van der Hulst & Smith 1982b). In chapter 2 we offer our own conception of sequential structure, in the light of some of the available evidence. In chapter 3 we suggest a characterisation of the properties of phonological sequences in terms of dependency stemmata (formal objects perhaps more familiar from syntactic studies), and propose that this characterisation is more adequate than that embodied in metrical trees. There, too, we argue further that the notion of dependency is also crucial to the characterisation of the internal structure of segments (given the properties of segments that are observed in chapter 1); hence the title of this book.

However, the relationship between sequential and segmental structure is not limited to formal similarity. Rather, we suggest, there are intimate connections between the detailed properties of the internal structure of segments and their potential for occurrence in sequence. Part II explores in more detail not only the characteristics of segment structure but also their consequences for the formulation of sequential regularities. The two 'enrichments' of phonological structure are, then, not unrelated. Sequential representation is a projection of the internal properties of the segments comprising the relevant sequence and the morpho-syntactic structure associated with it.

Rather than anticipate too much, however, let us focus in chapter 1 on the nature of the evidence for the internal structure of segments and the view of that structure which the evidence leads to, and, first of all, on the nature of what we hope are relatively uncontroversial assumptions – which, we claim, give our observations the status of evidence.

PART I

PHONOLOGICAL STRUCTURE

1   *The structure of phonological segments*

1.1   Some basic assumptions

In this chapter we consider the nature of the segments whose distribution is
the concern of phonological description. In particular, in common with
most phonologists, we shall look at the groupings or classes of segments
which must be invoked in the formulation of generalisations concerning
their distribution and behaviour. In the course of this we shall explore the
consequences of certain assumptions that are generally agreed on, but not,
we think, fully exploited: that is, our proposals concerning phonological
structure do not involve a reinterpretation of the domain of phonology.
Phenomena and assumptions which have been the central concern of
phonologists form the basis for the arguments which follow.

Let us illustrate these assumptions with a simple example from Old
English. The distribution of the vowels in the first of the two syllables in
the forms in (1.1) (here given in the traditional orthography) is rather
typical of Old English; ⟨æ⟩ is generally considered to represent a low front
vowel, and ⟨a⟩ the corresponding back vowel:

(1.1)   dæg   'day'   (nom./acc. sg.)   dagas   (nom./acc. pl.)
         dæges   (gen. sg.)   daga   (gen. pl.)
         dæge   (dat. sg.)   dagum   (dat. pl.)

We are not concerned here with the morphological correlations (singular
vs. plural), but rather with the relation of the vowel in the first syllable
with that in the following syllable, which is not limited to paradigms of
this type. For example, a word like that in (1.2):

(1.2)   fæder   'father'   (nom./acc./gen./dat. sg.)
         fæderas   (nom./acc. pl.)

has a single vowel throughout the paradigm, i.e. ⟨æ⟩, rather than ⟨æ⟩ *and*
⟨a⟩, correlating with the universal presence of a following ⟨e⟩, intervening before the inflectional vowel, if present.

Phonologists describing such situations generally make a two-part assumption, which (following Anderson 1980a) we shall label the NATURAL RECURRENCE ASSUMPTION, expressed informally as (1.3):

(1.3)   *Natural recurrence assumption*
      a. Classes of phonological segments are not random.
      b. Phonological classes and the regularities into which they enter have a phonetic basis.

In the present case, it will be observed that the vowels before which the ⟨a⟩-vowel appears belong to a class which is invoked by other rules in Old English and elsewhere – i.e. it is recurrent – and which can be labelled with the phonetically interpretable cover term 'back' – i.e. it is natural. Furthermore, the ⟨a⟩-vowel involved in the paradigmatic alternation of (1.1) itself belongs to this class: there is a natural relation between it and the class which determines its occurrence rather than that of ⟨æ⟩. Most phonologists adopt (1.3) as a unit; but it is appropriate to separate it into two sub-parts, the second of which presupposes the first, but is not presupposed by it, and, indeed, is not adopted by all (cf. Foley 1977, for example).

Most phonologists make a further assumption, that phonological regularities and the groupings established on this basis correlate with the 'content' of phonological segments. Segments belonging to a particular grouping share some component property, and it is these properties which can be associated with phonetically definable parameters. This assumption is crucial to the notion of FEATURE in standard generative phonologies and their antecedents, and to the associated proposal of a simplicity metric based on feature-counting, such that NATURAL CLASSES, i.e. groupings based on feature-sharing, can be formally more simply specified than individual segments or groupings of segments of disparate feature composition. The vowels which in (1.1) and (1.2) condition the appearance of ⟨a⟩ rather than ⟨æ⟩ share a property or property-value [n back], in these terms. A rule invoking such a grouping is in this respect easier to formulate than one involving a grouping of, say, /i/, /p/ and /h/, which cannot be distinctively characterised by a particular feature-value or by a (non-disjunctive) set of values.

This view of segment composition can be said to embody the COMPONENTIALITY ASSUMPTION, which may be formulated as (1.4):

(1.4)   *Componentiality assumption*
      The representation of the internal structure of segments optimises the expression of phonological relationships ('classes', 'regularities') that are (a) recurrent and (b) natural.

This requires that a theory of segment structure should permit recurrent regularities to be expressed more simply than non-natural, irregular and sporadic groupings and relationships, i.e. ones which do not show natural recurrence. Given this assumption, we can evaluate theories of segment structure with respect to two kinds of evidence: first, on the basis of their degree of correlation with independently established phonetic parameters, and second, in terms of their adequacy for expressing recurrent relationships.

In what immediately follows we examine the adequacy of some theories of segment structure with reference to the second kind of evidence. However, as far as we are aware, 'phonetic' evidence would not lead us to conclusions contrary to those we shall arrive at on phonological grounds concerning the relative appropriateness of the various theories of the segment which we shall consider. We return below to the relationship between the two kinds of evidence (e.g. §1.6.2).

In the following discussion we shall be looking at various putative phonological 'processes', or, more precisely (and less tendentiously), 'substitution relationships' – since only in diachronic terms are we necessarily dealing with genuine 'processes' (see Lass 1984a:ch. 8). It is not germane to our purpose to establish the precise status of these relationships with respect to particular phonologies: for example, whether, in relation to the phonology of a particular dialect, we have to do with a phonological or phonetic rule, a lexical or postlexical rule, or whatever. Rather, we are simply concerned with the phonological content of recurrent processes (in this loose sense) and the evidence this provides for the character of the internal structure of segments, given the componentiality assumption.

1.2   Non-componentiality

The null hypothesis concerning the internal structure of segments would consist in a denial of (1.4); i.e. phonologically, segments have no internal structure – segment labels are atomic. Let us refer to this as a NON-COMPONENTIAL THEORY. Some of the descriptions offered by American phonemicists come close to adopting such a position.

In Hockett's 'Peiping morphophonemics' (1950), for example, segment alternations are expressed in terms of atomic segment labels. It is only in determining the distinctive *phonetic* properties of individual phonemes, as in his 'Peiping phonology' (1947), that the content of segments is considered. Even then, the distinctive (or, in Hockett's terms, 'determining') features are simply listed and exemplified: the phoneme /p/, for example, is represented as (1.5):

(1.5) $/p/ = \dfrac{p}{S}$

i.e. it is defined as a simultaneous bundle of the two features 'bilabial position' (p) and 'unaspirated complete closure without nasalisation' (S) (1947:§7). The occurrence of non-distinctive (i.e. 'determined') features is also described (§9): only here is the internal structure of segments relevant to the expression of some regularity, such as the distribution of voice in syllables. But even this is not provided for by Bloomfield (1926:§16), for whom a phoneme is a 'minimum same of vocal feature', so that no proposal beyond this concerning internal structure is appropriate at all. Later descriptions in this tradition, such as Hockett's, do introduce some suggestions concerning componentiality; but even then the choice of features is language-specific, and there is no attempt to state the conditions governing feature combination (whether some are mutually exclusive, etc.). Thus the fact that componentiality is little invoked in the expression of phonological regularities is reflected in the absence of any explicit statement of principles specifying the composition of segments.

The Jakobsonian framework, whose notion of segment structure is generally adopted by generative phonology, is in marked contrast on both these counts. In the first place, a segment is comprised of a set of universally given properties or features, together with a specification of the value that each segment has with respect to that feature, where the number of values (as far as phonological regularities are concerned) is limited to two. On the second count, as we have already indicated, and as is again very familiar, the notions of feature and feature-value, and the natural classes they define, are crucial in this kind of phonological framework to the formulation and evaluation of phonological regularities, while the componentiality assumption is basic to the motivation of the individual features. These, and the assumption of componentiality, are supported to the extent that the Old English example which we started out with is typical, i.e. to the extent that recurrent regularities are indeed optimally expressible by the notation, and sporadic or non-occurring relationships are difficult (or 'expensive') to express.

We note in passing that Trubetzkoy (1969) in one respect occupies an intermediate position here, in that he systematically invokes components, which are, however, not universal. On the other hand, Trubetzkoy's conception of the internal structure of segments is rather richer than Jakobson & Halle's (1956), as we shall see below.

1.3   Minimal componentiality

1.3.1   Binary features

Let us now look in some detail at the adequacy of binary feature proposals for segmental structure, particularly those of Chomsky & Halle (1968; henceforth *SPE*). In such a framework, recurrence of a grouping of segments is to be expected to the extent to which the grouping can be specified by a non-disjunctive set of feature-values. The appropriateness of many of the groupings predicted as recurrent by the feature-assignments of *SPE* is not in doubt. However, there are some character-istic failures to separate the recurrent from the non-recurrent – failures which result from the particular claims being made concerning the nature of segment structure. For although the internal structure of a segment is indeed conceived of in this framework as being crucial to an explanation of its phonological behaviour, the degree of structural complexity invoked is minimal: a segment is an unordered set of features (or at least a set whose ordering plays no systematic role in the phonology), each feature having one of two values. Phonologically, the *SPE* framework is MINIMALLY COMPONENTIAL: internal structure is minimal, and the only structural variable is the value of the individual features. Though certain features may informally be thought of as more 'basic', hierarchisation of the features is not structurally relevant, nor (despite informal labels like 'major class features') are specific sub-groupings of features; the features themselves (except for the accentual) are atomic and uniform, in that they are all binary, for example. We turn now to examples that illustrate a need for two different kinds of increase in the complexity which should be attributed to the internal structure of segments.

In the first place, and perhaps less drastically, there are phonological relationships which invoke certain subsets of features in a very specific way, where once more the subsets are recurrent, and therefore, on the componentiality assumption, should be reflected as distinctive in our representation.

Lass (1976:§6.4), for instance, discusses the very common cross-linguistic phenomenon of homorganic assimilation of nasals to a following consonant. In terms of the minimally componential theory embodied in the *SPE* framework, such processes or relationships require for their expression something like (1.6), at least:

(1.6)
$$\begin{bmatrix} C \\ +\text{nasal} \end{bmatrix} \rightarrow \begin{bmatrix} \alpha\text{anterior} \\ \beta\text{coronal} \end{bmatrix} \;/\!\!-\; \begin{bmatrix} C \\ \alpha\text{anterior} \\ \beta\text{coronal} \end{bmatrix}$$

How adequate or complete this is will depend on whether the agreement of other feature-values is guaranteed by other rules (and on the number of distinctive places of articulation for postnasal consonants in the language in question). Some uncertainty over this is revealed by formulations such as that of Hooper (1976:194):

(1.7)
$$\begin{bmatrix} C \\ +\text{nasal} \end{bmatrix} \rightarrow \begin{bmatrix} \alpha\text{anterior} \\ \beta\text{coronal} \\ \vdots \end{bmatrix} \;/\!\!-\; \begin{bmatrix} C \\ \alpha\text{anterior} \\ \beta\text{coronal} \\ \vdots \end{bmatrix}$$

Such formulations are in one significant respect less adequate than traditional descriptions: they completely fail to capture the fact that what is involved in homorganicity is just the set of features that in articulatory terms specifies the place of the supralaryngeal stricture, and that what is crucial is agreement between *these as a whole* (rather than, say, some other fortuitous subset of features). Both Jakobson and Chomsky & Halle group their features into subsets, Jakobson on the basis of well-defined acoustic criteria. But these sub-groupings have no formal status, nor do they play a role in the formulation of phonological regularities. What homorganic assimilation involves is apparently the set of resonance features, in Jakobson's terminology, or the set of stricture and cavity features of *SPE*. The recurrence of phenomena such as nasal assimilation suggests that the relevant partitioning should be formally represented in phonological structure. Indeed, formulations like (1.6) and (1.7) clearly fail to satisfy the componentiality assumption.

It is in fact simpler to formulate, instead of (1.6), a rule in which, say, only two of the features assimilate, as in (1.8):

(1.8)
$$\begin{bmatrix} C \\ +\text{nasal} \end{bmatrix} \rightarrow \begin{bmatrix} \alpha\text{anterior} \\ \beta\text{high} \end{bmatrix} \;/\!\!-\; \begin{bmatrix} C \\ \alpha\text{anterior} \\ \beta\text{high} \end{bmatrix}$$

and equally simple to formulate agreement between the members of any arbitrary set of features, or indeed between different features in a set:

(1.9)

$$\begin{bmatrix} C \\ +\text{nasal} \end{bmatrix} \rightarrow \begin{bmatrix} \alpha\text{anterior} \\ \beta\text{coronal} \\ \gamma\text{low} \\ \delta\text{back} \end{bmatrix} / - \begin{bmatrix} C \\ \delta\text{anterior} \\ \alpha\text{coronal} \\ \beta\text{low} \\ \gamma\text{back} \end{bmatrix}$$

Notice that we cannot simply exclude the Greek letter variable convention from pairing instances of different distinctive features as in (1.9). In a componentially minimal phonology this convention is required for the expression of regularities such as that in (1.10):

(1.10)

$$\begin{bmatrix} V \\ -\text{low} \\ \alpha\text{back} \end{bmatrix} \rightarrow [\alpha\text{round}]$$

which, in pairing a non-low vowel's roundness and backness values, is appropriate as a redundancy condition applicable to many vowel systems, in allowing only /ieuo/ as non-low vowels.

If the processes represented by (1.8) and (1.9) are less natural and recurrent than that in (1.6), then the characterisation in (1.6) leaves this quite unexplained: the notation does not optimise the expression of the recurrent. A system is required in which appeal can be made directly to recurrent sub-groupings of this sort: we return to this in §1.6.

Before moving on to consider some phenomena whose description requires more drastic revision of our notion of phonological structure, including the character of the atomic primes themselves, let us note a further respect in which there is evidence that relations between the features of the minimal theory have to be enriched. S. R. Anderson (1976), for example, argues for the presence of sequential relations within the segment, so that, for instance, a prenasalised stop is characterised phonologically as showing a nasal initiation or onset only. We return in §§3.6.3 and 7.3 to a consideration of the nature of this evidence and to proposals, within the framework to be elaborated here, for the characterisation of 'segment-internal' sequence.

We will refer to a conception of phonological structure which differs from the minimally componential theory only in such ways as we have just considered (i.e. by making appeal to sub-groupings – see §1.6 – and incorporating some internal sequence) as an ENRICHED (minimal) theory. Such enrichments leave the atoms untouched: they are now simply grouped together and occasionally sequenced; otherwise, their intrinsic character and internal relationships remain the same.

1.3.2   Markedness and naturalness

In the last chapter of *SPE* Chomsky & Halle observe one set of problems associated with their phonetic framework, in particular some failures to predict natural classes and natural processes correctly, i.e. failures with respect to the componentiality assumption. For instance, the condition we formulated as (1.10) is no simpler than (1.11):

(1.11) $\begin{bmatrix} V \\ -\text{high} \\ \alpha\text{low} \end{bmatrix} \rightarrow [\alpha\text{round}]$

which requires agreement between the values for lowness and roundness among non-high vowels. In other words, the class /eʌæɔ/ is no more difficult to specify than the class /ieuo/. Yet, while (1.10), which specifies the latter class, seems to have a good chance of being true of a number of vowel systems (see Crothers 1978:139), unlike (1.11), and unlike a rule requiring the complementary class to either (1.10) or (1.11) (i.e. with '−α' to the right of the arrow), these classes do not require representations which differ significantly in cost.

Further, the minimally componential theory fails to discriminate between recurrent and non-recurrent processes. Chomsky & Halle point out that of the two processes involved in (1.12):

(1.12)   a. i → u   b. i → ɯ

(1.12a) requires for its expression more features than (1.12b), although, in their view, (a) is more to be expected as a phonological process. In both respects, then – in the expression of recurrent processes and of recurrent classes – the minimally componential theory is, as argued by Chomsky & Halle themselves, clearly inadequate; and the enrichments of the structure we discussed in §1.3.1 offer no help in resolving these particular problems.

As is familiar, Chomsky & Halle offer a single solution to (at least some instances of) both types of problem, involving the introduction of specifications for MARKEDNESS alongside '+' and '−' as values for features. The features in lexical entries may have as values any one of '*u*' or '*m*' or '+' or '−', of which only '*u*' is cost-free: all the others count towards the complexity of individual entries. Each '*u*' and '*m*' in an individual entry is associated with a ' + ' or a ' − ' by a set of 'marking conventions', such as that in (1.13), which applies to vowels:

(1.13)
$$[u \text{ round}] \rightarrow [\alpha\text{round}]/ \begin{bmatrix} \alpha \overline{\text{ back}} \\ -\text{low} \end{bmatrix}$$

The application of the marking convention here substitutes for [u round] in any lexical entry the specification [− round] if the segment, apart from being [− low], is also [− back], and [+ round] if it is already [+ back]. It is also to be interpreted as substituting for [m round] the reverse values in the same environments. This means that /i e u o/ are all [u round], while /y ø ɯ ʌ/ are [m round]. An underlying [− low] vowel system comprising only the former set, then, will be evaluated as simpler than one containing the latter vowels: the lexical entries will in this respect cost less. The recurrence of such systems, and of the redundancy condition (1.10) that characterises them, is accounted for by the marking convention (1.13) – and the redundancy condition itself can be eliminated from particular phonologies.

Chomsky & Halle also attempt to allow for some of the recurrent *processes* which the minimal theory fails to predict in terms of a principle whereby the marking conventions are LINKED to the output of phonological rules. If, say, a rule assigns to a segment a certain value for a feature F_i, then the value for each of the other features $F_j \ldots F_n$ in the output segment which is dependent on F_i for its markedness specification is the unmarked value for $F_j \ldots F_n$ in that particular environment. Consider again (1.12a), which can be characterised as (1.14):

(1.14)
$$\begin{bmatrix} V \\ +\text{high} \end{bmatrix} \rightarrow [+\text{back}]$$

where the output segment is automatically [+ round] by virtue of being linked to marking convention (1.13), which states that the unmarked value for a high back vowel is [+ round]. (1.12b), on the other hand, requires that we formulate a rule in such a way as to suppress the link to the marking conventions, as in (1.15):

(1.15)
$$\begin{bmatrix} V \\ +\text{high} \\ \alpha\text{round} \end{bmatrix} \rightarrow \begin{bmatrix} +\text{back} \\ \alpha\text{round} \end{bmatrix}$$

which keeps the roundness value constant, but which is thereby necessarily more complex than (1.14) and is thus predicted to be less likely to occur. If Chomsky & Halle's claim concerning the relative recurrence of the processes in (1.12) is correct, then linking the marking conventions to phonological rules permits us in this case to optimise the expression of the recurrent.

Similarly, in the *SPE* account of the English Vowel Shift, the stressed vowel in *profound* originates as a high back rounded vowel, and shifts to a low back unrounded one. It is, however, unnecessary to specify the change in roundness, either in the Vowel Shift rule itself, or as a separate rule, in that the unmarked value for low vowels is [−round], as specified by the marking convention in (1.16):

(1.16)
$$[u \text{ round}] \rightarrow [-\text{round}]/ \begin{bmatrix} \overline{} \\ +\text{low} \end{bmatrix}$$

The actual shift (1.17a) requires a less complex formulation than one such as (1.17b):

(1.17)   a. ū → ā   b. ū → ɔ̄

(where, in the notation of *SPE*, [ɑ] and [ɔ] are both low and back, and differ only in roundness). The linking convention assigns optimality to this aspect of the Vowel Shift formulation.

Let us refer to a minimally componential theory which has grafted on to it the marking and linking conventions, together with an extension of the values for features to include '*u*' and '*m*', as an ELABORATED MINIMALLY COMPONENTIAL THEORY. Chomsky & Halle claim that this elaboration allows them to provide an account of the 'intrinsic content' of features. It is, however, difficult to see what they mean by this. As Lass (1975) notes, they have not provided an account of the composition of features or of anything else that could reasonably be described as intrinsic. Rather, they have devised a system for relabelling and, on the basis of this, costing feature-values in such a way that phonological representation ceases in various cases to be at odds with the simplicity metric, i.e. the componentiality assumption. But the relabellings are carried out specifically to conform with the recurrences they are intended to explain; they have no independent motivation. The markedness apparatus does not represent any increased insight into the nature of phonological structure, but is added on ad hoc to a conception of phonological structure based on binary features; its role is simply to repair flaws in this conception. (For a discussion of this circularity see particularly Lass 1980:ch. 2.) We lack any independent motivation for the accretions provided by the elaborated theory.

1.3.3 Rule naturalness

The emptiness of markedness theory has been discussed in some detail elsewhere (e.g. Botha 1971; Lass 1975; Lass & Anderson 1975: app. IV); and we shall not pursue this, although we return below to the relationship between the observational basis of markedness-assignment and the intrinsic content of phonological structures. But, in view of the failure of, for example, Cairns & Feinstein (1982) to recognise this point, it is perhaps worth stressing the vacuousness of any 'theory of markedness'. Chomsky & Halle provide not a theory, but a set of labels ('*u*', '*m*'), which remain uninterpreted. If '*u*' and '*m*' are to be regarded as primitives, then they add nothing in degree of generality or explanatory abstractness to the observations on which such labellings are based; they label recurrences that need to be accounted for by phonological theory. If they are not primitives, what is their place in a 'theory of markedness'? What is the natural basis for these recurrences?

Even a demonstration that markedness appears to be relevant to distinct domains (such as syllable structure – Cairns & Feinstein 1982; Anderson 1984b) merely underlines the need for a 'theory' which relates markedness to an explanatory account of this and other aspects of phonological structure. Chomsky & Halle's 'theory of markedness' in fact makes this more difficult by substituting uninterpreted labels for any attempt to arrive at an appropriate account of phonological structure.

Moreover, it is not at all clear that markedness is indeed directly relevant even to the two domains envisaged by Chomsky & Halle. In particular, given the dual role of markedness theory in optimising the expression both of recurrent classes and of recurrent processes, there is a contradiction between these two aims. Naturalness of process (as opposed to naturalness of domain), in terms of the proposals made in *SPE*, correlates with the naturalness (unmarkedness) of the output of the process. But this leads to wrong predictions in many cases, just one of which we consider here.

Part of Old English *i*-umlaut involves the shift in (1.18):

(1.18) $u \rightarrow y / - C_0 i$

whose application is illustrated by the alternation in (1.19):

(1.19) a. burg 'town' (nom. sg.) – no *i*-umlaut
       b. byrig (dat. sg.) – *i*-umlaut

This shift is rated, by linking to the marking conventions, as less natural than either of those in (1.20):

(1.20)   a. i → u   b. u → i

In order to give [y] as the output of this sub-part of *i*-umlaut we must incorporate additional feature specifications to ensure that roundness is retained, as in (1.21):

$$(1.21) \qquad \begin{bmatrix} V \\ +high \\ \alpha round \end{bmatrix} \rightarrow \begin{bmatrix} -back \\ \alpha round \end{bmatrix} \Big/ \!-\! C_0 \begin{bmatrix} +high \\ -back \end{bmatrix}$$

(1.20b), on the other hand, given the linking conventions, requires only (1.22):

$$(1.22) \qquad \begin{bmatrix} V \\ +high \end{bmatrix} \rightarrow [-back] \Big/ \!-\! C_0 \begin{bmatrix} +high \\ -back \end{bmatrix}$$

(assuming the same environment), in that an output high non-back vowel will be [−round] by virtue of marking convention (1.16).

There is, however, no reason to believe that the shift expressed as (1.22) is more natural than (1.18). In retaining its rounding, the back vowel fronted in *i*-umlaut is, as far as we are aware, not untypical: this retention is also found, for example, in the context-free frontings of [u] in Albanian, French, Scots, etc. If this is so, then it illustrates rather sharply that the naturalness of a rule cannot be equated with the markedness of its output. Notice, though, that it may be that *i*-umlaut should not be linked to the marking conventions, given the formal principle formulated by Chomsky & Halle (*SPE*: 431) as: 'a linking rule applies either to all or to none of the segments formed by a given rule'. *i*-umlaut forms low as well as non-low front vowels, as in *færð* (3rd pres. sg. indic. of *faran* 'go'). (1.16) (= *SPE*: XIb) applies only to non-low vowels (though XI as a whole applies to both). But (1.18) and (1.20) are then rated as equally natural, which is still inappropriate. In either case we need a characterisation of the internal structure of segments that enables us to separate the expression of markedness of input and output from that of naturalness of process.

Schachter (1969) comes to a rather similar conclusion on the basis of the asymmetry of recurrent processes, such that, for instance, while palatalisation of velar consonants before front vowels is a frequent phenomenon, retraction of palatals before back vowels is not. The processes, however, are equally simply characterised in terms of the minimally componential

theory, even if elaborated with respect to marking conventions. Compare
(1.23) with (1.24):

(1.23) $\begin{bmatrix} C \\ +\text{back} \end{bmatrix} \rightarrow [-\text{back}]/- \begin{bmatrix} V \\ -\text{back} \end{bmatrix}$

(1.24) $\begin{bmatrix} C \\ -\text{back} \end{bmatrix} \rightarrow [+\text{back}]/- \begin{bmatrix} V \\ +\text{back} \end{bmatrix}$

To allow for this asymmetry, Schachter proposes the introduction of yet
another value for features – '*n*' (for natural) – which is utilised in a
phonological rule when the value for a particular output feature is the
expected one in such an environment, and which counts for nothing in
costing the rule. This allows us to substitute for (1.23) the formulation in
(1.25):

(1.25) $\begin{bmatrix} C \\ +\text{back} \end{bmatrix} \rightarrow [n\ \text{back}]/- \begin{bmatrix} V \\ -\text{back} \end{bmatrix}$

while (1.24) remains unchanged, and as such is now more complex than
(1.25) (by one feature-value). [*n* back], of course, will require to be
interpreted by one of a new set of NATURALNESS CONVENTIONS, which will
tell us in the present case that the natural value for [back] for a consonant
followed by a [−back] vowel is [−back].

However, this SUPER-ELABORATED MINIMALLY COMPONENTIAL THEORY is
even more patently a case of labelling masquerading as explanation. The
naturalness of a rule in these terms does not relate to any independently
motivated aspect of the structure of the segments concerned: the label '*n*',
like '*u*' and '*m*', is uninterpretable with respect to any independent
empirical domain. We have simply devised an ad hoc label for recurrent
rules. Another piece of apparatus has been introduced to undo some of
the problems created by the adoption of a minimalist feature framework;
but this piece of apparatus, and markedness theory itself, are necessary
only if the atoms of phonological representation are related to each other in
the simple, undifferentiated manner inherent in the minimally componential theory. If we abandon the minimalist assumption, on quite different
grounds, the need for marking conventions and the like is much less
obvious, to put it no more strongly. Let us now look at one of these other
grounds.

1.3.4 Phonological scales

Jakobson observed the existence of various scalar relations between
individual features which are not, as such, captured by binary feature

theory. Indeed, Jakobson & Halle (1956) claim that all the inherent features rest upon two axes, the 'sonority axis' and the 'tonality axis'. For instance, a tense (true) plosive is one step away from the optimal lax stop defining one end of the sonority scale, and one step closer to the optimal lax vowel defining the other end. Problems arise in attempting to characterise processes or classes which involve these scalar relationships in terms of binary feature relationships. One such 'process' is the English Vowel Shift.

Chomsky & Halle's formulation of the central part of the Vowel Shift is reproduced as (1.26):

$$(1.26) \quad \begin{bmatrix} V \\ \gamma back \\ \gamma round \\ +tense \\ +stress \end{bmatrix} \rightarrow \begin{cases} [-\alpha high] / \begin{bmatrix} \overline{\quad} \\ \alpha high \\ -low \end{bmatrix} & a. \\ \\ [-\beta low] / \begin{bmatrix} \overline{\quad} \\ \beta low \\ -high \end{bmatrix} & b. \end{cases}$$

The two parts of (1.26) are conjunctively ordered; so that whereas the derivation of the second vowel in *obscene* involves only Vowel Shift (a) ($\bar{e} \rightarrow \bar{\imath}$) and that in *profane* only (b) ($\bar{æ} \rightarrow \bar{e}$), that of *deprive* includes first (a), then (b) ($\bar{\imath} \rightarrow \bar{e}$, $\bar{e} \rightarrow \bar{æ}$).

The Vowel Shift, in invoking in part the dimension of vowel height, is not an isolated phenomenon; our characterisation of the structure of segments should enable us to express this by rendering its formulation simpler than non-occurrent processes involving a similar set of vowels. This the notation in (1.26) fails to do.

Notice in the first place that (1.26) requires the deployment of braces. The brace notation is a very poorly supported abbreviatory device (for discussion, see Anderson 1977b); it does not adequately separate recurrent schemata from the adventitious. Indeed, where a genuine generalisation is involved, the use of braces in its formulation is simply an admission that there has been a failure to arrive at an adequate characterisation: we put inside the braces the aspect of the process we have failed to find the common factor in. The non-unitary formulation in (1.26) is thus not an adequate account.

In the present instance this evaluation is confirmed by the fact that (1.26) is no simpler a formulation than (1.27):

(1.27)

$$
\begin{bmatrix} V \\ \gamma high \\ \gamma round \\ +tense \\ +stress \end{bmatrix} \rightarrow \left\{ \begin{array}{ll} [-\alpha back] / \begin{bmatrix} \overline{} \\ \alpha back \\ -low \end{bmatrix} & \text{a.} \\ \\ [-\beta low] / \begin{bmatrix} \overline{} \\ \beta low \\ -back \end{bmatrix} & \text{b.} \end{array} \right\}
$$

which would involve bizarre shifts – e.g. assuming an initial /ī ē æ ū ō ā ɔ/ system and a link to the marking conventions: ū → ē, ē → ō, ē → æ, æ → ē. Indeed, there is no reason to prefer (1.26) over a rule such as (1.28):

(1.28)

$$
\begin{bmatrix} V \\ \gamma tense \\ \gamma stress \end{bmatrix} \rightarrow \left\{ \begin{array}{ll} [-\alpha high] / \begin{bmatrix} \overline{} \\ \alpha round \end{bmatrix} & \text{a.} \\ \\ [-\beta low] / \begin{bmatrix} \overline{} \\ \beta back \end{bmatrix} & \text{b.} \end{array} \right\}
$$

(1.28) highlights the extent to which the parallelism between the two sub-parts of (1.26) remains uncaptured, and apparently accidental in that formulation: (1.26) looks more symmetrical on the page, but the evaluation metric doesn't reckon with the shape and balance of rules. (1.27), on the other hand, reveals that the degree of parallelism does not give a recurrent process with all pairs of features. Part of the reason that (1.26) corresponds to a recurrent, natural process is that [high] and [low] belong to a single phonetic dimension or axis, whereas [back] and [low] do not; the latter are 'orthogonal' (Saltarelli 1973). However, the notion of features belonging to the same dimension is not expressible in the minimally componential theory of *SPE*, in which no two (or more) features are more intimately related than any others.

That this is the basic reason for the failure of (1.26) is confirmed by an examination of one attempt to provide a formulation consonant with the binary feature framework which avoids the use of braces, i.e. the account given by Wang (1968). Wang argues on other grounds that the features for vowels should be capable of allowing for four vowel heights rather than merely three, and he accordingly substitutes for Chomsky & Halle's [high] and [low], with respect to which [+ high, + low] is universally empty, the pair [high] and [mid], providing the four possibilities in (1.29):

$$(1.29) \quad \begin{bmatrix} +\text{high} \\ -\text{mid} \end{bmatrix} \quad \begin{bmatrix} +\text{high} \\ +\text{mid} \end{bmatrix} \quad \begin{bmatrix} -\text{high} \\ +\text{mid} \end{bmatrix} \quad \begin{bmatrix} -\text{high} \\ -\text{mid} \end{bmatrix}$$
$$\qquad\qquad\quad i \qquad\qquad\quad e \qquad\qquad\quad \varepsilon \qquad\qquad\quad æ$$

However, for English he envisages only three systematic heights; the redundancy rule in (1.30) is accordingly applicable:

$$(1.30) \quad [+\text{mid}] \rightarrow [+\text{high}]$$

In the formulation of the Vowel Shift he utilises instead of braces simply two paired Greek letter variables which 'cross over' features:

$$(1.31) \quad \begin{bmatrix} V \\ \gamma \text{back} \\ \gamma \text{round} \\ +\text{tense} \\ +\text{stress} \end{bmatrix} \rightarrow \begin{bmatrix} \beta \text{high} \\ -\alpha \text{mid} \end{bmatrix} \Big/ \begin{bmatrix} \overline{\qquad} \\ \alpha \text{high} \\ \beta \text{mid} \end{bmatrix}$$

((1.31) keeps the rest of the *SPE* proposals constant.)

This certainly states the appropriate relationships, as is apparent from the expansions in (1.32):

$$(1.32) \quad \text{a.} \quad \begin{bmatrix} +\text{high} \\ +\text{mid} \end{bmatrix} \rightarrow \begin{bmatrix} +\text{high} \\ -\text{mid} \end{bmatrix} \qquad\qquad \textit{obscene}$$
$$\qquad\qquad\qquad\quad \bar{e} \qquad\qquad\qquad\ \bar{\imath}$$

$$\qquad \text{b.} \quad \begin{bmatrix} -\text{high} \\ +\text{mid} \end{bmatrix} \rightarrow \begin{bmatrix} +\text{high} \\ +\text{mid} \end{bmatrix} \qquad\qquad \text{(empty: see (1.30))}$$
$$\qquad\qquad\qquad\quad \bar{\varepsilon} \qquad\qquad\qquad\ \bar{e}$$

$$\qquad \text{c.} \quad \begin{bmatrix} -\text{high} \\ -\text{mid} \end{bmatrix} \rightarrow \begin{bmatrix} -\text{high} \\ +\text{mid} \end{bmatrix} \rightarrow \begin{bmatrix} +\text{high} \\ +\text{mid} \end{bmatrix} \quad \textit{profane}$$
$$\qquad\qquad\qquad\quad \bar{æ} \qquad\qquad\qquad\ \bar{\varepsilon} \quad (1.30) \quad \bar{e}$$

$$\qquad \text{d.} \quad \begin{bmatrix} +\text{high} \\ -\text{mid} \end{bmatrix} \rightarrow \begin{bmatrix} -\text{high} \\ -\text{mid} \end{bmatrix} \qquad\qquad \textit{deprive}$$
$$\qquad\qquad\qquad\quad \bar{\imath} \qquad\qquad\qquad\ \bar{æ}$$

(1.32b) applies vacuously, given the absence of vowels which are [− high, + mid]; and the output of (1.32c) is required by redundancy rule (1.30) to be [+ high].

However, the componentiality assumption is again not satisfied; once more spurious candidates for naturalness can be provided with formulations as simple as (1.31). Indeed, the crossing over of paired variables offers considerable scope for the inventor of crazy rules. Consider, for example, (1.33):

$$(1.33) \quad \begin{bmatrix} V \\ \gamma mid \\ \gamma round \\ +tense \\ +stress \end{bmatrix} \rightarrow \begin{bmatrix} \beta high \\ -\alpha back \end{bmatrix} / \begin{bmatrix} \overline{\alpha high} \\ \beta back \end{bmatrix}$$

which, in allowing for just the shifts in (1.34) (given the same input as (1.27), but with no link to the marking conventions) is a rather implausible process:

$$(1.34) \quad \bar{\imath} \rightarrow \bar{æ}, \bar{æ} \rightarrow \bar{a}, \bar{o} \rightarrow \bar{ø}, \bar{ɔ} \rightarrow \bar{o}, \bar{a} \rightarrow \bar{ŭ}$$

It is, however, only mildly crazy on the scale of bizarreness permitted by the utilisation of crossed paired variables. The reason that this device is appropriate in (1.31) is again that [high] and [mid] characterise a single dimension, whereas [high] and [back] do not. But in this respect, Wang's feature system differs from that of *SPE* only in its choice of features for bifurcating the dimension; as a binary framework it too provides no characterisation of the notion 'belonging to the same dimension' (i.e. being non-orthogonal) as applied to distinctive features.

Our criticism here is directed primarily at the characterisation of raising in the Vowel Shift: it is not given a unitary status. However, it is in any case not clear that the high vowel development should be collapsed with the characterisation of the raisings, as in the accounts provided by *SPE* and Wang. The device of conjunctive ordering (or crossed variables) enables us to collapse two apparently distinct phonetic phenomena: the raising of non-high vowels and the diphthongisation of high vowels. If these are indeed distinct, we have here a violation of part (b) of the natural recurrence assumption. Compare the treatment proposed in §1.5 below.

To remedy the failure of binary systems in relation to scalar phenomena, two obvious strategies are available: (a) the revision of the set of basic feature-values (from just '+' and '−'), and (b) the reinterpretation of the relationship between the atoms of segment structure. Since the first option is apparently less drastic, let us consider whether such a limited modification will lead to a more satisfactory description of the internal structure of segments.

1.4 Scalar features: an alternative minimal theory

Say we allow some features, at least, to have more than two systematically relevant values, after the fashion of, for example, Contreras (1969), Ladefoged (1971) or Saltarelli (1973): i.e. the number of values for each feature is independent of those for every other, and is not determined by general principle applicable to all features. It is possible to imagine a stronger and weaker form of such a theory of structure, a proposal we shall refer to as the ALTERNATIVE MINIMALLY COMPONENTIAL THEORY. The strong form would require that all languages need phonologically the same number of values for any particular feature; this would appear to be untenable, however. In the weaker form, languages are free to have either a binary or ternary or whatever distinction for a particular feature, within some universal limits. We shall not pursue here the consequences of this distinction; what concerns us, rather, is the adequacy of the alternative theory in those respects in which the binary theory fails to satisfy the componentiality assumption.

A unitary characterisation of the Vowel Shift becomes available once we recognise height as an independent dimension by dispensing with [high] and [low] (or [high] and [mid]) in favour of a single multi-valued scalar feature [high]. Thus a three-height vowel system will have the values [1 high], [2 high] and [3 high]. Let us also assume, provisionally, that they are ordered in terms of an intransitive, asymmetric, binary relation, as in (1.35):

(1.35)   [1 high]≪[2 high], [2 high]≪[3 high], [3 high]≪[1 high]

where '≪' denotes 'ranks immediately below': i.e. the vowels are ordered cyclically so that [3 high]=[2+1 high], [2 high]=[1+1 high], and [1 high]=[3+1 high]. (We re-examine the cyclicity assumption in a moment.) If we admit a variable 'x' over the feature-values 1, 2 and 3, we can then formulate the Vowel Shift as in (1.36) (where we assume three values for [high]):

(1.36) $\begin{bmatrix} x\text{high} \\ y\text{back} \\ y\text{round} \\ +\text{tense} \\ +\text{stress} \end{bmatrix} \rightarrow [x+1 \text{ high}]$

which effects the individual shifts in (1.37):

(1.37) a. [2 high] → [2 + 1 high] = [3 high]   *obscene*
            ē   ī

        b. [1 high] → [1 + 1 high] = [2 high]   *profane*
            ǣ   ē

        c. [3 high] → [3 + 1 high] = [1 high]   *deprive*
            ī   ǣ

In this way, the scale of height and the proper domain of processes which involve shifts along (or around) such scales are given formal recognition. And no spurious non-scalar shifts are predicted. It looks as if our characterisation holds some promise of satisfying the componentiality assumption in this area. Moreover, if extended to place of articulation (Ladefoged 1975), such a view resolves some of the problems to do with homorganicity discussed above (§1.3.1), in that only a single variable is involved in expressing agreement between a nasal and a following obstruent: i.e. the value of the segment for place of articulation (see further §6.3).

But we have also created some fresh problems, both in the characterisation of the Vowel Shift and in the representation of vowels in general. There is, for instance, a historical problem with the formulation in (1.36). At an earlier period, the high vowel shifted only to a mid, rather than a low, position. Chomsky & Halle (*SPE*:§6.2) characterise the relevant aspect of the system described by John Hart as in (1.38):

(1.38) a. $\begin{bmatrix} V \\ \alpha high \\ -low \\ +tense \\ +stress \end{bmatrix} \rightarrow [-\alpha high] \quad \begin{matrix} \bar{e} \rightarrow \bar{\imath} \\ \bar{\imath} \rightarrow \bar{e} \end{matrix}$

        b. $\begin{bmatrix} V \\ +low \\ \alpha back \\ \alpha round \\ +tense \\ +stress \end{bmatrix} \rightarrow [-low] \quad \ǣ \rightarrow \bar{e}$

This seems to represent a plausible intermediate stage in the historical evolution, given Chomsky & Halle's two-part characterisation of the

Vowel Shift: Vowel Shift (a) is fully formed first; Vowel Shift (b) results from the generalisation of the raising rule (1.38b).

However, given the cyclical hierarchy of (1.35), and the formulation in (1.36), the intermediate stage represented by Hart's dialect is quite unexpected. A different hierarchisation seems to be involved. Suppose then that we abandon the cyclical order of (1.35) in favour of simply (1.39):

(1.39)   [1 high] ≪ [2 high], [2 high] ≪ [3 high]

We shall then need to supplement (1.36) with a convention for the present-day phonology of the character of (1.40):

(1.40)   [3 + 1 high] = [1 high]

whereas for Hart's dialect the appropriate requirement is (1.41):

(1.41)   [3 + 1 high] = [2 high]

This at least allows us to express the earlier situation. But we nevertheless fail to account within the notation for why there should have been such an intermediate stage.

However, as noted above, this characterisation of the Vowel Shift, which adopts the same strategy as that of *SPE*, may be simply inappropriate, in attempting to include the development of the high vowels as part of the same process as the raising. If the high vowel development is excluded, as being determined not by the same phonetic process as raising but by systemic factors, then (1.36) is an adequate characterisation of the Vowel Shift, with the development of the 'illegitimate' vowel [4 high] being essentially outside the domain of notation. This, however, is not available to a binary approach.

Unfortunately, in substituting a scale for binary features, we have lost as well as gained in notational expressiveness. Any componential notation leads to the establishment of natural classes, i.e. sub-groups of segments which satisfy the componentiality assumption. The classes established by the binary features [high] and [low] (or [high] and [mid]) are not relevant to (in fact they impede, if used) the characterisation of the Vowel Shift; but they are crucially involved in the expression of other regularities, such as those formulated in (1.10) and (1.13), which require a bifurcation of the dimension of height into [− low] vowels, which are affected, and [+ low] vowels, which are not. A scalar feature of height cannot express this bifurcation: the vowels that are affected are [2 high] and [3 high]; a [1 high] vowel does not participate in roundness and backness agreement. But

[2 high] and [3 high] do not emerge, in terms of this notation, as a natural class. Recurrent rules and markedness relationships which depend upon bifurcations (or, in general, any non-minimal division) of the height dimension cannot be expressed in a componentially satisfactory way.

Attempts to allow for bifurcatory properties in terms of limited extensions to a scalar feature framework meet with serious problems. Say, for instance, we introduce the binary relation '$<$', i.e. 'ranks below', as the transitive closure of the non-cyclic interpretation of the binary relation of (1.35), such that the particular relations in (1.42) hold:

(1.42)   [1 high]$<$[2 high], [1 high]$<$[3 high], [2 high]$<$[3 high]

We can thus define the class relevant to backness and roundness agreement as in (1.43):

(1.43)   [x high], where $1<x$

Notice, however, that the interpretation of x does not involve a universal convention, unlike the Greek letter variables. Its value must be specified for the particular rule it is involved in, i.e. as part of the formulation of the rule. But such a notation then fails to satisfy the componentiality assumption. Specifically, the class of [x high] vowels is more complex in its expression, since it must include a specification of the value x, than is the class of, say, [2 high] vowels.

The introduction of an operator, '$\sim$', such that [$\sim$1 high] denotes the class of vowels that are not [1 high], is perhaps appropriate in this case, in that this specification distinguishes the class of non-low vowels. It does not, however, lead to a generally viable solution. Consider, for instance, the problem of specifying the class of non-high vowels in a four-height system (e.g. (1.29)), i.e. [1 high] and [2 high].

Of course, it is possible to supplement the notation employed in (1.35) in various more extensive ways, the effect of which is to make such binary characterisations possible. But a scalar theory including these supplements is, if they are widespread, difficult to distinguish from a theory which assigns to segments a dual (binary and scalar) description (for some properties at least). Each relevant segment would then have a double representation, one in terms of binary features, the other with respect to scales of height, etc. Vennemann & Ladefoged (1973), indeed, propose allowing for phenomena determined by a scale of phonological strength in terms of 'feature redundancy rules', which associate particular segment-types (specified in terms of binary features) with particular (numerical) strength-values (where strength is a 'cover' feature), giving just such dual representations. However, in failing to allow, in terms of a single representation, for the duality of the relationships which segments enter into, this again simply suggests that features are inappropriate phono-logical atoms. The same objection can be directed at the introduction of 'second-order' features, proposed by Lass (1976:ch. 7).

Neither binary nor scalar features are adequate, then, to represent the full range of phonological phenomena. An adequate feature-based description must apparently invoke simultaneous binary and scalar classification. This suggests that we should now take into account a structural variable so far ignored. Up to now we have considered segments to be characterised by a simple unordered set (or sets) of omnipresent features, possibly grouped (in an enriched theory) into subsets. But suppose that we eliminate the possibility of variation in the value of features, which are then 'single-valued'. The relation between features or properties is itself a variable, even within very simple limits; properties need not necessarily always be present, or they may be hierarchised in some determinate manner. We want now to give a preliminary outline (to be developed later) of how such a view–that the relation between properties is a strictly defined variable–can accommodate in terms of a single small set of primitive properties both the phenomena readily characterised by scalar features and the classifications appropriately expressed by binary features. The notation to be proposed will also allow the expression of notions of markedness of segment and naturalness of process without contradiction and without recourse to additional ad hoc apparatus such as marking and naturalness conventions.

1.5   Vowel components

In defining the vowel space, we shall provisionally recognise three relevant perceptual properties, presented with articulatory/acoustic glosses in (1.44):

(1.44) |i| 'frontness'   (or 'acuteness' and 'sharpness')
         |a| 'lowness'   (or 'compactness')
         |u| 'roundness'   (or 'gravity' and 'flatness')

We shall refer to these properties (enclosed between verticals) as RESONANCE or VOWEL COMPONENTS (cf., for example, Donegan (Miller) 1973; Schane 1984b); they correspond to the locational features that characterise vowels, among other things. Given that these components constitute perceptual properties, the 'acoustic' glosses are less approximate than the 'articulatory'.

Unlike binary or multi-valued features, however, these components are not individually omnipresent: segments can be characterised by their absence as well as their presence. (1.45), then, represents a front, non-low, unrounded vowel:

(1.45)   {|i|}

The enclosing within braces of the representation for one of the components, flanked by verticals, indicates that the segment is characterised phonologically (as far as the locational gesture is concerned) by the presence of that component alone. The familiar triangular system of (1.46) is the simplest possible using all three components in (1.44), if each segment is characterised by one component only:

(1.46)   {|i|} (= /i/)   {|u|} (= /u/)

                   {|a|} (= /ɑ/)

where {|u|} represents a rounded, non-front, non-low vowel; and {|a|} is low, non-front and unrounded.

However, the components can also be combined into complex labels, as in (1.47):

(1.47)   a. {|i,a|}   b. {|u,a|}   c. {|i,u|}

(1.47a) is a vowel composed of |i| and |a|, where the comma specifies simply combination. Each component in the label is equal, but each is perceptually less strong than when it appears as the only component in the label for a segment, so that, for instance, (1.47a) represents a segment that is perceptually 'front', but not as 'front' as (1.45), and 'low', but not as 'low' as {|a|}, and is not rounded: i.e. it is a frontish, mid, unrounded vowel. Utilising all these possibilities, we have the system indicated in (1.48):

(1.48)   {|i|} (= /i/)   {|i,u|} (= /y/)   {|u|} (= /u/)

                   {|i,a|} (= /e/)   {|u,a|} (= /o/)

                          {|a|} (= /ɑ/)

i.e. with mid vowels and a high front rounded vowel. Combining all three components yields a frontish mid rounded vowel, represented as (1.49):

(1.49)   {|i,u,a|} (= /ø/)

It will be apparent that such a notation allows in principle for the expression of both scalar and binary phenomena. For instance, a process involving raising can be characterised in terms of a decrease in the preponderance of the |a| component. On the other hand, we can still express (for example) the natural class of non-high vowels as {a}, i.e. segments containing |a|, not necessarily as the only component – hence no verticals: a segment containing only |a| would be the more complex {|a|}. Non-low vowels are specified as {∼a}, i.e. the class of segments containing some component other than the |a| component (though, of course, they can contain |a| as well). Thus the verticals may be omitted in the case of the front rounded and mid vowels in (1.48): these are the only vowels in the system containing the two components in question, and hence there is no opposition with any other such vowels. But in a system which includes both the vowels in (1.48) and that in (1.49) the verticals are unnecessary only in the case of the latter: /y/, /e/ and /o/ are not the only segments containing {i,u}, {i,a} and {u,a} respectively, while /ø/ exhausts the set of segments containing all three components, and so can be represented as {i,u,a}. (Indeed, the vowels in (1.46) may also be represented as {i}, {u} and {a} respectively: each of these is the only vowel in the system containing the component in question.)

In terms of such representations, the relative markedness of a segment is an intrinsic property of its representation: the mid vowels and the front rounded vowel, involving combinations of components, are intrinsically the most complex of the representations in (1.48); the front mid rounded vowel in (1.49) is the most complex of all, involving all three components. Further, although the output of the sub-part of *i*-umlaut given in (1.18) is a relatively marked vowel (combining two components), the process itself is predicted to be natural and recurrent, as a simple assimilation involving addition of |i| to a {|u|} segment in the environment of an {|i|} segment, giving {|i,u|}.

However, further vowel distinctions are obviously needed, even if we consider only what is appropriately represented in terms of just these three components; and these distinctions involve further hierarchical and cross-classificatory relationships. They can be suitably represented if we allow combinations to be asymmetrical, so that one of the components may preponderate, as in (1.50):

(1.50)   a. {|i⇉a|} (= /e/)   b. {|a⇉i|} (= /ɛ/)

where the preponderant component is at the tail of the double arrow. Such representations will obviously count as less simple than the simple juxtaposition of components in (1.47): (1.50a) is structurally more complex than (1.47) in being opposed to (1.50b), and this is reflected in the notation, given that '⇉', the asymmetrical relation, is appropriately reckoned as more costly than ',', simple combination.

Utilising such possibilities, we can extend our system, as far as relative lowness is concerned, to that in (1.51):

(1.51)   {|i|} (= /i/)   {|u|} (= /u/)

         {|i⇉a|} (= /e/)   {|u⇉a|} (= /o/)

         {|a⇉i|} (= /ɛ/)   {|a⇉u|} (= /ɔ/)

                  {|a|} (= /ɑ/)

Given the relational character of the notation, the phonemic symbols given in round brackets in (1.51) and the like should not be given an absolute interpretation. For instance, /e/ in (1.48) can be realised at any point in the front mid vowel area: i.e. it 'covers' the area represented by /e/ and /ɛ/ together in (1.51). As is proper for a phonemic representation, the phonetic value of /e/ is a variable; specifically, it is partially determined by the number of distinctions occurring in a particular system.

A more complex system still (indeed the most complex utilising just these components – and not combining |i| and |u|) would involve both asymmetrical and symmetrical combinations (the latter represented by '⇄'), as in (1.52):

(1.52)   {|i|} (= /i/)   {|u|} (= /u/)

         {|i⇉a|} (= /e/)   {|u⇉a|} (= /o/)

         {|i⇄a|} (= /ɛ/)   {|u⇄a|} (= /ɔ/)

         {|a⇉i|} (= /æ/)   {|a⇉u|} (= /ɒ/)

                  {|a|} (= /ɑ/)

{|i ⇄ a|} involves both {|i ⇉ a|} and {|a ⇉ i|}, and is thus more complex than either. Notice that '⇄' is not equivalent to ',', simple combination, which would be inappropriate here: the simple combination of two components in a system implies that there is no other combination of the components in question. Whether (1.52) is required empirically is uncertain (see Basbøll 1985 on Maddieson 1984); but what is important is that each of the systems (1.46), (1.48), (1.51) and (1.52) is intrinsically ranked in complexity in terms of the complexity of the representations utilised. (1.52) represents the maximal system as far as combinations of |i| and |u| with |a| are concerned. As this is an empirical maximum, we can limit combinations of the components to one per segment. For the articulatory components associated with the representation of consonants and for those of the 'categorial gesture' (see ch. 4), however, it is appropriate to allow up to two instances of each component per segment, provided the two instances are asymmetrically related.

The strength of a segment with respect to a particular component is represented by the preponderance of that component in relation to the other components, so that upward movement through (1.51) and (1.52) involves decreasing strength of the |a| component. Similarly, more or less inclusive classes can be expressed in terms of how preponderant we require a component to be, so that we have the class-inclusion relations of (1.53):

(1.53) $\{a\} \supset \{a,\} \supset \dfrac{\{a\rightrightarrows\}}{\{a\leftleftarrows\}} \supset \{a\rightleftarrows\}$

where $\{a\}$ is the class of segments containing |a|; $\{a,\}$ contains |a| together with some other component; $\{a\rightrightarrows\}$ requires that |a| be preponderant over another component; $\{a\leftleftarrows\}$ requires that another component preponderate over |a|; $\{a\rightleftarrows\}$ requires that |a| be mutually or equally preponderant with some other element. Thus the class constituted by the lowest three segments in (1.51) is expressed by $\{a\rightrightarrows\}$. $\{\ \}$, $\{,\}$, $\{\rightrightarrows\}$, and $\{\rightleftarrows\}$ involve successive additions to the complexity of representation.

Assuming a 'tense' vowel system like (1.51) as input to the Vowel Shift, and adopting the *SPE* approach, i.e. including the development of the high vowels as part of the Vowel Shift process, we can offer as an appropriate formulation that in (1.54):

(1.54) $\begin{bmatrix} \{\sim a\} \\ \text{'tense'} \\ \text{'stress'} \end{bmatrix} \rightarrow \ |\sim a|$

CONDITION: $\{|\sim a|, |\sim a|\} = \{|a|\}$

We ignore here the characterisation of 'tenseness' and 'stress', with the condition of backness and roundness agreement being dispensed with in favour of the $\{\sim a\}$ specification, thus excluding the first vowel in *father*, which contains *only* |a|. (1.54) stipulates that a non-|a| component is added to tense stressed vowels which already have some non-|a| component. This is interpreted by universal convention as moving the affected vowel one step further away from $\{|a|\}$, i.e. converting it into that vowel which differs from the affected one only in terms of a minimal decrease in the preponderance of |a|, as indicated in (1.55):

(1.55) a. {|i ⇉ a|} → {|i ⇉ a|,|~a|} → {|i|}
      ē   ī

      b. {|a ⇉ i|} → {|a ⇉ i|,|~a|} → {|i ⇉ a|}
         æ   ē

      c. {|i|} → {|i|,|~a|} → {|a|}
       ī   æ

Thus the derived representations in (1.55a) and (1.55b), which include too many non-|a| components, are simplified in a direction away from {|a|}. (1.55c), which creates a segment which is so far away from {|a|} as to lie outside a legal system, is resolved with respect to the condition in (1.54), which converts a representation containing only two non-|a| components into the segment characterised by |a| alone; as it were, it exits from the system and re-enters from the opposite pole.

Note that Hart's dialect, in which the vowel in (1.55c) stops at mid, can be allowed for if the condition in (1.54) is modified as in (1.56):

(1.56)   {|~a|,|~a|} → {|~a|,|a|} → {|~a ⇉ a|}
                                              ē

in which the |a| component is substituted for only one of the two non-|a| components resulting from the application of (1.54), rather than for the whole sequence. The effect of this is to create a specification which is resolved by moving the original {|~a|} one step nearer to {|a|}, i.e. to {|~a ⇉ a|}. In this case, the later condition of (1.54) is a plausible successor to the earlier (1.56), in that it involves the substitution of a less complex or marked output: {|a|} rather than {|i ⇉ a|}. (1.56), however, represents the initial stage in the development of the condition, involving a simple internal 'dissimilation' rather than total substitution.

Once again, a decision to omit the diphthongisation from the Vowel Shift process is simply handled within this approach: the condition is simply dropped from (1.54), and the development of /ī/ will again fall outside the domain of the rule, which is thus appropriately simpler.

The implementation convention invoked here (if /ī/ is ignored) either adds a new segment to the system, as with [y] from the *i*-umlaut of [u] (see (1.18) and (1.19) above), or it 'moves' the segment affected into a slot vacated as a result of the application of the same schema, as in the case of the Vowel Shift. Merger must be specified language-specifically: on the characterisation of this see Anderson (1985a).

Such a characterisation of the Vowel Shift leaves a number of issues unresolved. For example, why are such 'tense' vowel shifts typically away from {|a|}? And there are more general questions raised by the representations: for example, why are combinations of |i| and |u| with |a| more generally utilised in the languages of the world than combinations of |i| and |u| with each other?

We return to such questions in §6.1.2 and in Part III; however, we can anticipate a little by recalling that Donegan (Miller) (1973) groups |i| and |u| together as vowel COLOURS, whereas |a| is simply SONORANCY: a resolution of the questions we have just posed may lie in an appropriate characterisation of this distinction (see also Schane 1984b). In §3.6 we offer a more detailed consideration of the formal character of the representations proposed in the present section.

1.6   Multi-gestural representations

We return now to some of the arguments of §1.3.1, where we observed that in the minimally componential feature systems of *SPE* and Ladefoged (1971) there is no formalisation of the notion of sub-grouping of features; i.e. there is no attempt to introduce subsets of features, each of which may operate independently in phonological processes involving homorganicity, for example.

Lass & Anderson (1975:app. II), however, within an otherwise minimal theory, propose formulating such processes in terms of a Greek letter variable outside a sub-bracketing that includes just the appropriate recurrent grouping of features, those constituting the ARTICULATORY GESTURE, as in (1.57):

(1.57)   [α[artic]]   [α[artic]]

This replaces representations of the *SPE* type, involving 'pairwise agreement of arbitrary features'.

The interpretation of (1.57) is not straightforward. Elsewhere, Greek letters are variables over '+' and '−' values for a particular feature; in (1.57), on the other hand, the value of 'α' is not simply '+' or '−', and a different, more complex convention is required for the interpretation of rules with pairs of Greek letters associated with gestures. Each Greek letter is a variable ranging 'over any combination of the values "+" and "−" on any feature in the inner brackets: the only condition being that as usual all values covered by any given pair of variables agree' (Lass & Anderson 1975:263). However, we are not concerned here with the details of this formalism, particularly since we consider that the use of variables over feature coefficients is in general quite unwarranted.

Since, as will become apparent, the notion of gesture is basic to our concept of segmental structure (even though, as noted in the previous section, the traditional notion of feature-value does not play a role in our system of representation), we shall here devote some space to a rather more formal discussion of this notion; in particular, we will consider the nature of the phonological representations of [h] and [ʔ]. For purposes of exposition, we shall in this section continue to use binary features to illustrate our arguments.

In an enriched componential theory incorporating gestures, the segment might have a structure something like (1.58):

(1.58)
$$\begin{bmatrix} \begin{bmatrix} & \\ & \end{bmatrix} \\ \begin{bmatrix} & \\ & \end{bmatrix} \\ \begin{bmatrix} & \end{bmatrix} \\ \begin{bmatrix} & \\ & \end{bmatrix} \end{bmatrix}$$

in which the number of sub-groupings would depend on arguments such as those to be developed in the introduction to Part II.

Although Chomsky & Halle do not formalise the notion of such sub-groupings, they nevertheless appear to suggest that some such idea can be appealed to. The use of terms such as 'major class features', 'tongue-body features', etc., seems to imply an intuitive (or at least expositorily convenient) acceptance of the possibility of sub-groupings. However, the only well-established approximation to a formal device which has the effect of creating sub-groupings is the use of the shorthand notation N for the groupings [+ consonantal, + nasal].

There are, though, as demonstrated by Lass's model, no formal impediments within feature theory to creating sub-groupings within a feature matrix (in spite of the objections of Hyman 1985, who claims that this is 'incoherent within the standard distinctive feature approach'). Indeed, this is a central property of autosegmental phonology (Thráinsson 1978; Goldsmith 1979; and in particular, Clements 1985), in which the minimal theory is enriched by dividing (sequences of) segments into autosegmental tiers. Thus, in a language in which a vowel may carry a contour tone (a sequence, say, of high and low tones), two autosegmental tiers can be set up; one a 'tonal' tier, carrying two tonal feature specifications, and the other a 'segmental' tier, containing a single set of feature specifications. This approach, then, goes some way towards incorporating two of the modifications envisaged in §1.3.1, i.e. sub-grouping of the features and the possibility of segment-internal sequence (albeit in a rather different form from that proposed by S. R. Anderson).

Even within the standard autosegmental approach, however, the notion of gesture is not appealed to in any formal fashion. Rather, tiers (or sub-matrices) are established with reference to particular phonological phenomena, rather than on general grounds; that is, it is not clear just which (sets of) features can potentially form distinct tiers. Thráinsson (1978:36), for example, offers the following representation for the voiceless aspirated stops of Icelandic involved in various preaspiration processes:

(1.59)

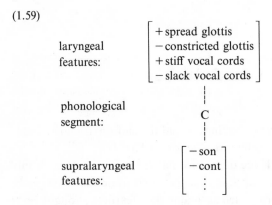

with a division of the segment analogous to that proposed by Lass & Anderson. (For a discussion of the features used here, see §5.1.) It is not, however, entirely clear whether this division is appropriate for all voiceless stops in all languages, or merely for this particular case, although Thráinsson does note that it is to be expected that subsets of features behaving as a unit will be well-defined rather than arbitrary combinations of features. That is, specific sub-groupings of features are involved in phonological processes, and this leads us to suggest that the notion of gesture must be incorporated formally in the phonological framework, in a way not fully exploited by the autosegmentalists (although the proposals of Clements 1985 show considerable similarities to those of Lass 1976; we return to this in §7.2). Let us now consider some of the motivations for this claim, and the nature of the resulting representations.

1.6.1 Arguments for greater componentiality

Lass & Anderson (1975) and Lass (1976) adduce various arguments supporting the organisation of features into sub-matrices after the fashion of (1.58). One of these, as we have seen, involves the characterisation of homorganicity, which, Lass & Anderson argue, requires bigestural representations, with an articulatory and a phonatory gesture. A process such as Old English Homorganic Lengthening, involving lengthening of a vowel before a sonorant followed by a homorganic voiced obstruent, is characterised as (1.60) (Lass & Anderson 1975:275):

$$(1.60) \qquad \emptyset \to V \ / \ V \text{---} \begin{bmatrix} \alpha[\quad \text{artic}] \\ \beta \begin{bmatrix} \text{phon} \\ -\text{obs} \end{bmatrix} \end{bmatrix} \begin{bmatrix} \alpha[\quad \text{artic}] \\ \beta \begin{bmatrix} \text{phon} \\ +\text{obs} \\ +\text{voice} \end{bmatrix} \end{bmatrix}$$

where 'α' and 'β' are variables over entire gestures. The environment of (1.60) involves two successive segments with identical specifications for the features of the articulatory gesture, and identical specifications for the features of the phonatory gesture, with the exception of those features specified in the rule.

Further evidence for the need for representations involving sub-groupings such as these comes from the behaviour of [ʔ]. Lass (1976:145–51) argues that [ʔ] in English is a 'reduction-stop' in the same way as [ə] is the 'reduction-vowel': it is the neutralisation of the /p/:/t/:/k/ contrast. Instead of the complex rules required to characterise the changes /p/ → [ʔ]; /t/ → [ʔ]; /k/ → [ʔ] in the *SPE* framework, each involving a change of four or five features as in (1.61):

$$(1.61) \qquad \begin{bmatrix} -\text{son} \\ +\text{ant} \\ +\text{cor} \\ -\text{cont} \\ -\text{voice} \end{bmatrix} \to \begin{bmatrix} +\text{son} \\ -\text{cons} \\ -\text{ant} \\ -\text{cor} \\ +\text{low} \end{bmatrix}$$
$$\qquad\qquad\quad /t/ \qquad\quad [ʔ]$$

Lass suggests that what is involved is deletion of all supralaryngeal articulatory information. That is, the articulatory gesture (or 'oral' gesture, in Lass's terms) is entirely deleted, as in (1.62):

(1.62)

$$\begin{bmatrix} \begin{bmatrix} \text{oral} \\ -\text{cont} \end{bmatrix} \\ \begin{bmatrix} -\text{son} \\ -\text{voice} \end{bmatrix} \end{bmatrix} \rightarrow \begin{bmatrix} \emptyset \\ [-\text{cont}] \end{bmatrix}$$

Glottal stops in English, then, are seen as 'defective', in that they lack an entire component or parameter that is present in 'normal' segments. ((1.62) also involves the transference of [−cont] from the articulatory to the phonatory gesture: we return to this in the Introduction to Part II, in §II.1.)

Similarly, [h] is viewed as standing in the same kind of relationship to voiceless fricatives as [ʔ] to voiceless stops. A change from a voiceless fricative to [h], then, again involves the deletion of the articulatory gesture. Further, [h] is less resistant to complete deletion than the other voiceless fricatives. The sequence voiceless fricative > [h] > ∅ is a typical occurrence in historical change. Lass formalises the sequence as (1.63):

(1.63)

$$\begin{bmatrix} \begin{bmatrix} +\text{ant} \\ +\text{cor} \\ +\text{cont} \end{bmatrix} \\ [-\text{voice}] \end{bmatrix} \rightarrow \begin{bmatrix} \emptyset \\ \begin{bmatrix} +\text{cont} \\ -\text{voice} \end{bmatrix} \end{bmatrix} \rightarrow \begin{bmatrix} \emptyset \\ \emptyset \end{bmatrix}$$

The propensity of [h] to delete is appropriately characterised by a representation in which it lacks a specification for one of the matrices – it is already on its way to '∅'. (For a similar treatment of [h] within the autosegmental framework, see Thráinsson 1978.)

These proposals in no way exclude the possibility of there being more than two sub-matrices in the representations of segments. For languages other than English there are a number of areas which require phonological characterisations not dealt with by Lass & Anderson, such as the various phonation-types involved in phonological oppositions – for example, breathy voice and creaky voice – and the different airstream mechanisms used in speech. Whatever the nature of the dependency representations which must be established to characterise these phenomena (see chapter 5), we must also decide whether it is necessary to establish further gestures, and if not, in what way such phenomena should be incorporated into the two gestures (whatever their precise nature) discussed above.

We discuss these matters further below; in the meantime it should be noted that the 'notational independence of the two parameters implies that each is a possible proper domain for a phonological rule: in addition to the whole segment being such a domain' (Lass 1976:155). For example, rules affecting the natural class of voiceless stops irrespective of their place of articulation would refer only to the phonatory gesture, while, as we have seen, homorganicity can be characterised by reference to a variable over the entire articulatory gesture, irrespective of the features of the phonatory gesture.

1.6.2 Phonetic evidence for greater componentiality

Support for the claim that the segment should be represented as a set of sub-matrices comes from various phonetic aspects of speech-sounds. Phonetically, the production of speech-sounds involves various parameters, which are less atomistic than non-gestural feature theories would suggest. Ladefoged (1971:2–3), for example, distinguishes four processes which are required in the specification of speech – the airstream process, the phonation process, the articulation process, and the oro-nasal process, while Catford (1977:15–16) suggests that the production of speech involves three functional components, of which two are more basic than the third. The two basic functional components are INITIATION (also called 'air-stream mechanism') and ARTICULATION:

> By *initiation* we mean a bellows-like or piston-like movement of an organ or organ-group (an initiator), which generates positive or negative pressure in the part of the vocal tract adjacent to it, that is, between the initiator and the place of articulation. The term 'initiation' is used for this component of speech production since it is the activity that 'initiates' the flow of air essential for the production of almost all sounds. (1977:63)

> *Articulation* is a movement or posture of an organ (an *articulator*) that interrupts or modifies the air-flow in such a way as to give rise to a specific type of sound. (1977:15)

> After initiation has set in train a flow of air, articulation acts upon the air-stream to 'shape' it, as it were, into a sound of specific type and quality. (1977:117)

Articulation can be divided into two sub-components, STRICTURE-TYPE and LOCATION, with the oro-nasal process being part of the location sub-component. The third functional component of speech production is PHONATION:

> By *phonation* we mean any relevant activity in the larynx which is neither initiatory nor articulatory in function . . . It is clear that phonation can occur only when we have a column of air passing through the larynx. (1977:16)

Thus all pulmonic sounds, and some glottalic ones, have phonation, while velaric sounds are phonationless. Various kinds of phonation are distinguished: for example, vocal cord vibration, voiceless phonation, whisper, etc.

In view of the principles discussed in §1.1 – in particular part (b) of (1.3), the natural recurrence assumption – it seems clear that we must investigate whether the division of the matrix characterising a segment into phonological sub-matrices should correspond to divisions such as these, which are established on purely phonetic grounds. We take it as desirable that it should in principle be possible to map phonological units (of whatever nature) on to (pseudo-)phonetic parameters – whether they be of an articulatory, acoustic or perceptual character. However, although there is, on the view taken here, an intimate relationship between phonology and phonetics, this does not imply that there is a necessary one-to-one correspondence between the two levels. We take a rather weaker standpoint – that there should be an asymmetry between phonological and phonetic units only when there is convincing phonological evidence for it. This is adopted in the light of the kind of consideration noted elsewhere by Anderson & Jones:

. . . there may indeed be independent psychological organizing principles in the internal classification of sound systems, while at the same time what appear at the moment to be purely phonological criteria may turn out to have anatomical or acoustic correlates of a type of which we are as yet ignorant. (1977:5)

Whatever the resolution of these problems may be, it is clear that the phonetic evidence supports the view that the representation of segments should incorporate this additional attribute, thus further increasing the degree of componentiality in the system. Our segmental representations, then, will incorporate the notion of gesture, together with the properties outlined in §1.5. However, for the moment we leave open the question of whether the phonological matrix characterising a segment should consist of three sub-matrices reflecting Catford's three functional (phonetic) components of initiation, articulation and phonation, and, indeed, the question of how many gestures are required in phonological representations. Before returning to this in Part II, we consider now the other 'dimension' of phonological structure – that displayed by sequences of segments rather than individual segments.

2 The structure of phonological sequences

In chapter 1 we looked at various kinds of evidence relating to the internal structure of segments, including some phenomena involving sequential constraints. We turn now to a consideration of phonological sequences as such, and specifically to the question of their structure, if any.

The past few years have seen a wide range of work on different models of suprasegmental structure, notably on variants of metrical and autosegmental phonology. It nevertheless seems appropriate to us to approach the notion of phonological constituency and related properties from an initially agnostic standpoint. Much of this chapter will therefore be concerned with establishing the validity of concepts which are now commonly taken for granted. Often this confidence is, we would suggest, to some extent unwarranted; and this is in part reflected in debates over the precise character of suprasegmental structure – debates such as that concerning the status of the 'metrical grid' (see Prince 1983; Hayes 1984; Giegerich 1986). We delay until chapter 3 an exposition of our own view of the nature of this structure. Here our aims are rather more limited.

We begin by considering what properties should be attributed to sequences of segments, and whether these include constituency. Questions like the following arise. Are some sequential constraints to be associated with a structure that is not simply a concatenation of segments? And even if this structure (e.g. grouping into syllables) is reducible to, or predictable from, the sequence of segments, is generality lost if any other generalisations are attributed directly to the sequence rather than to the structure? We approach these questions via the same kind of strategy as we employed in §1.2. Consider in the first place an 'anti-structuralist' position.

2.1 Non-constituentiality

2.1.1 Introduction

For Chomsky & Halle, 'a phonetic representation . . . is actually a feature matrix in which the rows correspond to a restricted set of universal phonetic categories or features (voicing, nasality, etc.) and the columns to successive segments'; and further, 'each formative of the surface structure can also be represented as a feature matrix interpreted in a rather similar way, with rows corresponding to the universal phonetic and grammatical categories' (*SPE*: 14). It is clear from their discussion that phonetic representations and the non-morpho-syntactic content of phonological representations comprise a simple concatenation of segments: there are no higher phonological units apart from the 'phonological phrase', which is the 'maximal domain for phonological processes' (*SPE*: 9), and even this is not explicitly characterised (see *SPE*: 372). Let us refer to such a view of phonological sequences as NON-CONSTITUENTIAL.

Chomsky & Halle do not offer any explicit arguments against constituentiality. But despite constant references throughout their discussions to syllables, in particular, the notion has for them no systematic status, and, as far as we can determine, 'syllable' can simply be equated with '(sequence containing at most one) vowel (or most sonorant consonant in certain environments)' wherever it is used; see further §2.1.2. (Their index has no entry for 'Syllable', but it does have one for 'Stressed Syllable Rule'.) We have, then, an argument from non-use: no regularities of, for instance, English phonology require for their optimal expression reference to phonological units more inclusive than the segment, the minimal sequential element. In the sections that follow we shall be considering various kinds of phenomena which invoke syllable-sized units or their boundaries. Here we turn to the related notion of syllabicity (of a segment).

2.1.2   The status of syllabicity

In the course of their discussion (*SPE*: 353–5), Chomsky & Halle do introduce the feature [syllabic]. But this is not associated with the recognition of the syllable as a systematic unit, either in that work or in subsequent discussions in the same tradition, such as Halle & Keyser's (1971) on English stress.

We use the term 'syllable' here as the equivalent of 'sequence of speech sounds consisting of one syllabic sound (vowel) preceded and followed by any number of consecutive non-syllabic sounds (consonants)'. In particular, we do not take a position on the vexing question of whether or not utterances can be uniformly segmented into syllables. (1971: 141)

The status of the feature itself, however, is problematical, in that, unlike others proposed in *SPE*, it is inherently combinatorial (syntagmatic) rather than simply relative: a syllabic sound is a segment constituting a syllabic peak (*SPE*:354), i.e. a peak of prominence relative to immediately adjacent segments. On the other hand, a low segment is low in terms of the position of the body of the tongue relative to the 'neutral' position (*SPE*:305)–though of course in actual communication it may be *perceived* as low in relation to surrounding segments. Jakobson & Halle (1956:§3.1) are careful to distinguish syllabicity from the contrast of successive features whereby it is manifested:

. . . ordinarily the crest is formed by vowels, while the slopes contain the other types of phonemes; less frequently the contrast of crest and slope phonemes is displayed by liquids *vs.* pure consonants, or by nasal *vs.* oral consonants . . . and in exceptional cases by constrictives *vs.* stops.

In their framework vowels are not *defined* as syllabic; rather, given the inherent prominence of vowels relative to other segment-types, it is typically a vowel that constitutes the crest of a syllable. The status of syllabicity as combinatorial is obscured by giving it the same formal status as inherent features such as [consonantal].

Further, as a combinatorial property, syllabicity in languages is predictable, either completely or in the vast majority of cases, from the sequence of segments: typically, then, it is not lexically contrastive. Thus in Lumasaaba, a [−cons] segment is syllabic unless it is also [−low] and followed by another [−cons] segment; and a consonant is syllabic only if it is immediately followed by another consonant (Brown 1972:§3.2.4):

(2.1)   a. [cikalaßu]   'a hand'
        b. [madjoːfu]   'bubbles'
        c. [iːsiṃbicila]   'a pin-tailed widah bird'

In (a) all and only the [−cons] segments are syllabic; in (b) only [−cons] segments are syllabic, but the [−low, −cons] segment preceding [oː] is non-syllabic [j] (on the assumption that [j] is [−cons]); and in (c) all the [−cons] segments and the preconsonantal [ṃ] are syllabic.

More generally in language, a vowel ([−cons, +son]) between non-vowels will be [+syllabic]; and, typically, a consonant can be syllabic only if it, too, constitutes a peak of prominence: i.e. if it is not juxtaposed to a vowel (rather than a consonant or a boundary) and is a [+son] surrounded by [−son] segments, or, if that is not the case, if it is a [+cont] surrounded by [−cont], or is the unique [−cont] segment in a syllable. We return in chapter 4 to the syllabicity hierarchy (see also Bell 1978): it again involves a scalar phenomenon not amenable to characterisation in terms of binary features. All that is of interest at the present moment is that syllabicity is determinate (non-contrastive) in such cases with respect to the sequences of segment-types. Of course, syllabicity is not entirely determined by universal principles: in Lumasaaba, as we have seen, a pre-consonantal nasal is syllabic; in other languages this is not the case. However, it remains true that for individual languages syllabicity assignment is determinate (relative to particular tempi). Moreover, in Lumasaaba, syllabicity is *necessarily* derived rather than lexical (if the lexicon contains formatives rather than words) in that the determining sequences may arise only as a result of the juxtaposition of formatives (see again Brown 1972:§3.2.4).

It seems that the only occasion for potential indeterminacy in syllabicity assignment in languages is with respect to sequences of [− cons] segments, if 'glides' like [w] and [j] are distinguished from vowels solely as [− syllabic]. However, actual indeterminacies are rarer than this situation might suggest, since, for example, particular languages may reject hiatus and allow only falling diphthongs, in which case the first of two [− cons] segments is necessarily the syllabic. Moreover, in English, at least, which at first appears to present just such indeterminate possibilities in having both glide + vowel and vowel + glide sequences (*well, yell vs. now, nigh*), there are motivations for regarding prevocalic glides as [+ cons], i.e. as sonorant consonants (Lass & Anderson 1975; Lass 1976). In that case, syllabicity is determinate with respect to other properties of segments plus their sequential arrangement; i.e. it is PROJECTIVE.

If syllabicity is typically, if not universally, non-contrastive, as being determined by the sequence of segment-types (despite Bell & Hooper 1978b:5, who merely show that syllabicity is not uniquely determined by universal principles), it is even more inappropriate to represent it in the same way as inherent features. Rather, we should explicitly recognise that, like stress level in English, it is both combinatorial and typically determinate, relative to the context. Accordingly, we propose to introduce at this point the auxiliary symbol '∗' to mark a syllabic segment, which is thus associated with the syllabic peak, all other segments being part of the troughs. This symbol is typically absent from lexical representations, which lack indications of combinatorially determined properties. The phonology of Lumasaaba will contain redundancy rules associating ∗ with particular segments on the basis of the sequence, as in (2.2):

(2.2)

a. ki + kalaßu → $\overset{* \ \ \ * * * \ \ \ * * * *}{\text{ki + kalaßu}}$ → cikalaßu

b. ma + diofu → $\overset{* \ \ \ * * \ \ \ * * *}{\text{ma + diofu}}$ → madjoːfu

c. i + N + siNbikila → $\overset{* \ * \ ** *** \ * ** ***}{\text{i + N + siNbikila}}$ → iːsimbicila

We take up below the formal characterisation of ✳: this in itself requires recognition of a structural property of phonological sequences that is not given recognition in *SPE*, for example. All that we are concerned with at this point, however, is to distinguish such a combinatorial notion from the status of inherent features; and secondly to try to establish the plausibility of suggesting a derivative (non-contrastive) status for this property. Notice that the use of ✳ is traditional in dependency grammars (see Hays 1964). It is also employed in the notation of metrical phonology as a grid element (Liberman & Prince 1977; Prince 1983). We return below to the status of the metrical grid, after first developing a dependency characterisation of phonological sequences.

2.1.3 Recurrence, markedness and constituentiality

All of the phenomena alluded to in the previous section are, it would appear, quite compatible with non-constituentiality. We have merely uncovered another structural variable which (like those discussed in chapter 1) is concealed by a simple feature matrix. Certainly, the property is combinatorial: it is a feature of sequences. However, it does not as such depend on constituency: the identification of peaks does not require division of, say, the intervening troughs, such that the segments in the troughs are grouped with particular peaks. What we must turn to now is a consideration of the evidence for such divisions and for the grouping of segments in this way.

Let us approach the question of phonological constituency via the formulation of an assumption concerning what should be required of an account of permissible sequences in language and languages, which we shall refer to as the CONSTITUENTIALITY ASSUMPTION, given as (2.3):

(2.3)   *Constituentiality assumption*

The representation of sequences of segments optimises the expression of phonological relationships ('sequences', 'regularities') that are (a) recurrent and (b) natural.

Again (as in the componentiality assumption), this incorporates the natural recurrence assumption, provided that for 'classes' we substitute 'sequences'. A formulation of this latter principle which would allow for both classes and sequences is given as (2.4):

(2.4)   *Natural recurrence assumption*

   a. Paradigmatic and syntagmatic groupings of phonological segments are not random.
   b. Phonological groupings and the regularities into which they enter have a phonetic basis.

The phonological theory proposed and exemplified in the first eight chapters of *SPE* makes no constituentiality claim as such, although in so far as universal sequential conditions might be established, recurrence of sequence can at least be given recognition. But the notation gives us no reason to expect this; it does not make the expression of recurrent sequences simpler than that of the non-recurrent or non-occurrent. Nor does it enable us to distinguish, except by listing, between non-recurrence and non-occurrence, i.e. between RELATIVE and ABSOLUTE universals (assuming that there are instances of the latter in the area of sequential conditions: for some suggestions, see, for example, Greenberg 1978b). Even if we lay this latter problem aside, it is clear that certain sequences are recurrent. For example, given a sequence such as is indicated in (2.5):

(2.5) $+ C_1 C_2 V \ldots$

the values for C_1 and C_2 given in (2.6):

(2.6) $C_1 = [-\text{sonorant}]$
       $C_2 = [+\text{sonorant}]$

are much more likely, to put it no more strongly, than the reverse (see Greenberg's (1978:257–8) generalisation 17 concerning clusters). The theory of representation presented in the first eight chapters of *SPE* gives us no reason to expect the sequence $[-\text{sonorant}]$ $[+\text{sonorant}]$ to recur in this environment.

This kind of recurrence (relative universality) could perhaps be described using the machinery of marking conventions proposed in chapter 9 of *SPE*. Chomsky & Halle (*SPE*:§9.2.1) propose only six 'sequential' marking conventions, four of which (IIa,b; IIIc,d) designate as unmarked initial and postvocalic true consonants (as opposed to glides and liquids, which are more marked, and vowels, which are most marked), together with postconsonantal $[+\text{vocalic}]$ segments. Five of these conventions (from *SPE*:404) are reproduced as (2.7):

(2.7)   a.

$$[u \text{ cons}] \rightarrow [+\text{cons}]/ \left\{ \begin{bmatrix} + \\ +\text{voc} \\ -\text{cons} \end{bmatrix} \right\} \quad - \quad \text{(IIa,b)}$$

b.

$$[u \text{ voc}] \rightarrow \left\{ \begin{array}{l} [+\text{voc}]/ \quad C- \\ [-\text{voc}]/ \left\{ \begin{array}{l} + \\ V \end{array} \right\} - \end{array} \right\} \quad \text{(IIIa,c,d)}$$

IIIa is too general, in that a consonant following another in final position has [−vocalic] as its unmarked value. However, the conventions in (2.7) could be restricted to assign, say, the unmarked value [+vocalic] to a segment in the context in (2.8):

(2.8)   +[−voc]—

thus providing for the recurrence referred to in our discussion of (2.5). Further conventions are required to account for terminal constraints.

The sixth convention (XXIVa), reproduced as (2.9):

(2.9)   [u cont] → [+cont]/+ —[+cons]

seems to be simply wrong (cf. Greenberg's 1978b generalisations 7, 9, 17, 24, which involve different kinds of counterexample), and we shall ignore it.

It is clear once again (as in our discussion of *SPE* 'markedness' in chapter 1) that the strategy embodied in (2.7) is non-explanatory. We are simply cataloguing as '*u*' those feature-values that recur in a particular context. The reason for the recurrence does not emerge from the notation. In introducing their discussion of markedness, Chomsky & Halle observe, concerning the previous chapters of *SPE*:

Suppose . . . that we were systematically to interchange features or to replace [αF] by [−αF] (where α = +, and F is a feature) throughout our description of English structure. There is nothing in our account of linguistic theory to indicate that the result would be the description of a system that violates certain principles governing human languages. (*SPE*:400)

But the marking conventions do not provide these principles: they merely provide a device for labelling segments and sequences with respect to the extent to which they conform to the (unformulated) principles. It is in itself quite arbitrary in terms of this notation that the unmarked value for [consonantal] initially or after a vowel is [+consonantal]. What principle does this evaluation follow from?

Cairns (1969) provides an elaborate attempt to extend the theory of markedness in such a way as to permit the formulation of universal sequential constraints. He provides a mechanism for stating absolute rather than relative universals. The former are not provided for by markedness theory. Specifically, he adds to the apparatus of marking conventions a universal set of 'neutralisation rules', each of which 'specifies that a particular feature or set of features may not have the marked value in given environments' (1969:866). Consider, for example, his neutralisation rule 4, reproduced as (2.10):

$$(2.10) \quad N(\text{voc})/ + \begin{bmatrix} \underline{} \\ m\,\text{cons} \end{bmatrix} [m\,\text{cons}]$$

That is, [vocalic] is neutralised, such that its marked value is not permitted to a formative-initial segment that both has the marked value for [consonantal] and is followed by another segment marked [*m* consonantal].

Cairns' marking conventions for [consonantal] and [vocalic] are given in (2.11) and (2.12) respectively:

$$(2.11) \qquad [u\,\text{cons}] \rightarrow \begin{cases} [+\text{cons}]/ + \begin{cases} \underline{} \; [u\,\text{cons}] \\ [m\,\text{seg}][u\,\text{cons}] \underline{} \end{cases} & \text{a.} \\[2ex] & \text{b.} \\[1ex] [-\text{cons}]/ + \begin{cases} \underline{} \; [m\,\text{cons}] \\ [m\,\text{seg}][m\,\text{cons}] \underline{} \\ [m\,\text{seg}] \quad \underline{} \end{cases} & \text{c.} \\ & \text{d.} \\ & \text{e.} \end{cases}$$

$$(2.12) \qquad [u\,\text{voc}] \rightarrow \begin{cases} [+\text{voc}]/ \begin{cases} + \begin{bmatrix} +\text{cons} \\ -\text{voc} \end{bmatrix} \begin{bmatrix} \underline{} \\ u\,\text{nas} \end{bmatrix} \\[2ex] \begin{bmatrix} \underline{} \\ -\text{cons} \end{bmatrix} \end{cases} & \begin{matrix} \text{a.} \\[2ex] \text{b.} \end{matrix} \\[3ex] [-\text{voc}]/ \begin{bmatrix} \underline{} \\ +\text{cons} \end{bmatrix} & \text{c.} \end{cases}$$

The marked value for [consonantal] before a segment that is [*m* consonantal] is [+consonantal], by (2.11c); the marked value for a segment that follows a marked segment is also [+consonantal], by (2.11e). Thus (2.10) states that the first of two initial [+consonantal] segments necessarily has the unmarked value for [vocalic] in that environment, i.e. [−vocalic]. Similarly, by neutralisation rule 5, given as (2.13):

$$(2.13) \quad N(\text{voc})/ + [m\,\text{cons}] \begin{bmatrix} \underline{} \\ m\,\text{cons} \end{bmatrix}$$

the second segment in such a sequence is necessarily [+vocalic], by (2.12a) ([*u* nasal] → [−nasal]). Together, (2.10) and (2.13) allow initial sequences of true consonant followed by liquid, but not vice versa.

However, it is clear that (2.10) and (2.13), though they may specify a very common situation in the languages of the world, cannot be maintained as universal rules, i.e. as being necessarily true of any language where their structural description is met. It is just not the case that the excluded sequences are not attested. Both initial sequences of liquid + obstruent and of two obstruents are found (in Aguacatec, for example – see Greenberg 1978b). Thus, at best (2.10) and (2.13) are either relative rather than absolute universals, or (equivalently) they constitute another layer of marking conventions; they are 'meta-conventions' of markedness – and they are *a fortiori* open to the same objections. Moreover, even as universal rules (of whatever status), their relationship to the internal structure of the segments comprising the relevant sequences is again quite arbitrary. The theory, and specifically the notation, offers no explanation of why just these rules are appropriate; they are not related in any systematic way to the structure of segments and sequences. The notation as such does not even reflect in its form the physical origins of neutralisation suggested by Cairns (1969:§4): there is no natural relation between the notation and the physical factors which may underlie neutralisation. The character of the neutralisations that occur is not predictable from the representations provided by the notation.

Thus the universality or the recurrence of sequences across languages can be described within the *SPE* framework only arbitrarily, by listing or in terms of the ad hoc device of marking conventions (and, possibly, conventions of conventions – Cairns' 'neutralisation rules'). Symptomatic of the arbitrariness of the marking conventions is the fact that there seems to be no empirical basis for choosing between those conventions proposed in *SPE* and those suggested by Cairns, which make the markedness of different features predictable (see Hooper 1976:§9.3). Once more, then, there are structural properties not provided for by the notation. This also remains true of the markedness relations ascribed to syllable structure by Cairns & Feinstein (1982). As we have already observed, their discussion quite misses the point of criticisms of markedness such as Lass's (1975, 1976) concerning the circularity of the proposals made in *SPE*. They suggest, moreover, that the marking conventions might receive some support from their role in the explication of recurrent restrictions on syllable structure. However, they do not in fact show this; rather, they propose a new set of equally circular markedness conventions for syllable structure.

Again, this recurrence of sequential restrictions in itself does not necessarily argue for constituentiality; just as in the case of syllabicity, the mere existence of combinatorial restrictions does not require reference to constituency. If, however, the sequential domain of a number of these restrictions is the same, and this domain cannot be specified with reference to non-phonological bracketings, then it is appropriate to associate the restrictions with a phonological unit. Our characterisation of that unit must form a natural basis for the observed restrictions. Before turning to the characterisation of phonological units, in particular the syllable, and of the associated property of syllabicity, we must therefore first establish the appropriateness of the syllable as a domain for sequential conditions.

2.2   The syllable as a constituent

2.2.1   The syllable as a domain for sequential conditions

In the preceding section we have uncovered structural properties, such as syllabicity and the recurrence of sequential conditions, which are problematical within the non-constituential notation proposed in *SPE*. In the following sections we shall examine the extent to which these problems are resolved within a constituential theory. Here we consider, in the first instance, whether there are reasons for associating sequential restrictions with phonological units like the syllable rather than simply with words (or morphemes).

Consider any word containing more than one syllabic; for simplicity's sake, one with two syllabics. In English and many other languages consonant clusters can occur before the first syllabic, as the onset, after the second, as the coda, and between the two, as the interlude. In terms of a non-constituential notation, each of these positions is unique. If sequential conditions depend on word structure alone, then no predictions are made about the relationship between the constraints operative at each position. And there is no reason to expect the occurrence of a segment with the inherent feature [+syllabic] to impose specific restrictions on preceding and following sequences. In fact, the sequences occurring in the coda are typically the mirror image of those in the onset (note many of the universals formulated by Greenberg 1978b); and the interlude is a sequence of an allowable coda preceding a lawful onset. We take up the former regularity in chapter 4; here we are concerned with the decomposability of interludes.

Consider, for example, the status of the potential English interlude /tkt/, discussed by Kahn (1976:34). Such clusters, and others involving a medial

/k/ flanked by obstruents, must be ruled out as viable English interludes. There are partially similar constraints, however, on English initial and final clusters, if a formative boundary or word boundary is substituted for the initial and final obstruent respectively. All three of the sequences in (2.14) are ill-formed for English formatives:

(2.14)   a. *t   k   t
         b. *#   k   t
         c. *t   k   #

The expression of these regularities can be collapsed in various ways using arbitrary devices such as the brace notation. Kahn suggests (2.15):

$$(2.15) \quad *t \quad k \quad \begin{Bmatrix} C \\ \# \end{Bmatrix} \quad * \begin{Bmatrix} C \\ \# \end{Bmatrix} \quad k \quad t$$

These, however, involve the unnatural grouping $\{C, \#\}$. This grouping is indeed a recurrent one in non-syllabic formulations of phonological regularities; Kahn (1976) discusses a number of examples. He notes, for instance, that in English [g] may not appear in the sequence [ŋ]—$\{C, \#\}$: *tungsten, sing* (cf. prevocalic *anger*). This recurrence has led some writers to look for a natural relationship between # and (voiceless) obstruents. Lass (1971) argues for this on the basis of assimilatory phenomena in Old English and Modern German. Thus, in Old English, a fricative is voiceless in the immediate environment of voiceless obstruents or of #, as in (2.16):

(2.16)   a. æfter, mæst
         b. healf, smītan, mūs

Each of the fricatives (represented as ⟨f s⟩) is voiceless. A voiced fricative is excluded from any of the positions occupied by the voiceless fricative in (2.16). In examples like those in (2.16a) this can be associated with the adjacent voiceless obstruent. In (2.16b), however, the fricative is adjacent to a sonorant and #; # thus has the role of a voiceless obstruent if the distribution of voicelessness in fricatives is to be given a unitary formulation. However, the distribution of voicing in Old English fricatives seems to be adequately characterised in terms of associating voice only with occurrence between voiced sounds; otherwise, the simpler (see §4.1) voiceless variant appears. Moreover, attributing voicelessness or obstruency to # on the basis of phenomena such as (2.14)–(2.16) is inappropriate – as some further regularities reveal.

There are, indeed, other regularities which apparently equate # with V rather than with C or obstruent. Consider, for example, the distribution of tenseness/length in most varieties of Modern English. A vowel in a stressed syllable must be tense/long in two particular situations: (a) before #, and (b) before another vowel. This is illustrated in (2.17):

(2.17)   a. knee, pie
         b. neon, bias

Only tense segments can appear as the (first) vowels in examples such as these. Lax vowels are excluded from the environment in (2.18):

(2.18) $*\breve{V}\begin{Bmatrix} V \\ \# \end{Bmatrix}$

(In some dialects, such as RP, however, there is a tendency to lax a high stressed vowel in hiatus – thus ['nɪɒn] *neon*; see Wells 1982:§3.2.9 – whereas [ɪ] is preferred to *unstressed* [i] both in hiatus and word-finally.)

Here, then, is a regularity which (whatever its status in the phonology of English) apparently involves a grouping of # with V. It seems to us that this makes very clear the inappropriateness of attributing to # features such as [−voice] or [−son]. How, then, is the recurrence of the groupings {C, #} and {V, #} as environments to be accounted for?

Let us return in the first place to the restriction on interludes discussed by Kahn, and illustrated in (2.14a). A distinct interlude constraint (to exclude (2.14a) and the like) is unnecessary if interludes are segmented as syllable-final followed by syllable-initial. (2.14a) is not a well-formed interlude in English because the sequence cannot be exhaustively apportioned to a well-formed final + initial sequence. If the first /t/ alone in such an interlude constitutes a syllable-final (i.e. the syllable boundary falls between it and the following /kt/ sequence), then the syllable that follows lacks a permissible initial: as evidenced by (2.14b), /kt/ is not an initial. Equally, if the second /t/ alone is taken as an initial, then the preceding final is deviant (see (2.14c)). Such constraints on interludes as underlie the deviance of (2.14a) follow from the requirements of syllabification. Both formative and word structure constraints are syllable-based. (We return below (§2.4) to a further consideration of this, and of the difference between formative and word constraints. See also Haugen 1956; Hooper 1976:ch. 2.)

Further, notice that the environment from which stressed lax vowels are prohibited in Modern English reduces to 'end of syllable' (given the syllabifications for medials argued for below). Similarly, in English [g] may not follow [ŋ] if it cannot initiate the following syllable. Notice that this accounts for the absence of [ŋg] word- and formative-finally, as in *sing*, and also before consonant sequences like that in *tungsten*; it also allows for the well-formedness of the sequence *anglicise*, where [g] initiates the following syllable. Thus, both the unnatural groupings {C, #} and {V, #} can be eliminated if syllable segmentation is invoked. (The principles of segmentation remain to be motivated, of course: see §2.5.)

2.2.2   The syllable as a domain for phonological processes

The specification of sequential constraints is facilitated if they are related to syllable groupings rather than simply to formatives or words. This forms one kind of evidence for constituentiality. Before considering the various issues associated with the character of syllabification, we should also give some attention to the role of the syllable in segmental and suprasegmental processes. Syllables and their boundaries have been invoked in the formulation of a number of regularities in different languages (see Hooper 1972; Vennemann 1972; Anderson & Jones 1974a:§1; Kahn 1976; Selkirk 1982; Anderson 1984b:§1). We will consider here only a few instances, though the evidence for the relevance of syllabification is essentially cumulative, particularly since, unsurprisingly, it is difficult to establish cases where appeal to syllabification is completely unavoidable. Syllable boundary placement, as well as the selection of syllabic nuclei, is interpretive of the sequence of segments (see §2.5): boundaries are assigned on the basis of (partially universal) principles formulated in terms of segment sequences. Thus phonological formulations can refer directly to these sequences rather than to the syllabifications which they subtend. Syllabic formulations, however, are to be preferred to the extent that there are recurrent regularities whose domain is the syllable and/or which are more complex to characterise in a non-syllabic notation. It seems clear that the most natural expression for a range of phonological regularities makes reference to the syllable as a domain, or to a syllable boundary as a crucial determinant.

Consider in both these respects Saib's (1978) discussion of 'emphasis' or pharyngealisation in Berber. In careful speech, pharyngealisation spreads out from 'independent' emphatic consonants to an extent that is regulated, Saib claims, by syllabic structure. Pharyngealisation spreads to all segments in the same syllable, to those in the preceding if it is open, and to those in the following if the syllable containing the independent emphatic is itself open. Example (2.19a) illustrates spread of pharyngealisation over an open syllable, and (2.19b) over a syllable and its open predecessor:

(2.19)   a. /ðu $ raθ/ → [ðu̞ $ ra̞θ]   'go around' (imp. pl.)

b. /θa $ ðər $ ɣalθ/ → [θa̞ $ ðə̞r $ ɣalθ]   'blind' (fem.)

c. /a $ βərr $ i $ ## um $ lil/ →
       [a̞ $ βə̞rr $ i̞ $ ðu̞m $ lil]   'the white goat'

where, by the usual convention, '$' indicates a syllable boundary. In (2.19c) emphasis spreads in both directions (despite the word boundary), whereas spread to the final syllable in (2.19b) is blocked by the closed emphatic syllable. (On the syllabifications, see Saib 1978, and references there.) Pharyngealisation spread might thus be characterised as in (2.20) and (2.21):

(2.20) $[+\text{seg}] \rightarrow [+\text{phar}]/[+\text{phar}]$

(2.21)

$$[+\text{seg}] \rightarrow [+\text{phar}]/ \left\{ \begin{array}{l} \begin{bmatrix} - \\ V \end{bmatrix} \; \$ \, [+\text{phar}] \\[12pt] \begin{bmatrix} V \\ +\text{phar} \end{bmatrix} \; \$ - \end{array} \right\}$$

(2.20), which can apply both before and after (2.21) and involves possible reiteration in a mirror-image environment, spreads pharyngealisation to any tautosyllabic segment adjacent to a pharyngealised segment; and (2.21) allows spread over a syllable boundary to or from a preceding vowel. (2.21) must not reapply to the results of applying (2.20) a second time, so that spreading is limited to (at most) one syllable on either side of an independent emphatic. (For an alternative formulation, which invokes the syllable as a unit, rather than simply its boundaries, see Saib 1978:101.)

(2.20) and (2.21) make crucial reference to syllabification, given the convention that (2.20) has a tautosyllabic domain, and the specification of the syllable boundary in (2.21). However, a formulation that is syllabification-free is not impossible. Indeed, the reformulation offered by Bell & Hooper in their introductory essay to the book which includes Saib's discussion moves somewhat in this direction (1978b:15), though still mentioning the syllable as a domain. A rough approximation of a non-syllabic formulation would involve restricting spread of pharyngealisation to the following two circumstances:

(2.22)   a. If the independent emphatic immediately precedes a vowel, then the maximal spread is represented as:

$$C^1 \quad V \quad Ç \quad V \quad C^1 \quad V \quad C^1$$

(where geminates are counted as C) and pharyngealisation will spread continuously over as much of this domain as is available to it.

b. If the independent emphatic immediately precedes a consonant, then the maximal spread is represented as:

$$C^1 \quad V \quad C^1 \quad V \quad Ç$$

This allows for the examples in (2.19) as well as the others discussed by Saib, and it avoids reference to the syllable or its boundaries. However, even if it can be provided with an adequate formal characterisation, it is an awkward and unilluminating formulation, which invokes apparently arbitrary sequences of segments. This follows directly from the failure to make reference to a syllabic domain, given the correlations formulated in (2.20) and (2.21): syllable boundaries and syllable-type (i.e. open or vowel-final *vs.* closed) are both relevant to the determination of the spread of pharyngealisation. To put it slightly differently, (2.20) exhibits a prosodic process whose domain is the syllable, while in (2.21) the boundary marker figures as a crucial component in the structural description. Pharyngealisation spread in Berber, then, is constituential, and specifically syllable-bounded.

Syllable bounding has also often been invoked in another case, the characterisation of the distribution of aspiration in Modern English: for example, in the discussion in Selkirk (1978). The occurrence of aspirated stops seems to be limited to syllable-initial position. If there is an aspiration rule it is thus perhaps of the character of (2.23):

(2.23)
$$\begin{bmatrix} C \\ -\text{voice} \\ -\text{cont} \end{bmatrix} \rightarrow [+\text{asp}] / \$ \,—$$

Accordingly, both the word-initial (a) and the word-medial (b) stops in (2.24) are aspirated:

(2.24)   a. [tʰ]alon, [tʰ]orment, [tʰ]attoo
        b. a[tʰ]ain, ta[tʰ]oo

while those occurring after *s* in (2.25), which are thus not syllable-initial, are not aspirated:

(2.25)   a. s[t]ar, s[t]igma
        b. es[t]ate, as[t]ir

However, this range of data can obviously also be accommodated by a non-syllabic formulation such as (2.26):

(2.26)
$$\begin{bmatrix} C \\ -\text{voice} \\ -\text{cont} \end{bmatrix} \rightarrow \begin{cases} [-\text{asp}]/s- \\ \\ [+\text{asp}] \end{cases}$$

Neither formulation provides insight into the restriction: why is aspiration disallowed after *s*, or required syllable-initially? Moreover, there are some problems which are difficult to resolve with respect to either framework. However, we approach these via some observations that do indeed support the syllabic formulation in (2.23).

Notice that, as it stands, (2.23) predicts that aspiration is absent word-finally, as in the forms in (2.27) – where, indeed, for many speakers the stop is normally unreleased and glottalised:

(2.27)   ha[ʔt], malle[ʔt]

whereas this is not allowed for in (2.26). Rather, for such varieties an additional environment for non-aspiration must be added to that in (2.26), perhaps as (2.28):

(2.28)
$$\begin{bmatrix} C \\ -\text{voice} \\ -\text{cont} \end{bmatrix} \rightarrow \begin{cases} [-\text{asp}]/\begin{cases} s- \\ -\# \end{cases} \\ \\ [+\text{asp}] \end{cases}$$

However, this again involves the brace notation; and it clearly offers a lesser generalisation than (2.23). (Neither version is favoured, however, with respect to pronunciations in which the final stop is released and aspirated.) Once more we derive support for constituentiality in phonological representations. This is confirmed by some further considerations.

In accordance with both accounts, initial stop + liquid clusters show aspiration, manifested primarily as devoicing of the liquids, in examples such as (2.29):

(2.29)   a. [tr̥]ain, [tr̥]easure
        b. de[tr̥]act, a[tr̥]ition

again provided they are not preceded by *s*:

(2.30)   a. s[tr]ain, s[tr]etch
        b. as[tr]ingent, res[tr]ict

)wing *t* is not devoiced (in British English, at least);
aviour of the clusters in (2.31):

ic *vs.* a[p]]aud

stop in the latter receives aspiration (giving devoicing of
t in the former being typically glottalised. This can be
by a non-syllabic formulation only by way of a further
ldition to the environments for non-aspiration listed in
as indicated in (2.32):

$$
\left.\begin{array}{c} \text{ice} \\ \text{ont} \\ \text{>} \end{array}\right] \rightarrow \left\{ \begin{array}{l} [-\text{asp}]/\left\{ \begin{array}{l} \langle -l\rangle \\ s- \\ -\# \end{array}\right\} \\ [+\text{asp}] \end{array}\right\}
$$

However, given a syllabification for English formatives which is in
accordance with the 'law of initials' (see, for example, Vennemann 1972;
also this volume §2.3), whereby the constraints on formative- or word-
medial syllable-initials conform with those on formative- or word-initials,
the sequence *tl* cannot constitute a syllable-initial cluster: the syllable
boundary comes between the two consonants. The first *t* in *Atlantic* is thus
not syllable-initial (whereas the *p* in *applaud* is), and it is correctly
predicted to be non-aspirated by (2.23). It shows only the partial devoicing
associated with initials like the *l* in a compound verb such as *uplift*, where
the morphological boundary is observed (on the fragility of morphological boundaries, see further §2.3).

   Once again, the unmodified syllabic formulation of (2.23) is compatible
with phenomena which require a further ad hoc extension to the non-
syllabic account. The conditioning environment for lack of aspiration is
now, in terms of (2.32), even more heterogeneous. And a reformulation
which attempts to specify the conditions under which [+asp] rather than
[−asp] is found does not represent any improvement, as the reader can
readily verify (see, too, Selkirk 1978). There are varieties of English in
which devoicing of a liquid takes place after *any* voiceless sound,
irrespective of the syllabifications predicted by the 'law of initials', so that
both the examples in (2.31) display devoicing. In these varieties (such as
the New York one pointed out to us by Roger Lass) the lateral in *athlete*
also devoices – see the discussion below. Such varieties offer no evidence
concerning the relevance of syllabification in this case.

It seems clear that an adequate formulation of aspiration in the relevant varieties of English should invoke syllable boundaries. However, there is a problem with (2.23) as it stands. Although, as predicted by (2.23), aspiration is associated with a voiceless stop preceding a liquid whether or not the following vowel is stressed, a single intervocalic stop is not aspirated if the following vowel is unstressed, whether or not *s* precedes. Thus (2.33a) shows unstressed vowels preceded by an aspirated stop + liquid (cf. (2.29)), and (2.33b) shows that, as usual, such stops are unaspirated after *s*:

(2.33)   a. a[tr̩]ophy, seduc[tr̩]ess
          b. as[tr]al, mis[tr]ess

while (2.34) shows the unaspirated stop preceding an unstressed vowel, whether or not *s* precedes:

(2.34)   a. fe[t]id, phone[t]ic
          b. fes[t]ive, mas[t]iff

Given a syllabification whereby the stop in both (2.33a) and (2.34a) initiates a syllable, (2.23) fails to predict the lack of aspiration in (2.34a). We return to this problem in the sections that follow, in that stress assignment is crucially involved here (cf. the aspiration of the pre-stress stops in (2.24b)). Clearly, though, stress variation is insufficient in itself to explain the contrast between (2.34a) and (2.24b): as we have seen, the pre-liquid medial stops in both (2.29b) (preceding a stressed vowel) and (2.33a) (preceding an unstressed vowel) are aspirated, and the word-initial stop in *tattoo* or *tomato*, though it immediately precedes an unstressed vowel, is nevertheless aspirated.

2.3   Syllable boundaries

There is some support, then, for the relevance of a phonological unit of syllable size, such that there are regularities which invoke it as a domain, and/or invoke its initiation or termination as crucial determinants. If such a unit is to be made viable, we must now give some attention to the vexed questions concerning the placement of syllable boundaries – basically when and where? We consider first the location of boundaries in representations which are close to the phonetic.

2.3.1   Principles of syllabification

Intersubjective agreement among native speakers concerning location of syllabicity is high; and (partially universal) principles of syllabicity assignment can be formulated with respect to the sequence of segment-types (see §§2.1, 4.5). In addition, division into syllables appears to be relatively straightforward for some languages, for example, those in which utterances involve only sequences of the form (C)V. In such cases, intersyllabic (medial) segments are unambiguously syllable-initiating, if the formulation of syllable boundary placement is to be maximally general.

However, in many languages consonants can be both utterance- and word-initial and final. Intersyllabic occurrences of consonants are therefore potentially syllable-initiating or terminating or both: there is a distributional, as well as often a 'physical' indeterminacy, in locating syllable boundaries. This can frequently be resolved with reference to principles of syllable structure, either universal or language-specific.

For instance, the second segment in an intersyllabic sequence of the character of /-θr-/ or /-θl-/ will not be taken to belong to the preceding (rather than the succeeding) syllable: with exceptions to which we return below, a segment must be no more sonorous than any intervening between it and the nucleus of its syllable: 'Between a given sound and the peak are only found sounds of the same, or a higher, sonority class' (Jespersen 1950:131). In general, syllabic slopes coincide with decreasing sonority.

Further, in a language like English which lacks utterance-initial clusters of the character of /θl-/ (i.e. dental fricative + lateral), the fricative in the intersyllabic sequence in (2.35) cannot initiate the second syllable, if the principles of syllabification (in this instance language-specific) are to be maximally general:

(2.35)   athlete

The syllabification is thus distributionally determinate in this case; and the syllable boundary intervenes between the two consonants. Similarly, the boundary must follow the stop in (2.36):

(2.36)   atlas

as is confirmed by its lack of aspiration (recall §2.2.2) and, in the relevant dialects, by the clearness of the /l/.

This conjunction of universal and specific principles means that even in those (few) languages that show intersyllabic sequences that cannot be decomposed into two sub-sequences such that the first is a viable utterance-terminal and the second an utterance-initial, syllabification can still be determinate. In Telugu, for example, only the consonant /m/ can occur utterance-finally (Reddy 1979), while utterance-initial three-member clusters are limited to /str-/. However, in a form such as (2.37):

(2.37)   /aːndʰraː/   (place name)

we can on universal grounds only segment the intersyllabic sequence before or after the stop, with the language-specific existence of stop + liquid initials and absence of terminal clusters requiring that the boundary fall before the stop. Thus, as Reddy points out, the rules of syllable structure for Telugu will differ word-medially, word-initially and word-finally. The situation is in this respect non-optimal: we require positionally sensitive rules of syllable structure. However, syllabification is still determinate. In other circumstances, though, such distributional principles are not in themselves decisive: we consider some examples in a moment.

We have invoked universal principles of syllable structure together with language-particular conditions on finals and initials, conditions which are optimal if they are not sensitive to position in, for example, the word. These conditions constitute applications of the 'law of finals' and the 'law of initials' (see again Vennemann 1972). Pulgram (1970:46) provides a rather strong interpretation of the application of these laws, such that any 'syllable boundary in any part of the utterance must obey the constraints that prevail in the language under scrutiny at the word boundary'. This is untenable in this strong form, in that there are intersyllabic sequences in Telugu and other languages (see on Finnish, for example, Fischer-Jørgensen 1952; Anderson 1975:10) which on such conditions totally resist syllabification. Rather, a more plausible interpretation of the laws, as involving relative markedness, follows from the assumption that the basic phonotactic unit is the syllable: the phonotactic constraints are simpler if they apply to all syllables rather than having to embody restrictions on particular positions (word-medial, word-final, etc.). This assumption, which we argued for above, and universals of syllable structure, which we consider further below, thus significantly reduce distributional indeterminacy in the assignment of syllable boundaries to medial sequences of consonants.

There are, however, rather frequent indeterminacies in language-specific syllabification which cannot be resolved by appeal to universals of syllable structure, and which, indeed, arise from the availability of contrary syllabifications compatible both with these universals and with the independently established initial and final cluster structures for the language. In many languages this is the case with single consonant intersyllabics, such as the English forms in (2.38):

(2.38)   cassock, bonnet

The intervocalic consonant could form a legitimate part of either the preceding or following syllable. This is equally true of the stop in clusters such as those in (2.39):

(2.39)   a. cobra, petrol
          b. veranda, filter

while in (2.40) the entire *st* sequence is ambivalent in this way:

(2.40)   a. custom
          b. mistress

Such segments or sequences could belong to either syllable or both. It is our contention (following Anderson & Jones 1974a, 1977; Anderson 1975) that, after short vowels at least, such segments are to be interpreted as ambisyllabic unless the segment is adjacent to either a morpho-syntactic or a phonological, specifically a FOOT, boundary. We take up now the question of the domain of ambisyllabicity.

2.3.2   Syllabification and morphology

The inhibition of ambisyllabicity by morphological boundaries may be illustrated in terms of the familiar contrasts in (2.41):

(2.41)   a. linger *vs.* singer
          b. neutron *vs.* foot-rot

The second word in each pair in (2.41) lacks ambisyllabicity. In (b) the ambisyllabic stop in *neutron* shows both the aspiration associated with syllable-initial position (giving devoicing of the following sonorant) and the glottal reinforcement of syllable-final stops; whereas in *foot-rot* /r/ lacks the devoicing that it shows following a tautosyllabic voiceless stop. In (a) the ambisyllabic /g/ in *linger* does not drop; contrast the lack of final /g/ in *sing, long, tungsten*, etc. The morphological boundary in *singer*, however, apparently inhibits ambisyllabicity and thus requires the absence of final /g/.

Some morphological boundaries are not phonologically relevant. In (2.42), for instance:

(2.42)   longer, stronger

the boundary is quite transparent to phonological processes. For the purposes of the present discussion, we represent a phonologically salient boundary as #; words are stretches between ##, and phonologically salient word-internal divisions involve # (cf. Hyman 1975:§1.2.2). These separate the elements of compounds, and the stem from inflections and (in English, for example) other 'stress-neutral' affixes. The word is taken to be the minimal unit of the syntax. (For instance, we do not regard positioning of affixes, like tense and number in English, as syntactic; this is independent of the syntactic regularities of the language – see further Anderson 1980b.) Let us refer to stretches between # as FORMATIVES; a word will thus contain one or more stem or affixal formatives.

The relevance of formative boundaries to phonological processes can be illustrated by the operation of Aitken's Law (Aitken 1962, 1981; Vaiana Taylor 1974; Ewen 1977) in Scots and Scottish English. Consider in particular the diphthongs in (2.43):

(2.43)   a. rise, ties, tie, tire
          b. ride, tide, tile

In (a), before a voiced fricative, /r/ or ## we find the long diphthong [ɑ·e]; whereas in (b) there is a short diphthong that is also distinct in quality, i.e. [ʌɪ]. We also find the same contrast between the pair in (2.44):

(2.44)   tied [tʰɑ·ed] *vs.* tide [tʰʌɪd]

This conforms with the pattern established in (2.43), provided that the conditioning factor is # (as in *tie#d*) rather than necessarily ##. The long diphthong is formative-final.

Morphological units that are parts of formatives, separated by +, are MORPHEMES, either root or affixal, and are, we assume, not phonologically active, or, at least, less independent. Their occurrence, at any rate, does not block the application of rules. Hyman (1975:196) entertains the possibility (with some attempt at documentation) that + cannot have phonological consequences. However, any such strong account will have to accommodate phenomena like the conditions on medial voicing of *s* (in, for example, *resist*; cf. *consist*), which Siegel (1974:§3.2.1) relates to, among other things, the occurrence of +.

The forms in (2.41) and (2.42) can thus be represented in the appropriate respects as in (2.45):

(2.45)   a. ##linger##, ##sing#er##, ##sing##
         b. ##neutron##, ##foot#rot##
         c. ##long+er##

Ambisyllabicity is inhibited by #.

Of course, within this account, as in others, there remains, in the case of the distribution of [ŋ], the problem of sporadic forms like the nineteenth-century loanword *hangar*, which do not appear to be morphologically complex but nevertheless seem to show /g/-drop. Presumably, these represent a marginal contrast, such that there is no underlying /g/ in these forms and /ŋ/ is lexical. However, in that case, we could and should attribute /ŋ/ to *sing* and *singer* as well (in the absence of any alternation displaying [ŋg]). If so, it is then unnecessary to appeal to a # boundary here, whose presence before such derivational affixes is in any case doubtful on non-phonological grounds. This would mean that the absence of ambisyllabicity in *singer*, etc. would not be due to a morphological boundary, but to the fact that /ŋ/ cannot constitute a syllable-initial in English.

The relevance of the # boundary to compounds and between stem and inflection does not appear to be similarly vulnerable. But, of course, # boundaries can weaken over time to +, and this is reflected in the acquisition of ambisyllabicity. Contrast pronunciations of *newspaper* in which the sibilant, being immediately pre-#, is only partially devoiced, with ones in which it is voiceless, as being shared between the two syllables. Similarly, *teaspoon* may be either ambisyllabic or not: the first syllable is in the latter case open (and, other things being equal, longer). Ambisyllabicity and the lack of it correlate with the difference in the morphological representations given in (2.46):

(2.46)   a. news#paper ⎫
            tea#spoon   ⎬ no ambisyllabicity
                        ⎭

         b. news+paper ⎫
            tea+spoon ⎬ ambisyllabicity
                       ⎭

Again the presence of + has no phonological effect; we find the same ambisyllabicity as in simple morphemes.

Likewise, a root-containing formative is the proper domain for the erection of foot and word structures (on the generalisations governing this see §3.4): #-affixes are 'stress-neutral' (e.g. Siegel 1974). However, we pursue such considerations no further here, given that it is not part of our aim to elaborate a theory of morphological structure and the interaction between morphology and phonology.

We shall argue further in §2.4 that though it is appropriate to reject simple, undifferentiated morpheme-structure constraints (operative between + +) in favour of syllable-structure constraints (or rather lexical syllable-structure rules), there can be a difference (even within such a simplistic account of morphological domains) between the syllable constraints operative within the formative and the morpheme, and those associated with the word, and that in that case the sub-word constraints are more basic. However, at this point, let us return to our consideration of limitations on ambisyllabicity.

2.3.3   Ambisyllabicity and the foot

The other limit on ambisyllabic assignments for intersyllabic clusters is phonological: ambisyllabicity is prevented by an intervening foot boundary. We take the foot to be, among other things, the basic unit of timing: in stress-timed languages salient syllables are perceived as occurring at roughly isochronous intervals (given a constant tempo); see, for example, Abercrombie (1967), Giegerich (1980). In French, if we follow Selkirk's (1978) analysis, the foot consists of a single syllable (or two if the nucleus of the second is [ə]): French is syllable-timed. (For some scepticism concerning this distinction, see Roach 1982.)

Within the foot, ambisyllabicity is preferred, whereas foot boundaries inhibit it: specifically, the salient initial syllable of the foot resists sharing of consonants with the final syllable of the preceding foot. We thus have contrasts such as those in (2.47):

(2.47)   fabric *vs.* abrupt, pasta *vs.* pistaccio, sedentary *vs.* sedan, petrol *vs.* patrol

The consonant (cluster) shows ambisyllabicity only in the first example in each pair, in which it is foot-medial. In the second examples this consonant (cluster) initiates the foot. In the relevant dialects, the ambisyllabic *t* in *petrol* shows both the glottal reinforcement associated with syllable-final position and the aspiration of the initial, whereas the syllable- (and foot-) initiating *t* of *patrol* shows only the characteristics of an initial stop (see Anderson 1969). We can represent the distinction as in (2.48):

(2.48)   a. [pe[t]rol], [pe[d]ant]
         b. [pa][trol], [pe][dan[t]ic]

We now replace the $ symbol with square brackets, which mark the initiation and termination of individual syllables. This enables us to allow both for uniqueness of syllable boundary assignment and for ambisyllabicity; the former with respect to proper bracketing ([[), the latter in terms of overlapping, such that an ambisyllabic consonant is preceded by the initiation ([) of one syllable and followed by the termination (]) of another. Only the syllable junction between the first and second syllables in (2.48b) shows a proper bracketing in which the intersyllabic consonant is assigned exclusively to the following foot-initial salient syllable. All the foot-internal junctions involve overlap.

We have seen that (with the exception of *hangar*, etc.) dropping of /g/ after [ŋ] occurs only when the /g/ cannot be syllable-initial. The ambisyllabic /g/ in (2.49a) fails to drop:

(2.49)   a. [lin[g]er], [lon[g]er]
         b. [sing], [sing][er]

Even if we reject the /g/-dropping analysis (see §2.3.2), the /g/ in (2.49a) remains rather uncontroversially syllable-initiating. A nasal is assimilated to a following /g/ or /k/, however, only if they are tautosyllabic, as in the examples in (2.49). If a foot boundary intervenes, then for many speakers there is no assimilation (except with certain prefixes); contrast the pairs in (2.50) (see Hoard 1971):

(2.50)   a. congress, kinky, Sínclair
         b. congressional, Kinkáde, Sincláir

In the (b) examples the foot boundary falls between the nasal and the velar stop and there is no assimilation, whereas the foot-internal syllable junctions in (a) show ambisyllabicity, and thus assimilation. Notice that the second /k/ in *kinky* shows the aspiration we expect of initial voiceless stops, and we therefore cannot allow for the assimilation and lack of it by virtue of syllabifications such as those in (2.51):

(2.51)   kink $ y *vs.* Kin $ kade

Rather, the second /k/ in *kinky* must simultaneously end the first syllable, to provide for the assimilation, and initiate the second, to account for the aspiration, which is absent in a stop which is not syllable-initial. This is as predicted by our proposal concerning the domain of ambisyllabicity.

At this point, however, we should also try to resolve the problems left over from the discussion of aspiration in §2.2.2. There we found that aspiration does not occur with syllable-final stops such as those in (2.52):

(2.52)   [at][las], [hat]

while the syllable-initial stops in (2.53) do show aspiration:

(2.53)   [tʰap], [a][tʰire]

Syllable-initial stops that are also final, such as the second in *kinky*, or those in (2.54):

(2.54)   [an[tʰ]ic], [ma[tɹ]ess]

show aspiration, too, except in cases like (2.55):

(2.55)   [fre][ne[t]ic]

where the stop is the sole intersyllabic consonant. These generalisations concerning the distribution of aspiration depend on the assumption of foot-bounded ambisyllabicity.

Even more directly related to the occurrence of a foot boundary is the distribution of 'tenseness' of consonant groups. As Hoard (1971) points out, foot-initial clusters (not simply syllable-initial) are 'tenser' than groups in other positions.

Notice too that just as weakening of a morphological boundary leads to the development of ambisyllabicity within the foot, so such weakening may lead to a shifting of the foot boundary. Consider, for instance, the development of *mistake*, as represented in (2.56) (Abercrombie 1967:78):

(2.56)   [mis][take] > [mi][stake]

In other formatives with *mis-* the morphological boundary corresponds with a syllable break and a foot-initiation if the following syllable is stressed:

(2.57)   mis][time

However, with *mistake* the absence of aspiration associated with the *t* indicates that it is tautosyllabic with the *s*.

2.3.4   Middle English Open Syllable Lengthening

In the preceding two sub-sections we have looked at limitations on the spread of ambisyllabicity. One consequence of our discussion is that if the foot is universally a domain for ambisyllabicity then ambisyllabicity will characteristically occur only in languages in which the foot has a complex structure in terms of syllables, and which possess both initial and final consonant clusters. (Rudes 1977 specifically associates ambisyllabicity with stress-timed languages.) However, it is our assumption that within such limits segments are ambisyllabic in accordance with the constraints on syllable structure, both universal and language-particular. We return below to one further illustration of this.

First, however, let us note one other apparent limitation on phonetic ambisyllabicity. Specifically, a stressed syllable containing a long (or tense) vowel may not include following consonants in polysyllabic feet. Jespersen, for example, observes that in words like *better, upper, jester* and *biscuit* it is impossible to fix the point of syllable division and determine where the first syllable may be said to end and the second to begin (1950:135). The vowel–consonant transition here he describes as 'close contact', and his description is suggestive of ambisyllabicity. However, after a long vowel 'we have to do with *open contact*' (p. 136), as at foot boundaries, i.e. 'where a syllable is followed by a more strongly stressed syllable'. Such observations are confirmed by Fallows' (1981) experimental findings. Notice too that it is only in the case of stressed short vowels that syllable-final position would violate the constraint discussed in §2.2.1: ambisyllabicity in this instance circumvents this. Thus, phonetic and distributional evidence strongly supports ambisyllabicity only after stressed short vowels.

In the course of the history of English, stressed vowels in certain originally disyllabic words have been lengthened. This is thought to have occurred around 1200 (later in the case of /i/ and /u/), and is usually referred to as Middle English Open Syllable Lengthening (see Malsch & Fulcher 1975; Lass 1976; Anderson & Jones 1977; Minkova 1982). Typical products of MEOSL are given in (2.58):

(2.58) name < OE nama   basin (< French)
        nose < OE nosu   capon (< French)
        steal < OE stelan   able (< French)

As the traditional title suggests, the occurrence of MEOSL can be associated with a vowel which immediately precedes a syllable boundary (but cf. Minkova 1982). However, as far as these examples are concerned, appeal to syllable boundaries is unnecessary: the presence of a single intervocalic consonant also characterises the appropriate set. (2.58) contrasts in both respects with (2.59):

(2.59)   help < OE helpan

where two consonants intervene, and the second syllable begins with the second consonant.

There are many exceptions to this pattern, some of which can be related to paradigmatic levelling or to gemination of a medial sonorant (*gallon*) or to the intervention of a morphological boundary (*throttle*; cf. *throat*) – see Malsch & Fulcher (1975), and also Bliss (1952–3). However, of particular interest here are words such as those in (2.60):

(2.60)   April, chaste, haste (< French), maister (Scots)

in which lengthening has occurred before a cluster, thus favouring an interpretation of the lengthening whereby syllabification is invoked. Notice that in each case the cluster is a viable syllable initiator, unlike the non-lengthening clusters in such disyllables as (2.59): that is, the vowel is lengthened only if it is immediately followed by the initiation of the following syllable.

This again illustrates that, despite the tendency for stressed syllables to be maximalised (i.e. to be of the maximal size compatible with constraints on syllable structure – recall Hoard 1971; Rudes 1977), this is not at the expense of the following unstressed syllable, which shares with the preceding stressed syllable consonants or clusters that are eligible for inclusion in both syllables. Thus, on this assumption, the words in (2.61) cannot simply contrast in the junction of the first two syllables in the manner shown:

(2.61)   Cast $ rol *vs.* ca $ strate

In the former the *st* cluster belongs equally with the second syllable. These phenomena (and recall (2.50)) are incompatible with any notation that does not allow ambisyllabicity – i.e. where] and [always coincide as $, as in Hooper (1976); or that allows only one ambisyllabic consonant at any junction, as apparently in Rudes (1977), though the precise interpretation of his notation, which involves superposition of $ with respect to the allegedly ambisyllabic segment, is unclear to us.

Typically, then, syllable-bracketing, like the selection of the syllabic (§2.2.1), is predictable on the basis of universal and language-specific constraints; only sporadic instances of contrastive syllabification have been recorded (the Northern Iroquoian languages have been cited in this respect). Further, given certain conditions, ambisyllabicity is to be expected. Whether or not ambisyllabification occurs depends on foot-formation and the nature of the stressed syllabic, as well as the occurrence of morphological boundaries. But the placement of stress depends in an intimate way on syllabification, as shown in Anderson (1975), Anderson & Jones (1977:ch. 4), and as we shall attempt to demonstrate in §2.5. This presupposes a level of pre-stress syllabification, a syllabification assigned to lexical items in accordance with (universal and language-particular) constraints on syllable structure. Pre-stress syllabifications must differ, then, in one crucial respect from the relatively superficial syllabifications which we have been concerned with so far: the ambisyllabic/non-ambisyllabic distinction must be absent. It is only after foot-formation, and thus stress-assignment, that the non-morphological limitations to ambisyllabicity are established. Either (within the morphological limits) pre-stress syllabification is uniformly ambisyllabic (unless in a particular instance segment-sharing is incompatible with the constraints on syllable structure), or ambisyllabification is totally absent. We shall argue in what follows that the pre-stress syllabification assigned to individual morphemes or formatives is ambisyllabic. Firstly, let us look briefly and in a preliminary way at the proper domain with respect to which basic syllable constraints should be stated.

2.4 The basic domain of syllabification

2.4.1 Words, formatives and morphemes

It is well known that in English the constraints on the internal phonological structure of formatives (in the sense of §2.3.2) are much more restrictive than those governing word structure. Specifically, the range of word-final consonant clusters is greater than that associated with simple formative-finals. Consider the sample of (formatively complex) word-finals in (2.62):

(2.62)   ##path#s##, ##last#s##, ##bulb#s##
         ##film#d##, ##ease#d##, ##bulge#d##

None of these final clusters occur word- or formative-medially: i.e. word- or formative-medial syllable-finals conform to the constraints on formative-finals rather than those associated with word-finals. The limited apparent exceptions to this statement largely involve borrowed heterosyllabic clusters such as that in *Gazdar* and *Mazda*. Therefore, the formative rather than the word is the more appropriate domain with respect to which the generalisations concerning the structure of English syllables can be stated. The clusters unique to word-final position are extensions of the basic patterns which are only possible where there is an intervening # (see, for example, Fujimura 1981). Indeed, they constitute, by virtue of their violation of the basic syllable constraints, signals that a word is morphologically complex.

Notice, moreover, that if forms such as those in (2.63) show only the weaker internal boundary:

(2.63) $\#\#$ six + th $\#\#$, $\#\#$ eight + th $\#\#$

then the appropriate domain for the statement of syllable structure may be even smaller than the formative, in that here we have clusters that are possible only formative- (and word-) finally, and are therefore syllabically irregular. The most general pattern for English syllables is that which holds within the morpheme; here we have maximum congruence between the syllable margins found initially and finally (in the morpheme) and those occurring medially. Formative- and word-final clusters are extensions of this basic pattern. Notice also, for instance, that the postvocalic stop in *eighth* shows the glottal reinforcement associated with syllable-final stops.

Say, then, that the basic domain for syllabification is a stretch between + +, i.e. a morpheme. Some such morphemes – specifically some suffix morphemes (see (2.63)) – will lack a syllabic, and their status with respect to syllable structure will be undefined at this level. They will syllabify with whatever syllable is to their left in the formative. Similarly, undefined suffix formatives (as in (2.62)) will syllabify with the preceding syllable in the word (with the exception of /s/ following a sibilant and /d/ following an alveolar stop, which acquire a syllabic of their own). Some of the clusters created by the accretion of these undefined morphemes and formatives will violate the basic syllable constraints. It is, however, unnecessary to formulate distinct formative and word constraints. The range of formative- and word-final clusters is a simple product of the range allowed for by the basic constraints, together with the set of undefined segment sequences in accordance with the demands of morphological structure.

2.4.2   Beyond the word

The extent to which these syllabification constraints are manifested across grammatical boundaries (or between them, for that matter) in continuous speech is dependent on tempo. Faster tempi, however, approximate in their syllabification to the basic (intra-morphemic) constraints. Within the foot, sequences like [tθ] or [ʃt], which constitute formative- or word- but not morpheme-final clusters, do not develop ambisyllabicity across the word boundary: the syllable boundary remains between the two consonants in stretches like (2.64):

(2.64)   rush to Daddy   ‖[rʌʃ][tə]‖[dædɪ]

(where ‖ = foot boundary). However, with the potentially morpheme-medial cluster in (2.65):

(2.65)   run to Daddy   ‖[rʌn[t]ə]‖[dædɪ]

ambisyllabicity (and possible glottalisation of the [t]) develops, given the viability of [nt] as a final cluster. We return to such consequences of foot-formation in the following sections. Here we are concerned with the failure of word-final clusters that are not morpheme-final to behave like syllable-final clusters in other circumstances. The marked status of these clusters with respect to English syllable structure is quite clear.

We note in passing that our observations concerning fast tempi do not, of course, imply that foot structure ignores word division in general. Indeed, we can recognise encliticisation in terms of the obliteration within the foot of the normal effects of a word boundary. As Abercrombie (1965) and others have observed, in a disyllabic foot in RP the first syllable is normally longer than the second (whatever their internal structure) only if a word division intervenes: contrast the second and third syllables in *Take Grey to London* and *Take Greater London*, which are ˉ˘ and ⌣⌣ respectively in Abercrombie's notation. However, a clitic does not result in a foot which is ⌣⌣, but in one whose quantities are determined by the nature of the component segments (as word internally), so that *Stop her* is ˉˉ and *Take it* ⌣⌣.

It is nevertheless the case that, just as syllabification ignores some morphological boundaries (in *congress* the *g* is included in the preceding syllable, thus triggering assimilation of the preceding tautosyllabic nasal – see §2.3.3), so the foot (or even a combination of feet) is not coterminous with the word. Many words contain initial unstressed syllables which are apparently not assigned to a foot within the word (given that each foot begins with a stressed syllable). This is the case with the initial syllable in *patrol* or *abrupt*: these words appear to consist of a single foot (consisting of the one syllable *trol* and *brupt*) and an unassigned initial syllable. In a sentence like *Guards patrol*, this syllable is assigned to the foot initiated by

Guards, the grouping into feet thus cutting across the word divisions. Such a syllable may also be assigned to a foot initiated by a 'silent stress' (see Abercrombie 1967:36), as in *Patrol the grounds*. Similarly, many 'grammatical words' (pronouns, prepositions, etc.) do not themselves constitute feet but are assigned to a preceding stressed (including 'silent') element, as in (2.64) and (2.65). See further §§3.4 and 3.5, however.

2.5   Syllabification and stress placement

In §2.3 we found some support for the notion that syllabification and stress are intimately related; specifically, the foot, the unit initiated by a stressed syllable, forms the maximal phonological domain for ambisyllabicity, in that a foot boundary co-occurs with a proper bracketing into syllables. This, and other phenomena (such as relative 'tenseness'), require reference to a unit such as the foot. However, we must now investigate rather more carefully the interaction between syllabification and stress, given that there is evidence not only for the dependence of syllabification on stress placement, but also for the converse. We consider the latter aspect of this apparent paradox in §2.5.1.

2.5.1   The Main Stress Rule, weak clusters and syllabification

Placement of stress is rather obviously dependent on the nature of subparts of the sequence of segments to which stress is assigned. The formulation of the Main Stress Rule of *SPE*, and its various subsequent modifications, involve reference to the number of consonants following a vowel as well as to whether a vowel is tense or lax. It is, for instance, only if the penultimate vowel of a noun ending with a sequence containing a lax vowel occurs in a sequence of the character:

$$(2.66) \quad \begin{bmatrix} V \\ -\text{tense} \end{bmatrix} C^1 \begin{bmatrix} V \\ -\text{tense} \end{bmatrix} C_0 \ ]$$

that stress will be assigned to the antepenult, as in (2.67a):

(2.67)   a. vítamin, ásterisk
         b. veránda, pentáthlon
         c. aréna, angína
         d. degrée, domáin

In (b) the penultimate lax vowel is followed by two consonants, and thus receives the stress; and the tense penult in (c) is similarly stressed. (Example (2.67d) illustrates stress associated with a tense final vowel.)

However, here and elsewhere in English phonology, as Chomsky & Halle (*SPE*: 241) concede, an adequate characterisation of the relevant sequence-type, in this instance the penultimate vowel-containing sequence that rejects stress, as in (2.67a), does not seem to be available to the notation. This is because there are penultimate vowels which show the same stress pattern as in (2.67a) but which are followed by more than one consonant, as exemplified in (2.68):

(2.68)   álgebra, péregrine, Páraquat

Chomsky & Halle therefore modify their characterisation of the stress-rejecting sequence, or 'weak cluster', as in (2.69):

(2.69)
$$\begin{bmatrix} V \\ -\,\text{tense} \end{bmatrix} C_1 \begin{bmatrix} \alpha\text{voc} \\ \alpha\text{cons} \\ -\,\text{ant} \end{bmatrix}_0 \cdots$$

whereby the single consonant following the lax vowel can be optionally followed by a liquid or glide that is not [+ anterior], i.e. is not [l]. This correctly characterises *pentathlon* as having a strong, and thus stress-taking penultimate, as opposed to the forms in (2.68).

This characterisation, however, is simply non-explanatory. This type of sequence is appealed to elsewhere in English phonology (see again *SPE*: 241) and in the phonologies of other languages: it is recurrent. But in a non-constituential representation it is no simpler to express than a sequence in which, say, the positions of the consonant and the following liquid/glide are interchanged, i.e. (2.70):

(2.70)
$$\begin{bmatrix} V \\ -\,\text{tense} \end{bmatrix} \begin{bmatrix} \alpha\text{voc} \\ \alpha\text{cons} \\ -\,\text{ant} \end{bmatrix}_0 C_1 \cdots$$

However, (2.70) groups together the penultimate syllables in (2.67a) and (2.67c) with those in the forms in (2.71):

(2.71)   laburnum, detergent

This is an inappropriate, non-recurrent grouping of sequence-types. The demands of the constituentiality assumption are not met in this case.

The characterisation in (2.69), as it stands, is scarcely even observationally adequate, in that whereas it is true that some *Cl* sequences behave as strong clusters, as predicted by (2.69), there are others where the sequence is undeniably weak, as illustrated in (2.72):

(2.72)   díscipline, dísciplinary

(On the latter, see *SPE*:140; notice that the form *disciplinary*, with antepenultimate stress, does not bear on the discussion here.) There seems to be no option for allowing for this within a non-constituential framework other than simply listing the subset of *Cl* clusters that are weak.

On the other hand, the notion of weak cluster receives a straightforward interpretation in terms of the law of initials: a weak cluster is one that is a permissible syllable-initial. This is true of the penultimate clusters in (2.67a), (2.68) and (2.72), whereas *nd*, *thl*, *rn*, etc. in (2.67b) and (2.71) are not permissible initials. If, moreover, 'tense' vowels are interpreted as divocalic sequences (Anderson 1970; Lass & Anderson 1975; Lass 1976; and see §3.3) in which the first vowel is syllabic, a simple generalisation allows for all the types illustrated in (2.67)–(2.72):

(2.73)   *Weak syllabic*
          A penultimate syllabic is weak (and therefore stress-rejecting) if it is
          immediately followed by a possible syllable-initial cluster.

This excludes from being weak all the penultimate syllabics in (2.67b) and (2.71), and those in (2.67c), in that in each instance the segment immediately following the syllabic cannot be included in the following syllable-initiating cluster.

This situation is most adequately characterised if the sequences to which the rules of stress placement apply are already syllabified at the point at which stress is assigned, such that each final syllable begins as indicated in (2.74):

(2.74)   a. vita[min
          b. veran[da
          c. areː[na
          d. alge[bra
          e. labur[num

That is, stress placement is directly related to syllabification. And in so far as the syllabification involved is the placement of the initiation of syllables, it obeys the same regularities as we have already established for post-stress syllabification, as involving crucially the law of initials. Once again, as with syllabification, stress placement is a projection of the sequence of segments – and their morpho-syntactic bracketing – but the segments are themselves organised into syllables.

However, although stress placement does not affect the location of syllable-initial boundaries, we have also seen that the location of the ends of syllables (where these may be distinct from the initiation of the following syllable) is dependent on the location of stress. Ambisyllabicity is foot-internal: recall the contrasts of (2.47). To put it another way: with respect to their terminations, stressed syllables (with a short vowel) obey the law of finals, and are thus (final) MAXIMALIST in their extent (Anderson 1975); unstressed syllables are MINIMALIST, in simply ending where the following (stressed) syllable begins, as shown by [pé[d]ant] and [pe][dán[t]ic] (see (2.48)).

The distinction between maximalist and minimalist finals is dependent on stress placement, then. But syllabification is present prior to stress placement. Prior to stress assignment, therefore, syllabification must be either uniformly maximalist or uniformly minimalist (unless some independent factor supervenes in terms of which different principles of syllabification (maximal, minimal or whatever) can be applied appropriately). We consider now some evidence favouring a (final) maximalist interpretation of pre-stress syllabification. (For a fuller discussion of these issues and a more generally applicable characterisation of the notion 'weak syllable' see, especially, Anderson 1975; Anderson & Jones 1977:ch. 4; and see further §3.4.2.)

2.5.2 Evidence for pre-stress-assignment ambisyllabicity

We can define a weak (penultimate) syllable in the nouns we have been looking at as one containing a syllabic which meets the condition given in (2.73), i.e. that it immediately precedes the initiation of the following syllable. If pre-stress syllabification is (final) minimalist, then the syllabic in a weak syllable also terminates its syllable, as represented in (2.74a) and (2.74d) (in contrast to the other penults in (2.74), which are all strong). However, if pre-stress syllabification is maximalist, then the penultimate syllable in the forms concerned will also include the consonant which immediately follows the syllabic, and which is thus ambisyllabic, as indicated in (2.75):

(2.75)   a. vita[m]in
          b. alge[b]ra

In these instances, this does not seem to be crucial. And we certainly cannot define weak syllables as, say, containing only one consonantal segment following the syllabic; this is contradicted by forms like *pentathlon*, which have a strong penult:

(2.76)   pentath][lon

The crucial determinant of weakness for a syllable is apparently simply the location of the initiation of the following syllable. These phenomena are thus neutral as evidence in the decision concerning the maximalist *vs.* minimalist character of pre-stress syllabification. Either view of syllabification is compatible with this characterisation of weak syllable.

Notice, however, that there are some forms which are problematical for the notion of weak syllabic embodied in (2.73). Lax penultimate vowels which immediately precede an *sC* cluster should be weak by (2.73), given a (final-)minimalist syllabification as in (2.77):

(2.77)   a. péde][stal, móde][sty, ári][ston, órche][stra
         b. asbé][stos, phlogí][ston, domé][stic, orché][stral

But only the (a) examples show the expected lack of stress on the penult. Moreover, many of these can have their stress placement accounted for in terms of other factors. The *-y* suffix on *modesty*, for instance, characteristically throws stress two syllables forward, even over syllables that are uncontroversially strong, as in *cálumny*, for example. The stress in *modesty* and the like thus shows us nothing about the nature of the penultimate syllable. Further, examples of the character of *pedestal* may be underlyingly bisyllabic (or at least contain only two syllabic vowels), with a final *stl* cluster, and again irrelevant to the issue. Even examples like *ariston* and *arista* we found to be more often accorded penultimate stress by speakers to whom the items were unfamiliar. Thus, at best, from the point of view embodied in (2.73), there is fluctuation in the status accorded to such antepenults. For many speakers they are almost consistently strong. We can allow for both situations if pre-stress syllabification is ambisyllabic.

We can exclude from being weak the $\breve{V}sC$ syllables in (2.77) if we invoke not just the initiation of the final syllable, but also the termination of the penult (where, on the maximalist assumption, these are distinct), to give (2.78) rather than (2.73):

(2.78)   *Weak syllabic*
         A penultimate syllabic is weak if it is immediately followed by a single ambisyllabic segment, i.e. where the syllabic initiates a V[C] . . . sequence.

This condition is met by the forms in (2.75) but infringed by (2.79):

(2.79)   asbe[st]os

in which the entire *sC* cluster is ambisyllabic.

Where the sequence $\breve{V}sC$ is ambivalent, we suggest that there is a conflict between the characterisation of weak syllabic in (2.78) and one in which only the initiation of the final syllable is invoked, as in (2.73). In either case, whether $\breve{V}sC$ is strong or ambivalent, a characterisation like (2.78) is relevant to the determination of stress; and we thus have evidence for ambisyllabicity in pre-stress syllabification. And there are other cases where sC is incontrovertibly strong, and thus where a formulation such as (2.78) will again be necessary for the definition of weak syllable.

Consider, for example, nouns and adjectives in *-ate*, such as those in (2.80):

(2.80)   a. édentate ~ edéntate
          b. célibate

Both (a) and (b) may have initial (i.e. antepenultimate) stress; however, the strong penult in (a), but not the weak in (b), can also bear primary stress. Similarly, the weak (lax) penult in (2.81):

(2.81)   cérebrate

shows only initial stress (though there is an alternative pronunciation with a tense penult in which the stress is of course penultimate). However, a form with a $\breve{V}sC$ penult such as that in (2.82):

(2.82)   ápostate ~ apóstate

shows both stress possibilities: i.e. $\breve{V}sC$ behaves like a strong syllable. Our definition of weak syllable must therefore be as in (2.78), which, as we have observed, is only available if pre-stress representations are ambisyllabic.

Similar examples, involving adjectives in *-oid* and verbs in *-ate*, are discussed by Chomsky & Halle (*SPE*:152–5). The forms in *-oid* again show quite straightforwardly that sC clusters are strong, as demonstrated by (2.83):

(2.83)   a. amýgdaloid, sólenoid
          b. érythroid
          c. aráchnoid, cylíndroid
          d. mollúscoid

in which the sC cluster in (d) behaves like the uncontroversially strong clusters in (c) in taking stress. Again, the sC cluster can be distinguished from the weak cluster in (a), and especially that in (b), only if ambisyllabicity can be invoked. Only the penultimates in (a) and (b) meet the condition in (2.78):

(2.84)   sole[n]oid, ery[th]roid *vs.* cylin[d]roid, mollu[sc]oid

Notice finally that after stress assignment, *sC* belongs entirely with a following stressed syllable, unlike those strong clusters which contain an initial segment that can belong only to the preceding syllable. This is one factor underlying availability for vowel-reduction: an initial unstressed non-prefixal syllabic will reduce only if it is syllable-final, as shown in (2.85):

(2.85)   a. po][líce, a][spáragus
          b. ban][dána, psy][chólogy

where only the (a) forms show reduction (again, assuming that the tense initial syllabic in *psychology* involves two segments, thus rendering the syllabic element non-final); for some further examples, see Liberman & Prince (1977:284). The difference in behaviour of pre- and post-stress-assignment of *sC* clusters is perfectly in accord with the proposals concerning syllabification and foot-formation that we have made.

There is evidence for ambisyllabicity in pre-stress representations in English, then. It is simplest to suppose that such representations are ambisyllabic in general: that is, morphemes and formatives are first syllabified maximally in accordance with universal and language-particular conditions on syllable structure. After stress assignment, final clusters in unstressed syllables (and after long vowels) are reduced to eliminate ambisyllabicity (§2.3.3), and ambisyllabicity may be extended to final clusters in stressed syllables within the foot but not across word boundaries (§2.4.2). Syllabic weight is adjusted in accordance with the distribution of stress.

2.6   Preliminary remarks on the foot and the tone group

As already indicated, we take the foot to be the basic unit of rhythmic organisation, constituted by a stressed syllable and any unstressed syllables to its right. But the foot is also a domain for distributional restrictions. For example, in most varieties of English no short vowels may appear finally in the first syllable of a foot. Thus, as we have seen, *buy*, *knee*, *bias* and *neon* are not paralleled by forms in which the relevant syllable is terminated by a short vowel. Long vowels, on the other hand, are limited to the first syllable of a foot (see further below). /h/ in English is typically limited to foot- or word-initial position: *history*, *hysterical*; see Anderson (1986b).

Division into feet is also relevant to the determination of various phonological processes. For example, (fast speech) weakening of stops in English is excluded from foot-initial position, as in (2.86):

(2.86)   ['træxɪŋ 'deɪşə]   tracking data

but not from word-initial position, unless it is also foot-initial:

(2.87)   [ɸa'lɪtɪkl̩]   political

(examples, and transcription, from Brown 1977:74). Similarly, 'flapping' of /t d/ is impossible in foot-initial position.

It is also arguable that the preference for enclisis over proclisis in language is related to foot structure: a clitic prefers to attach itself to the same foot as the element undergoing cliticisation, which requires postposition of the clitic. Thus in Buryat unstressed pronouns have encliticised themselves to the verb, even though, as Comrie (1980) has shown, the language has been syntactically verb-final as far back as we can reconstruct. Further, proclitics tend to lose syllabicity in order to be able to attach themselves to the cliticee. Contrast the behaviour of the Middle English proclitic *ne* in (2.88):

(2.88)   nolde 'didn't want to', nat 'didn't know', nis 'isn't'

with the Modern English enclitic *not*:

(2.89)   shouldn't, hasn't, doesn't, wasn't

which typically (despite *won't, shan't, aren't, can't,* for which there are particular explanations involving [l] and [r] vocalisation) retains syllabicity. Given the (stress-initial) structure of the foot, enclitics require less radical structure change, if any, to attach themselves to the same foot as the cliticee.

Feet are grouped into TONE GROUPS, the stretch associated with a major tone-shift. These constitute the maximal domain for assimilations and deletions in casual speech. For example, in English fast speech syllable-final /t/ and /d/ are omissible between consonants, no matter where in the foot they occur:

(2.90)   ['kɒnflɪkstɪl]   conflict still
         ['ɪntres'reɪts]   interest rates
         [ðə'fækðət]   the fact that

(from Brown 1977:61), but not across a tone group boundary. Compare the Gorgia Toscana, i.e. the weakening of voiceless stops between vowels in Tuscan Italian, which cannot occur across a tone group boundary:

(2.91)   //Le c̦ase c̦arine//costano molto c̦are in America//
       'Cute houses are very expensive in America'

The double slashes enclose tone groups, within whose domain the underlined intervocalic plosives may be weakened, even across a foot boundary, as with *molto care*. However, the initial *c* of *costano* does not weaken, since the preceding vowel is in a separate tone group. This phenomenon is discussed by Nespor & Vogel (1982:§2.3.2), from whom our example is taken, as is nasal assimilation in Spanish, which also has the tone group as its domain.

Tone groups are assembled into utterances – what we shall term in chapter 3 'second level groups' (G^2), or 'tone groups' in Halliday's (1967) terms. Halliday distinguishes a 'pre-tonic' and a 'tonic segment' within the 'tone group'. The relative independence of these is recognised within the present framework in terms of the status of each as a group. The hierarchisation between 'pre-tonic' and 'tonic' is characterised by the subordination relations proposed in what follows. Following Halliday, we take the G^2 (utterance) construction to be the appropriate domain for 'tune–text association' (Liberman 1975; Ladd 1978).

We return in chapter 3 to a more formal characterisation of these various construction-types. In the concluding section of this chapter we consider in a preliminary way some of the structural properties of phonological units.

2.7   The nature of syllabicity, stressedness and tonicity: an informal outline

2.7.1   The headedness of phonological constructions

Crucial to an approach to the characterisation of 'syllabic' is not just sequential placement of the syllabic segment but specifically, as argued in §2.1.2, its status in the syllable as a unit. As the traditional terminology suggests, there is an intimate relationship between the syllable and its syllabic element: this segment is the obligatory core of the syllable; a syllable necessarily includes a syllabic peak – or, in terms more familiar in relation to syntactic constructions, a syllabic HEAD. In many languages, the syllabic is the only obligatory element of a syllable. But even in languages in which, say, every syllable also contains an onset, it is still the very presence of a syllabic peak that identifies the construction as a syllable. In chapter 3 we attempt to provide a more careful specification of

the notion of head and related phenomena in terms of an application of
the concepts of dependency grammar to phonological structure. At this
point, we merely observe that syllables are headed constructions: the
*-notation of (2.2) identifies the head of each syllable, its peak.

Similarly, within a foot the stressed segment is the head. Again, the
stressed segment is normally the only obligatory part of the foot, and it is
the presence of a stressed segment that identifies or characterises the
construction as a foot. As we have seen, foot-formation is based on the
occurrence of stressed segments: each foot is initiated by a syllable
containing a stressed syllabic. The syllabic and the stressed segment are
thus distributional heads of their respective constructions. They are also
identified as heads substantively, in terms of greater PROMINENCE relative
to the other elements in the construction.

Given this interpretation of the structure of syllables and feet, it is clear
that in each foot there will be a single segment which will serve as head of
both a syllable and the foot. That is, contrary to one traditional view of
the notion 'head' (see Matthews 1981:86–8), a single element may be head
of more than one construction-type, provided the types consistently differ
in their relative inclusiveness: a foot includes syllables (and never vice
versa). This is quite compatible with the head being a 'characteristic' or
defining element of its construction: a single element may be both syllabic
with respect to other parts of a syllable, and stressed with respect to other
syllabics. Both the phonetic content of the headship (syllabicity *vs.*
stressedness) and the character of the MODIFIERS (non-syllabic *vs.* syllabic)
differ in the two cases.

We can extend the *-notation of (2.2) to represent these relationships, as
in (2.92):

(2.92) a. $\quad$ *
$\qquad\quad$ * $\quad$ *
$\qquad$ [[bo[nn]et]]

$\quad$ b. $\qquad\qquad\qquad$ *
$\qquad\quad$ * $\qquad\quad$ *
$\qquad\quad$ * $\quad$ * $\quad$ * $\quad$ *
$\qquad$ [[[run[t]o] [Da[dd]y]]]

The (a) example contains a single foot consisting of two syllables. The
head of each syllable is marked by *, as is the head of the foot – i.e. the first
vowel, which thus bears a double marking. The (b) example contains two
successive feet of this character, and the notation has been further
extended to indicate that the second stressed syllable, i.e. the head of the
second foot, is also the head of the tone group (the syllabic of the tonic

syllable – Halliday 1967), and as such bears yet another mark: it is thus the head of three successively more inclusive constructions.

The auxiliary symbols *s* and *w* deployed within the notation associated with 'metrical phonology' (Liberman & Prince 1977; etc.) in part appear to serve the same function as *: within a phonological construction *s* corresponds to * and *w* to absence of *. This, of course, is made explicit in the associated metrical grid, which employs grid marks to indicate relative prominence in a way similar to that in (2.92). We do not pursue the consequences of either notation at this point. (See, however, Ewen 1986 for a discussion of the redundancy of the grid in a dependency-based model.) Rather, we take up the characterisation of these and other aspects of phonological structure more explicitly in the chapter that follows. However, notice at this point that the notion of successive headship also applies to the internal structure of syllables. Thus, given the range of evidence for the rhyme as a unit (see for example Anderson 1984b; and for a contrary view Clements & Keyser 1983), a syllable such as *pat* has something like the representation in (2.93), rather than a tripartite structure:

(2.93)   *
            *
         [p[at]]

The vowel is both head of the rhyme, with the (optional) rest of the rhyme (the coda) to its right, and head of the syllable, with the onset to its left; again, syllables and rhymes differ in asymmetric inclusivity. This hierarchisation is in accord with the widely held view that syllable structure displays a hierarchy of binary cuts: in terms of the even more restrictive notions discussed here, each construction contains a head and one other constituent (see further §3.2).

It can also be argued that feet display a similar binarity of internal organisation. We turn now to consider some motivations for adopting this rather more controversial position, and thus a tentative adoption of the proposal that the structure of phonological sequences is universally of this restricted character. (We refine this notion in chapter 3, however.)

2.7.2   The binary character of phonological constructions

In §2.3.3 we associated ambisyllabicity in stressed representations with the foot: foot boundaries inhibit ambisyllabicity. And we associated the absence of aspiration of the alveolar stops in (2.94) with their ambisyllabicity, permitted by the absence of an intervening foot boundary:

(2.94)   [fre][ne[t]ic]], [psy][cho[t]ic]]

The foot-initial velar stop in the second example is strongly aspirated.

Notice, however, that many speakers do aspirate the alveolar stops in (2.95):

(2.95)   here[tʰ]ic, arithme[tʰ]ic

even though they appear to meet the conditions for ambisyllabicity, in that they are foot-internal, i.e. between the second and third syllabics of a three-syllable foot. This is the case if (2.96) is appropriate:

(2.96)   [[he[r]e[tʰ]ic]]

But suppose that foot structure is also binary. Then such forms can display a complex foot structure of the character of (2.97), which reflects the greater intimacy of the first two syllables and the greater prominence of the third syllable relative to the second:

(2.97)   ₂[₁[[he[r]e]]₁ [tʰic]]₂

i.e. there is a more inclusive foot, or SUPERFOOT, subscripted 2 in (2.97), and a lesser or SUB-FOOT, subscripted 1, which includes only the first two syllables in (2.97). The first two syllables thus belong to a unit that does not include the last. The stressed syllable is successively head of its syllable (and rhyme), of the sub-foot, and of the superfoot. In this case, the bracket closing the sub-foot inhibits ambisyllabicity, and the syllable-initiating alveolar stops of (2.95) will show aspiration.

Similarly, the restriction on the sequence [stl] illustrated by (2.98):

(2.98)   castle, wrestle, tussle, apostle

where in many cases a historical [t] has disappeared, is associated with the absence of a foot boundary. The sequence [st] is not allowed foot-medially before [l] (except, for some speakers, in a few uncommon items such as *pestle* and *astel*). However, this sequence is quite permissible in the trisyllabic foot in (2.99):

(2.99)   pedestal

Again, we can attribute this to the failure of ambisyllabicity-retention at foot boundaries, given that the second syllable in (2.99) terminates a sub-foot. See further Anderson (1984b:§11).

An internal structure of this sort for trisyllabic feet also relates in a very direct way to the conditions governing the deletion of non-foot-initial high vowels in Old English, as discussed by Keyser & O'Neil (1983). Consider the alternations in (2.100):

(2.100)   a. neut. nom. and acc. pl. nouns:
scipu 'ships' ~ folc 'people', bān 'bones'

b. masc. and fem. nom. and acc. sg. nouns:
sunu 'son', talu 'tale' ~ hond 'hand', flōr 'floor'

c. fem. nom. sg. and neut. nom. and acc. pl. adjectives:
gramu 'fierce' ~ blind 'blind', lāð 'hostile'

If we define a strong syllable as one containing two segments after the syllabic, then we can say (again assuming that long vowels are geminate) that in disyllables final -*u* is lost after a strong syllable, giving us the forms on the right of these alternations. However, -*u* in a final syllable is 'protected' by a following consonant, as in datives in -*um*: e.g. *bānum*.

In medial syllables in trisyllabic inflected forms, such a vowel (written ⟨o⟩) is lost under the same conditions as finally in disyllables, as shown by the alternation in (2.101):

(2.101)   neut. dat. pl. nouns:
weorodum 'troops' ~ hēafdum 'heads'

Again -*u/o*- is lost after the strong initial syllable. But notice that this -*u/o*- is not protected by the following consonant, suggesting that the *d* does not belong to the same syllable as the originally preceding -*u/o*-. This is in accordance with the internal structure for trisyllabic feet proposed here, whereby such a consonant belongs uniquely with the following syllable.

We associate with phonological constructions, then, the requirement that each head have only one modifier, i.e. that each construction be binary, thus severely limiting the structural possibilities available. Similarly, in metrical phonology, the *s* and *w* of each construction are defined as unique (on this, see further §3.2.3, where we argue that such an approach to relational notions in terms of definitions of 'category' labels is inappropriate).

We return in the following chapter to a further consideration of the internal structure of feet and their organisation into tone groups, and indeed of suprasegmental structure in general; but this must await a rather more explicit formulation of the notion of dependency, which we argue to be basic to phonological structure.

3 Dependency structures in phonology

3.1 Dependency and syntax

In the preceding chapters, particularly §2.7, we introduced in an informal way some notions from the conception of linguistic structure associated with dependency grammars. Here we examine the notions more precisely, in particular their appropriateness for the characterisation of phonological structure. We begin, however, with a consideration of dependency in syntax, where the concept is perhaps rather more familiar.

3.1.1 Constituency and precedence

The currently most widespread representation of syntactic structure invokes the notions of CONSTITUENCY and PRECEDENCE (linear order). The minimal syntactic elements form sets (or sentences) endowed with the binary asymmetric relation of immediate strict precedence. A unique element in each set immediately precedes no other; a unique element is immediately preceded by no other; otherwise, each element immediately precedes a unique element and immediately follows another. The elements ordered by immediate strict precedence, as in (3.1):

(3.1) $a_1 \ll a_2, a_2 \ll a_3, a_3 \ll a_4 \dots a_{n-1} \ll a_n$

constitute a STRING, henceforth represented as in (3.2):

(3.2) $a_1 \, a_2 \, a_3 \, a_4 \dots a_{n-1} \, a_n$

such that each a_i immediately strictly precedes a_{i+1}. The relation ' $<$ ', strict precedence, is the transitive closure of ' $\ll$ ', such that:

(3.3)   a. $a_1 < a_2, a_1 < a_3 \dots a_1 < a_n$
        b. $a_2 < a_3, a_2 < a_4 \dots a_2 < a_n$
        c. ...

Any continuous sequence in a string such as (3.2) forms a SUB-STRING.

The elements of a sub-string may be structured by the n-ary symmetric relation of CO-CONSTITUENCY, or sisterhood. A sub-string of co-

constituent elements is a CONSTITUTE. Let us require that the string is exhausted by the relation of co-constituency; and that no element belongs to more than one constitute: i.e. the division of the string into co-constituent sub-strings is PROPER. The string in (3.4) is analysed into proper constitutes, where the [] brackets enclose co-constituent sub-strings:

(3.4) $[a_1 a_2][a_3][a_4 a_5 a_6][a_7 a_8]$

If we now extend the relation of co-constituency to constitutes, such that adjacent constitutes may form more inclusive proper constitutes, until the string is exhausted, then bracketings such as (3.5) may be superimposed:

(3.5) $[[[a_1 a_2][a_3]][[a_4 a_5 a_6][a_7 a_8]]]$

where the ultimate constitute is the entire string.

Typically, in characterisations of the syntax of natural languages, constituency structures of the character of (3.5) are supplemented with CATEGORY LABELS which identify instances of the same constitute-type in the set of strings making up the language, on the basis of structural properties internal to the constitute and distributional parallels through the set of strings, as in (3.6):

(3.6) $[_A [_B [_C a_1 a_2][_D a_3]][_E [_F a_4 a_5 a_6] [_C a_7 a_8]]]$

where both $[a_1 a_2]$ and $[a_7 a_8]$ are identified as instances of the same constitute-type C.

We can define a binary asymmetric relation of IMMEDIATE CONSTITUENCY as holding between any constitute and each of the co-constituents which it includes. Thus a_4 is an immediate constituent or daughter of F in (3.6). CONSTITUENCY is the transitive closure of immediate constituency, such that a_4 is a constituent of all of F, E and A.

Many current conceptions of syntactic structure can be characterised in these terms (of labelled constituents and precedence), or as enrichments of this notion of constituent structure – as in the various proposals concerning $\bar{X}$-notation (see particularly Jackendoff 1977), which introduce conventions whereby additional structural relations can be defined over (some) constituency relations.

3.1.2   The notion 'head of a construction'

Constituent structure representations which are not enriched with some extrinsic apparatus such as the $\bar{X}$-conventions fail to reflect one property

that has often been attributed to some syntactic constructions at least: the
HEAD–MODIFIER relation. Thus the constituent structure which is typically
attributed to the English sentence in (3.7) does not distinguish headship:

(3.7)   [s [NP [D the][N Australians]][Aux will][VP [V come][PP [P to][NP [N London]]]]]

In the subject NP, for instance, the Determiner and Noun constituents are
of equal status, as co-constituents; the atomic labels NP, VP, PP, etc.,
unless interpreted via some extrinsic conventions, are not specifically
related by the representation to any one of their constituents.

Such a representation can be supplemented with definitions designating
headship. For instance, in constitutes with only one OBLIGATORY constituent, this can be defined as the head. However, this attributes heads only to
endocentric constructions, such as the NP and VP in (3.7). This treatment
is problematical in so far as syntactic regularities which invoke headship
defined in this way also refer to elements in other constitutes which
cannot be defined in these terms, in that they occur in exocentric
constructions.

Consider, for example, the tendency expressed as the principle of
NATURAL SERIALISATION (Bartsch & Vennemann 1972; Vennemann 1974;
Anderson 1976, 1979a), whereby languages can be said to prefer
construction-types in which modifiers consistently either precede or follow
their heads. Thus, in Japanese, for instance, noun and adjective modifiers
precede the element they modify. If these are endocentric constructions,
such that the noun and adjective can be designated heads, then we can
express this correlation in Japanese and other languages as an instanti-
ation of natural serialisation. But the same principle can be claimed to be
manifested by the typical occurrence of postpositions rather than
prepositions in languages like Japanese – provided that such adpositions
(despite the exocentricity of the construction) are, like nouns and
adjectives, heads of their constitutes.

Below, we will extend the definition of head to allow for the scope of
such generalisations, and we will also provide an independently appropriate characterisation of headship. But we should note at this point that
headship can be assigned directly in relation to the string of basic elements
without reference to constituency structure, which in turn can indeed be
directly extrapolated from the head–modifier relations. Since head–
modifier, or DEPENDENCY, structure makes in itself a rather more
restrictive claim about the nature of syntactic representation (in requiring
constructions to have heads), it is to be preferred over constituency, other

things being equal. And other things in fact select dependency structures in so far as reference to heads is recurrently required, and in so far as headship can be provided from constituency structures only via the kind of additional apparatus we have been looking at.

However, as a preliminary to our examination of dependency structure, let us extend our characterisation of headship so that it will encompass exocentric constructions. We can restrict the set of potential heads for a construction to constituents which are not only obligatory but also LEXICAL – i.e. the least inclusive constitutes in (3.7). This selects the Preposition as the head of the PP, in that the other constituent of the PP, though arguably obligatory, is not lexical: it is an NP, which includes a Noun. Similarly, the head of that sentence is the Auxiliary: neither of the other constituents (NP and VP) is lexical.

We might also require that the head be DISTINCTIVE, in the sense that the same category must not be head of different construction-types (see, for example, Robinson 1970). However, as anticipated by our preliminary discussion in §2.7, we shall find that such a requirement needs some refinement in the light of phenomena we shall be considering in §3.1.5, as well as in relation to headship of phonological constructions. Furthermore, the requirements of obligatoriness and lexicalness are sufficient to characterise the heads of the central construction-types we have been concerned with. We now turn to the association of dependency structures with strings of basic elements.

3.1.3   The dependency relation

Let us assign each element in the basic string in (3.7) to a lexical category: *the* – D, *Australians* – N_1, *will* – Aux, *come* – V, *to* – P, *London* – N_2. Let us then designate pairs of elements, i.e. lexical categories, in the derived string in (3.8):

(3.8)   D N_1 Aux V P N_2

as related by the binary asymmetric relation of dependency, '$\Rightarrow$', so that: $N_1 \Rightarrow D$ (i.e. N_1 is a head modified by D and D depends on N_1), Aux $\Rightarrow N_1$, Aux $\Rightarrow$ V, V $\Rightarrow$ P, P $\Rightarrow N_2$. Subordination, '$\rightarrow$' is the transitive closure of dependency, so that D is subordinate both to N_1 and Aux, and Aux $\rightarrow N_1$, Aux $\rightarrow$ V, Aux $\rightarrow$ P, V $\rightarrow$ P, Aux $\rightarrow N_2$, V $\rightarrow N_2$, P $\rightarrow N_2$. V is the ULTIMATE HEAD with respect to its subordinates, and is thus head of the construction VP; Aux is the ultimate head or CENTRE of the entire string, and is thus not subordinate to any other category. Notice now that: (a) there is a unique ultimate head associated with the string; (b) as observed, all other categories in the string are subordinate to this ultimate head; and (c) all the other categories depend on only one other category. Such a string is said to be a simple structured string (see, e.g., Marcus 1967:§6.3).

If we now impose a general requirement that each category (as the ultimate head of a construction) and all its subordinates form a sub-string, then we can always derive a proper constituency bracketing from the dependency relations, as indicated in (3.9):

(3.9)
$$
\begin{array}{ll}
\text{a.} & [\text{D N}_1 \text{ Aux } \overset{*}{\text{V}} \text{ P N}_2] \\
\text{b.} & [\text{D N}_1 \text{ Aux } [\overset{*}{\text{V}} \text{ P N}_2]] \\
\text{c.} & [\text{D N}_1 \text{ Aux } [\overset{*}{\text{V}} [\overset{*}{\text{P}} \text{ N}_2]]] \\
\text{d.} & [[\text{D } \overset{*}{\text{N}}_1] \text{ Aux } [\overset{*}{\text{V}} [\overset{*}{\text{P}} \text{ N}_2]]] \\
\text{e.} & [[\text{D } \overset{*}{\text{N}}_1] \text{ Aux } [\overset{*}{\text{V}} [\overset{*}{\text{P}} [\overset{*}{\text{N}}_2]]]]
\end{array}
$$

For the moment, we indicate the ultimate head of each constitute as *. In step (3.9a) Aux, designated *, is grouped with all its subordinates into a constitute; in (3.9b), V and all its subordinates; and so on. (3.9e) creates a one-element constitute; the necessity for this stage follows from the status of Ns as heads in general. Each category indexed as * is head of the construction of which it is an immediate constituent.

Such representations express the headedness of syntactic constructions, and are supported to the extent that headship is determinate throughout syntactic constructions. They are thus to be preferred to unenriched constituent structures, which embody no such hypothesis, and also to enriched ones, which are inelegant (particularly in their specification of headship) and over-structured. Notice in this last connection that dependency structures embody another empirical claim resulting from the absence of non-lexical or phrasal category labels. V, for instance, labels both a lexical category and, as its head, the constitute of which the lexical category is a daughter. No ambivalence is involved if a further hypothesis can be maintained, viz. that if V, say, is invoked by a syntactic regularity, then the regularity involves V and all of its subordinates, unless one or more of the subordinates is invoked by the same regularity, in which case only the lexical category V (apart from the invoked subordinate(s)) is involved. That is, whether V is involved as constitute label or head is predictable from the character of the regularity, specifically whether other members of the constitute are essentially referred to: this is discussed as the HEAD CONVENTION in Anderson (1984b).

3.1.4   Dependency trees

We now sketch out briefly a graph-theoretic interpretation of dependency structure, in that this will considerably facilitate the exposition which follows in the remainder of this work. Let us associate with a string like (3.8) a GRAPH such that each category in (3.8) labels a VERTEX or node in the graph and each pair of categories contracting a dependency relation is linked by an ARC, or directed line, in the graph, as in (3.10):

(3.10)

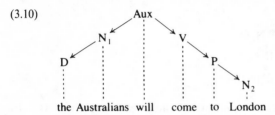

or, alternatively, (3.11):

(3.11)

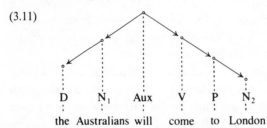

N_2 is dependent on P – it TERMINATES an arc INITIATED by P – and P is dependent on V; while both N_2 and P are subordinate to V – they are connected by a PATH of arcs. We have also assumed a category assignment function which associates appropriate lexical elements in the basic string with the categories of the derived string projected onto the graph in (3.10). In (3.11) the ASSOCIATION LINES (which are represented as discontinuous) map both derived and basic strings onto the graph. Henceforth we suppress the arrow-head on the dependency arcs, in that the direction of the dependency relation is given by placement on the vertical axis, as precedence is by the horizontal.

This directed graph displays certain further properties corresponding to those described in §3.1.3 as defining a simple structured string. So: (a) there is a unique vertex or ROOT, here Aux, which terminates no arc; (b) all other vertices are subordinate to the root; and (c) all other vertices terminate one and only one arc. Such a graph is a TREE FROM A POINT, sometimes also referred to as a 'proper' tree (Marcus 1967:205). Consistently with the discussion in §3.1.3, we shall reserve the designation PROPER for a tree which also lacks TANGLING (i.e. which displays projectivity in the sense of Lecerf and Ihm – see Marcus 1967:§6.10), such that the elements in the basic string associated with vertices subordinate to a single vertex are required to form a sub-string with the element associated with that vertex. The tree from a point in (3.12):

(3.12)

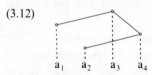

$$a_1 \quad a_2 \quad a_3 \quad a_4$$

displays tangling (a_2 and a_4 do not form a sub-string) and is thus not proper in this sense.

3.1.5   VP and subjunctions

A question arises in English (and in other languages in relation to which a VP node can be justified) in so far as there occur sentence strings which, unlike (3.7), apparently lack an Auxiliary and thus, it would seem, a head. The various resolutions of the question that we know of typically sacrifice the lexical character of heads, in suggesting, for example, that the tense marker (an inflection) and/or intonation realise the head of the sentence (see again, e.g., Robinson 1970). There are, however, no problems associated with allowing a single element in the basic string to function as the head of two different constructions, if it is associated with two distinct categories. That is, in relation to a string such as (3.13):

(3.13)   The Australians come to London

come can be simultaneously, as V, head of the VP, and, as Aux, head of the Sentence, as represented in (3.14):

(3.14)

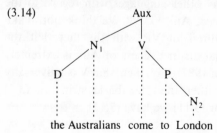

where Aux and V are equivalent in precedence: Aux = V, but Aux ⇉V. This means that the set of categories (as opposed to the basic string) is not TOTALLY ORDERED by the precedence relation; the relation is not strict; it is merely NON-SYMMETRIC rather than asymmetric. In (3.14) V is SUBJOINED to Aux, whereas in (3.10) it is ADJOINED. As Aux, *come* bears the tense and concord inflection; but nevertheless also forms a constitute (VP) with *to London*, as evidenced by the coordination in (3.15):

(3.15)   The Australians came to London and went to Earls Court

This dual categorisation is embodied in the representation in (3.14). We shall invoke such dual categorisations in the description of the internal structure of phonological segments in §3.6.

Notice, however, still with respect to syntactic structure, that the evidence for VP as a constituent is limited to SVO languages such as English. In other language-types subject and object are members of the same constitute. This constitute is the Sentence, and its head, in accordance with our criteria, is the Verb, as indicated in the representation for a sentence of Old English given in (3.16):

(3.16)

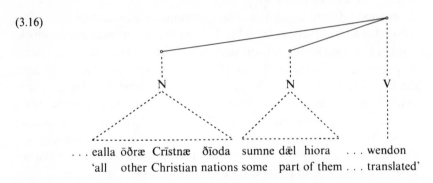

```
... ealla ōðræ Crīstnæ  ðīoda  sumne dæl hiora   ... wendon
    'all    other Christian nations some   part of them ... translated'
```

(from the letter prefixed to the Alfredian translation of Gregory the Great's *Cura Pastoralis*).

Does this mean that we need to recognise a rather drastic distinction between Modern English and many other languages with regard to the identity of the head of the sentence: Aux *vs.* V? We think not. Take together the typological restrictedness of VP with the fact that the syntactic evidence for the categorial distinctiveness of Aux is extremely weak (for an assessment, see Pullum 1981). Say, then, that V is universally head of the sentence. That is, rather than the basic string in (3.7) displaying the structure in (3.10) or (3.11) we have (3.17):

(3.17)

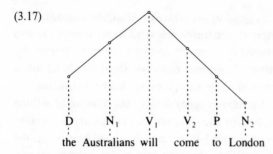

D   N₁   V₁   V₂   P   N₂

the Australians will   come   to London

Thus auxiliaries are simply Verbs that take another Verb as an adjacent dependent. We drop the categorial distinctiveness requirement on the heads of S and VP; the constructions are distinguished in other terms. And V is the head of both VP and Sentence; the distinction being that as head of the Sentence (V_1 in (3.17)) it takes its non-verbal modifiers to the left, and as head of the VP (V_2 in (3.17)) it takes its modifiers to the right. Alternatively, we can say that V as head of the Sentence takes modifiers in both directions but as head of VP it takes modifiers only to the right. This is the crucial difference between Sentence and VP.

(3.13), then, should be associated not with (3.14), but rather with the structure in (3.18) with, once more, subjunction, but no distinction in labelling, between the nodes associated with *come*, such that the verb is simultaneously head of the Sentence and the VP:

(3.18)

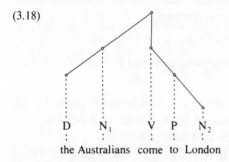

D   N₁   V   P   N₂

the Australians come to London

As such it meets the requirement of being both left-modified (as head of the Sentence) and right-modified (as head of the VP); it is not an auxiliary (it has no adjacent dependent verb); and it takes the concord and tense inflections, as head of the Sentence, but nevertheless exhibits the VP-headship behaviour evidenced in (3.15).

In general we hypothesise that, as in (3.18), the nodes in a syntactic subjunction relation are not categorially distinct, while the categories are totally ordered by immediate strict precedence. Subjunctions like (3.14), on the other hand, are, we suggest, appropriate for the characterisation of local structure, i.e. the internal structure of lexical items (see Anderson 1971c, 1977a:§2, 1984a, 1985a).

Given configurations like (3.18), we can say that the head of a construction must be lexical and obligatory; it must also be distinctive (i.e. the head of only that construction-type) unless the character of the modification is distinctive, and/or the different headships are associated with distinct properties. With S and VP in English, as we have seen, the modification of the head uniquely to the right makes the distinction, and the respective headships (of VP and S) are associated with distinctive syntactic properties.

This proposal concerning the headship identity of S and VP also involves a claim that a succession of non-initial auxiliaries and a main verb all head the same construction-type, VP, as in (3.19):

(3.19)

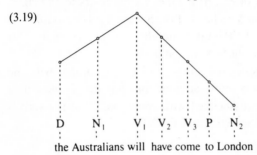

$$D \quad N_1 \quad V_1 \quad V_2 \quad V_3 \quad P \quad N_2$$

the Australians will have come to London

as is confirmed by their shared susceptibility to 'VP-deletion':

(3.20)   The Australians intend to come to London, and by June they will (have (done/come))

In (3.20) only the head of the sentence, *will*, is obligatorily present in the second conjunct; the entire VP headed by V_2, *have*, i.e. *have done/come to London*, may be absent, or only that headed by V_3.

Notice too that if we define VP in the way suggested, as differing from S not in its headship but rather in the direction of modification, then we have an explanation of why VP arises only in SVO languages but not in SOV or VSO. (The status of VP in VOS languages – see Keenan 1978 – and OVS and OSV languages – see Derbyshire & Pullum 1981 – is unclear.) In SVO, unlike in SOV and VSO, the subject and object are on opposing sides of the verb, thus permitting a differentiation between Sentence and VP in terms of direction of modification. The history of English illustrates the development of 'VP' and the associated differentiation between 'auxiliary' and other verbs, including the development of a 'dummy' auxiliary *do* to be present in various circumstances in which it is necessary to separate the Sentence-head role of the verb from its role as head of VP. Compare (3.21a) with (3.21b):

(3.21)   a. Bobsie wanted to entertain Mike, and entertain him she did
         b. Bobsie wants to entertain Mike, and entertain him she will

(The rise of VP in English, together with the concomitant development of *do* as an auxiliary, is charted in DeArmond 1984. See too Anderson ms a.)

The imposition of a distinctiveness criterion on heads introduces a limitation on the expressive capacity of dependency representations, the lack of which is the basis for Matthews' (1981:86–8) main criticism of such representations for syntactic structure. Matthews argues that in phrases like *up till Friday*, *till* governs both *up* and *Friday*, but that two different constructions are involved, one included within the other. This is problematical only if we assume distinctiveness for heads rather than construction-types. Just as in the case of V with respect to S and VP, *till* can be head of both constructions, which are distinguished by their direction of modification.

In §3.2 we shall suggest that, as well as characterising syntactic configurations, representations of the type embodied in (3.18) are appropriate for the representation of layers of relative prominence, whereby a single segment may function as head of successively more inclusive constructions (syllable, foot, tone group).

If all subjunctions were of this character then we could say with respect to the categorial status of vertices that the precedence relation is 'antisymmetric': symmetry, i.e. the existence of both $a_i \leqslant a_j$ and $a_j \leqslant a_i$, where $\leqslant$ indicates (non-strict) precedence, implies $i=j$, i.e. reflexivity. We shall be proposing below that whereas the dependency representation of suprasegmental structure involves associating antisymmetry with precedence, the characterisation of the internal structure of segments (as well as the internal structure of lexical items – see above) requires precedence relations between nodes that are merely 'non-symmetric', in that the existence of a symmetric relation between two elements does not imply their categorial identity. That is, segment-internally we find subjunction structures in which the vertices are distinctly categorised, whereas suprasegmental structure includes subjunctions whose nodes are not categorially distinct.

We return now to our discussion of phonological structure, in the light of the properties of dependency representations that we have attempted to illustrate in the present section in relation to syntactic structure.

3.2   The dependency structure of phonological sequences: a first approximation

3.2.1   Syllabicity, stressedness and tonicity

In §2.6 we suggested a characterisation of syllabicity, stressedness and tonicity of segments in terms of headship of their respective constructions, the syllable, the foot and the tone group. In each instance, the head is, in accordance with the criteria of §3.1.5, segmentally atomic and obligatory. Even though a single segment may be head of constructions of all three types, its headships are distinguished both in terms of the modification involved and the properties associated with the respective headship, which follow from the place of the construction in the hierarchy of construction-types. As head of the tone group a segment governs stressed segments; as head of the foot it governs syllabics; while the modifiers of a syllabic segment are not themselves syllabic. These headships correlate with placement of tonic, placement of stress, and syllabicity, respectively.

We can thus associate with the string in (2.92b), repeated below, a dependency structure such as that in (3.22):

(2.92)   b.
```
              *       *
       *      *       *
    [ [run[t]o] [Da[dd]y]] ]
```

(3.22)

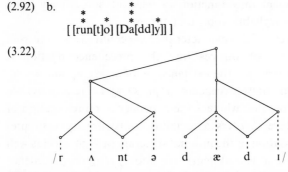

$$/\text{r} \quad \Lambda \quad \text{nt} \quad \text{ə} \quad \text{d} \quad \text{æ} \quad \text{d} \quad \text{ɪ}/$$

(We ignore for the moment the internal structure of clusters such as /nt/, as well as the other details of syllable structure.) Each * in (2.92b) corresponds to a headship: /ə/ and /ɪ/, with one *, are heads of their syllables; /ʌ/, with two, is head of both the initial syllable and the first foot, with the second syllable as its dependent; /æ/ is head of its syllable, head of the second foot, with the final syllable as its dependent, and head of the tone group, whose sole dependent is the preceding foot-head, /ʌ/.

Notice, however, that in contrast to the syntactic structures discussed in the preceding section (but cf. Anderson 1979b), (3.22) displays ambidependency (in this case ambisyllabicity) within the foot, whereby a single vertex may terminate more than one dependency arc. Thus, condition (c) of §3.1.4 (on page 91) must be weakened to allow for this within the foot. However, we hypothesise that no vertex terminates more than two arcs and that such dual dependencies remain compatible with the 'no tangling' condition; dependency arcs do not cross, either with each other or with association lines, except at vertices. Further, we assume that condition (c) is relaxed only in the pre-stress intermediate structures imposed on lexical items (§2.5). In post-stress structures it is relaxed only within a foot (which does not contain another foot – i.e. within sub-feet (§2.7.2)) – or, more exactly, between tautopodal elements.

3.2.2 Prominence, sonority and syllable structure

Within all these constructions, headship is associated with greater relative prominence (see §2.7.1). In a similar way, headship within the constituents that make up the syllable involves relative prominence, so that structures like (3.23) are appropriate:

(3.23)

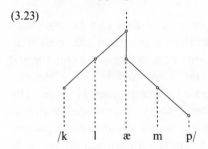

/k   l   æ   m   p/

where /æ/ is head of both syllable and RHYME and /l/ and /m/ are heads of their respective clusters, the ONSET and the CODA. /æ/ is both the syllabic and the NUCLEUS of the rhyme. (We again assume the validity of the onset *vs.* rhyme division.)

Within clusters, however, the general criteria for headship are inapplicable, in that neither atomic element (/k/ or /l/, /m/ or /p/) can be argued to be more or less 'obligatory' than the other. Only the greater prominence we have associated with phonological headship differentiates between the two elements. But this receives further confirmation from various phonological regularities, including particularly the phenomenon of 'reversed dependency', which we discuss further in §3.3.

Within the syllable, there is a universally preferred correlation between closeness to the syllabic and SONORITY (inherent prominence); on the sonority hierarchy and the characterisation of relative sonority, see further §4.5. A simple mapping of relative sonority onto distance from the syllabic peak is the unmarked possibility, such that sonority decreases, or at least does not increase, with distance. In English (and other languages) this is violated by initial sequences containing *sC* clusters (where *C* is a plosive). If we characterise the syllable (and onset, rhyme and coda) as a dependency structure in which the more sonorous and thus more prominent heads of component constructions are serialised naturally with respect to their modifiers, then representations like (3.23) are appropriate. But this unmarked situation is violated by *sC* clusters, as shown in (3.24):

(3.24)

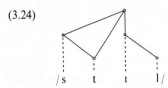

(assuming, again, ambidependency, as the extension of ambisyllabicity, within the foot).

These clusters exhibit distinctive behaviour that can be associated specifically with their configuration. For instance, in the system of alliterative verse found in the early Germanic languages, it is only the first consonant of other initial clusters that is invoked by the alliterative pattern: thus *pV-*, *pr-* and *pl-* all alliterate with each other. However, *sV-*, *sp-*, *st-* and *sk-* do not alliterate; *sp-* alliterates only with *sp-* (see Kuryłowicz 1971:195). For the purposes of alliteration, *s-* and any adjacent dependent are considered to be a single unit. A similar pattern is evident in the reduplication associated with some verbal paradigms in Gothic.

Notice too that it is clear from a configuration such as (3.24) that the *s* constitutes a sub-syllabic peak of prominence. This correlates with the fact that in such clusters it typically takes a distinct chest pulse, or 'burst of muscle drive' (Catford 1977:90).

Only *s* can occur before a plosive in initial clusters. This relationship is also captured by their forming a constituent (rather than, say, being mutually independent dependents of the following vowel). This is also expressed in forms of the constituent structure representation proposed by Selkirk (1980), as indicated (in simplified form) in (3.25):

(3.25)

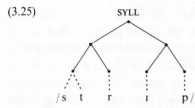

But, as Durand (1981) points out, this proper constituency assignment fails to express the close relationship between the post-*s* plosive and the following liquid: for instance, *stl* is no more a valid initial cluster in English than is *tl*. The constituency breaks in (3.25) are in this respect inappropriate. In (3.26), however:

(3.26)

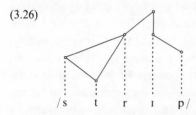

the ambidependent status of *t* makes this quite transparent, in that the *t* depends both on the preceding *s* and, as in (3.24), on the following liquid, which is the head of two distinct constructions. (We consider in §3.4 the assignment of such dependency structures.)

Notice too that a structure of this sort for *sC* clusters allows for the overlap of two segments without infringement of the 'no tangling' condition (despite the objections of Kahn 1976), as illustrated in (3.27):

(3.27)

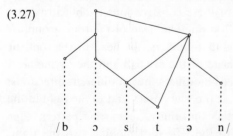

It is, indeed, a defect of the autosegmental notation employed by Kahn that this unique aspect of *sC* clusters cannot be captured.

We are assuming, as a further refinement of the notion that the syllable is the basic domain for the statement of phonotactic restrictions, that mutual restrictions between segments are associated with unique co-

constituency: only segment positions that uniquely belong to the same constituent display phonotactic constraints. Thus, both /st/ and /tr/ in (3.26) belong to particular constructions, to the exclusion of anything else, and so constitute domains for constraints. All three segment positions belong uniquely to a further construction, which itself displays unique restrictions: thus, whereas both /st-/ and /tw-/ (*still, twist*) are permissible initials, */stw-/ is not. Phonotactic constraints cannot be reduced to pairwise restrictions on adjacent segments, but reflect the constituent structure of the syllable.

This constraint on the domain of phonotactic constraints provides motivation for onsets, codas and *sC* constructions, which each display particular restrictions. Similarly, the rhyme as a whole exhibits phonotactic constraints. Thus, the syllabic nucleus /aʊ/ does not permit non-coronal codas: compare /-aʊd/ (*loud*) with */-aʊb/ and */-aʊg/. Similarly, simplex (short) nuclei in stressed syllables require a following coda: *bit, build,* */bɪ/. Such restrictions are not uncontroversially paralleled by constraints holding between onset and nucleus: the onset does not belong to a construction which contains only it and the nucleus, but forms a syllable together with the whole rhyme.

3.2.3   The configurational expression of phrasal categories and of relative prominence

We return now to those constructions in which the general criteria for headship are met (rather than simply manifestation as greater relative prominence): i.e. the tone group, the foot, the syllable and the rhyme. As we have seen, the head of each of these constructions is obligatory and associated with distinctive modification. The head of the tone group, or TONIC, takes stressed segments as its modifiers; the head of the foot, or ICTUS, takes syllabics. Both the head of the syllable and the rhyme-head take consonants as their (adjoined) modifiers, but in different directions: to the left in the case of the syllabic (i.e. the onset), and to the right in the rhyme (i.e. the coda). Notice further that this is a recurrent pattern: tone group (adjoined) modifiers are to the left, foot modifiers to the right, syllable modifiers to the left, rhyme modifiers to the right. That is, as we encounter each more, or less, inclusive construction-type the direction of modification reverses.

This means that, among other things, (prosodic) phonological category labels of the kind proposed by Selkirk (1980) ('syllable', 'foot', etc.) are redundant. If each of these construction-types is obligatory, so that a syllable necessarily contains a rhyme, a foot at least one syllable, and a tone group at least one foot, the identity of the construction-type is apparent from its place in the fixed hierarchy of types together with the direction of modification shown by the construction. This is apparent if we expand the representation in (3.22) to give (3.28):

(3.28)

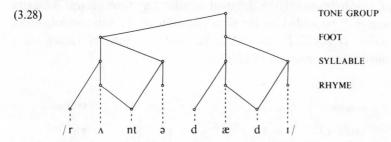

TONE GROUP

FOOT

SYLLABLE

RHYME

/ r ʌ nt ə d æ d ɪ /

(in which we once again ignore the internal structure of clusters). If we trace upwards from /æ/ the pattern of adjunctions to the succession of heads with which it is associated, we find that at each level the direction of modification reverses. Even if the rhyme, say, is not universally ob-ligatory, the hierarchy of construction-types remains determinate (see Anderson 1984b).

Notice that as well as not requiring category symbols like 'syllable', phonological structure has no need for auxiliary symbols such as 's' and 'w' (Liberman & Prince 1977). Like the X̄-notation in syntax, these are necessary only in a constituency-based system of representation which – in the case of phonological structure – fails to model prominence relations directly, in terms of dependency.

It has been objected that dependency structures, unlike s/w relations, do not embody the hypothesis that constructions are necessarily binary (one head but also only one modifier): see, e.g., Giegerich (1986:225). This is, however, fallacious, as already noted in §2.7.2 (and see too Ewen 1986). Binarity is no more inherent in the s/w notation than in the dependency. It is, in principle, available to the former notation to have more than one w per s: binarity is not inherent in the contrast strong/weak or the relation 'stronger than'. Moreover, unlike the notion of head in dependency structures, there is no exclusion of multiple s in a construction. Of course, this makes nonsense of what the employment of this notation is intended to claim about phonological structure. So a requirement is imposed on s and w that only one of each is available per construction. But in this respect the notation is in fact inherently less restrictive than dependency

structure. The inherently relational character of phonological structure is
only indirectly expressed (see too Anderson 1984b; Ewen 1986).

3.2.4   Complex feet and complex rhymes

The depth of layering displayed in (3.28) by the successive headships of the
/æ/ of *Daddy* is merely the minimal one for any tone group. An extra
layering may be added by the incorporation of the sub-foot/superfoot
distinction (see §2.7.2). Consider the foot structure of (3.29) (as a
dependency interpretation of (2.97)):

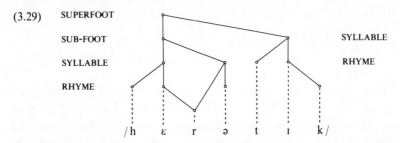

(3.29)   SUPERFOOT   SUB-FOOT   SYLLABLE   RHYME   SYLLABLE   RHYME   /h ɛ r ə t ɪ k/

The /ɛ/ of *heretic* in (3.29) is successively head of both the sub-foot *here-*
and the whole (super) foot including *-tic*. But both constructions meet the
criterion for being a foot. Given that the direction of modification is not
altered, it is apparent that we are still concerned with the second layer of
right-modifying structures (the first layer being the rhyme).

Similarly, within the rhyme we may have an additional layering
constituted by a complex rhyme, as in (3.30):

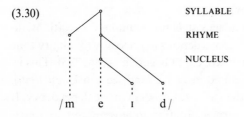

(3.30)   SYLLABLE   RHYME   NUCLEUS   /m e ɪ d/

This representation, in which modifiers are assigned to /e/ as head of the
rhyme on two different levels, is intended to capture the unity both of the
nucleus (the lowest construction headed by /e/), given the idiosyncrasies of
diphthong-formation, and of the rhyme, given that there exists a number
of restrictions holding between nuclei and a following consonant (cluster):
consider, for example, the rejection by [ŋ] of preceding complex nuclei.

Thus, a complex rhyme introduces an extra layering to the sequence of headships attributed to the /e/ segment in structures such as (3.30). But this layer, we suggest, has the same status as the sub-foot: it is a sub-rhyme. Like the sub-foot, it is optional; like the sub-foot, the direction of modification is the same as that of the including obligatory construction, the rhyme and the (super) foot respectively. It thus does not disturb the identificatory efficacy of the pattern of successive modification reversals associated with the *obligatory* layers of structure.

3.2.5   Layering of feet and tone groups

Observe, however, that we must associate a rather different kind of optional additional layering with higher levels of structure. Both feet and tone groups show CONSTRUCTIONAL ITERATION, though, particularly in the case of the foot, only in rather special circumstances. Consider in the first place the tone group.

A sequence of tone groups is subordinated to the head of the final group, which then forms a G^2 or utterance head. Such a construction differs from a group only in that its modifiers are groups rather than feet: the direction of modification is identical. The head is also identical to a group-head, though it is accorded greater prominence as locus of the major tone-shift in the utterance. In (3.31):

(3.31)

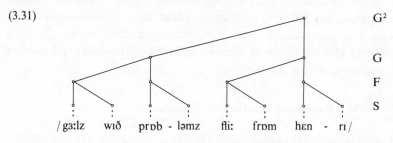

the first tone group, headed by /prɒb(ləmz)/ is subordinated to the second, headed by /hɛn(rɪ)/, which carries the utterance tonic. If we regard hierarchical placement and direction of modification as critical in distinguishing constructions, then it is appropriate to regard G^2 as a sub-type of group. And this is confirmed by the fact that in both cases headship is associated with a tone-shift.

If the head of a tone group is not the head of the final foot (i.e. we have 'de-accentuation' – see Ladd 1978:ch. 3), then the final foot is subordinated to the preceding ictus, which is also the tonic, creating an F^2 construction, as in (3.32) and (3.33):

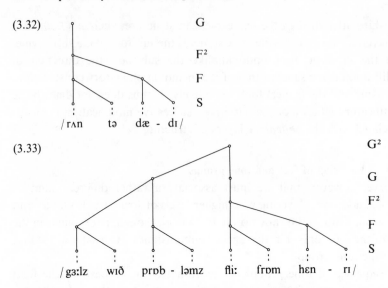

with (3.33) displaying both an F^2 and a G^2 construction.

Both foot and group may thus be iterated, such that an ictus may be subordinated to an F^2 head, and a tonic to a G^2 head. However, given that this does not occur in the lower layers (rhyme and syllable), the identification of the constituent-type in terms of the direction of modification remains determinate: any left-modifying construction above the syllable is a tone group. This potential for layering is sufficient to allow for the structural properties of even the most complex utterances. However, still another distinction in level is required.

3.3   Word structure *vs.* utterance structure

A consideration of the immediately preceding examples makes it clear that the foot and group structures associated with a particular string of segments may vary (even if the overt morpho-syntactic structure remains constant): cf., for instance, the headships of G^2 in (3.31) and (3.33). Thus, as is well known, group structure cannot be entirely predicted from the sequence of syllables that constitutes an utterance, or even from this sequence in conjunction with the syntactic structure. It depends in particular on the INFORMATION STRUCTURE associated with the utterance: what is being presented as new, contrastive, parenthetical, etc. Foot structure is also affected as a consequence (by 'de-accentuation', for example).

As is familiar, foot structure is also sensitive to rhythmic requirements, as evidenced by STRESS-REVERSAL (or 'iambic reversal') – see Giegerich (1985:§4.3.1). Compare (3.34a), with ictus marked with an acute accent and tonics underlined, with (3.34b):

(3.34)   a. //Thirtéen//cáme to dínner//
            //Bílly//persevéres in it//
         b. //Thírteen línguists//cáme to dínner//
            //Bílly//pérseveres gládly//

in which the ictus in *thirteen* and *perseveres* appears to be 'shifted' to the left away from an adjacent tonic to the right. An adequate characterisation of this and related phenomena depends on an explication of the relationship between word and utterance structure, i.e. between intralexical and extralexical structure. We offer some suggestions in this direction in §§3.5 and 7.6, where we also note some of the phonological and syntactic factors that interact with information structure and rhythm (and tempo) in determining extralexical foot and group (and syllable) structures; here we give the distinction a preliminary airing.

Up to now our discussion has implied that suprasegmental structure may be characterised in relation to a single hierarchy of construction-types, as delineated in §3.2. What we want to suggest in this section is that two such hierarchies are involved, one assigned to words in the lexicon, the other associated with utterances. In the preceding section our concern was with utterance structure (though it was not there distinguished as such). It is our contention that the hierarchy formulated there also characterises the internal structure of words. However, in word structure, unlike extralexical structure, the assignments are not sensitive to syntactic and information structure, and thus are not variable (except with respect to 'free variation'); rather, lexical or word structure is a projection of the segments composing words and the morphological character of these words. As such, it is 'frozen'; headships, for instance, are invariable and lexicalised. But we can nevertheless establish for words the same hierarchy of construction-types, differentiated both by placement in the hierarchy and by direction of modification.

Of course, there are further differences between the two hierarchies which are a consequence of the lexical/utterance distinction. For instance, word-tonics, unlike utterance-tonics, are not as such associated with variations in tone, unless tone is also lexicalised in the language. However, they are the locus of the tonic when the word is spoken in isolation.

Furthermore, lexical representations are no more sensitive to tempo than they are to the requirements of information structure or of the rhythmic organisation of the utterance.

Languages vary in the constraints they impose on lexicalised foot and group structure. For instance, Hayes (1980), in his typology of intralexical feet, distinguishes quantity-sensitive assignment of foot structure from non-quantity-sensitive and bounded from unbounded – English being quantity-sensitive and bounded. Languages also vary in the 'prominence' they accord to the foot word-internally: foot-prominence is evidenced by 'initial-stress' languages; lack of it by 'final-stress'. (On the initial/final dichotomy see, e.g., Dogil 1981.) English is relatively foot-prominent.

We turn in the following section to a consideration of some of the crucial constraints on the intralexical phonological structure of English. Central to these are rules which build up word-trees by making dependency assignments. We assume that no suprasegmental structure is stored as such in the lexicon. Each word is represented as a sequence of morphologically bracketed segments only.

Segments are internally complex, of course. The components or features that characterise them are grouped into two or more gestures or sub-segments (though these groupings are themselves predictable) – specifically, for our purposes, a categorial gesture (which specifies major class/manner of articulation/phonation-type) and an articulatory gesture (which specifies place of articulation/vowel dimension – see §II.1). They may also display internal adjunctions (as in the case of affricates, prenasalised and postnasalised stops, or diphthongs that are not contras-tively long – see §3.6 below).

Intralexical suprasegmental structure is a projection of such represent-ations, whereby each segment is associated with one or more nodes in a word-tree built up out of the constructions we have surveyed. The existence of exceptions (some of which we shall note below) to the regular processes of word-tree formation does not disguise the essentially projective character of this relationship, nor does it require the storage of suprasegmental structure, even in the case of these exceptions.

Extralexical structure is in turn a set of alternative projections of sequences of word-trees, determined by factors such as syntactic and information structure and rhythm. The account of suprasegmental structure sketched out in §3.2 is crucially inadequate in neglecting the interaction between word and utterance structure, among other things.

We take this up in §3.5; meanwhile, we illustrate some of the principles determining the assignment of word structure in English.

3.4   Remarks on the assignment of word structure

Our concern in this work is with the character of phonological structure, i.e. with the most appropriate representation of the phonological properties which can be attributed to natural language utterances. However, given our contention that suprasegmental structure is a projection of the sequence of segments and their non-phonological organisation, we must say something about these rules of projection, with respect to English, at least. Accordingly, the present section is concerned with outlining some of the principles by whose application strings of segments are associated with word structures, as well as with providing some illustration of English word structures. The section which follows this provides an informal outline of some of the principles governing word–utterance association.

3.4.1   Syllable-formation

Structure within the syllable is a straightforward projection of the sequence of segments. Syllabification itself, given the interaction with stress discussed in chapter 2, involves slightly different factors. Consider firstly the assignment of basic syllable structure.

Dependency relations within the syllable are assigned in accordance with the sonority of the segments concerned, where sonority is measured in terms of the relative preponderance of the |V| ('vocalic') component in the representations of these segments (see further §4.5). We might thus formulate the syllable structure rule as in (3.35), which applies to the sequences supplied by the lexicon:

(3.35)   Given segments a, b, where a < b (i.e. a precedes, not necessarily immediately, b), a ⇉ b iff b is weak, i.e. is not more sonorous (does not have a greater preponderance of |V|) than a; otherwise b ⇉ a.

In accordance with this, the sequence represented by *stink* will be assigned the dependency relations in (3.36):

(3.36)   s ⇉ t
t ⇇ ɪ
s ⇇ ɪ
ɪ ⇉ ŋ
ŋ ⇉ k

given that projectivity is required (thus ruling out /s/ $\rightrightarrows$ /k/, etc.), and that dependency arcs which entirely coincide with a subordination path, such as /ɪ/ $\rightrightarrows$ /k/, are discarded. This gives (3.37):

(3.37)

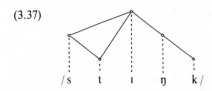

/ s   t   ɪ   ŋ   k /

(3.35) also selects the first of two adjacent vowels as syllabic, as in a diphthongal sequence such as /aɪ/. Similarly, sequences of equisonorous consonants, such as that in *apt*, will have the second subordinated to the first, in accordance with the binarity assumption (see §2.7.2). The viability of (3.35) clearly depends on the presyllabic segments in, for example, *you* and *woo* being interpreted as non-vowels – say, as liquids (see Lass & Anderson 1975:ch. 1; Anderson & Jones 1977:ch. 3). (3.35) is simply an interpretation of a viewpoint with a rather long tradition: for example, Grammont (1933), Jespersen (1950:ch. 12), and, more recently, Vennemann (1972), Anderson & Jones (1974a), Kiparsky (1981) and Selkirk (1984).

As it stands, however, (3.35) does not allow for rhyme structure. We accordingly suggest that syllable structure is assigned in two stages. Firstly, rhyme-formation:

(3.38)   Given segments a, b, where a≪b, a $\rightrightarrows$ b iff b is weak, i.e. is not more sonorous than a.

which gives the dependency relations for *stink* in (3.39):

(3.39)   s $\rightrightarrows$ t
            ɪ $\rightrightarrows$ ŋ
            ŋ $\rightrightarrows$ k

i.e. the structure represented graphically in (3.40):

(3.40)

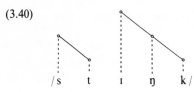

/ s   t   ɪ   ŋ   k /

or for *prick*:

(3.41)   ɪ $\rightrightarrows$ k

i.e. (3.42):

(3.42)

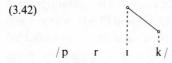

/ p   r   ɪ   k /

Syllable-formation, which follows, is (3.43):

(3.43)   Given segments a, b, where a ⩽⩽ b, and a ⤳̸ b by (3.38), b ⤳ a.

Applied to (3.40), this gives (3.44):

(3.44)

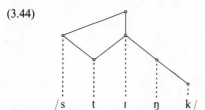

/ s   t   ɪ   ŋ   k /

and applied to (3.42), it gives (3.45):

(3.45)

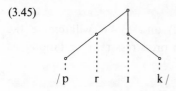

/ p   r   ɪ   k /

These representations embody the binarity assumption discussed in §2.7.2: given that by (3.38) /ɪ/ already has one dependent (to the right), application of (3.43) introduces a new layer of structure (via subjunction). (3.43) also allows a = b. Thus, even if a vowel has no segment to its right, it will nevertheless constitute the head of a syllable, as in the second syllable of *hurry*. This ensures an obligatory status for the syllable as a construction.

(3.43) assigns a dependency relation to both /sɪ/ and /tɪ/. (On the motivations for the ambidependency of /t/ in (3.44) see §3.2.2 above.) Notice too that, given prior application of (3.38), both (3.43) and (3.38) can be formulated in terms of immediate precedence rather than (unconstrained) precedence. Once /t/ is assigned as a dependent to /s/ in (3.40), /s/ immediately precedes /ɪ/, given the head convention (§3.1.3 above; Anderson 1984b): i.e. the construction headed by /s/ immediately precedes /ɪ/.

As it stands, this account of syllable structure does not allow for configurations containing complex nuclei such as were proposed in §3.2.4

and exemplified by (3.30). We assume that all long vowels, monoph-
thongal or diphthongal, constitute complex nuclei. This presupposes a
rule of nucleus-formation applying prior to (3.38) and (3.43), where a and
b are both vowels. On this see Anderson (1986a), where it is also suggested
that the /juː/ sequence in forms like *mute* constitutes a complex nucleus in
which /j/ modifies a nucleus containing a long vowel: [j[uː]]. That is,
nucleus structure in this case replicates the configuration associated with
syllable structure, as shown in (3.46):

(3.46)

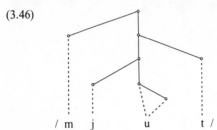

/ m   j   u   t /

3.4.2   Foot-formation

Applied to polysyllabic sequences, (3.38) and (3.43) will create the
ambisyllabic structures we associated with pre-stress representations, as
for *debit* in (3.47), for example:

(3.47)   a. after (3.38)

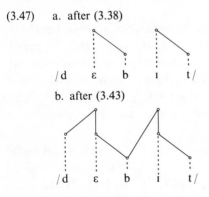

/d   ε   b   ɪ   t/

b. after (3.43)

/d   ε   b   ɪ   t/

or for *petrol* in (3.48):

(3.48)   a. after (3.38)

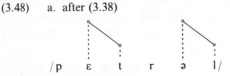

/p   ε   t   r   ə   l/

b. after (3.43)

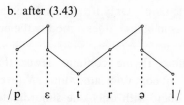

/p ε t r ə l/

Notice now that if we apply (3.38) as it stands to the structures in (3.47b) and (3.48b) it will select the first of the two vowels as having the second subordinate to it, since the second is no more sonorous, giving the appropriate foot structure for the examples in (3.47) and (3.48). But, as is well known, ictus selection in English is not dependent solely on the inherent sonority of the syllabic vowel: the character, specifically the weight, of the rhyme as a whole is relevant to the determination of stressability. The first vowel in, for example, the verbs *attend* and *maintain* does not in fact outrank the second; rather, as discussed in §2.5, final syllables ending in strong clusters are selected as ictus (and ultimately tonic), as in (3.49):

(3.49)   a.

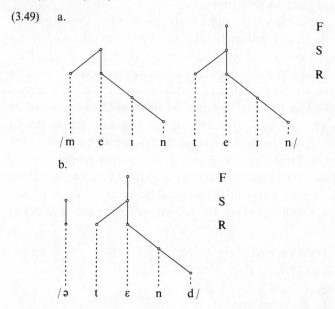

/m e ɪ n t e ɪ n/

b.

/ə t ε n d/

We return below to the footing of the first syllable. The representations in (3.49) also introduce the proper syllabification associated with foot boundaries: the preceding unstressed syllable loses any segments that could belong to the following one alone. Only if the second syllable in a disyllabic word is weak, or light, as in *punish*, does it modify the preceding syllable-head.

A weak · syllable is one whose rhyme contains fewer than two subordinates. Moreover, it must not contain a subordinate V (even if it is the only subordinate): contrast *obey*, with only one subordinate in the rhyme, but that a V, with *hurry*, with no subordinates in the final rhyme. Accordingly, we might formulate foot-formation as (3.50):

(3.50)   Given syllabics a, b, where a ≪ b], a $\rightrightarrows$ b iff b is weak; otherwise b $\rightrightarrows$ b, where weak is defined as having a rhyme containing fewer than 2 subordinates, and no subordinate V; and where] indicates (for the moment) word-termination.

In (3.47b) the second syllabic is weak; the first is thus the head of a foot containing the second. This is not true of the second syllabics in *maintain* and *attend*, which are therefore assigned the structures in (3.49). Again, we interpret application of the rule as adding an extra level of structure, extending the subjunction path upwards.

However, foot-formation is apparently even more dependent on morpho-syntactic structure than is syllabification. For instance, as has frequently been observed (and recall §2.5), nouns (and derived adjectives) allow a final syllable with a short vowel to count as weak, even if its rhyme is complex in the sense of (3.50), as in *pedant, modest*. Contrast *degree*, with a long vowel in the final syllable. In these instances this can be allowed for in (3.50) simply by modifying the definition of 'weak' for forms in these categories, such that it involves a rhyme with a short vowel.

However, in trisyllabic forms belonging to the same categories, the first syllable is the head if the final syllable is weak in this new sense, and if the second syllable is also weak, in the original sense of (3.50). Compare *asterisk* or *cinema* with *attendant*. We accordingly reformulate (3.50) as (3.51):

(3.51)   Given syllabics a, b, c, where (a ≪) b (≪ c)],

   (a): b $\rightrightarrows$ b iff b is not weak$_1$
   (b): otherwise, a $\rightrightarrows$ b
   (c): c $\rightrightarrows$ c iff c is not weak$_2$
   (d): a, b $\rightrightarrows$ c iff a, b $\rightrightarrows$ b or c $\not\rightrightarrows$ c

where weak$_1$ is a syllabic whose rhyme contains fewer than 2 subordinates, and no subordinate V, and weak$_2$ is a syllabic in a noun or derived adjective whose rhyme contains a short vowel.

This formulation accounts for the assignments in (3.52):

(3.52)

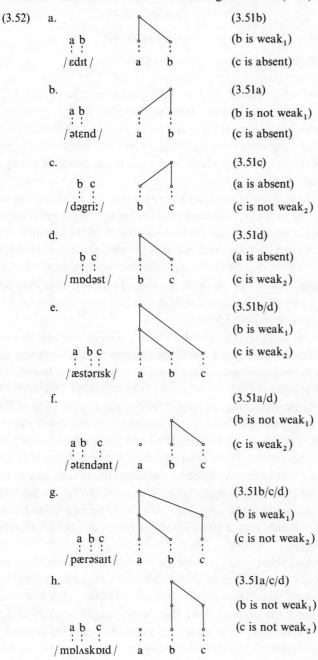

a.

a b
/ ɛdɪt /

(3.51b)
(b is weak₁)
(c is absent)

b.

a b
/ ətɛnd /

(3.51a)
(b is not weak₁)
(c is absent)

c.

b c
/ dəgriː /

(3.51c)
(a is absent)
(c is not weak₂)

d.

b c
/ mɒdəst /

(3.51d)
(a is absent)
(c is weak₂)

e.

a b c
/ æstərɪsk /

(3.51b/d)
(b is weak₁)
(c is weak₂)

f.

a b c
/ ətɛndənt /

(3.51a/d)
(b is not weak₁)
(c is weak₂)

g.

a b c
/ pærəsaɪt /

(3.51b/c/d)
(b is weak₁)
(c is not weak₂)

h.

a b c
/ mɒlʌskɔɪd /

(3.51a/c/d)
(b is not weak₁)
(c is not weak₂)

i.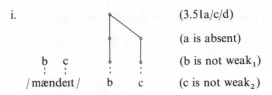

           (3.51a/c/d)

           (a is absent)

b   c   (b is not $weak_1$)

/mænde ɪt/   b   c   (c is not $weak_2$)

In (3.52e) a superfoot is created, and in (3.52g–i) a second level foot, F^2. Compare the utterance level constructions proposed in §3.2.

Trisyllabic verbs with strong suffixes and weak penults follow the same pattern as similar nouns and derived adjectives: *déprecate*, *éxplicate*, *anticipate*, etc. But so also do trisyllabic verbs where the penult is strong: *désignate*, *ínculcate*.

The extension to (3.50) proposed in (3.51) also requires modification to our characterisation of $weak_1$. Notice in the first place that if we assume that a monosyllabic word is assigned a foot structure – as those which are not weak will be by (3.51) – then the denial of ictus status to monosyllables which are $weak_1$, as is done by (3.51) as it stands, must be avoided. All monosyllables are footed: *sin* as well as *sink*. However, this can be provided for in terms of an independently motivated modification to the notion of $weak_1$ suggested in (3.50).

In terms of (3.50) and (3.51) a syllable is $weak_1$ if its rhyme contains at most one subordinate that is not a vowel: this allows for the weakness of the final syllable in the verbs *punish* and *debit* as well as in *hurry*. But in the presence of the syllabic labelled c in (3.51) – i.e. in nouns and derived adjectives – b is typically strong, in that it attracts the ictus, even if its rhyme contains only one consonantal subordinate: thus *arachnoid* shows the same pattern as *molluscoid* in (3.52h). If we assume pre-foot formation ambisyllabicity, the second syllable in *arachnoid* differs from that in *celebrand* or *parasite* in having a rhyme whose subordinate is unique to it: it is not shared with the following syllable. This seems to be the general pattern, despite exceptions like *anecdote*, with weak penultimate. Thus, $weak_1$ non-final syllables lack a subordinate to the rhyme-head which is unique to the rhyme.

We can generalise this to the circumstance in which b is word-final in verbs if a final consonant in non-monosyllabic verbs may be 'ignored' in assessing $weak_1$-ness (see Hayes 1982; Anderson 1984b). This allows a simpler characterisation of $weak_1$, in that it no longer need refer to whether a subordinate is a vowel or a consonant. Further, we can now allow for the fact that all monosyllables are footed: with the exception of reduced forms (e.g. /ðə/ *vs.* /ðiː/), where absence of footing can be related to utterance structure (see §3.5), monosyllables contain a rhyme with at least one unique subordinate, and are thus not weak$_1$.

This characterisation of weak$_1$ fails to allow for the strength of *sC* clusters, in that here (as in *molluscoid*, for example) neither segment belongs uniquely to the preceding syllable. Thus, weak$_1$ appears to involve a conjunctive definition: to be strong a rhyme must contain either a subordinate that is unique to it or at least two not necessarily unique subordinates. The penultimate in *arachnoid* meets the first condition, that in *molluscoid* the second, that in *salamander* both. Notice that it is only the first condition that is violated by *anecdote*, etc.; the second is less prone to exceptions.

We propose, then, that the definitions of weak$_1$ and weak$_2$ be revised as in (3.53):

(3.53)   In (3.51), b is weak$_1$ iff its rhyme contains no unique subordinate, or no more than two subordinates; c is weak$_2$ iff its nucleus contains no subordinate.

Conditions:
(i) In verbs and simple adjectives, if a is present, then b is weak$_1$ even if its rhyme contains a unique subordinate consonant.
(ii) c is present only in nouns and derived adjectives.

(3.53) defines a hierarchy of weakness. In addition, the less specific the restriction (weak$_2$ excludes fewer rhymes than weak$_1$), the more specific the morpho-syntactic condition: weak$_1$ applies to all word classes, weak$_2$ only to a subset of these (as indicated in condition (ii)). We consider now some evidence from the behaviour of verbal prefixes that the hierarchy should be further extended.

Monosyllabic prefixes typically, but again with some exceptions, reject ictus status in favour of a following monosyllabic stem:

(3.54)   permít, upsét

unless they contain a complex nucleus, in which case both prefix and stem are footed:

(3.55)   ré-sét, bý-páss

With disyllabic prefixes, again both prefix and stem are footed:

(3.56)   únder-bíd, íntercéde

We can allow for this situation if we extend (3.51a) as in (3.57):

(3.57)   b $\rightrightarrows$ b iff a is weak$_3$ or b is not weak$_1$.

Weak$_3$ is characterised as in (3.58):

(3.58)   a is weak$_3$ iff it is part of the prefix of a verb and b is in the stem.

The stress on the prefixes in (3.55) and (3.56) is assigned by another application of (3.51) with respect to which the (second) syllabic in the prefix is the b element. We return to this below, as well as to the selection of the group-tonic or word-ictus in such forms.

Observe now that weak$_3$ is even more inclusive than weak$_2$: any syllabic is eligible. And its morpho-syntactic domain is correspondingly even more specific. This confirms the pattern established for weak$_1$ and weak$_2$, whereby the greater inclusiveness of what counts as weak is matched by an increasing specificness in the morpho-syntactic conditions in which the weakness holds.

An even more restricted set is that constituted by nouns like those in (3.59) (see Schane 1979:490):

(3.59)   a. directee, devotee
          b. volunteer, expertise, brigadier

in which c $\rightrightarrows$ c but c is not governed by a or b. That is, both a and b are what we shall now term weak$_4$ with respect to (3.51d), such that a $\rightrightarrows$ c or b $\rightrightarrows$ c iff a and b are not weak$_4$. The final syllable is thus made head of the word in accordance with the formulation of group-formation suggested in §3.4.3 below. 'Weak' here thus includes two syllables, whatever their character; and the morpho-syntactic restriction is accordingly even tighter, in that weak$_4$ is limited to nouns with certain suffixes, and sometimes only to certain instances of these: contrast *princéss* with *wáitress* (where *-ess* in *princess* is exceptionally not weak$_2$ with respect to (3.51)).

3.4.3   Group-formation

(3.51) must apply twice to forms with more than three syllables, i.e. those whose syllable count exceeds what is allowed for by its various provisions. Exceptional here, however, are leftmost syllables which are weak and which precede a syllable eligible for ictus, as in *attend* (3.52b), *degree* (3.52c), *attendant* (3.52f) and *molluscoid* (3.52h): application of (3.51) must exhaust the string at its right edge, but a weak leftmost syllable will be left unassigned. Consider too forms such as *America*, in which the final three syllables constitute a superfoot but the initial is not footed.

Contrast with these the forms in (3.60):

(3.60) a. maintain
        b. Pertwee, Attlee
        c. creator
        d. edentate

in which the initial syllable either forms a foot by itself (a,c,d) or forms the head of an F^2 with the following ictus dependent on it (b), as allowed for by (3.51a,c,d).

These and other initial sequences preceding a sequence eligible for application of (3.51) are footed in accordance with the same rule, as in (3.61):

(3.61)

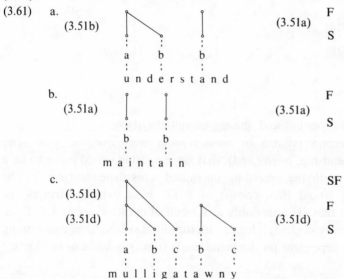

except that if b is not weak₁ a non-final c element may be absent in nouns and derived adjectives, as illustrated in (3.62):

(3.62)

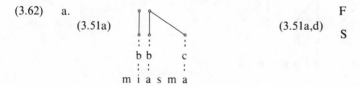

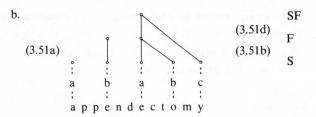

Notice too that in the application of (3.51b) c is absent twice in (3.63):

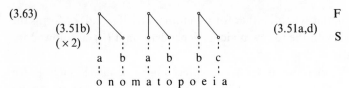

in preference to the analysis in (3.64):

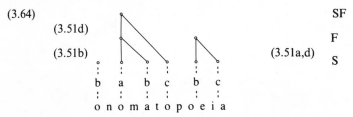

with medial superfoot and unassigned initial syllable.

If the second syllable in *onomatopoeia* were assigned foot- and superfoot-headship, as in (3.64), that same syllabic would come to be a group-head with the preceding unrealised ictus dependent on it. The penultimate would then consist of a G^2 head, which infringes the requirement that G^2 arises only as a result of cyclicity: see §3.4.4. Thus, only the footing in (3.63) is legal, with the initial syllabic then constituting an F^2 head dependent on the penultimate (tonic) syllabic, as in (3.65):

(3.65)

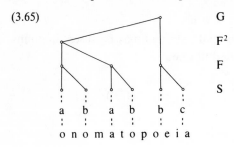

In all instances where independent foot-heads are created within the same word, it is the rightmost which governs as head of the group:

(3.66)   a.

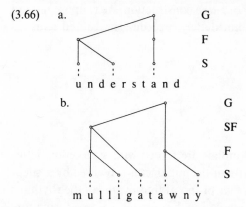

G²
structures involve cyclicity (see §3.4.4):

(3.67)

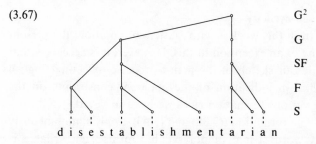

with again the rightmost of the two Gs being the governor.

Group-formation can therefore take the form of (3.68):

(3.68)   Given suprasyllabics a, b, where (a ≪) b, b⇉.

The suprasyllabic b is selected as group or G² head: i.e. it is the most prominent syllabic in the word, and the site of any tonicity that may be assigned to the word by the utterance phonology. Where there is only one ictus in a word, it will be assigned word-tonic status, as in (3.69):

(3.69)

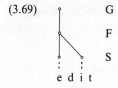

There remain, however, the weak initials in *applause, applaud* and the like, left unattached by foot-formation (3.51); see, for example, (3.52b,c,f). Rather than suggesting that these syllables are left unattached or are attached directly to the group-head, both of which involve violations of the principles of word-tree construction, we propose instead that they are footed with an immediately preceding unrealised ictus, as shown in (3.70):

(3.70)

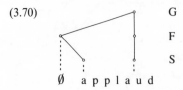

In utterances, such weak word-initials are footed with a preceding ictus, which thus replaces the Ø in (3.70), or the initial ictus is realised by a 'silent stress' (see Abercrombie 1965). Our proposal thus expresses the rhythmic potential of such forms, without violating the principles of tree-formation.

3.4.4   Iteration and cyclicity

Our central concern in this work is with matters of notation; the present section is something of an exception to this. However, it is necessary that we should conclude our sketch of the major processes effecting English word structure with an indication of the apparent constraints on the application of the various formation rules we have surveyed.

Rhyme and syllable-formation ((3.38) and (3.43)) apply simultaneously at all points in a word string: in polysyllabic forms each syllable is constructed simultaneously, giving a typically overlapping pre-stress syllabification. They are constrained only by restrictions on particular combinations: */tl/, etc.

With foot-formation, however, we have some evidence for iteration, specifically right-to-left iterative application. Consider, for example, *sC* clusters. In foot-formation a syllable preceding an *sC* cluster is strong, as evidenced by *phlogíston*, etc. Even when the same application of (3.51) foots the following syllable, *sC* is still strong: *mollúscoid*. However, a syllabic followed by another syllabic which is assigned foot-headship by a distinct application of (3.51) is weak if *sC* intervenes between the two syllabics. Only the initial syllables in (3.71a) form feet:

(3.71)   a. cárnívorous, mándrágora, ómnívorous
         b. cadáverous
         c. aspáragus

whereas those in (b) and (c) show vowel-reduction and absence of ictus status. Thus, the presence of the following /sp/ in (3.71c) does not render the preceding syllable strong. This is provided for if footing of the syllables to the left of the stressed syllable marked in (3.71) follows the formation of the foot to the right (initiated by the marked syllabic). Given that a stressed syllable deprives a preceding one of segments which were ambisyllabic prior to the acquisition of stress, the initial syllables in (b) and (c) will be rendered weak, whereas those in (a) will retain a closing consonant and so be strong. The foot structure of the forms in (3.71) thus suggests that foot-formation is right-to-left iterative.

Similarly, apparent irregularities with respect to group-formation can be related to cyclic application. Thus, for example, the expected word-tree for a form like *participation* is given in (3.72):

(3.72)

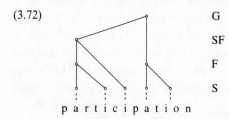

G
SF
F
S

(cf. (3.66b)). However, the pronunciation associated with the structure in (3.73) is at least equally common, with the second syllable being more prominent than the first:

(3.73)

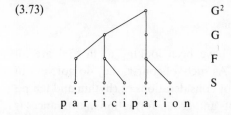

G^2
G
F
S

This is allowed for if groups are established cyclically: specifically, they are formed first with respect to the least inclusive lexical category in derived forms at the same level or stratum. Given a morphological structure of the character of (3.74):

(3.74) $[[\text{participate}]_V \text{ ion}]_N$

group-formation applies firstly to the sequence enclosed in the V-bracket, yielding (3.75):

(3.75)

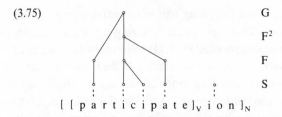

[[p a r t i c i p a t e]$_V$ i o n]$_N$

as in the independent verb *participate*. *-ion* then foots with, and thus confers tonicity on, the immediately preceding syllable. By group-formation (3.68) the second of the two group-heads will govern the first. This gives (3.73), with suppression of the F^2 node consequent upon the removal of the dependency of the penultimate syllable upon the antepenult. For further exemplification see Kiparsky (1979) and Hayes (1982).

In this instance, both the 'cyclic' and the 'non-cyclic' structures are well-formed. It is not our purpose here to consider how general such a conclusion might be, nor, indeed, to examine further the role of this and other suffixes in the determination of phonological structure. This whole area – in particular the 'classic treatment' of *SPE* – is currently the subject of a profound re-examination in terms of the theory of LEXICAL PHONOLOGY (e.g. Kiparsky 1982, 1985; Kaisse & Shaw 1985). Rather, we have simply tried to illustrate that some obvious apparent anomalies in word structures with respect to the formulations suggested here are systematically eliminated if appeal to cyclicity is allowed.

3.5   Word–utterance associations

The dependency assignments we have been looking at in §3.4 are all intralexical: they form word-trees. As such, of course, they do not vary in response to information structure or considerations of rhythm and tempo within the utterance. Syllable-, foot- and group-formation in utterances is sensitive not just to the lexical structures we have just been considering but also to these non-lexical factors. And any sequence of word structures may be associated with several distinct utterance structures. We can draw an analogous intralexical *vs.* extralexical distinction with respect to tune assignment (tone *vs.* intonation). Group-formation in utterances provides the basic unit with respect to which tune–text associations may be formulated, and both utterance groups and utterance tunes (INTONATION contours) are in part determined by information structure. In 'tone languages' certain tunes are lexicalised, as TONE contours, associated with word rather than utterance groups; and are thus idiosyncratically or morphologically determined (and subject to local phonological constraints). The distinction between the phonological structure of the word and that of the utterance is thus similar to that between tone and intonation.

This is not the place for us to try to provide a theory of information structure (but see Ladd 1980 and Gussenhoven 1983 for some proposals concerning its phonological role). However, to the extent that alternative information structures can be regarded as 'variations' associated with a particular syntactic structure, we can at least outline potential utterance patterns on the basis of lexical and syntactic information, without in most cases being able to specify motivations for the choice between alternative potential patterns. We take it that in its phonologically determined aspects, utterance structure is a projection of sequences of word-trees, just as word-trees are projections of sequences of segments. Let us consider, then, potential projections deriving from sequences of word-trees and relevant syntactic information.

We offer some tentative suggestions concerning word-to-utterance associations in (3.76):

(3.76)   *Dependency assignment in utterances*
    (i) Each word-syllabic is a potential utterance-syllabic (with variation according to tempo).
    (ii) Each non-subordinated tonic in a lexical word and each ictus and subordinated tonic which is not adjacent to a group is a potential utterance-ictus (again with variation according to tempo and, as illustrated below, rhythmic requirements).
    (iii) The last utterance-ictus of each disjoint syntactic phrase (i.e. one that is not immediately part of another) is a potential utterance-tonic (with ultimate selection and variation from this pattern being based on information structure).
    (iv) a. A syllabic which is not an utterance-ictus depends on the left-adjacent ictus; if there is no ictus to the left in the same group, it depends on an unrealised ictus ('silent stress').
        b. An ictus which is not an utterance-tonic depends on the right-adjacent tonic; if there is no tonic to the right in the same group ('deaccentuation'), it is F^2-subordinated to the left-adjacent tonic.
        c. The last of several tonics in an utterance (defined by information structure) is a G^2 head; each non-final tonic depends on such a G^2 head.

Consider the application of (3.76) in relation to (3.31) above, whose structure we can now provide with a more adequate characterisation than was given at that point. We can associate with such a sequence the (abbreviated) word-trees and phrasal bracketings in (3.77):

(3.77)

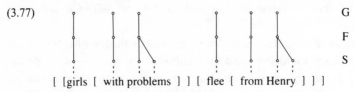

[[girls [with problems]] [flee [from Henry]]]

Application of the principles suggested in (3.76) will give us the associations represented in (3.78):

(3.78)

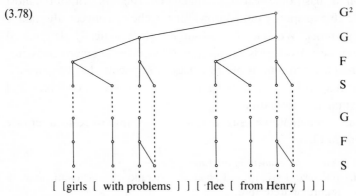

[[girls [with problems]] [flee [from Henry]]]

or, with 'de-accentuation' in the second utterance group, those in (3.33). (3.76) associates each of the word syllables in (3.77) with an utterance syllable in (3.78), on the assumption that the tempo is not too fast. Each of the tonics in the lexical words corresponds to an utterance-ictus. There is in this case no ictus which is not a tonic, nor any subordinate tonics. *With* and *from* as non-lexical words are normally not associated with an utterance-ictus; rather, they are adjoined to the preceding ictus by (iv.a) in (3.76). However, it seems clear that even non-lexical words should be assigned word-ictus and tonics: we need, for instance, to distinguish between the two syllables in *about* and *over* – even though it is only in contrastive or rhythmically appropriate circumstances that the distinction shows up in utterances. There are only two disjoint phrases in (3.77) (note (3.76iii)): the prepositional phrases are immediate constituents of the noun phrase and the verb phrase. We thus have two tone groups in (3.33), with heads *prob-* and *flee*. The second utterance foot follows its tonic, and so is subordinated to it by (iv.b) in (3.76).

An ictus in a lexical word that is not the word-tonic may or may not be an utterance-ictus, depending on the rhythmic environment. An ictus adjacent to another which outranks it (as in (3.62)) is normally not an utterance-ictus. Non-adjacent word-ictus depend for their utterance status on tempo and the rhythmic environment. Compare, for example, the two utterances in (3.79) (where the tonics are again underlined, and Δ marks a silent stress):

(3.79)   a. //all the/indi/cations//Δ are/positive//
          b. //Δ there's/no indi/cation of//bad/faith//

in which after an unstressed syllable the first word-ictus in *indication* is associated with an utterance-ictus (a), but not after a stressed syllable (b).

Non-lexical words are normally footed with a preceding stressed syllable (note (3.76iv.a)), as with *with* and *from* in (3.78), or with a preceding unrealised ictus (if no ictus precedes in the same group), as with *are* in (3.79a) and *there's* in (3.79b). Similar options are available (though provided lexically – see §3.4.3) to the initial unstressed syllables of lexical words, as in *applaud/applause*.

But a non-lexical word may receive utterance-footship, either to break up a sequence of unstressed syllables or so that it can receive (contrastive) tonic status, as in (b) and (c) respectively in (3.80):

(3.80)   a. //John's//Δ gotta/leave//
          b. //John//Δ has/got to/leave//
          c. //John//Δ has/got to/leave//

Similarly, a sequence of two or more non-tonic-bearing monosyllabic lexical words may have the utterance-ictus denied to a non-initial instance (see Giegerich 1980: §3.2.2):

(3.81)   //Δ the/two old/men//

Characteristically, the last ictus is also a tonic.

We return in §7.6 to the general question of associations between levels of representation and to the constraints on these and the levels of representation themselves. At this point we turn to a consideration of the relevance of dependency structure to another level of representation, the segmental.

3.6   Dependency within the segment

In §3.2 we provided an interpretation of headship in relation to phonological constructions. The phonetic property associated with head-ship of a construction is relative prominence with respect to modifiers. In the case of the rhyme and above, however, each head also has a subjoined modifier realised by the same segment; each head takes itself as modifier. These are unlabelled subjunctions; the category status of the head and modifier is the same. We turn now to the internal structure of segments, for which we suggest that subjunction paths with categorially distinct nodes are appropriate as a characterisation of some of the properties observed in chapter 1.

3.6.1 Preponderance and dependency

In chapter 1 we proposed that segments displayed various internal structural properties which are not adequately represented by a simple column of features whose only variation in structure is the binary option associated with each feature. Within gestures, we allowed for the atoms of the representations, components (or single-valued features), to be either present or absent: thus, /u/ is characterised by the presence of the |u| component and the absence of the other articulatory components associated with vowels; /y/ shows presence of both |i| and |u|. Further, components may be present in varying proportions, such that one may preponderate over another: /e/, in a four-height vowel system, involves the preponderance of |i| over |a|, whereas the direction of preponderance is reversed for /ɛ/.

(Relative) preponderance, like (relative) prominence, is appropriately modelled by the dependency relation. That is, as anticipated by the '⇉' notation of chapter 1, we can equate 'preponderate over' with 'govern'. In a four-height vowel system, then, |i| ⇉ |a| in the representation for /e/, and |a| ⇉ |i| for /ɛ/. Given that '⇉' is more costly than ',' (mere co-occurrence) and that both are more costly than non-co-occurrence (i.e. occurrence of a single component), the complexity relations are thus adequately expressed. Moreover, the gradient of 'preponderance' is modelled by the representations, given that in a sequence such as {|i|}, {|i ⇉ a|}, {|a ⇉ i|}, {|a|}, the preponderance of |i| and |a| is directly expressed in terms of the dependencies involved: |i| is the only component; it governs |a|; it is governed by |a|; it is absent. The fact that 'preponderate over' generalises over cases both of absence *vs.* presence and of 'relative strength' of presence is appropriately expressed.

'Mutual preponderance' or 'equal preponderance' is interpreted as mutual government. Thus, as noted in §1.5, we can express the extra level in a five-height system as {|i ⇄ a|} (/ɛ/, in a system which also contains /e/ and /æ/), which abbreviates {|i ⇉ a|, |a ⇉ i|}. As is appropriate, this is the most complex possibility and is ranked in terms of height between /e/ and /æ/. Of course, the admission of such a possibility requires that the dependency relation be non-symmetric rather than antisymmetric or asymmetric. It is thus an interesting empirical question whether such a possibility is ever required in the characterisation of any particular dimension. We shall see in chapter 4 that it is well-motivated with respect to representations in the categorial gesture (specifically the phonatory sub-gesture). We shall, moreover, be proposing there representations in which the subjunction path is extended beyond two nodes: i.e. segments which include paths such as $a_i \rightrightarrows a_j$, $a_j \rightrightarrows a_k$, where $a_i = a_j = a_k$, abbreviated as $a_i \rightrightarrows a_j \rightrightarrows a_k$.

Recall that, as we observed in §1.5, representations which incorporate relative preponderance also provide appropriate characterisations of the notion of natural class. The class-inclusion relations embodied in (1.53) are correctly reflected in the increasing complexity of the dependency relations involved. We add here only one refinement to that account. It is clear that the costing of representations including the complementarity operator '$\sim$' is dependent on the number of relevant components. If three components are involved, say |i|, |u| and |a|, then $\{\sim a\}$ is less costly than $\{a\}$. If only two non-combinable components are involved, '$\sim X$' and 'X' are equivalent in cost. We thus arrive at a hierarchy of relative complexity in the articulatory gesture of the following character:

(3.82)	$\{\sim a\}$	(a segment whose articulatory gesture contains a component other than |a|)
	$\{a\}$	(a segment whose articulatory gesture contains |a|)
	$\{\|\sim a\|\}$	(a segment whose articulatory gesture contains only a component other than |a|)
	$\{\|a\|\}$	(a segment whose articulatory gesture contains only |a|)
	$\{a, \sim a\}$	(a segment whose articulatory gesture contains |a| and a component other than |a|)
	$\{\|a, \sim a\|\}$	(a segment whose articulatory gesture contains only |a| and a component other than |a|)
	$\begin{Bmatrix} \{\|\sim a \rightrightarrows a\|\} \\ \{\|a \rightrightarrows \sim a\|\} \end{Bmatrix}$	(a segment whose articulatory gesture contains only |a| and a component other than |a|, in which one governs the other)
	$\{\|\sim a \rightleftarrows a\|\}$	(a segment whose articulatory gesture contains only |a| and a component other than |a|, in which each governs the other)

In terms of the graph-theoretic interpretation of dependency proposed in §3.1.4, we can offer as alternatives to the representations of the articulatory gesture for vowels suggested in §1.5 those in (3.83), for example (see (1.51)):

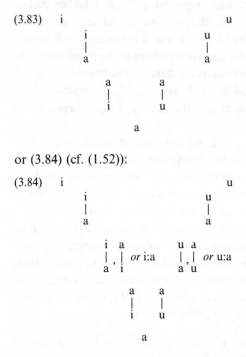

(3.83)

or (3.84) (cf. (1.52)):

(3.84)

The subjunctions in (3.83) and (3.84) involve vertices which are labelled with distinct categories (in contrast to the subjunctions of suprasegmental structure discussed in §3.2).

The parallel treatment of prominence and preponderance proposed here (i.e. in terms of dependency) embodies a claim that these relations can be identified with each other. We suggest that this is substantively plausible: preponderance is the intrasegmental analogue of prominence. Moreover, there is evidence that, other things being equal, prominence relations between segments are preserved in terms of preponderance if these segments are fused into one. We consider this in §3.6.2. Notice too that, whereas suprasegmental structure involves unlabelled dependencies and segmental structure labelled, thus far we have associated the subjunction/adjunction distinction only with suprasegmentals. In §§3.6.3 and 3.6.4 we consider the possibility that the internal structure of segments may involve not only the subjunction of labelled vertices but also adjunction.

3.6.2   Preponderance and prominence

Various phonological developments involve the fusion of distinct segments into one. We hypothesise that where the segments are related by
(asymmetric) dependency this will be preserved, where appropriate, within
the segment that results from their fusion: i.e. (relative) prominence will be
reflected in (relative) preponderance.

Consider in this respect the development of the Middle English
diphthongs /ai̯/ and /au̯/, as exemplified in *day* and *claw*. The development
of the latter is clearer. It emerges as a half-open long back rounded vowel
/ɔː/, distinct from original (Southern) ME /ɔː/, which is vowel-shifted
to /oː/ (*stone*, etc.). The development is as represented in (3.85):

(3.85)

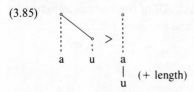

where the dependency relation is preserved. Similarly, /ai̯/ develops to /ɛː/,
i.e. a long half-open front (unrounded) vowel. As such, it develops along
with some descendants of ME /ɛː/ to give /eː/ by the Vowel Shift. Most
ME /ɛː/ fall together with ME /eː/ to give (vowel-shifted) /iː/: contrast *day*
from /ai̯/ and *break* from /ɛː/ with *read* from /ɛː/ and *feed* from /eː/. The
picture is further complicated by the fact that ME /ɑː/ also develops to /ɛː/
and /eː/ by the Vowel Shift, as in *name*. Nevertheless, the diphthong again
develops initially to a segment which preserves the original dependency
relation between its components.

Of course, where a language does not display a vowel-height system that
necessitates appeal to (asymmetric) dependencies (i.e. there is only one
mid vowel, front and/or back), the dependency relation shown by such a
diphthong is redundant intrasegmentally. This is what occasions our
caveat 'where appropriate' in relation to the hypothesis of dependency
preservation under fusion. Sanskrit may be such a case, where, in 'internal
sandhi', the *-i* of the locative inflection fuses with the final *a* of a stem such
as *kān-ta* 'beloved' to give a simple mid vowel {i,a}: *kānte*. Sanskrit shows
only three vowel heights; thus no dependency relation between the vowel
components is relevant.

3.6.3   Intrasegmental adjunctions: consonantal

Suprasegmental structure displays vertices which are unlabelled, the
category of each vertex being given by the category of the segment

associated with the most deeply subjoined vertex which is connected by a subjunction path to the vertex in question. Thus the leftmost node in *pit* is assigned to a segment which bears the categorial gesture shown in (3.86) (which assumes for illustrative purposes two distinct gestures – see §II.1):

(3.86)

where {|C|} is the representation for voiceless stops (see §4.1), and the articulatory gesture is here left unspecified. All of the vertices assigned to the second segment are associated with the category {|V|}:

(3.87)

Suprasegmental structure does not introduce new categories. Specifically, as we have observed, 'categories' such as 'syllable', 'foot', etc. are simple projections from the dependency structures associated with phonological sequences.

The unlabelled suprasegmental dependency structures involve both subjunctions, as in (3.87), and adjunctions, as in the relationship between the two segments in (3.86) and (3.87), represented in (3.88):

(3.88)
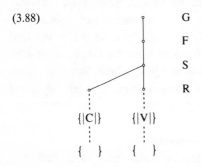

The distinct vertices of intrasegmental structure are labelled. Moreover, up to this point we have allowed only for subjunctions within the segment. This might seem appropriate, given a conception of the segment as the atom of sequential structure. However, there exist certain phenomena which suggest that segment-internal adjunctions, i.e. labelled adjunctions, should also be invoked in phonological representation. (For fuller discussions of the phenomena considered here, see Ewen 1980b, 1982 and the works referred to there.)

We are concerned here with phonetic events which exhibit more than one phase but whose status as belonging to a single segment or sequence has been controversial. Consider, for example, the prenasalised stops of a language like Nyanga, illustrated in (3.89a) (see Herbert 1977:257), which contrasts with the sequence of syllabic nasal and (voiced) stop shown in (3.89b):

(3.89)   a. [m͡bale] 'plate'
         b. [m̩bale] 'brother'

Though exhibiting two clearly differentiated phases (a nasal followed by a non-nasal), prenasalised consonants have the duration of single segments rather than of sequences. Moreover, as sequences they would be phonotactically aberrant in showing a syllable-initial sequence of nasal followed by a less sonorant consonant.

On the other hand, it is misleading, both phonetically and phonologically, to regard them as simple segments which differ from other segments only in terms of, say, the feature [prenasality], as is suggested by Ladefoged (1971:35). S. R. Anderson (1976), for example, observes that Apinayé possesses a series of voiced stops which may be nasal, prenasal, postnasal, or oral, depending on the nasality of the adjacent vowel. The various possibilities for clusters of voiced stops are shown in (3.90):

(3.90)   a. [V b d V]
         b. [Ṽ m d V]
         c. [V b n Ṽ]
         d. [Ṽ m n Ṽ]

Between oral vowels (a) both stops are non-nasal; after the nasalised vowel in (b) the first stop is nasal, whereas the second, adjacent to an oral vowel, is non-nasal; in (c) this situation is reversed; and in (d) both stops are adjacent to a nasalised vowel and are thus themselves nasal.

With a single intervocalic voiced stop we find the possibilities in (3.91):

(3.91)   a. [V b V]
          b. [Ṽ m̂b V]
          c. [V b̂m Ṽ]
          d. [Ṽ m Ṽ]

As before, with an oral vowel on both sides, the stop is non-nasal (a); it is fully nasal only between vowels which are both nasalised (d). After a nasalised vowel and before a non-nasalised one the stop is prenasalised (b); and if the sequence is reversed, it is postnasalised (c). S. R. Anderson sums this up as follows:

> The generalization to be drawn from these facts is: the first portion of a consonant (cluster) between vowels has the nasality of the preceding vowel, while its second portion has the nasality of the following vowel. Where the vowels differ, the result is a 'complex nasal contour'. If there are two segments on which to realize this contour, each specification takes one segment as its domain; but if there is only one, a complex nasal consonant results. (1976:337)

The distribution in (3.91) cannot be explained by assuming that the stop segment in (b) is uniformly [+prenasalised] whereas that in (c) is [+postnasalised]. Such segments are, both phonetically and phonologically, 'sequentially' complex.

Similar considerations apply in the case of affricates, such as those in *church* and *judge* in English. Again we have events which have the duration of one segment and which as sequences are phonotactically anomalous, but which display some of the properties of sequences. (For further discussion, see again Ewen 1982:§6.)

In both these instances it seems appropriate to attribute internal sequential structure to the segment. Moreover, in both cases the less sonorous SUB-SEGMENT is dominant: affricates are a kind of stop, as are prenasalised and postnasalised stops. Historically, the source of both affricates and prenasalised and postnasalised stops is typically a stop; and in formulations of synchronic distributions such as those exemplified in (3.90) and (3.91) the stop is the basic allophone (see again S. R. Anderson 1976).

Accordingly, we might propose that prenasalised stops display the segment-internal structure in (3.92):

(3.92)   {|'voiced stop'|}

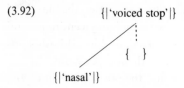

                                    { }

          {|'nasal'|}

where the content of the articulatory gesture of the (necessarily homorganic) dependent nasal sub-segment is predictable from that of its
governor (here left unspecified), and where the categorial representations
will be those to be developed in chapter 4. Affricates may be represented as
in (3.93), where both the articulatory gesture and the presence or absence
of voicing in the case of the dependent fricative is predictable from the
character of its governor:

(3.93)   {|'stop'|}

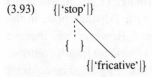

          {|'fricative'|}

These representations, then, involve labelled adjunctions. And, if warran-
ted, this means that we can associate subjunctions and adjunctions with
both suprasegmental and segmental structure.

Ewen (1982) provides a rather different interpretation of pre- and
postnasalisation and analogous phenomena, whereby the ambivalence of
such segments with respect to mono- *vs.* multi-segmentality is related to
their infringement of the sonority hierarchy: the more sonorous element is
further from the syllabic peak. This property is shared with initial *sC*
sequences in, for example, English (for which, again, monosegmental
analyses have been proposed – see, e.g., Fudge 1969). In terms of such an
approach we can view segmentality as a gradient property rather than as
once-and-for-all. Thus, /st-/ and /mb-/ are intermediate between a
straightforward cluster such as /tr-/ and a simple segment like /s-/.

The alternative offered here above makes a simple binary distinction
between segment and sequence, so that /mb-/ is grouped with /s-/ as a
single segment, in accordance with its duration. /st-/ is a cluster whose
component segments enter into independent restrictions: recall the ban on
/stl-/ in English parallel to that on /tl-/. This alternative account fails,
however, to explain the limitation of prenasalised stops to syllable-initial
position, whereas this follows immediately from the proposal made in
Ewen (1982): the sequence /mb/ is anomalous only initially; a final
sequence of this character is quite in accordance with the sonority
hierarchy.

We therefore offer these phenomena only rather tentatively as instances
of intrasegmental adjunctions. If this position is adopted, affricates will
also exemplify an adjunction within the segment, of a fricative to a stop.
However, once more the ambivalence of these might be related to another

sonority-based infringement, given that the fricative element (more sonorant) is interpreted as governed by the stop (less sonorant).

3.6.4   Intrasegmental adjunctions: 'short' diphthongs

A further area in which appeal to intrasegmental sequence may be appropriate is in the characterisation of the diphthongs in certain vowel systems. Diphthongs often pattern with long vowels in constituting heavy or strong syllables. In such cases a representation like (3.30), in which the second element of the diphthong is associated with a distinct node in the suprasegmental structure, is perhaps appropriate. However, say that we are dealing with a vowel system which shows no (surface) length contrast, as is arguably the case in Modern Scots and Scottish English. The contrast between the vowels in *beat*, *bite* and *bit*, for example, is purely one of quality, and not of length. A representation of diphthongs involving a (superficially) complex nucleus is inappropriate here: the system lacks a complex/simplex nucleus distinction.

Once again, we suggest, the internal sequencing of the elements of the diphthong (its initial posture and the target posture) should in this case be attributed to the segment, so that it can be represented as (3.94):

(3.94)

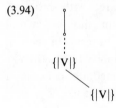

where this complex segment is assigned to a single vertex in the suprasegmental dependency structure.

A rhyme containing a 'long' diphthong may now be characterised as in (3.95):

(3.95)

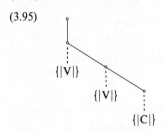

rather than the needlessly complex (3.30). We can now also dispense with the notion of a sub-rhyme: the relationship between the elements of a diphthong or geminate vowel sequence is expressed as part of the segmental structure.

Some systems show an opposition between 'short' (purely segment-internal) and 'long' (involving a heavy syllable) diphthongs. This may have been the case in Old English, which has a set of 'long' diphthongs, associated in their phonological behaviour with long vowels. Thus, for example, the -*u* of the nominative and accusative plural of neuter *a*-stem nouns, shown in (3.96):

(3.96)   scipu 'ships', hofu 'dwellings'

is dropped if the rhyme is heavy (as noted in §2.7.2), i.e. if the head of the rhyme of the stem syllable has more than one segment subordinate to it to its right, as exemplified in (3.97):

(3.97)   word 'words', wīf 'women'

Both of these types show the rhyme structure in (3.98):

(3.98)

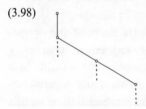

differing only in whether the dependent of the rhyme is vocalic or consonantal. We can associate the same structure with the 'long' diphthongs; they too require the dropping of -*u* in such stems:

(3.99)   dēor 'animals'

In pre-Old English there developed a series of diphthongs associated with various environments, involving 'sound changes' such as Breaking and Back Mutation. When these diphthongs develop from a long vowel, they fall together in their subsequent behaviour with the 'original' long diphthongs. But the diphthongs resulting from Breaking or Back Mutation of short vowels remain systematically short (other things being equal). The -*u* of the nominative and accusative plural neuter *a*-stems remains in Old English:

(3.100)   featu 'vessels'
          (Back Mutated form, from the Vespasian Psalter Gloss)

suggesting that the diphthong structure is segment-internal, as in (3.94). It

shares with *scipu* the property of having a rhyme-head with only one
subordinate.

3.7   Conclusion

In this chapter we have provided a characterisation of various aspects of
phonological representations in terms of the structural properties made
available by dependency grammar (as described in relation to syntax in
§3.1). In §3.2 we characterised the notion 'head of a phonological
construction', and established the layers of obligatory constructions
(rhyme, syllable, foot, tone group) in terms of alternations in the direction
of modification. §3.3 drew a distinction between those aspects of
phonological structure assigned in the lexicon and those which depend on
extralexical considerations; and §3.5 offered some suggestions as to how
lexical and utterance representations are associated. §3.4 illustrated the
generalisations governing assignment of word or intralexical structure in
English, crucially head selection. In the immediately preceding section we
have been concerned to demonstrate the appropriateness of the dependency relation to the expression of what we termed in chapter 1
'preponderance', i.e. the dominance of one component (or several) in a
gesture over the other(s). (Thus far we have not invoked any dependency
relations involving the gestures themselves; in the representations in this
chapter they simply co-occur. But we return to this question in Part III.)
Finally, we have been concerned with some evidence that sequential
relations – and thus adjunction rather than simply subjunction – are relevant to the internal structure of segments. (We return in chapter 7 to the
characterisation and status of the notion 'segment'.) It is perhaps not
without interest that the heads of such intrasegmental constructions are
the categorially simplest (sub-)segment-types, i.e. vowels and (voiceless)
stops. That is, this particular kind of additional complexity is permitted
only to the otherwise simplest segment-types.

Overview of Part I

In Part I we have presented arguments, notably in chapters 1 and 2, in favour of a particular view of phonological structure. In this view, the properties of segmental structure are most adequately characterised if the atomic elements (components) out of which segments are constructed are conceived of as being organised into systematic subsets (gestures) within which particular components may be present or absent and within which components may or may not preponderate over one another. Sequential structure is organised into constituents of a particular kind; they are binary, headed constructions – i.e. each construction has two members, one the (sequentially simplex) head of the construction, the other its (possibly complex) modifier. Headship is manifested in terms of relative prominence.

Chapter 3 provides a characterisation of preponderance and prominence in terms of the binary relation of dependency more familiar from work on syntactic structure. Crucial to the representation of the obligatory constructional layers of tone group, foot, syllable and rhyme is the notion of successive headship for an element, whereby a single element may be head of successively more inclusive constructions. These constructions are unlabelled, even though they are not differentiated in terms of the nature of their head; each differs from that which it immediately includes and that which immediately includes it in terms of direction of modification. The successive headships of a single element are characterised by subjunction paths. It is also in terms of subjunctive dependencies, but in this instance with labelled vertices, that relations of preponderance within the segments are given an appropriate expression.

The basis for arguments for these structural properties is what we have termed the natural recurrence, componentiality and constituentiality assumptions, which we take to be a formulation of notions underlying any attempt to arrive at a principled characterisation of phonological structure. In Part II we pursue further the consequences of these assumptions in relation to the detailed content of the gestures which make up each segment, i.e. the basic components and their combinatorial possibilities. We will also be concerned with the character of the gestures themselves, and the relationship between them, which our discussion in §1.6 left rather unresolved. The resolution of this will depend in large part on our investigation of the nature of the atoms of phonological representation. These, then, will be the concerns of Part II.

PART II

PHONOLOGICAL GESTURES AND THEIR STRUCTURE

Introduction

Our primary aim in Part II will be to work out some of the notions partially developed in chapters 1 and 3, i.e. those concerned with the structure of segmental representations in dependency phonology. Before we can discuss any further the nature of the phonological primes and their interaction, however, we must devote some space to refining the notion of gesture, which we considered in a preliminary way in §1.6. In particular, we must establish exactly how many gestures are required, and how the components characterising a segment are divided amongst them.

In §1.6 we noted that both Lass (1976) and Lass & Anderson (1975) propose that the matrix characterising a segment be divided into (at least) two sub-matrices – the articulatory gesture and the phonatory gesture – and that phonological rules and processes may have as their domain just one of these gestures. Further, we noted that [ʔ] and [h] can be characterised as lacking all supralaryngeal articulatory information, so that rules changing voiceless stops to [ʔ], or voiceless fricatives to [h], involve merely deletion of all articulatory features – the resulting segment being specified only for features in the phonatory gesture. In other words, [ʔ] is viewed as the 'minimal' stop and [h] as the 'minimal' fricative.

Notice, however, that the proposal made by Lass differs in some interesting ways from that of Lass & Anderson. Instead of two gestures labelled [articulatory] and [phonatory], he proposes an [oral] and a [laryngeal] gesture. In this model, there are two distinct operations involved in the 'de-oralisation' of a voiceless stop to [ʔ] (Lass 1976:155). First there is a 'gesture-shift' involving the copying of [−continuant] from the oral to the laryngeal gesture; then deletion of the [oral] gesture, as in (1.62) (repeated here as (II.1)):

$$\text{(II.1)} \quad \begin{bmatrix} \begin{bmatrix} \text{oral} \\ -\text{cont} \end{bmatrix} \\ \begin{bmatrix} -\text{son} \\ -\text{voice} \end{bmatrix} \end{bmatrix} \rightarrow \begin{bmatrix} \emptyset \\ [-\text{cont}] \end{bmatrix}$$

141

or, in the case of de-oralisation of a voiceless fricative to [h], a gesture-shift in which [+continuant] is copied into the laryngeal gesture, with subsequent deletion of [oral]. For Lass & Anderson, however, a feature like [continuant] forms part of the phonatory rather than the articulatory gesture, and so changes from voiceless stops to [ʔ] involve only the latter stage, i.e. deletion of one of the sub-matrices. The Lass model is based on the distinction between the two gestures being laryngeal *vs.* supra-laryngeal, so that voicing is a property of the laryngeal gesture, with degree of stricture, place of articulation and lip setting being properties of the supralaryngeal or oral gesture. However, he appears to accept that, phonologically, the gestures need not correspond with this division. He suggests that there are two kinds of linguistically relevant information, apportioned between two gestures: (a) a categorial gesture ('vowel', 'voiceless stop'), and (b) a locational or distinctive gesture ('back vowel', 'palatal'). Nevertheless, he does not utilise this distinction in his present-ation, and rather, maintains his convention whereby features may be copied from one gesture to another. Thus, the de-oralisation of a voiceless stop to [ʔ], illustrated above, involves two distinct operations. In a model in which the basic division is in terms of the categorial/locational dichotomy, on the other hand, [continuant] is already a feature of what Lass & Anderson call the 'phonation' gesture, and deletion of the 'articulation' gesture in, say, [t] → [ʔ] leaves the specifications within the phonation gesture unaffected.

In the following section we cite evidence from lenition processes which appears to show that this treatment is more appropriate, even though it deviates from various proposals which have been made with regard to the establishing of gestures or components on phonetic grounds (such as those of Catford 1977; see again §1.6.2). Catford's (phonetically based) articulation component consists of two sub-components, 'stricture-type' and 'location' (i.e. in traditional terms, manner and place of articulation), while his phonation component is concerned with activity in the larynx.

II.1   Articulation *vs.* phonation

It is clear that the distinction between Catford's articulation and phonation components corresponds more closely to Lass's distinction between an oral and a laryngeal gesture than to the articulatory/phon-atory split in the Lass & Anderson model. However, as noted above, this division appears to introduce certain unfortunate complexities at the phonological level, in that [voice] and [sonorant] will form part of the laryngeal gesture, while [continuant] and any other stricture features will form part of the oral gesture.

A further argument against Lass's model involves the behaviour in various types of phonological hierarchies of segment-types such as voiced and voiceless stops, voiced and voiceless fricatives, and sonorant consonants. In lenition processes, for example, voiceless stops can weaken to voiced fricatives along two paths, either via voiceless fricatives or via voiced stops (see, e.g., Lass & Anderson 1975:156–8). In the Lass (1976) model, these changes must be viewed as belonging to two different gestures, voicing being a change in the laryngeal gesture, fricativisation a change in the oral gesture:

(II.2)
$$
\begin{bmatrix} [-\text{cont}] \\ \begin{bmatrix} -\text{son} \\ -\text{voice} \end{bmatrix} \end{bmatrix}
\rightarrow
\begin{bmatrix} [-\text{cont}] \\ \begin{bmatrix} -\text{son} \\ +\text{voice} \end{bmatrix} \end{bmatrix}
$$
voiceless   voiced
stop   stop

(II.3)
$$
\begin{bmatrix} [-\text{cont}] \\ \begin{bmatrix} -\text{son} \\ +\text{voice} \end{bmatrix} \end{bmatrix}
\rightarrow
\begin{bmatrix} [+\text{cont}] \\ \begin{bmatrix} -\text{son} \\ +\text{voice} \end{bmatrix} \end{bmatrix}
$$
voiced   voiced
stop   fricative

Sonorisation, too, will involve a change in the laryngeal gesture, while weakening from a sonorant consonant to, say, a semi-vowel is presumably a change in the oral gesture, from [+consonantal] to [−consonantal].

However, a set of changes like those outlined above clearly represents weakening along a *single* hierarchy (see for example Lass & Anderson 1975:ch. 5; also §4.4 below). Lass & Anderson (1975:50) observe that the sequence of changes in (II.4) is one that tends to recur in the histories of languages:

(II.4)   a. (intervocalic) voiceless stop → voiced stop
           b. voiced stop → voiced fricative
           c. voiced fricative → approximant consonant
           d. approximant → vowel
           e. vowel → ∅

If schemata such as (II.4) do in fact represent single, unidimensional recurrent processes, a division between oral and laryngeal gestures disguises the unitary nature of such processes. Features like [continuant], [sonorant] and [voice] seem rather to be of the same phonological type – we might, in Lass's terms, refer to them as categorial features (or, using *SPE* terminology, as major class features; although Chomsky & Halle, *SPE*:299, do not treat either [continuant] or [voice] as major class features).

Similar evidence can be found in the behaviour of elements in syllabicity hierarchies (see for example Vennemann 1972; Basbøll 1974; Hooper 1976). Like lenition hierarchies, syllabicity hierarchies seem to involve a single scale, in which the features [voice] and [continuant], for example, interact. Hooper (1976:199) claims that the intrinsic structure of the syllable involves the hierarchisation of segment-types in (II.5), where we give the characterisation of the various categories in terms of *SPE* features:

$$(II.5) \quad \begin{bmatrix} +\text{cons} \\ -\text{son} \end{bmatrix} \quad \begin{bmatrix} +\text{cons} \\ -\text{cont} \\ +\text{son} \end{bmatrix} \quad \begin{bmatrix} +\text{cons} \\ +\text{cont} \\ +\text{son} \end{bmatrix} \quad \begin{bmatrix} -\text{cons} \\ +\text{cont} \\ +\text{son} \\ -\text{syll} \end{bmatrix} \quad \begin{bmatrix} -\text{cons} \\ +\text{cont} \\ +\text{son} \\ +\text{syll} \end{bmatrix}$$

$$\text{obstruents} \qquad \text{nasals} \qquad \text{liquids} \qquad \text{glides} \qquad \text{vowels}$$

We again see the features of the two gestures interacting. Again, it seems reasonable to suppose that the sequence in (II.5) represents a unitary scale, but a system in which [continuant] and [consonantal] are assigned to one gesture and [sonorant] to another fails to show this.

Evidence of this sort (to which we will return in chapter 4) strongly suggests that all the features of (II.5) belong to a single gesture, so that the relevant *phonological* distinction is between, on the one hand, a purely locational gesture, and, on the other, a gesture which combines Catford's phonation component with the sub-division of the articulation component which he labels stricture-type (i.e. manner of articulation). What we are claiming, then, is that this gesture involves a set of segmental primes which correspond to parameters which, when viewed from a particular phonetic perspective, may be of two different types. Thus it seems that a strict adherence to the components established by Catford on the apparently most salient phonetic grounds can only disguise the fact that the *linguistically* relevant distinction between the two gestures is clearly based on other factors.

However, even on phonetic grounds, it is possible to argue that the association of stricture-type with location rather than with phonation is at least debatable; notice that, as opposed to locational 'features', both stricture-type and phonation 'features' are concerned (at least partly) with characterising the sound-source itself, rather than its modification or 'shaping' by the vocal tract configuration. This is (roughly) the informal division made between 'source features' on the one hand and 'resonance features' on the other in the Jakobsonian framework.

The term CATEGORIAL GESTURE is more appropriate than the label 'phonatory gesture' which was used in earlier work within dependency phonology (Anderson & Jones 1977; Ewen 1977), seeing that the gesture does not entirely correspond to the phonation component proposed by Catford; rather, our categorial gesture includes certain aspects of the segment (i.e. stricture-type) not assigned to Catford's phonation component.

II.2   Phonation *vs.* initiation

We turn now to the division between Catford's phonation and initiation components, and to the issue of whether there should be a phonological distinction corresponding to Catford's phonetic one. We suggest that there should indeed be a sub-division of the segment in this area, but that, again, the sub-division should be rather different from Catford's. In the first place, we consider that the phonation and initiation components (or their equivalents) should not correspond to two independent gestures, but that they should represent sub-divisions of a single gesture. That is, we envisage an essentially bipartite segmental structure, rather than the tripartite one proposed by Catford. We return below to the motivations for this claim. In the second place, we believe that the phonetically based component of phonation should be spread over both of the sub-gestures envisaged above; that is, the categorial gesture is made up of two sub-gestures, one of which corresponds to certain aspects of Catford's phonation component, together with his initiation component. The arguments for both these claims will involve some anticipation of matters dealt with in greater detail in chapter 5.

In characterising phonation, Chomsky & Halle use the binary feature [voice] (cf. Jakobson, Fant & Halle 1969). Ladefoged (1971:7–22), however, proposes a multi-valued scalar feature [glottal stricture], which may have up to three phonological values for any particular language, and a number of phonetic values. This non-binary feature is required at the phonetic level to characterise the difference between the various phonation-types, and at the phonological level in those languages which make an opposition amongst more than two states of the glottis – for example, Gujarati, with contrasts involving voicelessness, breathy voice and voice.

However, the presence in a model of a scalar feature such as Ladefoged's [glottal stricture] does not necessarily imply the absence of a (binary) [voice] feature. We have already argued that, phonologically, [voice] is a feature like [continuant] and [sonorant], in that categories like voiced stops and voiceless fricatives appear to behave in the same way with respect to various kinds of hierarchies. However, the important distinction in this respect appears to be between the presence and absence of voice, rather than between various *degrees* of voicing. Thus a feature indicating degree of glottal stricture might be kept separate from one denoting voicing as such. Notice, too, that a particular degree of glottal stricture does not necessarily imply [+ voice]: whisper shows a greater degree of glottal stricture than voicelessness, but does not involve vocal cord vibration. Phonetically, there are two parameters involved: degree of glottal stricture, and vocal cord vibration.

This evidence is suggestive of a treatment in which there are two phonological features corresponding to the two phonetic parameters. Indeed, a rather similar approach is adopted by Halle & Stevens (1971), who propose two (non-orthogonal) pairs of binary features to character-ise various laryngeal states. The first pair, [stiff vocal cords] and [slack vocal cords], are essentially concerned with the state of the glottis itself, and the other, [spread glottis] and [constricted glottis], with degree of glottal opening.

However, there is evidence to suggest that the two (pairs of) features should be assigned to different sub-gestures within the categorial gesture. We suggest that [voice] (or [stiff vocal cords] and [slack vocal cords]) is a feature of what we shall call the phonatory sub-gesture, while [glottal stricture] (or [spread glottis] and [constricted glottis]) belongs to the initiatory sub-gesture.

A solution of this sort allows us to capture the notion of phonological complexity in a natural way. In the characterisation of segments in languages in which only a voiced/voiceless opposition is found (and in which only a pulmonic egressive airstream mechanism is utilised), no representations in the initiatory sub-gesture will be required phonologically; that is, segments in these languages will require phonological representations in which the categorial gesture involves only a single sub-gesture. For languages in which a three-way opposition in phonation-type is made, and which are therefore phonologically more complex, representations of the initiatory sub-gesture will also be present at the phonological level. Thus, /b/ and /p/ in English (in which only a two-way opposition is made) have representations such as (II.6):

$$
\text{(II.6)} \quad
\begin{bmatrix} \begin{bmatrix} +\text{slack v.c.} \\ \vdots \end{bmatrix} \\ \\ \begin{bmatrix} +\text{ant} \\ -\text{cor} \\ \vdots \end{bmatrix} \end{bmatrix}_{/b/}
\qquad
\begin{bmatrix} \begin{bmatrix} +\text{stiff v.c.} \\ \vdots \end{bmatrix} \\ \\ \begin{bmatrix} +\text{ant} \\ -\text{cor} \\ \vdots \end{bmatrix} \end{bmatrix}_{/p/}
$$

in which the initiatory sub-gesture is not present, while the phonological representations of /ɓ/, /b/ and /p/ in Margi are as in (II.7) (where we give only the representations of the categorial gesture):

$$
\text{(II.7)} \quad
\begin{bmatrix} \begin{bmatrix} +\text{slack v.c.} \\ \vdots \end{bmatrix} \\ \\ \begin{bmatrix} +\text{constr.gl.} \\ \vdots \end{bmatrix} \end{bmatrix}_{/ɓ/}
\quad
\begin{bmatrix} \begin{bmatrix} +\text{slack v.c.} \\ \vdots \end{bmatrix} \\ \\ \begin{bmatrix} -\text{spr.gl.} \\ -\text{constr.gl.} \\ \vdots \end{bmatrix} \end{bmatrix}_{/b/}
\quad
\begin{bmatrix} \begin{bmatrix} +\text{stiff v.c.} \\ \vdots \end{bmatrix} \\ \\ \begin{bmatrix} +\text{spr.gl.} \\ \vdots \end{bmatrix} \end{bmatrix}_{/p/}
$$

/b/, /p/ and /pʰ/ in Thai will have the representations in (II.8):

$$
\text{(II.8)} \quad
\begin{bmatrix} \begin{bmatrix} +\text{slack v.c.} \\ \vdots \end{bmatrix} \\ \\ \begin{bmatrix} +\text{constr. gl.} \\ \vdots \end{bmatrix} \end{bmatrix}_{/b/}
\quad
\begin{bmatrix} \begin{bmatrix} +\text{slack v.c.} \\ \vdots \end{bmatrix} \\ \\ \begin{bmatrix} -\text{spr. gl.} \\ -\text{constr. gl.} \\ \vdots \end{bmatrix} \end{bmatrix}_{/p/}
\quad
\begin{bmatrix} \begin{bmatrix} +\text{stiff v.c.} \\ \vdots \end{bmatrix} \\ \\ \begin{bmatrix} +\text{spr. gl.} \\ \vdots \end{bmatrix} \end{bmatrix}_{/pʰ/}
$$

The specification of the representations of the initiatory sub-gesture is necessary because of the presence in the language of the opposition amongst three phonation-types. The complexity of such systems in comparison with those in which only a two-way opposition in phonation-type is made is appropriately characterised by this additional notational complexity.

However, notice too that a language may make a choice out of the two sub-gestures in the representation of particular segments. That is, as well as it being possible for a segment to be characterised by the presence of the phonatory sub-gesture alone (English), or by the presence of both sub-gestures (Margi, Thai), there are also cases where various primes within the phonatory sub-gesture for a particular set of segments are absent phonologically, and the distinction is made entirely by the representations of the initiatory sub-gesture. This appears to be the case in languages such as Korean and Icelandic, in which the opposition amongst the various members of the stop series is one of aspiration rather than of voicing. (Of course, an analysis of this sort might also be postulated for languages such as English, in which voicelessness might also be held to be predictable from aspiration.) For Icelandic, where we find a series of voiceless unaspirated stops and a series of voiceless aspirated stops, the following representations seem appropriate:

$$(II.9) \qquad \begin{bmatrix} \begin{bmatrix} -\text{spr.gl.} \\ \vdots \end{bmatrix} \end{bmatrix} \qquad \begin{bmatrix} \begin{bmatrix} +\text{spr.gl.} \\ \vdots \end{bmatrix} \end{bmatrix}$$

$$\qquad\qquad \text{unaspirated stop} \qquad \text{aspirated stop}$$

where the phonatory sub-gesture is lacking (with the exception of those features identifying the segments as stops). Similarly, Korean, which has three series of voiceless stops, distinguished by degree of aspiration (Kim 1970), will have the following initiatory representations:

$$(II.10) \quad \begin{bmatrix} \begin{bmatrix} +\text{constr.gl.} \\ \vdots \end{bmatrix} \end{bmatrix} \qquad\qquad \begin{bmatrix} \begin{bmatrix} -\text{spr.gl.} \\ -\text{constr.gl.} \\ \vdots \end{bmatrix} \end{bmatrix} \qquad \begin{bmatrix} \begin{bmatrix} +\text{spr.gl.} \\ \vdots \end{bmatrix} \end{bmatrix}$$

$$\qquad\quad \text{unaspirated stop} \qquad\quad \text{slightly aspirated stop} \quad \text{heavily aspirated stop}$$

Notice finally in this section that features (or components) characterising airstream mechanisms other than the pulmonic will also form part of the initiatory sub-gesture. These matters are worked out in detail in chapter 5.

II.3   The representation of the segment

The matrix characterising the segment will from now on be viewed as a composite of two sub-matrices: the ARTICULATORY GESTURE and the

CATEGORIAL GESTURE, with the categorial gesture being further divided into two sub-gestures: the PHONATORY SUB-GESTURE and the INITIATORY SUB-GESTURE. As we shall see in detail in chapter 6, a similar structure is perhaps not inappropriate for the articulatory gesture. Recall that while Catford's phonetic account involves the positing of three functional components, Ladefoged (1971) distinguishes four processes required in the specification of speech, adding the oro-nasal process to Catford's three components. In Catford's treatment, nasality is handled within the articulation component, although no strong motivation is offered for this. It seems possible, then, to account for the oro-nasal process as a distinct sub-gesture within the articulatory gesture, thus giving the articulatory representations in (II.11):

(II.11)
$$\begin{bmatrix} \begin{bmatrix} +\text{ant} \\ -\text{cor} \\ \vdots \end{bmatrix} \\ \begin{bmatrix} -\text{nas} \end{bmatrix} \end{bmatrix} \qquad \begin{bmatrix} \begin{bmatrix} +\text{ant} \\ -\text{cor} \\ \vdots \end{bmatrix} \\ \begin{bmatrix} +\text{nas} \end{bmatrix} \end{bmatrix}$$
voiceless stop   nasal

where [nasal] is assigned to a distinct sub-gesture within the articulatory gesture. Let us label the two sub-gestures the LOCATIONAL SUB-GESTURE and the ORO-NASAL SUB-GESTURE. Such an account successfully represents the fact that the oro-nasal sub-gesture is a distinct domain for phonological processes, although its formulation in terms of binary features, as in (II.11), rather obscures the privative nature of nasality. We return to these matters in §6.9.

The segment now has the structure shown in (II.12):

(II.12)

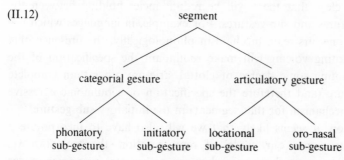

while (II.13) is an abstract matrix representing the kinds of properties present within each of the gestures:

(II.13)

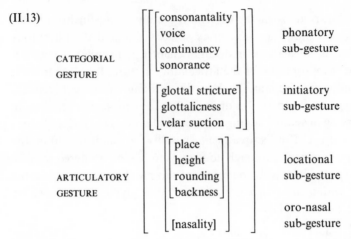

(II.13) is thus a formalisation of the notion of gesture, and of particular groups of features forming recurrent domains for phonological processes. As such, it is to be preferred both to Thráinsson's (1978) approach (see §1.6), where the notion of gesture is appealed to but where no attempt is made to establish the groups of features which form gestures, and to approaches such as that of Chomsky & Halle (*SPE*:299), who, although providing groups of features with labels (major class, cavity, manner of articulation, source, prosodic) make no attempt to characterise or utilise the sub-divisions in any formal way. This deficiency has also been observed by Clements (1985), who proposes a hierarchical model of segment structure within an autosegmental framework which is similar to, but in some respects even more extensive than, that discussed here (see §7.2).

It seems clear that there will be redundancies holding between the various gestures and sub-gestures. For example, in languages which use more than one airstream mechanism phonologically, the presence of a feature denoting voicing will make redundant the specification of the feature denoting some degree of glottal stricture other than complete glottal closure (and therefore the specification of a pulmonic egressive airstream mechanism for that segment) in the initiatory sub-gesture.

In addition, it seems likely that we will also have to incorporate a further gesture into our model of representation – the TONOLOGICAL. However, as tone is rather obviously a suprasegmental phenomenon (see Goldsmith 1976), we postpone discussion of this gesture until Part III (see §7.4). In the meantime, we consider in the next three chapters the representations of the gestures and sub-gestures constituting a segment.

4   *The categorial gesture: phonation*

4.1   The phonatory components

Jakobson, Fant & Halle (1969:18–19) distinguish two 'Fundamental Source Features', i.e. vocalic *vs.* non-vocalic, and consonantal *vs.* non-consonantal:

> Phonemes possessing the vocalic feature have a single periodic ('voice') source whose onset is not abrupt . . . Phonemes possessing the consonantal feature are acoustically characterized by the presence of zeros that affect the entire spectrum.

Thus vowels are vocalic and non-consonantal, while obstruents are consonantal and non-vocalic. Liquids are characterised as having both the consonantal and vocalic features, i.e. they have some of the acoustic properties both of vowels and of (true) consonants.

For Jakobson, these features are, of course, binary. The appropriateness of the properties characterised by these features, and the way in which they classify segments, are not in doubt, although we interpret them (following Anderson & Jones 1977:123) in a rather different way. We propose two dependency components in the phonatory sub-gesture: |V|, a component which can be defined as 'relatively periodic', and |C|, a component of 'periodic energy reduction'. However, |V| and |C| differ from the vocalic and consonantal distinctive features in that the presence of, say, |V| in a segment does not necessarily imply that the segment is in a simple binary opposition to an otherwise identical segment not containing |V|. Rather, as we noted in §3.4, the more prominent a particular dependency component in a subjunction tree, the greater the preponderance of the property characterised by that component. Notice too that |V| and |C| can characterise segments either alone or in combination. Thus |V| and |C| have to this extent the same attributes with respect to the phonatory sub-gesture as |i|, |u|, and |a| have with respect to the vowel space, as discussed in §1.5.

|V| and |C| alone, then, represent either end of a hierarchy, at one

extreme of which we find segments with maximum |V|-ness and non-existent |C|-ness (i.e. maximum periodicity and lack of energy reduction due to the presence of acoustic zeros), and at the other extreme segments which show the reverse characteristics, i.e. maximum |C|-ness and non-existent |V|-ness. Accordingly, vowels have the representation in (4.1), and voiceless plosives, the 'optimal' consonants, that in (4.2):

(4.1)   {|V|}   (4.2)   {|C|}
        vowel   voiceless
                              plosive

Sonorant consonants have traditionally been viewed as being in some way combinations of vowels and true consonants. Thus Jakobson *et al.* characterise liquids as having both the vocalic and the consonantal features: 'like vowels, the liquids have only a harmonic source [hence they are vocalic]; like consonants, they show significant zeros in their spectrum envelope [hence consonantal] . . . The formant structure of the liquids is broadly similar to that of vowels' (1969:19). Nasals, too, are seen as combining the characteristics of vowels and consonants: 'nasality, by super-imposing a clear-cut formant structure upon the consonantal pattern, brings consonants closer to vowels' (Jakobson & Halle 1956:56). Sonorant consonants, then, are combinations of |V| and |C|, as in (4.3):

(4.3)   {|V ⇉ C|}
        sonorant
        consonant

Because sonorant consonants have a clearly marked formant structure, we propose a representation in which |V| governs |C|, rather than one in which |C| (unilaterally or bilaterally) governs |V|. Sonorants are thus character-ised, uncontroversially, as being nearer the |V| end of the continuum than the |C| end.

However, it is clear that we need to be able to distinguish the two sub-classes of sonorant consonants (i.e. nasals and liquids), each of which may form a natural class (as opposed to the other) in some phonological process. In acoustic terms, liquids are more |V|-like and less |C|-like than nasals – Jakobson treats nasals as non-vocalic, while, as we have seen, liquids are vocalic. Notice that for Jakobson this leads to problems in characterising nasals and liquids as a natural class, something which can only be achieved by using a cumbersome formula such as (4.4):

(4.4)
$$\begin{bmatrix} [+\text{cons}] \\ \left\{ \begin{array}{c} ([+\text{voc}]) \\ \left[\begin{array}{c} -\text{voc} \\ +\text{nas} \end{array} \right] \end{array} \right\} \end{bmatrix}$$

There is a great deal of evidence, however, that nasals and liquids may function as a natural class; consider, for example, their behaviour with respect to Dutch diminutive suffix selection (Ewen 1978), or in the system of strong verb classes in Germanic (Anderson 1970, 1986a). A representation such as (4.4), then, is componentially inadequate. Equally, however, nasals and liquids can function independently in phonological processes. We suggest that the representations in (4.5) and (4.6) reflect these similarities and differences:

(4.5) $\{|V \rightrightarrows C|\}$ (4.6) $\{|V \rightrightarrows V:C|\}$
nasal liquid

In these representations, liquids have an additional subjoined $|V|$, mutually dependent with $|C|$, as compared with nasals. However, both involve the sub-structure $\{V \rightrightarrows C\}$, whose presence in the representation of a segment therefore specifies a sonorant consonant. As we observed in §II.3, nasals are also distinguished from other segments by virtue of a component within the oro-nasal sub-gesture. That is, nasals have both a unique categorial characterisation and a unique articulatory representation. We return to this in §6.8.

We turn now to the representation of fricatives. Acoustically, we find in the production of a fricative attenuation of the consonantal reduction of energy as compared with the optimal stop consonant (Jakobson & Halle 1956:55). Fricatives are therefore less $|C|$-like than their corresponding stops. The following representation for voiceless fricatives can thus be established:

(4.7) $\{|V:C|\}$
voiceless
fricative

namely a representation in which $|V|$ and $|C|$ are mutually dependent (more explicitly, $\{|V \leftrightarrows C|, |V=C|\}$), and in which the $|C|$-ness of the segment is 'diluted' by the presence of a $|V|$ component. Notice that, like

the nasals, the voiceless fricatives have a representation containing both
|V| and |C|. The nasals, however, differ from the voiceless fricatives in
having |V| in governing position – in other words, their representation is
more |V|-like (and hence less |C|-like) than that of the fricatives, in
accordance with their acoustic, and, as we shall see, phonological
characteristics.

Voiced phonemes are characterised by the 'superposition of a harmonic
sound source upon the noise source' of the voiceless phonemes (Jakobson
et al. 1969:26). Voicing, then, increases the periodicity of the consonant,
by virtue of the addition of the harmonic source, vocal cord vibration. We
can interpret voicing in obstruents as involving the addition of a |V|
component, but this time in dependent position, as in (4.8) and (4.9):

(4.8)   {|C ⇉ V|}   (4.9)   {|V:C⇉ V|}
         voiced   voiced
         plosive   fricative

Although these voiced obstruents are characterised by the addition of a
subjoined |V| component, we have seen that sonorant consonants do not
show this configuration, but rather have |V| alone in governing position
(as do vowels). We suggest that this reflects the fact that 'voicing must be
considered as an accompanying feature of vowels and can be absent only
optionally' (Jakobson 1968:69), while for obstruents voicelessness is
basic. 'The optimal consonant is voiceless and the optimal vowel voiced'
(Jakobson & Halle 1956:56). Like vowels, sonorant consonants are
optimally voiced. Our representations appropriately reflect the fact that
for obstruents voicing is an additive component, while for sonorants it is
inherent.

Notice that we have now created a system in which both voiceless
fricatives and voiced stops have representations with a single |V| and a
single |C|, differing from each other in that for the voiceless fricatives |V| is
mutually dependent with |C|, while for the voiced stops it is unilaterally
dependent. Thus voiceless fricatives appear to be 'more |V|-like' (or,
equivalently, 'less |C|-like') than voiced stops. This claim, we suggest, gains
support from the acoustic evidence, specifically with respect to the status
of |C|. Recall that |C| (like the Jakobsonian consonantal feature) is
characterised by energy reduction, manifested as acoustic zeros. In the
production of the fricatives, this property is, as already noted, heavily
attenuated – indeed, in the production of what we might term the 'optimal'
fricative, [s], the spectrogram is characterised by the presence of random

high intensity noise, with little damping. The other (voiceless) fricatives display similar characteristics, with, however, a rather greater degree of energy reduction. This suggests that the |C|-ness of such segments is heavily reduced, indeed, that the class of fricatives represents a kind of mean between the two extremes of the |V|–|C| cline. A representation in which |V| and |C| are mutually dependent appropriately reflects this status: notice, too, that voiceless fricatives show a substantial reduction of the acoustic properties associated with |V|.

In the case of voiced stops, however, we are confronted with a rather different situation. As noted above, voicing is superimposed on the acoustic configuration for the voiceless stops. These segments retain their 'original' acoustic characteristics, but show additional properties associated with the presence of vocal cord vibration. In this sense, then, it is reasonable to treat voiced stops as 'basically' |C| with 'superimposed' (dependent) |V|, giving the representation in (4.8).

This evidence, we suggest, supports the claim inherent in the notation that voiceless fricatives are less |C|-like than voiced stops, and we will continue to characterise voicing of an obstruent as involving addition of unilaterally dependent |V|, and fricativisation of a stop as involving addition of a mutually dependent |V|. (For further discussion of the status of [s] as opposed to the other voiceless fricatives, see §4.1.4.)

Our distinction between the representations of nasals and liquids, i.e., (4.5) *vs.* (4.6), can also now be given further motivation. Nasals, like oral stops, are non-continuant in that they show complete closure in the oral tract, while liquids are continuant (but see the discussion of láterals in §4.1.3). Further, liquids may form a natural class with fricatives in phonological processes, as opposed to nasals and stops (see, e.g., Vaiana Taylor 1974:418–19; Ewen 1977:324–5). In the representations established here, the non-continuancy of nasals is indicated by the presence of |C| alone in subjoined position (cf. |C| alone in governing position for the plosives), while for the (continuant) liquids, we find subjoined |V:C| (cf. governing |V:C| for the fricatives). However, for both, the fact that |C| and |V:C| are dependent on governing |V| alone shows that they are sonorants. (In §§4.1.2 and 4.1.3 we propose some refinements to the representations of 'liquids'.)

This treatment of the phonatory sub-gesture allows the interpretation of segment-types as manifestations of different points on the |V|–|C| continuum, whereas binary distinctive feature phonologies must characterise the gradient of the various segment-types by a combination of *different* features. For example, fricatives differ from stops in being [+continuant], and voiced obstruents from voiceless obstruents in being [+voice]. Moreover, as well as being able to characterise the different segment-types as forming in some sense a 'gradual' opposition (Trubetzkoy 1969:75), the dependency notation allows us to characterise the various types of opposition holding between individual members of this gradual opposition. For example, as we have noticed, voiced obstruents differ from their voiceless counterparts in showing an extra subjoined |V|. Thus the opposition between any pair of voiced and voiceless obstruents is shown to be a privative one – the voiced term of this opposition shows a 'mark' which is absent from its voiceless counterpart.

We suggest that the various facts surveyed above lend support to the view, inherent in the treatment within this section, that the 'major classes' of segment-types should be viewed as points on a continuum such as (4.10):

(4.10) |V| ————————————— |C|

i.e. a continuum, one end of which represents maximum |V|-ness, and minimum (i.e. non-existent) |C|-ness, and the other maximum |C|-ness and non-existent |V|-ness. Notice that (4.10) differs from the kind of representation which could be established with respect to the vowel components of §1.5, which might have the form:

(4.11) |i|

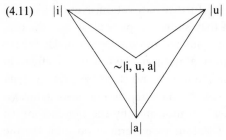

|a|

i.e. a characterisation which does not represent a single continuum, but rather a complex of possible paths. Notice that for each of the components |i|, |u|, and |a| we can find paths like (4.12) (in which |X| denotes any of the three components):

(4.12) |X| ————————————— ~|X|

i.e. a continuum in which one extreme represents maximum |X|-ness, and the other non-existent |X|-ness, with points in between representing gradually decreasing |X|-ness.

While, by and large, increasing |V|-ness correlates with decreasing |C|-ness, it would nevertheless be inappropriate to replace (4.10) by a continuum such as (4.12), for example by using |C| as the only basic component within the phonatory sub-gesture. Such an interpretation of the phonatory sub-gesture would preclude the characterisation of the classes as interactions of the two components, linked by the type of dependency relations developed in this model. Indeed, there would be no other component with which |C| could interact in any way in such a model. Rather, the differences between classes would presumably have to be characterised as differences in 'degrees' of |C|-ness; i.e. we would, essentially, have a scalar feature of the type proposed by Ladefoged (1971), and, in particular, Williamson (1977). This in turn would prohibit the characterisation of the various hierarchical relationships holding between segment classes (to be surveyed in §4.3), and the characterisation of relative complexity (see §4.2).

Thus it appears that, phonologically, (4.10) is an appropriate characterisation for major class segments. Notice, too, that this is given additional support from the fact that, although |V| and |C| occupy opposite ends of a unidimensional scale, they are nevertheless associated with distinct phonetic properties (cf. Jakobsonian vocalic *vs.* consonantal).

The representations of the phonatory sub-gesture also differ from those of the articulatory gesture established in §1.5 in having the structural property displayed by the liquids in (4.6) and the voiced fricatives in (4.9). Such representations have *two* occurrences of |V|, related by unilateral dependency. It seems appropriate to allow just this extension to the types of representations in the dependency system, i.e. to allow two instances of a particular component in a representation. We shall see that such an interpretation is phonologically appropriate in that it allows for the expression of hierarchies within the phonatory sub-gesture. Notice too that this additional structural property correlates with the fact that the |V|-ness of a segment may be increased by different phonetic means, e.g. by addition of vocal cord vibration (i.e. a harmonic sound source), or by the attenuation of the consonantal reduction of energy. Thus, while voiced stops and voiced fricatives differ from voiceless stops and voiceless fricatives, respectively, in the presence of an additional harmonic sound source, and fricatives differ from stops in the attenuation of reduction of energy, voiced fricatives differ from voiceless stops in *both* respects. This difference is appropriately characterised by the presence of two extra |V| components in the representation for voiced fricatives, while the essentially consonantal nature of the voiced fricatives (as obstruents) is maintained by having |C| in (mutually) governing position. Thus, in the phonatory sub-gesture, where there are only two components, we require more complex combinatorial properties, while in the characterisation of the vowel space, with a greater number of components, only a single occurrence of each component is permitted in any representation.

The following table illustrates the representations established so far for the phonatory sub-gesture, presented as dependency trees:

(4.13)
$$
\begin{array}{ccc}
\text{V} & \text{V} & \text{V} \\
 & | & | \\
 & \text{V:C} & \text{C}
\end{array}
$$

vowel   liquid   nasal

$$
\begin{array}{cccc}
\text{V:C} & \text{V:C} & \text{C} & \text{C} \\
| & | & | & \\
\text{V} & & \text{V} &
\end{array}
$$

voiced   voiceless   voiced   voiceless
fricative   fricative   plosive   plosive

4.1.1   Natural classes in the phonatory sub-gesture

The system in (4.13) allows us to characterise natural classes of segments in a very transparent and componentially appropriate way. Some major classes that can be distinguished are shown in (4.14):

(4.14) vowels $\{|\text{V}|\}$
        sonorants $\{|\text{V}| \rightrightarrows\}$
        sonorant consonants $\{|\text{V}| \rightrightarrows \text{C}\}$ or $\{\text{C}\not\rightrightarrows\}$
        obstruents $\{\text{C}\rightrightarrows\}$
        consonants $\{\text{C}\}$

Other sub-classes which can be characterised are:

(4.15) fricatives $\{\text{V:C}\rightrightarrows\}$
        continuant consonants $\{\text{V:C}\}$
        non-continuant obstruents $\{|\text{C}|\rightrightarrows\}$
        voiceless obstruents $\{\text{C}\not\rightrightarrows\text{V}\}$
        voiced obstruents $\{\text{C}\rightrightarrows\text{V}\}$
        voiced continuants $\{\text{V,V}\}$

(where $\rightrightarrows$ = 'unilaterally governs' and $\not\rightrightarrows$ = 'does not unilaterally govern': notice that a representation such as $\{|\text{V}|\rightrightarrows\}$ includes $\{|\text{V}|\}$, which governs the identity element, thus correctly characterising vowels as a sub-class of sonorants). Again, componentiality is satisfied.

4.1.2 /r/-types

In §4.1 we tacitly assumed that all segments which we might label /r/ could be characterised as liquids, i.e. as {|V ⇉ V:C|}. However, this is clearly not the case; there are both phonetic and phonological reasons for wanting to treat various types of /r/ in other ways.

Consider, for example, the case of Aitken's Law in the history of Scots. Aitken's Law (after the original formulation by Aitken 1962; cf. Aitken 1981) consists of two processes, both dating from the late 16th to early 17th centuries, and summarised by Lass (1973:14) as:

(4.16)   *Aitken's Law* (a): All long vowels shorten EVERYWHERE EXCEPT before
         /r v z ð #/.
         Aitken's Law (b): All NON-HIGH short vowels lengthen before
         /r v z ð #/.

These processes took place in many Scots dialects, and leave a system in the modern dialects in which there is no phonemic opposition between long and short vowels in stressed syllables – rather, the distribution of length is predictable according to the environment (Lass 1974:317).

Lass shows that in the dialects in which Aitken's Law occurs:

there are both phonetic and phonological arguments for taking /r/ as a voiced fricative rather than a 'liquid' . . . /r/ is usually a fricative and slightly retroflex [ř]; initially it is often a retroflex affricate . . . In dialects . . . with fairly extensive terminal obstruent devoicing, /r/ also devoices, but not /l/ or the nasals . . . Thus /r/ classes phonologically with the obstruents. (Lass 1974:338–9)

At first sight, then, we might want to suggest that /r/ in such cases has simply the representation for a voiced fricative, i.e. {V:C ⇉ V}, thus leaving the normal representation for a liquid ({V ⇉ V:C}) free for /l/, which does not pattern with /r/ and the voiced fricatives. However, there is also phonological evidence that similar sounds can behave *differently* from the voiced fricatives. Again in Southern Scots, we find dialects in which some sort of breaking process is taking place before /l/ and /r/, where /r/ is an alveolar trill, but not before fricatives (Vaiana Taylor 1974:410–11). In Czech, too, /ř/ behaves distributionally like a sonorant (Kučera 1961:31). Although this [ř] is phonetically not the same as the Scots sound – it is defined by Abercrombie (1967:54) as a (voiced) alveolar fricative trill, rather than a trill with accompanying friction – it appears to have the same status: it is in some sense intermediate between the voiced fricatives and the 'normal' liquids.

It seems clear then that this type of /r/, whether it is of the Scots or

Czech variety, must have a representation which will enable it to be distinguished from /l/ and from the voiced fricatives but which will allow it to pattern with either. A dependency representation which is intermediate between those for /l/ and the voiced fricatives seems appropriate, and such a representation is available, provided that we allow complex nodes in a segmental representation to be related by symmetric dependency, rather than just asymmetric dependency as in (4.13). Utilising this possibility gives (4.17) as the representation for the fricative trill:

(4.17)   {|V:C ⇄ V|}
          fricative
          trill

Here the |V| node, which is unilaterally dependent on |V:C| for voiced fricatives, and unilaterally governs it for liquids, is mutually dependent, and as such the segment-type is shown to be intermediate between the other two categories. (Notice that in (4.17) the verticals are required: here there is an opposition between two segment-types containing a configuration in which |V:C| symmetrically or asymmetrically governs |V|.) Support for this intermediate status comes from the common pronunciation by many (rhotic) English speakers of *Dvořák* as [dvɔɹʒæk], with a sequence of sonorant consonant + voiced fricative corresponding to the Czech fricative trill. Notice, too, that the inherent complexity of a system utilising (4.17) is brought out by the need to invoke both symmetric and asymmetric dependency in relation to the complex node, thus giving a three-way hierarchical opposition involving a |V| node and a |V:C| node, and two occurrences of symmetric dependency in (4.17) – both within the complex |V:C| node, and between it and the |V| node.

Using this representation for the Scots system involved in Aitken's Law, the lengthening environment may be specified as (4.18):

(4.18)   {V:C ⇉ V}

i.e. as the set of segments containing |V:C| (unilaterally or mutually) governing |V|. Similarly, the Czech fricative trill can be shown to form a natural class with sonorant consonants:

(4.19)   {V ⇉ V:C}

This treatment of the voiced fricative trill allows it to be characterised as forming a natural class with either of the other two relevant categories, as opposed to the other ((4.18) and (4.19)), or as forming the middle term of a gradual relationship (see the discussion on the representation of vowel height in §1.5).

Further evidence supporting the characterisation of the fricative trilled [r̃], and also of the class of liquids as opposed to nasals (see again §4.1), can be found in Vaiana Taylor's comments on the contrasts between the histories of Southern English and Southern Scots (1974:418–19). She observes the following relevant differences:

(4.20)   a. In Sth ME breaking took place before voiceless palatal and velar fricatives, but not in Scots.
         b. In Early OE lengthening took place before nasal + homorganic stop clusters and before /ld/. In Scots, only lengthening before /ld/ occurred.
         c. In the history of Scots there occurred both vocalisation of /l/ and lengthening before /r/.
         d. In Scots, Aitken's Law lengthened vowels before /r/ and the voiced fricatives.

She views all these processes as types of '(vowel) strengthening', and points out that Scots evidences strengthening only before segments which are both voiced and continuant. This generalisation can be very naturally captured within the dependency framework. The relevant environments for strengthening in Scots are:

(4.21) $\{|V \rightrightarrows V:C|\}$ $\{|V:C \leftrightarrows V|\}$ $\{|V:C \rightrightarrows V|\}$
            /l/   /r/   voiced
                                             fricative

while the environments which cause strengthening in English, but not in Scots, are:

(4.22) $\{|V:C|\}$ $\{|V \rightrightarrows C|\}$
         voiceless   nasal
         fricative

The representations in (4.21) characterise the voiced continuants, and, as anticipated in (4.15), can be distinguished from the representations in (4.22), and indeed from any other segment-type, in a very obvious way. It is only in these three cases that we find a representation containing two |V| nodes. Thus the crucial environment for the strengthening process is:

(4.23) $\{V,V\}$

As well as voiced [r̃], voiceless [r̥] (with or without friction) is also found, as a phoneme in some Welsh dialects, for example (as in *Rhondda*), and allophonically in Czech and Scots. We postpone discussion of this segment-type until §5.2, in that it is more appropriately characterised with reference to the representations of the initiatory sub-gesture than by utilising the components of the phonatory sub-gesture alone.

4.1.3   Lateral consonants

In §4.1 we argued that liquids should be given the characterisation {|V ⇉ V:C|}, as opposed to nasals {|V ⇉ C|}. Within the class of liquids, the laterals can be distinguished from the non-laterals by means of a component within the articulatory gesture (see §6.7.4). However, there is evidence from some phonological processes that laterals can, on occasion, form a class with nasals, opposed to other liquids. Thus, Ó Dochartaigh (1978, ms) notes that in some dialects of Scottish Gaelic there are lengthening and diphthongisation processes which operate on short vowels preceding a syllable-final long sonorant. He summarises these processes, which operate differently in different areas, as (4.24):

(4.24)

	Area 1	Area 2	Area 3
bàrr	baːr	baːr	baːr
dall	dalː	daul	daul
ceann	kʼenː	kʼeun	kʼeun
cam	kamː	kamː	kaum

It can be seen from (4.24) that in all areas the lateral patterns with the alveolar nasal, while only the non-lateral liquid is associated with lengthening of the vowel. This leads Ó Dochartaigh to suggest that /r/ has a higher 'relative vocalicness' than /l/ and /n/, which in turn are more vocalic than /m/. In terms of dependency representations, he offers the following account:

(4.25)   V   V   V:C
          | | |
         V:C   C   V
         /r/   /l n/   /m/

with |V| becoming less prominent as we move from left to right. In addition, Ó Dochartaigh observes that there is phonological evidence from Gaelic to suggest that /l/ is more vocalic than /n/, thus giving the cline /r l n m/.

However, although the representations in (4.25) appear to capture the relationships between the segment-types in Gaelic, we have already seen that the liquids frequently form a natural class opposed to nasals. The adoption of (4.25), then, would mean that radically different phonatory representations would have to be established for different languages, a state of affairs which would lead to rather ad hoc analyses. It seems appropriate, therefore, to ask whether there is a way of characterising the laterals so that they may be shown to have categorial properties in common both with the other liquids and with the nasals.

Notice that laterals are phonetically unique, as far as the phonatory sub-gesture is concerned, in having effectively two manners of articulation. While there is a stricture of open approximation at one or both sides of the mouth (at least for sonorant laterals), there is also closure in the centre of the oral tract. This 'double characterisation' is, however, not captured by the representation $\{|V \Rrightarrow V:C|\}$. We might argue that an appropriate way of representing this is to allow a characterisation in which the normal constraints on phonatory representations (only two occurrences of each component per segment, and only two distinct nodes) are relaxed with respect to the second constraint, as in (4.26):

$$(4.26) \quad V \Rrightarrow V:C$$
$$\mid$$
$$C$$

In (4.26) the governing $|V|$ node characterises sonorancy, the $|V:C|$ node continuancy, and the $|C|$ node the central closure. Notice thát the form of the representation in (4.26) is adopted merely for convenience: (4.26) is clearly not different from either of the representations in (4.27):

$$(4.27) \quad V \qquad \{|V \Rrightarrow V:C \Rrightarrow C|\}$$
$$\mid$$
$$V:C$$
$$\mid$$
$$C$$

to which it is formally equivalent. However, (4.26) has certain graphic advantages in this context, in that it explicitly shows that $|C|$ is 'added' to the basic representation for liquids.

Essentially, then, the $|C|$ node characterises a secondary phonation-type (or, better, stricture-type within the phonatory sub-gesture). In §6.8 we give an account of secondary articulation in which the component characterising the secondary articulation is unilaterally dependent on that characterising the primary articulation; we suggest that this reflects in a very obvious way the hierarchisation of the articulation-types in question.

A similar strategy is appropriate here, given the clearly secondary status of the central closure of the laterals.

The various sonorant types (in systems in which laterals are categorially distinct from non-lateral liquids) will have the representations in (4.28):

(4.28)   V ⇉ V:C   V ⇉ V:C   V ⇉ C
                                  |
                                  C

      non-lateral   lateral   nasal
      liquid

Laterals can be shown to form a natural class with the other liquids, as these are the only segments containing {V ⇉ V:C}, or with nasals, as {|V| → |C|} (i.e. the only segments containing a |V| node superordinate to a |C| node). Thus the behaviour of the laterals in Gaelic can be characterised within the phonatory sub-gesture without resort to the language-specific representations proposed by Ó Dochartaigh. (We ignore here the problem of /m/; it is not clear to us whether Ó Dochartaigh's claim that /m/ is less vocalic than /n/ should be characterised by assigning different phonatory representations, or whether this is due to the articulatory difference.)

Representations like (4.26) will not be required, except phonetically, in the phonologies of most languages. That is, in languages in which the laterals form a natural class with the other liquids, and not with the nasals, the representation of §4.1 will be adequate. (4.26) is required only when the phonologically more complex situation described by Ó Dochartaigh occurs.

Notice that, if necessary, other lateral consonants can be given similar representations. Thus, the difference between a voiced /ř/-type segment and the voiced lateral fricative /ɮ/ may be characterised as:

(4.29)   V:C ⇆ V   V:C ⇆ V
                                  |
                                  C

    voiced fricative voiced lateral
      trill   fricative

The characterisation of the voiceless counterpart of the voiced lateral fricative, i.e. /ɬ/, as in Welsh *Llanelli*, again depends on the representations of the initiatory sub-gesture; we return to this in §5.2.

4.1.4   Sibilants *vs.* other fricatives

In this section, as in the previous two, we want to propose a refinement to the representations of the phonatory sub-gesture in (4.13). In §4.1 we suggested that $\{|V:C|\}$ is the appropriate representation for voiceless fricatives. However, there is a good deal of evidence for separating the sibilants (in particular /s/) from the other fricatives within this class. This evidence is both phonetic and phonological in nature. Phonetically, sibilants display a spectrum with virtually no damping, while the non-sibilants show considerably greater energy reduction, realised as zeros. Sibilants, then, are optimally 'strident', in Jakobsonian terminology (i.e. they have the most random distribution of energy, particularly at high frequencies). As such, therefore, although they are obstruents, they display the lowest possible preponderance of the consonantal feature (i.e. of |C|): that is, they are the most vowel-like fricatives (see the discussion on the class of fricatives in general in §4.1). Non-sibilants, on the other hand, have a greater preponderance of the consonantal feature than sibilants. Equally, the sibilants are further from the vocalic extreme (|V| alone) than any sonorants (or any of the /r/-types considered in §4.1.2); they display mixed periodicity. Hence we can view the sibilants, rather than the fricatives in general, as representing the simplest possible combination of the |V| and |C| components in this area; they are the segments which are optimally intermediate between |V| and |C|, and hence show |V| and |C| in a mutually dependent relation (i.e. having equivalent hierarchical status). We might thus characterise the sibilants as being the 'optimal' fricatives, constituting the intermediate category *par excellence* between the two extremes of the |V|–|C| continuum.

As is well known, /s/ also shows a number of phonological properties which set it apart from the other fricatives. In languages containing only a single fricative, this fricative is nearly always /s/ (see Lass 1984a:§7.6.2), and it is in general the most common fricative (Maddieson 1984:44). The constraints on the clustering of /s/ with other consonants frequently differ from those on the clustering of other fricatives: many languages allow initial clusters of /s/ followed by a voiceless stop, thus violating the normal constraints on the internal structure of the syllable (see §4.5). Clusters involving /s/ also show apparently deviant behaviour with respect to the alliterative patterns of Germanic verse (see Kuryłowicz 1971). This evidence has led various writers to treat clusters involving /s/ as 'complex segments' (see Ewen 1982:§5; and §3.4 above).

We return to the problem of the characterisation of such clusters in §7.3; for the moment we are concerned with the fact that it is just /s/ which typically shows this type of behaviour. How can we characterise the unique status of /s/ as opposed to the other fricatives, and is it appropriate to attempt to do so within the phonatory sub-gesture?

As noted above, /s/ may be interpreted as the optimal fricative phonetically; acoustically it shows the 'simplest' combination of consonantal and vocalic properties, while the other fricatives involve energy reduction in various frequency bands. In comparison with the sibilants, then, the other fricatives display extra /C/-ness. On the basis of the acoustic properties, we might suggest that the appropriate distinction is as in (4.30):

(4.30)   {|V:C|}   {V:C ⇒ C}
          sibilant   non-sibilant
                      fricative

where the non-sibilant shows an extra |C| node, dependent on the node characterising the sibilant. This |C| node, then, represents what we might term a 'secondary' acoustic property – note our discussion of secondary articulation in §6.8.

The phonological evidence, too, appears to favour (4.30). As we have seen, /s/ displays a number of properties which suggest that it is phonologically less complex than the non-sibilants: it shows greater potential for occurrence in phonological systems and also occurs more freely in combination with other consonants in clusters. It seems appropriate, then, to have a representation which reflects this relative lack of complexity (for more general discussion of the notion of complexity in the phonatory sub-gesture, see §4.2).

Notice that by adopting (4.30) we have not lost the ability to characterise fricatives as a natural class. This class can still be represented as {V:C⇒}.

4.2   Phonological complexity in the phonatory sub-gesture

In §4.1 we attempted to justify the representations of the phonatory sub-gesture primarily in terms of various phonetic characteristics, mostly acoustic. In the remaining sections of this chapter, we shall argue in more detail that various areas of phonological behaviour, in addition to those mentioned already, give support to these representations. In this section, we concentrate on the problem of the relative complexity of segment-types within the phonatory sub-gesture.

The question of the representation of relative complexity is one that has posed great problems for distinctive feature theory. In a feature matrix (whether or not we incorporate the proposals regarding gestures made above) there is no way of representing whether what we are dealing with is a phonologically complex or simple segment, and there is no way of comparing two feature matrices in terms of relative complexity. Each matrix (at least when fully specified) consists of a number of features, each of which has a particular value for the segment in question. As there is no difference in complexity between, say $[+F_x]$ and $[-F_x]$, or between $[0F_y]$, $[1F_y]$ and $[2F_y]$, all segments appear to be equally complex.

We have already shown (in §1.3.2) that the introduction of 'markedness theory' in an attempt to overcome these deficiencies must fail, irrespective of the success or otherwise of the theory on its own terms. The measure of complexity which can be established using the system does not arise out of the representations themselves, but results from the imposition of external conventions: the theory is basically an attempt to patch up the deficiencies of the representations.

It has been argued (particularly by Lass 1984a:§§7.4, 11.2) that all markedness and complexity considerations should be excluded from phonological characterisations, i.e. the fact that a particular segment-type is universally present in languages, or, alternatively, that its occurrence is restricted, should not be reflected in its representation: 'there is no reason for a particular language to code in its own segment specifications what are in essence facts about language-in-general'. However, we believe that this view is untenable, at least in this extreme form. As is well known, the 'structural laws' of Jakobson (1968), on which ultimately the notion of complexity is based, owe their origin to parallelism between various aspects of phonological behaviour – language acquisition, aphasia, and phonological inventories – which allow the setting up of implicational universals with respect to phonological systems. Thus, the presence of voiced stops in a system implies the presence of voiceless stops, front rounded vowels imply front unrounded vowels, and so on. In accordance with part (b) of the natural recurrence assumption, we take it that the cross-linguistic existence of such generalisations must have a phonetic basis. Indeed there is evidence that this must be the case (note the work of Stevens 1972; Lieberman 1976): less complex categories are in some sense perceptually more salient – indeed perhaps 'easier' – than more complex (see Stevens' discussion of the 'quantal' vowels). On the grounds of phonetic naturalness, then, it seems reasonable to demand of our system of representation that it can in principle provide some analogue of these properties; this analogue must be internal to the system, not externally imposed as in the case of markedness theory. Only by doing this can we also characterise the complexity of particular *systems* as opposed to others, i.e. phonological complexity arising from the oppositions made in a particular system, rather than from the inherent complexity of particular segment-types. And this, we maintain, is necessary even though Jakobson's structural laws have been shown to be idealised, and even though what appear to be cross-linguistic universal tendencies are violated quite spectacularly in individual language families or areas (see Lass 1984a:§7.6.3). Indeed, the logical conclusion of Lass's standpoint is to abandon the encoding of natural classes in the system of representation – here too we have the encoding of 'facts about language-in-general' in the segmental representations of a particular language.

   How, then, does the system of representation established in §4.1 for the phonatory sub-gesture reflect the notion of relative complexity? It is clear from (4.13) that certain representations are inherently less complex than others. The representation for voiceless stops, {|C|}, involving a single component, is clearly less complex (and hence less 'costly', in terms of any appropriate evaluation metric) than that for voiced fricatives, {|V:C ⇉ V|}, which involves three components and two types of relations. Notice, then, that there are potentially two types of parameters on which we can measure relative complexity. The first involves simple counting of components – a segment with one component {|a|} is simpler than one with, say, two {|a,b|} (here we assume no dependency relation between |a| and |b|: see, e.g., the representations for mid vowels in the three-height system in §1.5). However, as we have already seen (see again §1.5), *systems* may also be ranked in terms of complexity; consider, for example, the three systems involving only the two components |a| and |b| in (4.31):

(4.31)   a. a,b

         b. a   b
             | |
             b   a

         c. a   a:b   b
             | |
             b   a

These three systems can be hierarchically ranked in complexity according to the relations involved: (4.31a) involves simple combination only, (4.31b) unilateral dependency, (4.31c) both unilateral and mutual dependency. That is, it is not necessarily the case that any of the *segments* in

(4.31) is inherently more complex than any of the other; rather, relative complexity here refers to the systems involved.

We can now show that the dependency system gives a very transparent account of phonological complexity. Jakobson's structural laws predict (roughly) the following hierarchisation of the various (basic) phonatory segment-types in terms of complexity:

(4.32)

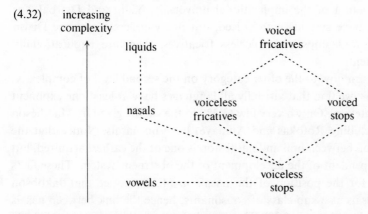

We shall not here examine the motivations for Jakobson's stratification of the various segment-types in any detail – these are familiar. If we now replace the segment-types in (4.32) with the corresponding dependency representations, we have (4.33):

(4.33)

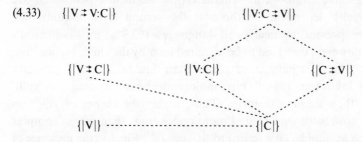

(4.33) reflects the hierarchisation of (4.32) in a very obvious way: the degree of complexity corresponds to the number of components required to specify the segment-type in question. The fundamental opposition in the phonatory sub-gesture (minimal vocalismus *vs.* minimal consonantismus, in Jakobson's terminology) is that between |V| alone and |C| alone, i.e. between the two extremes of the |V|–|C| scale (see (4.10)). On the second hierarchical level in (4.33) we find three segment-types, none of which implies either of the others but all of which imply the presence of the fundamental |V|–|C| opposition. Thus, as far as obstruents are concerned, languages may have voiceless stops alone (Burera, Western Desert), voiceless stops with voiceless fricatives (Maori, Hawaiian), voiceless stops with voiced stops (Nyangumata, Nasioi), or all three categories (Sentani, Papago). (Notice that some Australian languages provide an example of areal violation of the implicational universals: Yidiɲ and Dyirbal, for example, have systems with voiced, but not voiceless stops – see Dixon 1977.) Voiced stops and voiceless fricatives, then, are implicationally independent.

If we turn now to the other category on the second level of complexity, the nasals, we find that virtually all languages have at least one exponent of this category. Only a very few (3.2% in the survey given by Maddieson 1984, including Rotokas and Apinayé) have no nasals. Notice that the opposition between oral and nasal stop is one of the earliest acquired, but it is independent of the development of the obstruent system. These facts account for the position of the nasals in (4.32) – notice that Jakobson treats nasals as a sub-class of consonants; hence the link between nasals and voiceless stops in (4.32). Thus the elements on the second hierarchical level, all implicationally independent of each other, contain one more component than those on the first level.

Moving now to the most complex level in (4.33), we find representations containing three components, characterising segment-types which are implicationally dependent on those at the second level. Liquids, like nasals, are present in nearly all languages (95.9% in Maddieson's account); however, they tend to be acquired later by the child. Notice, too, that most languages have more nasals than liquids. This is a property noticed by Jakobson (1968:91): phonologically complex categories 'split' less easily than simple categories. Thus, within the classes of voiceless stops and vowels we tend to find more oppositions than within complex classes such as liquids. (We return to this in §7.4.) Finally, the presence of voiced fricatives in a system presupposes the existence both of voiceless fricatives and of voiced stops. Thus, English and French have obstruent systems with all four categories. (But notice that Rotokas violates this implication, in having /β/, but no voiceless fricative.)

There is, then, a simple correlation between complexity of segment and complexity of representation in the dependency system: the representations – established on independent phonetic grounds – provide an inherent measure of complexity, as indeed seems desirable, given our claim that relative complexity also has a phonetic basis. Contrast this with the externally imposed markedness conventions of distinctive feature systems.

Consider now a system with more than just liquids and voiced fricatives, e.g. one such as the Scots dialects discussed in §4.1.2 containing fricative trilled /r/ as a category distinct from both the liquids and the voiced fricatives. In such systems we have three categories containing three components, as in (4.21). Here, the relative complexity of a system containing {|V:C ⇄ V|} is characterised not by the complexity of the representation itself (which, like the other categories in (4.21), has three components), but by the need to introduce the relation of mutual dependency holding between |V| and |V:C| as well as the unilateral dependency relation already required (see (4.31c)). Notice, too, that the presence of {|V:C ⇄ V|} in a system depends on the presence of the other two: that is, the utilisation of the mutual dependency relation depends on the previous utilisation of unilateral dependency.

4.3 Hierarchies in the phonatory sub-gesture

There have been various proposals for a hierarchical ranking of segment-types in phonological frameworks, both in terms of categorial types and with respect to place of articulation. What we are concerned with here is the former, i.e. proposals which have been made for hierarchies within the phonatory sub-gesture. The evidence for the need for such hierarchies has been drawn from various phonological phenomena, and the phonetic correlates of the hierarchies have been interpreted in various ways.

Such hierarchies, established on diverse grounds, in general display a more or less identical ranking of segment-types, although the details of particular accounts vary, especially where there are attempts to offer hierarchisation of segments *within* particular categorial types. One important source of evidence for such hierarchies has been the behaviour of segments in historical change. We return to this in some detail in the following section; here we note only that such phenomena have led, among others, Vaiana Taylor (1974), Lass & Anderson (1975), Escure (1977), and, working within a framework which rejects part (b) of the natural recurrence assumption, Foley (1977), to set up scales, often referred to as 'strength scales', typified by that of Escure (1977):

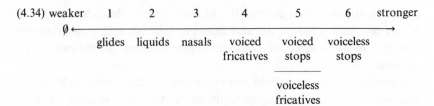

(4.34) weaker 　　1　　　2　　　3　　　4　　　5　　　6　　stronger

	glides	liquids	nasals	voiced fricatives	voiced stops	voiceless stops
					voiceless fricatives	

in which lenition processes progressively affect the segments from right to left on the scale.

A similar approach is adopted by Vaiana Taylor (1974:406), who draws her evidence from changes in the history of Scots, and proposes two scales which are the inverse of each other – a sonorance scale, in which strength is equivalent to acoustic energy output, and a consonant scale, in which strength corresponds to articulatory resistance:

(4.35) 　　*Sonorance scale*: 　t　s　d　z　l　j　i　ii

strength = acoustic energy

　　　　Consonant scale: 　ii　i　j　l　z　d　s　t

strength = articulatory resistance

Observe that Vaiana Taylor's hierarchy does not include the nasals; these tend not to participate in weakening processes in the same way as other segment-types (see §4.4 for further discussion).

In syllable structure, however, another major area providing the source of evidence for such hierarchies, nasals do participate. The internal structure of the syllable is generally predictable from what in this area is usually referred to as a 'sonority hierarchy'. Such hierarchies, in which nasals occupy a position intermediate between liquids and voiced fricatives, are proposed by Vennemann (1972), Hooper (1976), and Kiparsky (1979), among others. We discuss syllable structure in detail in §4.5.

Various other kinds of phonological processes have been used as evidence for such hierarchies: see Zwicky (1972) on fast-speech phenomena in English, and Hankamer & Aissen (1974) on assimilation in Pali. For a general discussion of the need for hierarchies in phonology, see Drachman (1977).

The evidence for incorporating hierarchies into our system of representation is clear, then. However, as we would expect, in view of our discussion of vowel height in §§1.3 and 1.4, minimally componential frameworks are unable to characterise the hierarchy in such a way as to allow for the expression of both hierarchical and binary classificatory phenomena in this area. Ladefoged (1975) and Williamson (1977), for example, propose multi-valued features to account for various stricture-types. Williamson's scalar feature [stricture], established on the basis of evidence from historical changes in various languages, has the values in (4.36):

(4.36)   2 stop
          1 fricative
          0 approximant
          − 1 high vowel
          − 2 low vowel

However, as we have seen with respect to vowel height, a scalar feature such as that in (4.36) cannot characterise in any natural way privative or equipollent oppositions such as that holding between obstruent and sonorant consonants. Consider the formulation which would be necessary within the system of (4.36):

(4.37)   [⩾1 stricture] *vs.* [0 stricture]

This wholly disguises the binary nature of the opposition.

Vennemann & Ladefoged (1973) propose an alternative system, with scalar 'cover features' in addition to the normal binary 'prime features' (see again the discussion in §1.4). A segment with a particular value for prime features such as [stop] and [fricative] in (4.38) also has a value for the cover feature [strength]:

(4.38)
$$[3 \text{ strength}] \leftrightarrow \begin{bmatrix} +\text{stop} \\ -\text{fricative} \end{bmatrix}$$

$$[2 \text{ strength}] \leftrightarrow \begin{bmatrix} -\text{stop} \\ +\text{fricative} \end{bmatrix}$$

$$[1 \text{ strength}] \leftrightarrow \begin{bmatrix} -\text{stop} \\ -\text{fricative} \end{bmatrix}$$

(where '↔' denotes equivalence). The value for the cover feature can be predicted from the values of the prime features by a set of 'feature redundancy rules' (1973:69). But this strategy, as we suggested in §1.4, while allowing a formal expression of the scalar strength relation and at the same time maintaining the possibility of expressing binary oppositions, merely shows that neither binary nor scalar features are in themselves adequate for the characterisation of the full range of phonological phenomena (see also Selkirk 1984).

In any case, like the purely scalar approaches, it fails to solve the second problem, which is that the order of segments on the scales discussed seems to be quite arbitrary in a minimally componential theory. For example, why, in Vennemann & Ladefoged's formulation, should [+stop, −fricative] be 'stronger' than [−stop, −fricative]? Similarly, formalisms like those in (4.39) (proposed by Vennemann – see Hooper 1976:207) would look equally natural with the values, or even, say, every alternate value, reversed:

(4.39)   strength [−voice] > strength [+voice]

strength [−sonorant] > strength [+sonorant]

strength [−continuant] > strength [+continuant]

While (4.39) may describe the relations correctly, the distinctive feature representations fail to show why this should be.

Consider now the elements in a strength hierarchy in terms of the dependency representations developed in §4.1:

(4.40)   {|V|} {|V ⇉ V:C|} {|V ⇉ C|} {|V:C ⇉ V|} {|V:C|} {|C|}

{|C ⇉ V|}

$$\overrightarrow{}$$

strength

The relationship between each element on the strength hierarchy is obvious. As an element becomes stronger, it becomes more |C|-like, and therefore less |V|-like, and vice versa as it becomes weaker. In dependency notation, there is no need to set up an independent feature of strength or sonorance, as the hierarchy is inherent in the segmental representations. Thus the problem of the apparently arbitrary relationship between the feature representation of segments and their relative position in the hierarchy is avoided. Similarly, there is no problem in expressing binary oppositions holding within the hierarchy – the privative opposition of voiced *vs.* voiceless (for obstruents) is characterised by the presence of dependent |V| *vs.* its absence, while the opposition of sonorant *vs.* obstruent is characterised by a single governing |V| *vs.* governing {C} (see (4.14)).

Having shown that the formal problems of characterising the concept of hierarchy do not arise in dependency phonology, we now examine in greater detail two areas in which such hierarchies are relevant – lenition processes, and the internal structure of syllables.

4.4   Lenition processes

Lass & Anderson (1975:159) observe that:

in lenition processes there are two basic options (assuming a hierarchical ranking where we start with a voiceless stop as the strongest type): opening, i.e. progressive continuantization without change of glottal attitude, and sonorization, i.e. voicing and then progressive opening, with increasing output of acoustic energy. The last stage in any lenition is deletion.

The options are realised by 'sequences of changes that tend to repeat themselves again and again in the histories of languages' (1975:150), and can be represented as (4.41):

(4.41)

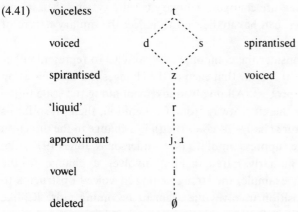

Here we have collapsed two hierarchies which are distinct in Lass & Anderson's treatment. The first, involving 'weakening of closure' (e.g. /t → s → h → ∅/), interacts with the second, 'sonorisation and opening', to give (4.41), in that a voiceless stop, for example, may weaken either to a voiceless fricative (by 'weakening of closure') or to a voiced stop (by 'sonorisation'). Notice that in (4.41) we have omitted the /s/ → /h/ stage in the 'weakening of closure' hierarchy. In terms of the gestural model developed above, this stage differs from the others in involving deletion of the articulatory gesture, rather than a change in the phonatory sub-gesture.

Lass (1976:163) proposes a universal progressive weakening schema for obstruents:

(4.42)   *Weakening I: feature change*   *Weakening II: matrix change*

$$[-\text{cont}] \rightarrow [+\text{cont}]$$
$$\text{or}$$
$$[-\text{voice}] \rightarrow [+\text{voice}]$$

$$\begin{bmatrix} [\text{oral}] \\ \\ [\text{laryn}] \end{bmatrix} \rightarrow \begin{bmatrix} \emptyset \\ \\ [\text{laryn}] \end{bmatrix} \rightarrow \begin{bmatrix} \emptyset \\ \\ \emptyset \end{bmatrix}$$

In (4.42) we see that although lenition appears to be a unitary phenomenon, in that it involves movement along a hierarchy like those discussed in §4.3, a binary distinctive feature phonology requires a choice between two apparently unrelated features, [continuant] and [voice], to characterise weakening in obstruents. And the situation becomes worse if we consider the rest of the stages in (4.41). Presumably, the change from [z] to [r] involves [−sonorant] becoming [+sonorant], while the change from sonorant consonant to vowel is [+consonantal] → [−consonantal]. 'Weakening I', then, if we are to extend it for use as a schema for progressive lenition in general, would involve a combination of four formally unrelated feature changes. A binary feature system, then, as we might by now expect, can hardly be said to reflect the unitary nature of lenition.

However, if we consider the components $|V|$ and $|C|$ to represent either end of a linear scale, it is clear that each of the changes is a manifestation of the same kind of process. All involve movement along the scale in the direction of $|V|$, and therefore away from $|C|$. Lenition, then (in so far as Lass's category 'feature change' is concerned), is a change in the direction of $|V|$, or progressive suppression of $|C|$ (see Anderson & Jones 1977:125; Ewen 1977:320). Similarly, strengthening involves a change in the direction of $|C|$. For example, the strengthening of voiced obstruents to voiceless in final position involves the segment becoming more $|C|$-like (specifically by deletion of the subjoined $|V|$ denoting voicing) (see Vaiana Taylor 1974:404).

The interpretation of lenition as a shift towards $|V|$ is illustrated in (4.43), the dependency equivalent of (4.41):

(4.43)

where we assume the [r] of (4.41) to be distinct from both [z] and [ɹ]. (4.43) is the equivalent for historical change of the universal strength hierarchy presented in (4.40).

We have made no mention of the nasals with respect to lenition.

Clearly, nasals do not participate in (4.43) (unless we interpret a change from voiced stop to nasal as lenition). In so far as they do undergo lenition as such, weakening gives a vowel as in (4.44):

(4.44) $\{|V \Rightarrow C|\} \xrightarrow{\hspace{1cm}} \{|V|\}$
$\phantom{(4.44)   \{|V \Rightarrow C|\}}$ vocalisation

in which we again see that lenition is characterised as a movement towards |V|. However, this is not a common process; rather, processes affecting nasal consonants typically involve nasalisation of the preceding vowel followed by deletion of the nasal consonant, with no intervening vowel stage.

Notice that there are various types of strengthening process which cannot be accounted for in the model developed in this section. The strengthening of nasals in Icelandic, where, for example, [n] → [n̥], is such a case. As noted in §4.1, the characterisation of voiceless nasals is appropriate to the initiatory sub-gesture, and this type of strengthening must be accounted for there.

4.5   Syllable structure

4.5.1   Strength hierarchies and syllable structure

In §4.2 we noted that there have been various approaches to the problem of syllable structure in relation to the kind of hierarchy which we have been discussing. One approach, that of Vennemann (1972) and Hooper (1976), involves predicting syllable structure from the (at least partly) independently motivated strength hierarchies discussed in §4.3. The 'partly universal, partly language-specific' relational hierarchy of segments which Vennemann (1972:7) sets up on these considerations can predict the order of consonants in a syllable. As far as syllabicity is concerned, 'the universal aspect . . . is that certain weak consonants cannot establish for themselves a syllable-initial position in the presence of certain strong consonants' (1972:11).

Similarly, Hooper (1976:199) views the syllable as a unit whose centre is the most vowel-like and whose outer margins are the least vowel-like, and suggests that 'it is reasonable to speculate further that any intervening segments will be intermediate between least and most vowel-like'. However, although the strength scale may be said to be adequate to predict this kind of patterning, it suffers from the same kind of difficulties as those discussed in §4.4, namely, that such scales appear to have no intrinsic motivation. The position of the elements on the strength scale appears to be totally arbitrary, while a corresponding scale in terms of dependency representations (such as (4.40)) can be shown to overcome this apparent arbitrariness.

In the metrical framework, too, in which a sonority hierarchy is mapped onto a syllabic template (Kiparsky 1979:432), the same problems apply:

(4.45)

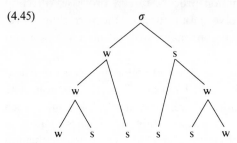

Within any pair of adjacent segments in a σ, the one marked *s* is the more sonorous in terms of the sonority hierarchy. But again, the sonority hierarchy is a given, without reference to the properties underlying the hierarchisation involved.

4.5.2   Distinctive feature hierarchies and syllable structure

Basbøll (1974, 1977) establishes a hierarchy, not of segments or segment-types, but of certain distinctive features, which, he claims, will predict the ordering of elements within the syllable in Danish:

(4.46)

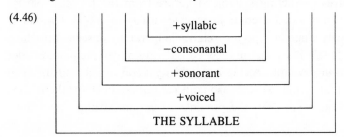

(4.46) allows the identification of various 'parts' of the syllable. Thus the syllabic peak, together with any adjacent [−syllabic, −consonantal] segments, constitutes the non-consonantal part of the syllable (i.e. the 'nucleus'), while the sonorant part together with any adjacent voiced obstruents forms the voiced part of the syllable, and so on (see Basbøll

1974:101). For Danish, the following ordering relations obtain (Basbøll 1977:145):

(4.47)

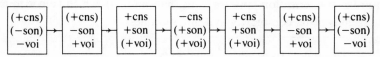

(4.47) correctly predicts the ordering relations in Danish monosyllables. This syllable hierarchy, which Basbøll claims might be considered the maximally 'natural' or 'unmarked' arrangement of distinctive features in the syllable, contains a number of 'hierarchical' features, i.e. a set of features which he distinguishes from other features, which are not involved in ordering relations and which he calls 'cross-classificatory' (1974:107). However, to account for the ordering relation of liquids and nasals (liquids being closer to the nucleus of the syllable than nasals), Basbøll is forced to characterise [continuant] as a semi-hierarchical feature, which is hierarchical only in the sonorant part of the syllable.

Basbøll claims the syllable hierarchy as a candidate for a universal model to predict ordering within the syllable, and indeed it appears to be adequate to account for a range of other languages. Notice that in languages other than Danish some of the order-classes which the model can predict may be redundant; for example, in Swedish (Sigurd 1965:81) the hierarchical feature [consonantal] is redundant in final position (Swedish having no [− syllabic, − consonantal] segments postvocalically). However:

the fact that some of the 'boxes' . . . have no descriptive justification in a given language does in itself not prove that the model is not universal. As long as a language . . . does *not* offer *counter-examples* to the orderings predicted by the general model, then it is in accordance with the model in the sense that a strict subset of the hierarchical features in the same order will be a relevant model for its syllabic structure . . . Each language takes all of these features or any subset of them *in the order given* to form its syllabic hierarchy. (Basbøll 1974:106–7)

In Norwegian, however, certain problems arise. Vogt's (1942) study of the monosyllable in Norwegian shows that only two order-classes seem to be involved in syllable-initial position:

(4.48)

```
┌─────────┐       ┌─────────┐
│  p  t  k │       │  r  l   │
│  b  d  g │ ─────→│  v  j   │ ────→
│     f  s │       │  m  n   │
└─────────┘       └─────────┘
```

In (4.48) the second position is not the 'voiced' part of the syllable, as /b d g/ occur in first position, nor is it the 'sonorant' part, on the assumption that /v j/ are not sonorant in Norwegian. The only distinctive feature characterisation appears to be that in (4.49), which is inadequate on grounds of its complexity and unnaturalness:

(4.49)

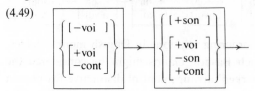

While Basbøll's theory has the advantage of imposing some structure on distinctive feature matrices, in that he establishes sub-classes of features (hierarchical *vs.* cross-classificatory), the choice of the particular features involved again appears to be fortuitous. Notice, for example, the treatment of [continuant] as a semi-hierarchical feature. In fact, although Basbøll treats [continuant] as hierarchical only within the sonorant part of the syllable, it can plausibly be argued that it is also hierarchical within the non-sonorant part. Basbøll's reason for not treating it as such is that it is not possible to predict the ordering relations of stops and fricatives. However, it seems that in nearly all languages stops are always further away from the syllabic peak than fricatives, provided that /s/ is ignored (see §3.4.3). Thus [continuant] is hierarchical within both the non-sonorant and sonorant parts of the syllable. But it is clear that, if this is the case, [continuant] will occur in two places in the hierarchy in (4.46) – it is still unlike the other hierarchical features in that it can only predict ordering relations *within* other parts of the syllable. There appears to be nothing inherent to the particular features involved which suggests that, for example, [sonorant] should be hierarchical, [continuant] semi-hierarchical, and various other features cross-classificatory.

In general, the kind of criticism offered with respect to the models in §4.5.1 is equally applicable to the Basbøll distinctive feature hierarchy. Specifically, we believe that the need for an independent hierarchy of this sort arises again from the inadequacy of the system of representation, in that the patterning of segments does not follow from the representations of the segments themselves.

4.5.3   Dependency phonology and syllable structure

Within dependency phonology, as anticipated in §3.3.1, the difficulties arising from the need for the sort of predictive hierarchies discussed in the previous two sections do not arise, because the representations are such that hierarchies of this kind are redundant, as shown in §§4.3 and 4.4. The syllabicity hierarchy is determined by the representations themselves, in that segments nearer the nucleus are more |V|-like than segments further away from the nucleus. And this alone accounts for the same set of data as Basbøll's distinctive feature hierarchy: ordering relations can be predicted from the segmental representations, and need not be predicted by an externally imposed hierarchy. Similarly, there is no need to make syllabicity dependent on a strength hierarchy. The relationship between segmental representations and syllabic structure is illustrated in (4.50), which shows the syllabic structure associated with English *clamp*, given earlier as (3.23), but now with the phonemic labels replaced by the segmental representations for the appropriate segment-types:

(4.50)

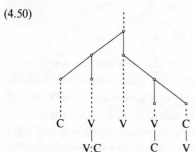

C   V   V   V   C
     V:C   C   V

Only in cases such as syllable-initial *sC* clusters (and the reverse clusters in syllable-final position) and instances of 'extrametricality' is this pattern violated, and here we might want to claim that the status of such sequences differs from that of normal clusters (see §3.4.3 above; Anderson to appear b).

The dependency model, then, can predict any ordering relations which can be predicted by the distinctive feature hierarchy, by virtue of the simple principle that more |V|-like segments will occur nearer to the nucleus of the syllable than less |V|-like segments, without the need for a hierarchy external to the representations themselves. This does not, of course, mean that the dependency model (or the Basbøll hierarchy) will predict the members of each order-class, or indeed the number of order-classes, in a particular language – this is a linguistic variable. Nor will either model be able to predict clusters which violate the sonority hierarchy (nor is it desirable that they should); hence the principle that linear distance from the syllabic peak corresponds with degree of dependency can be maintained.

Notice that the unnaturalness of (4.49) – the representation of the order-classes within the onsets of Norwegian syllables – is not apparent in (4.51), the corresponding representation utilising the dependency model:

(4.51)

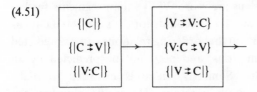

The problems associated with (4.49) are shown to be a result of the feature framework employed there; but in (4.51) the expected pattern operates, with the first box containing segments with a less prominent |V| than those in the second.

4.6   Neutralisation and Old English [v]

Crucial to an adequate characterisation of the sonority hierarchy is the equivalence of each step along that dimension: increasing sonority can be equated with increasing preponderance of |V|. Combinations of |V| and |C| articulate the entire dimension. This entails that distinctions which are formally quite unrelated in terms of a binary feature representation (such as stop *vs.* continuant and voiceless *vs.* voiced) will be represented as alike: in each instance the latter is more |V|-like.

Consider this in relation to a specific lenition process, as evidenced in the development of Gallo-Roman. In Late Latin and Gallo-Roman, Latin plosives weaken intervocalically to varying degrees. That is, in this highly |V|-ful environment plosives increase their |V|-ness, whether this involves simply voicing, or voicing and continuantisation, or even, as in the case of palatals, sonorisation. The major developments are illustrated in (4.52), whose labial examples are paralleled in the apical and velar series:

(4.52)

	Latin	*Late Latin*	*Gallo-Roman*	*French*
	faba	b → β		fève
	ripa	p	b → β	rive
	regina	ɟ → j	i	reine

(On these developments and the evidence for them, see, e.g., Pope 1934: particularly chs. 6 & 7.) We have, in this and many other instances, testimony to the equivalence of what are in one respect quite distinct processes, but which in another (as manifestations of intervocalic lenition) must clearly be characterised in such a way as to make obvious what is in common between them: voicing, continuantisation and sonorisation all involve an increase in the preponderance of the |V| component.

This aspect of the notation is also fundamental to the representation of other regularities. Consider, for example, the status of [v] in Old English. This voiced fricative is in complementary distribution with its voiceless congener. Thus, [f] occurs word- and stem-initially, word-finally, and adjacent to a voiceless segment, as in (4.53):

(4.53)   feoh   'money'
         befaestan   'fasten' (inf.)
         hlāf   'bread'
         eft   'afterwards'

Between voiced segments we find [v]:

(4.54)   hlafas   (nom./acc. pl. of *hlāf*)

As a consequence of this distribution, the two segment-types have generally been assigned to the same phoneme (see, e.g., Pilch 1970:58). However, [v] in Old English shows similar complementarity with respect to [b], as is shown by a comparison of (4.55) with (4.54):

(4.55)   blōd   'blood'
         tōbrecan   'break' (inf.)

[b], like [v], fails to occur word-finally or adjacent to a voiceless segment; but, like [f] and unlike [v], it does occur in gemination:

(4.56)   habban   'have' (inf.)
         pyffan   'puff' (inf.)

Thus, [v] occurs only in an environment from which both [f] and [b] are excluded. Further, it shares phonetic properties with both: like [f] but unlike [b], it is continuant; like [b] but unlike [f], it is voiced; like them both, it is an obstruent. Such a distributional pattern suggests not allophony (the phonemic assignment is not determinate), but rather neutralisation. [v] is the neutralisation product (see Anderson & Ewen 1981) for the [f] ≠ [b] contrast in this particular environment.

Within a binary feature framework the [f] ≠ [b] contrast is not neutralisable: more than one opposition is involved, viz. continuant *vs.* stop and voiced *vs.* voiceless. At best, such a suspension of contrast is unexpected, given this notation. The Old English situation is, however, not idiosyncratic. It is therefore a failure of the notation that it should not be able to predict the occurrence of this neutralisation-type.

In terms of a dependency notation, [f] and [b] both differ from [p], with which they are both in contrast in Old English, in terms of the presence of |V| – unilaterally dependent on |C| in the case of [b], and mutually dependent with it in the case of [f]:

(4.57)   {|V:C|}   {|C ⇉ V|}   {|C|}
              [f]   [b]   [p]

They have in common the presence of a |V| element, in addition to a |C| which it does not unilaterally govern. We can accordingly characterise the neutralisation of /f/ and /b/ as in (4.58):

(4.58)   {|V, ⇈̸ C|}

i.e. a segment containing a |V| component and a |C| which is not unilaterally dependent, or as {C ⇉ V}, on the assumption that this does not exclude {|V:C|}. Between voiced segments, i.e. in a highly |V|-ful environment, this archisegment is realised as a segment which differs from (4.58) in the presence of a further |V| element. The neutralisation is thus assimilatory (see again Anderson & Ewen 1981): the product is a segment whose characterisation is one step closer to {|V|}. If we add |V| to the specification in (4.58), we have a segment which contains two |V|s and a non-dependent |C|. The only possible segment-type comprising these which is compatible with the constraints on the structure of the phonatory sub-gesture is:

(4.59)   {V:C ⇉ V}

the characterisation of a voiced fricative, i.e., in the case of labials, [v].

Neither the neutralisation nor its assimilatory product is formulable unless 'continuancy' and 'voice' share some property; this is characterised in (4.58). For a fuller discussion of the voiced fricatives in Old English see Anderson (1985b); and see §8.2 below.

Such a conclusion coincides with what emerges from a consideration of syllable structure and lenition: 'distinct' feature oppositions like stop–continuant, voiceless–voiced, and obstruent–sonorant must be characterised in such a way as to reveal a similarity, in terms of orientation with respect to a hierarchy, as well as to express the individual differences between the pairs and their location on the hierarchy.

5   *The categorial gesture: initiation*

In §II.2 we outlined some arguments which showed that what has been interpreted as a single phonetic component of PHONATION, i.e. 'activities . . . described chiefly in terms of postures and movements of the vocal cords' (Catford 1977:16), is phonologically relevant to more than one of the sub-divisions of the categorial gesture. In particular, we showed that Ladefoged's (1971) scalar feature of [glottal stricture] can be given a more natural interpretation with respect to phonological phenomena if the two different phonetic parameters involved – degree of glottal stricture and presence or absence of vocal cord vibration – are separated, such that vocal cord vibration is characterised in the representations of the phonatory sub-gesture, while degree of glottal stricture proper is interpreted as being relevant to the other sub-division of the categorial gesture – the initiatory sub-gesture.

Our arguments in favour of this approach are given support by the phenomena surveyed in the previous chapter. As we have seen, what is crucial to the kind of hierarchies which we were able to establish in §§4.3 and 4.4 to account for lenition is the (privative) binary opposition between voicing and lack of voicing, i.e. between the presence and absence of vocal cord vibration, represented (at least for obstruents) by the presence *vs.* absence of a subjoined |V|. The physically independent parameter of glottal stricture, i.e. the degree of opening of the vocal cords, whether in vibration or not, appears to be phonologically relevant for three main types of languages. Firstly, there are languages which display an opposition amongst more than two states of the glottis, such as Indonesian (see §5.1), which distinguishes between voicelessness, 'lax' voice and 'tense' voice. Secondly, we find languages which utilise a phonological opposition between voiced and voiceless sonorants, such as Burmese, with oppositions between voiced and voiceless laterals and nasals (§5.2). Finally, some languages have an obstruent system involving two series of obstruents which are not distinguished by voicing, but which are both voiceless, and differ in degree of aspiration. Thus, Icelandic has an opposition between an aspirated set /pʰ tʰ kʰ/ and an unaspirated set /p t k/ (§5.3). All of these phenomena are characterisable with reference to degree of opening of the glottis, and, as such, are not accounted for within the representations of the phonatory sub-gesture developed in chapter 4.

We suggest that the greater phonological complexity of systems such as Indonesian, involving a three-way opposition of phonation-type rather than a simple binary one, is reflected by the need to introduce a component of glottal opening, whose nature is explored in §5.1.1. For languages in which no more than a simple binary opposition is made, and whose phonological systems are correspondingly less complex, the phonological representations will not require the presence of the component of glottal opening, and their relative simplicity is thus reflected in an obvious manner (see §II.2). It will become apparent that it is the nature of the interaction between glottal opening and the representations of the phonatory sub-gesture already established which leads us to propose that the component of glottal opening belongs to a separate sub-gesture rather than being a third distinct component (besides |V| and |C|) within the phonatory sub-gesture.

However, as we shall see, in obstruent systems of the Icelandic type, with an opposition based on aspiration rather than voicing, it is not the case that all three components are required in the representation: |V| is absent (as the obstruents are all voiceless), and only |C| and the component of glottal opening are found.

Other phenomena are also appropriately characterised within the initiatory sub-gesture: in particular, we shall see that the utilisation by languages of airstream mechanisms other than the pulmonic egressive involves an extra component in their initiatory representation. Languages using only a pulmonic egressive airstream mechanism, we will claim, are like languages making only a binary opposition between voicing and voicelessness, in requiring only phonatory representations within the categorial gesture to characterise their phonological systems. Languages having an opposition between airstream mechanisms require the introduction of specific components reflecting this, and are thus shown to be more complex.

5.1   Glottal stricture

We discussed briefly in §II.2 Ladefoged's characterisation of phonation by means of a scalar feature [glottal stricture]. Ladefoged (1971:18) notes that perhaps as many as nine states of the glottis (i.e. different degrees of glottal stricture) occur in languages, representing a continuum extending from a glottal stop to the most open position observed in speech, voicelessness. However, although there is such a wide range of possible phonation-types available, he shows that no language makes contrasts involving more than three states of the glottis phonologically, with most languages having only a binary opposition. In (5.1) (see Ladefoged 1971:17) we illustrate how the continuum is split up in various languages with a three-way distinction:

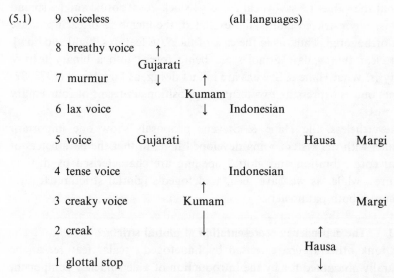

(5.1)   9 voiceless   (all languages)

Thus Gujarati (Ladefoged 1971:13) has voiceless, murmured and voiced stops (/por/ vs. /b̤ar/ vs. /bar/), and Margi (Ladefoged 1968:65) voiceless, voiced and laryngealised (creaky voiced) stops (/tátá/ vs. /bábál/ vs. /ɓàɓàl/).

Such data lead Ladefoged to propose the [glottal stricture] feature. He claims that there is a great deal of explanatory power in the concept of a feature on which some of the glottal states are rank ordered (1971:19). It shows, for example, that murmured or breathy sounds are 'between' voiced and voiceless sounds, and so may be phonologically grouped with either.

For the languages in (5.1), the feature [glottal stricture] has three phonological values /2 1 0/, which are rewritten phonetically as, for example, [9 8/7 5] in Gujarati, [9 6 4] in Indonesian, and [9 5 3] in Margi.

The feature is thus not binary, either phonetically or phonologically, unlike those used to characterise phonation by Jakobson *et al.* (1969), *SPE*, and particularly by Halle & Stevens (1971). As anticipated in §II.2, Halle & Stevens offer an analysis of phonation-type using four binary features, [stiff vocal cords], [slack vocal cords], [spread glottis] and [constricted glottis], which are claimed to be adequate to account not only for glottal stricture, but also for various tonal and voice onset time phenomena. The four features correspond to only two phonetic parameters: degree of stiffness of the vocal cords and degree of glottal opening, so that the values [+ stiff vocal cords, + slack vocal cords] and [+ spread glottis, + constricted glottis] are excluded: the members of each pair are non-orthogonal. Thus, as in the case of the *SPE* features [high] and [low], it is clear that scalar variables are being forced into a binary feature analysis. What Halle & Stevens are in fact doing, as Ladefoged (1973:82) points out, is expressing two ternary oppositions in terms of four binary features.

Nevertheless, the Halle & Stevens proposals show one important parallel with the system being developed here, in that the parameters of vocal cord vibration and glottal opening are characterised by distinct features, while, as we have seen, Ladefoged's [glottal stricture] feature subsumes both parameters.

5.1.1   The dependency representation of glottal stricture

The rank ordering characterised by Ladefoged's scalar feature can be naturally accounted for by the introduction of a dependency component within the initiatory sub-gesture – a component of GLOTTAL OPENING, which we represent as |O|. If, in the phonological representation of a segment (in those languages which make a three-way opposition in this area), the component |O| occurs, there will be some degree of glottal opening, with the degree of opening being reflected by the relative preponderance of the component. Thus, as anticipated above, the component |O| corresponds more closely to the [spread glottis] and [constricted glottis] features than to Ladefoged's scalar feature, in as much as it characterises *only* degree of glottal opening and leaves the state of the vocal cords out of account.

However, we clearly need to establish what relative prominence here means – in other words, with what does |O| show dependency relations? |O| cannot enter into the same kind of relations as the components of the phonatory sub-gesture. Specifically, while |V| and |C| show relations with each other, the difference between three phonation-types (e.g. /p/ *vs.* /b/ *vs.* /ɓ/ in Hausa) involves only a single component in the initiatory gesture: for /p/ |O| is more prominent than for /b/, and for /b/ |O| is more prominent than for /ɓ/. We propose that this situation is appropriately represented if the initiatory and phonatory sub-gestures enter into dependency relations with each other. Thus, while there will be some kind of dependency structure within the phonatory sub-gesture, dependency relations will also hold between the two sub-gestures, as in (5.2), in which |O| is taken to be the only component within the initiatory sub-gesture:

(5.2)   {O}   {O}:phon   phon
          | |
         phon   {O}

The three segments in Hausa will thus have the following representations:

(5.3)   {O}   {O}:{|C|;}   {|C|;}
          | |
        {|C|;}   {O}
         /p/   /b/   /ɓ/

For /p/, with the greatest degree of glottal opening, {O} (as the representation of the initiatory sub-gesture and the component of glottal opening) governs {|C|;}, the representation of the phonatory sub-gesture. (Here, for ease of presentation, we replace the '⇉' notation by a semi-colon, to which it is equivalent – cf. the use of the colon to denote symmetric dependency.) For /ɓ/, with the smallest degree of glottal opening, {O} is dependent; and for /b/, the representations of the two sub-gestures are mutually dependent.

(5.2) allows a maximum of three possibilities, correlating with the empirical maximum number of oppositions found in languages. The representations, then, reflect this maximum, while Ladefoged's scalar feature cannot be said to do this – there appears to be no motivation, within the notation which he employs, for allowing only the three values /0 1 2/, rather than /0 1 . . . n/, where *n* could be any integer.

Notice that (as in Ladefoged's system) different phonetic phonation-types may have the same phonological representations, and, indeed, the same phonetic types may have different phonological representations in different systems, as in (5.4):

(5.4)

	Gujarati	Kumam	Indonesian	Hausa	Margi
{O} | {|C|;}	←————————— voiceless stops —————————→				
{O}:{|C|;}	breathy voice	murmur/ lax voice	lax voice	voice	voice
{|C|;} | {O}	voice	creaky voice	tense voice	creak	creaky voice

(5.4) shows that the phonological notation employed reflects the function of a particular phonation-type within the phonological system of a particular language, and its position on the phonetic dimension relative to other types present in that language, rather than showing the 'absolute' phonetic realisation of that phonation-type.

5.1.2   Glottal stops

There is a fourth possibility in relation to the representations of the initiatory sub-gesture besides those in (5.2) (in which the initiatory sub-gesture is governing, mutually dependent, or unilaterally dependent); i.e. that it may be absent, even in a phonological system with a three-way opposition in the area under discussion. Absence of |O|, then, would correlate with lack of glottal opening, i.e. a representation lacking |O| would be that for a glottal stop. Thus Tagalog has the system in (5.5):

(5.5)

{O} | {|C|;}	{|C|;} | {O}	{|C|;}
voiceless stop	voiced stop	glottal stop

In §1.6 we discussed the view that the glottal stop is frequently a realisation of the neutralisation of a contrast amongst the voiceless stops, i.e. that it bears the same sort of relationship to voiceless stops as the reduced vowel does to full vowels. We argued there, following Lass (1976), that [?] differed from voiceless stops only in the absence of any supra-glottal locational information, i.e. in the complete absence of any representation in the articulatory gesture for the glottal stop. Further, there is a phonetic similarity between the two types of segment. Although the state of the glottis is quite different, both the glottal stop and the voiceless stops have the effect of blocking the airstream completely, thus causing a period of silence during the closure phase. In Catford's terms (1977:104), both the voiceless stops and the glottal stop may have an articulatory function.

These facts suggest that we should, if necessary, be able to characterise voiceless stops and the glottal stop as a natural class, and in the notation developed here this is easily achieved: only these segments have {|C|} as the representation of the phonatory sub-gesture. Thus, although the two types of segments occur at opposite ends of Ladefoged's scalar feature – and as such cannot readily be characterised as a natural class on the natural recurrence assumption – the system developed here allows just this possibility, in incorporating the notion of gesture.

5.2 Voiceless sonorants

Some languages have phonological oppositions between corresponding pairs of voiced and voiceless sonorants – both consonants and vowels. Examples of minimal pairs involving voiced and voiceless nasals and laterals in Burmese are given by Ladefoged (1971:11):

(5.6) mà 'healthy'   nà 'pain'   ŋâ 'fish'
       m̥à 'order'   n̥à 'nostril'   ŋ̊â 'rent'

                      la 'moon'
                      l̥á 'beautiful'

In the representations of the phonatory sub-gesture established in chapter 4, no allowance was made for the representation of voiceless sonorants. Indeed, the representations which were developed for sonorants, showing |V| alone in governing position, seemed appropriate in that they reflected the claim that sonorants are 'inherently' voiced, as opposed to obstruents, which may be naturally voiced or voiceless.

If it is the case that sonorants are naturally voiced, then it is reasonable to assume that a system such as (5.6), involving phonological oppositions between voiced and voiceless sonorants, should be characterised as more complex than a system involving only oppositions between voiced and voiceless obstruents. Our phonological notation should, in turn, reflect this relative complexity. We suggest that it is appropriate, in representing voiceless sonorants, to introduce the dependency component |O|, i.e. the component of glottal opening. Such segments will display both {O} and the phonatory sub-gesture (containing the usual representation for the sonorant in question):

(5.7)   {O},{V;V:C}   {O},{|V;C|}   {O},{|V|}
          voiceless   voiceless   voiceless
          liquid   nasal   vowel

In such a system, the voiced counterparts of the segments in (5.7) will show a structure in which |O| is simply absent phonologically; in this way the complexity of the voiced and voiceless sonorants is successfully represented. Here we are adopting a view of phonological representation similar to that of Archangeli (1984): the phonological representations are 'underspecified', in the sense that while both voiced and voiceless sonorants will display |O| phonetically (as noted above, a segment lacking |O| in its phonetic representation would have glottal closure), one member of the opposition lacks the component in phonological representations. This embodies a claim that we have here a property which *functions* privatively, although phonetically it is, in this case, scalar; while in the case of the various phonation-types discussed above, its function is also scalar, and hence all phonation-types (with the exception of glottal stops) display |O| in their phonological representations. In Archangeli's minimally componential approach, the choice of which of the members of the opposition lacks the component in phonological representations is not determined by the notation; here, however, as might be expected, the segment-type lacking |O| is the one with less of the property in question.

We are now in a position to formulate a condition on segments containing |O|, viz: a segment with |O|, either unilaterally governing or in simple combination with the phonatory representation, is voiceless. This condition holds only if all languages with a three-way opposition in phonation-type have, as one of these types, voiceless segments – a state of affairs which does, in fact, appear to be universally true. Thus, for voiceless sonorants the specification for glottal opening ({O}) overrides the inherent specification for vocal cord vibration in the phonatory sub-gesture (governing |V| alone). Segments with governing |O|, but without a voicing specification (e.g. the voiceless stops in (5.4)), of course, lack vocal cord vibration in any case. The naturalness of this condition is apparent in that segments with |O| in these positions show a relatively large degree of glottal opening. Such a glottal configuration is incompatible with the presence of vocal cord vibration, which can only occur with a relatively small degree of glottal opening. The claim that voiceless sonorants retain the sub-structure characterising voiced sonorants can be defended by the fact that such segments retain traces of the formant patterns associated with their voiced counterparts.

This treatment of voiceless sonorants allows us to show the relative complexity of phonological systems employing this segment-type, by the need to introduce representations of the initiatory sub-gesture in their characterisation. Compare this with a binary feature system, where it is not possible (except by using the ad hoc accretions discussed in chapter 1) to characterise the relative complexity of these segments, as shown in (5.8):

(5.8) $\begin{bmatrix} +\text{son} \\ -\text{voice} \end{bmatrix}$ $\begin{bmatrix} +\text{son} \\ +\text{voice} \end{bmatrix}$ $\begin{bmatrix} -\text{son} \\ -\text{voice} \end{bmatrix}$ $\begin{bmatrix} -\text{son} \\ +\text{voice} \end{bmatrix}$

   voiceless   voiced   voiceless   voiced
   sonorant   sonorant   obstruent   obstruent

5.3   Aspiration

We turn now to the representation of aspiration. It has been argued by, for example, Kim (1970), Pétursson (1976) and Catford (1977) that degree of aspiration correlates directly with degree of glottal opening. Thus Kim (1970:108) observes that Korean has three types of voiceless stops, which differ from each other in degree of aspiration, as in (5.9):

(5.9)   I   /p'ali/ 'washer'   /t'al/ 'daughter'   /k'ali/ 'villain'
   II   /pal/   'leg'   /tal/   'moon'   /kali/ 'stack'
   III   /pʰal/ 'arm'   /tʰal/ 'mistake'   /kʰal/ 'knife'

where series I is 'unaspirated', series II 'slightly aspirated', and series III 'heavily aspirated'.

Kim shows, by means of a 'cineradiographic film of the laryngeal area', that degree of glottal opening correlates with degree of aspiration. The film shows a 'narrow glottis in I, a moderately open glottis in II, and a wide open glottis in III'. Kim notes that there seems to be a direct correlation between the degree of the glottal opening at the time of the release and the degree of aspiration.

In the dependency model these stops differ from each other only in the relative prominence of |O|, as in (5.10):

(5.10)   {|C|}   {O}:{|C|}   {O}
            | |
           {O}   {|C|}

           /p'/   /p/   /pʰ/

in which {O} becomes more prominent as the degree of glottal opening, and hence of aspiration, increases.

It might be objected that in the 'unaspirated' series we would expect {O} to be absent, rather than dependent as in (5.10). However, such a representation would characterise a glottal stop (see §5.1.1); for the unaspirated series, there is, of course, some glottal opening, albeit less than for series II and III, and there seems to be no reason for treating these segments as 'underspecified' in the way that voiced sonorants were in the previous section.

A second objection to the representations in (5.10) might be that aspirated stops are treated as units, rather than as sequences of oral closure followed by a period of aspiration. However, there is phonetic evidence which appears to support this analysis. Pétursson (1972:66) and Thráinsson (1978:5) note that in Icelandic, where both preaspiration and postaspiration are found, the two phenomena are very different. Preaspiration typically has full segment length, and therefore preaspirated stops are appropriately analysed as bisegmental sequences, while postaspiration is much shorter. This leads Thráinsson to transcribe preaspirated voiceless stops as, for example, [ht], and postaspirated stops as [t^h]. In addition, the auditory correlate of postaspiration, i.e. the voicing-lag between the release of the oral closure and the onset of voicing, 'is only a symptom of what we may regard as a more fundamental characteristic of these sounds, namely, the state of the glottis' (Catford 1977:114). On distributional grounds, too, it has been argued that postaspirated stops should be treated as unit phonemes in various cases. Ternes (1973:21–2) claims that in the Applecross dialect of Scots Gaelic, which shows oppositions between stops based on aspiration rather than voicing, the aspirated stops should be treated as single phonemes, on grounds of phonetic realisation and pattern congruity with respect to the operation of initial consonant mutation.

Notice that these arguments tend to support this treatment of aspiration (i.e. as being determined by degree of glottal opening) rather than that of Ladefoged (1975:258), whose definition of the feature [aspiration] refers to time of onset of voicing with respect to release of the articulation.

Postaspiration, then, can be interpreted as a component of the stop itself, as in (5.10), while preaspiration differs in that the |O| component is sequentially distinct from the |C| component, as in (5.11) (see Ewen 1982:§7):

(5.11)   {O}
            \
        {|C|}

Here the dependency relation for a postaspirated stop is maintained, the |C| being adjoined rather than subjoined. (We do not here commit ourselves to a view on whether (5.11) represents a (complex) segment or a sequence: for discussion of the formal status of such representations, see §7.3.)

5.4 |O|-languages

We have distinguished three different ways in which the |O| component can be utilised phonologically in languages (in three-way oppositions of phonation-type, in a voicing opposition amongst sonorants and in the distinctive use of aspiration). It is interesting to notice that such languages tend to use more than one of these types in their phonological inventories. In particular, the presence of an aspiration opposition in a system seems to co-occur with the presence of voiceless sonorants. Thus, Icelandic, which, as we have seen, displays an aspiration opposition in the voiceless stop series, also has voiceless sonorants in words such as [heiḷt] *heilt* 'whole' and [fan̥tʏr] *fantur* 'villain' (Árnason 1980:9). Scots Gaelic, at least in some dialects, shows a similar state of affairs, having both preaspiration and voiceless nasals, while Burmese has oppositions between voiced and voiceless nasals and between aspirated and unaspirated fricatives. Notice too that the presence of aspiration does not preclude the occurrence of a three-way opposition in phonation-type: Gujarati (see Ladefoged 1971:13) has both a murmured stop series and an aspiration opposition amongst the voiceless stops. Burmese, too, has both breathy voice and creaky voice, associated with its tone system.

In languages with both phonological aspiration and voiceless sono- rants, indeed, the (allophonic) occurrence of these voiceless sonorants can be ascribed, at least partially, to constraints on consonant clusters involving stops from the aspirated series. Here we shall consider in some detail just one such case, the surface realisation of lexically aspirated stops in Icelandic. (Our analysis here is in some respects similar to that of Hermans 1985, who offers an account in terms of an autosegmental framework.) If a 'hard' stop (i.e. one of the aspirated series /p^h t^h k^h/) follows a vowel, any consonantal element that intervenes between it and a following short vowel must be voiceless. 'One may wonder whether this is a coincidence' (Árnason 1980:25). As Árnason implies, this is clearly not the case. Rather, we have here a manifestation of a constraint whereby in any cluster containing a stop which is phonologically aspirated, i.e., in dependency terms in any cluster containing |O|, this |O| may be realised phonetically at only one point in the cluster. Thus we find forms such as:

(5.12) a. titra   /tʰɪtʰra/   [tʰɪːtɽa]   'to shiver'
            plata   /pʰlatʰa/   [pḷaːtʰa]   'plate'
            tvisvar   /tʰvɪsvar/   [tfɪːsvar]   'twice'
            spara   /spʰara/   [spaːra]   'save'

        b. hempa   /hɛmpʰa/   [hɛm̥pa] or [hɛmpʰa]   'cassock'
            maðkur   /maðkʰʏr/   [maθkʏr] or [maðkʰʏr]   'worm'

        c. tappi   /tʰapʰpʰɪ/   [tʰahpɪ]   'cork'
            detta   /tɛtʰtʰa/   [tɛhta]   'fall'

        d. taka   /takʰa/   [tʰaːkʰa]   'take'
            vakka   /vakʰkʰa/   [vahka]   'walk to and fro'
            vakna   /vakʰna/   [vahkna]   'wake up'

        e. feit   /fɛitʰ/   [fɛiːtʰ]   'fat' (fem. sg.)
            ljót   /ljoutʰ/   [ljouːtʰ]   'ugly' (fem. sg.)

        f. heilt   /hɛiltʰ/   [hɛil̥t]   'whole' (neut.)
            maðk   /maðkʰ/   [maθk]   'worm'

        g. feitt   /fɛitʰ+tʰ/   [fɛiht]   'fat' (neut. sg.)
            ljótt   /ljoutʰ+tʰ/   [ljouht]   'ugly' (neut. sg.)

The lexical aspiration specification manifests itself phonetically in various ways. Initially, (5.12a), we find postaspiration or devoicing of a following consonant, while a preceding /s/ absorbs the aspiration. In final position we find postaspiration of a single consonant (5.12e), and devoicing of a preceding consonant (sonorant or fricative) (5.12f). A sequence of two aspirated stops is realised as a preaspirated stop, both intervocalically (5.12c) and finally (5.12g). A phonologically aspirated stop followed by a sonorant is preaspirated phonetically (5.12d), while a sequence of consonant and aspirated stop in intervocalic position (5.12b) may be realised in one of two ways: either as a sequence of voiceless consonant and unaspirated stop, or as a sequence of voiced consonant and aspirated stop, depending on dialect. In sequences of aspirated stop and voiced continuant we find both surface devoicing of the consonant, as in (5.13a), and preaspiration, as in (5.13b):

(5.13) a. titra   /tʰɪtʰra/   [tʰɪːtɽa]   'to shiver'
            skrökva   /skʰrœkʰva/   [skrœːkfa]   'to tell a lie'

        b. rytmi   /rɪtʰmɪ/   [rɪhtmɪ]   'rhythm'
            vakna   /vakʰna/   [vahkna]   'wake up'

The difference in realisation between (5.13a) and (5.13b) appears to depend on syllabification, as noted both by Árnason (1980) and by Hermans (1985), who, however, offer different analyses: for Árnason the syllable boundary in (a) falls after the stop, and in (b) after the sonorant consonant, while Hermans gives (5.14) as the appropriate syllabification:

(5.14)   a. ti][tra, skrö][kva
          b. ryt][mi, vak][na

The clusters in (5.12) all contain at least one segment lexically specified as containing |O|; a sequence of nasal and aspirated stop, for instance, will have the representation in (5.15a), and a geminate stop that in (5.15b):

(5.15)   a. {|V;C|}   {O},{|C|}
          b. {O},{|C|}   {O},{|C|}

In the course of the derivation of the appropriate surface forms for the clusters, the |O| component must lose its segmental status and become prosodic (or EXTRASEGMENTAL; see Anderson, Ewen & Staun 1985). This is shown by the fact that only one segment in a cluster may be phonetically aspirated, preaspirated or devoiced. Thus the derivation must involve three stages: lexical association of |O| with a particular segment, the creation of extrasegmental status for |O|, and finally, unique association of |O| with the appropriate segment for phonetic realisation.

The second stage is achieved by simply associating |O| with each of the {C} segments in its domain, which is any tautosyllabic consonant cluster, as in (5.16):

(5.16)

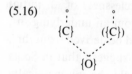

The derivation of the structure in (5.16) involves first scanning any sequence of {C} elements for the presence of |O|, which is then extracted from the lexical representation and associated with all the {C} elements in its domain, to give (5.16). Notice that if two |O|s occur in a string, as in the case of a geminate stop, one of them is simply deleted: only one |O| may occur in any single |O| domain.

The third stage – the specification of the phonetic realisation of the |O| prosody – involves association with the most sonorous element of the cluster forming the domain of the prosody, i.e. its governor, a process which we can formalise as (5.17):

(5.17)

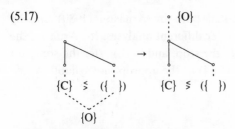

Thus we have here a case in which |O| characterises aspiration lexically, but may be realised as devoicing of a lexically voiced sonorant consonant.

The specification of the surface realisation of a geminate aspirated stop as preaspirated involves appeal to the constraint noted by Árnason that a voiceless continuant must intervene between a short vowel and a lexically aspirated stop. The interaction of (5.17) and this constraint requires that such rhymes have the surface structure in (5.18):

(5.18)   {|V|}{　}{|C|}

　　　　　{O}

i.e., |O| must be linked with the second element of the rhyme. For geminates this is achieved by deleting the first of the two {|C|}s in the structure in (5.16).

For languages such as Icelandic and Scots Gaelic, we often find discussion as to whether 'voiceless' sonorants are to be interpreted phonologically in various environments as monophonemic or biphonemic sequences. Árnason (1980:10) notes that the voicelessness of an initial voiceless sonorant in Icelandic might be derived from an underlying /h/, which only occurs initially. In this analysis, [r̥] would be derived from /hr/, rather than from /r̥/. Similarly, Ternes (1973:72ff) suggests that in Scots Gaelic a 'voiceless/aspirated' alveolar nasal could be phonemically represented either as biphonemic /hn/ or /nh/, or as monophonemic /n̥/ or /nʰ/. In the model proposed here, this corresponds at the phonetic level merely to a difference in the relative ordering of |O| and the phonatory representation, with the dependency relation between them being maintained, as in (5.19):

(5.19)

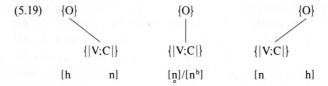

Phonologically, however, the segment/sequence is interpreted as a structure involving {O} governing the phonatory representation, as in the forms in (5.7), with the position of the phonetic realisation of {O} being specified by language-particular rules, to give (5.19). The likelihood of occurrence of such segments/sequences in languages such as these can again be attributed to the phonological utilisation of |O| in the consonant system. (For a fuller discussion of this problem, with a prosodic interpretation of aspiration, see Ewen 1982; and see §7.3 for the status of representations such as those in (5.6).)

5.5 Airstream mechanisms

We turn now to another aspect whose characterisation is appropriate to the initiatory sub-gesture – the use of different airstream mechanisms in speech production. In the preceding discussion we have tacitly assumed that all sounds are produced on one airstream mechanism, i.e. the pulmonic egressive. Although in many languages this is of course the case (at least systematically), there are two other airstream mechanisms used in the production of speech in many languages: the glottalic and the velaric. Ladefoged (1971:23) notes that four types of airstream are found in language: pulmonic egressive, glottalic egressive, glottalic ingressive and velaric ingressive. Two parameters can be distinguished in the use of these types: firstly, whether the airstream is egressive or ingressive, i.e. whether pressure or suction is involved; and secondly, the location of the initiation of the sound, i.e. which organs carry out the 'initiatory activity' (Catford 1977:64). The table in (5.20) (from Catford) shows the possibilities, together with examples of each of the mechanisms actually occurring in systematic linguistic communication:

(5.20)

Location	Direction	
	compressive	rarefactive
lungs	*pulmonic pressure* (plosives [p t k])	pulmonic suction
larynx	*glottalic pressure* (ejectives [p' t' k'])	*glottalic suction* (implosives [ɓ ɗ ɠ])
mouth	velaric pressure	*velaric suction* (clicks [ǀ ǂ ǁ])

According to Catford, pulmonic suction and velaric pressure, although anthropophonically possible, are not used linguistically.

Ladefoged points out that glottalic ingressive sounds are produced with a downward movement of the vibrating glottis, i.e. there is also a pulmonic egressive airstream mechanism involved in the production of these implosives. He notes further that glottalic ingressive sounds with no vocal cord vibration (i.e. implosives with a closed glottis) are possible, but rare. However, according to Greenberg (1970:126), most Munda languages have a full set of four voiceless implosive stops in final position, and in what follows we will include these sounds in our attempt to offer a characterisation of different airstream mechanisms.

5.5.1   Pulmonic airstream mechanisms

By definition, a sound produced on a pulmonic airstream mechanism must involve an open glottis. Thus any sound involving this airstream mechanism can be characterised phonetically, and, if necessary, phonologically, by the presence of the component |O|. Therefore, although |O| is defined as characterising glottal opening, its presence may also be taken to indicate the presence of a pulmonic egressive airstream mechanism. The fact that the pulmonic airstream mechanism is phonologically the least complex accords well with the interpretation offered here; it is not necessary to provide a component whose sole function is to characterise the use of this airstream mechanism.

5.5.2   Glottalic airstream mechanisms

As shown in (5.20), the glottalic airstream mechanism may be egressive (compressive) or ingressive (rarefactive). If it is egressive, the glottis is closed, and the whole larynx raised, so that the pressure of the air in the mouth and the pharynx is increased. Sounds produced on a glottalic egressive airstream are known as ejectives (or glottalic pressure sounds), and are usually stops, although ejective fricatives and affricates are also recorded. Ladefoged (1971:25) observes contrasts such as the following in Amharic:

(5.21)   t'ɨl   'quarrel'   tɨl   'warm'   dɨl   'victory'
          s'əgga 'grace'   səgga 'to worry'   zəgga 'to close'

Sounds produced on a glottalic ingressive airstream usually (but not always; see above) involve some vibration of the vocal cords. Whether or not the glottis is tightly closed, it is lowered, thus reducing the pressure between it and the articulatory stricture and causing air to enter the mouth when the articulatory closure is released. Only stops can be implosive. A series of voiced implosive stops is found in Sindhi (Ladefoged 1971:26), which also has series of voiced stops, voiceless unaspirated and aspirated stops, and breathy voiced stops. The contrasts involving the labial set are:

(5.22) ɓəni 'curse'   pʰəɳu 'snake hood'
        bənu 'forest'   b̤əneɳu 'lamentation'
        pənu 'leaf'

Ladefoged sets up a feature [glottalicness], which 'uses the fact that implosives and ejectives differ in terms of the single parameter of rate of vertical laryngeal movement toward the lungs' (1971:30). At the phonetic level, his system offers a characterisation such as the following:

(5.23) [−n glottalic] ejectives
        [∅ glottalic] plosives
        [+n glottalic] implosives

where the value of n indicates the degree of force with which the glottalic airstream mechanism is used.

Chomsky & Halle (*SPE*:322–4) use two binary features to characterise this mechanism: [implosion] (or [glottal suction]) and [ejection] ([glottal pressure]). Ejectives are [− implosion, + ejection], implosives [+ implosion, − ejection], and other sounds [− implosion, − ejection]. As in other similar cases noted above, the formally possible combination of [+ implosion, + ejection] is excluded by the definition of the features, both of which involve movement of the glottal closure – downward for [implosion] and upward for [ejection].

In the model which we are in the process of developing here, we propose that glottalic airstream mechanisms should be characterised by a component of GLOTTALICNESS in the initiatory sub-gesture, which we label |G|. As a component of the initiatory sub-gesture, |G| will show dependency relations with the phonatory representations in the same manner as |O|. In other words, dependency relations will hold between the two sub-gestures. A representation in which |G| governs the phonatory sub-gesture will characterise a glottalic egressive sound, while a representation in which the reverse holds will characterise a glottalic ingressive sound, as in (5.24):

(5.24)   G   phon
           | |
          phon   G

        glottalic   glottalic
        egressive   ingressive

Ordinary pulmonic sounds, represented as [∅ glottalic] by Ladefoged, will, we suggest, lack the component |G|. In other words, there is no representation in which |G| is mutually dependent with a phonatory representation. Although the position of the glottis in the production of a pulmonic sound is intermediate between the positions for glottalic ingressive and glottalic egressive sounds, the presence of |G| denotes the presence of glottalic initiation, and so pulmonics lack |G|. Only ejectives and implosives show |G|, whose relative prominence is determined by the height of the glottis. Thus glottalic egressives, involving glottalic initiation plus raising of the glottis, show governing |G|; glottalic ingressives (glottalic initiation plus lowering of the glottis) show dependent |G|; while glottal stops, like pulmonic egressives, lack |G|. Such a characterisation allows us to show that segments with the glottis in the 'normal' position are less complex than those with glottalic initiation.

Applying this system to various sounds produced with a closed glottis, i.e. to those not employing a pulmonic airstream mechanism, and therefore lacking |O|, we have the display in (5.25):

(5.25)   {G}   {|C|}   {|C|}
          | |
          {|C|}   {G}

          /p'/   /ʔ/   /ɓ/

We turn now to various sounds involving vocal cord vibration. We consider first a system in which there is a two-way opposition in phonation-type, e.g. /b̥/ vs. /b̤/, together with an opposition between a pulmonic egressive airstream and a glottalic ingressive airstream, such that each of /b̥/ and /b̤/ has a corresponding voiced implosive, i.e. /ɓ̥/ vs. /ɓ̤/. (Here we ignore the voiceless series.) The representations for the pulmonic egressive sounds, established in §5.1, are:

(5.26)   {O}   {|C;|}
          | |
          {|C;|}   {O}

          /b̥/   /b̤/

These representations lack |G|, in that the segments do not show glottalic initiation. The series of voiced implosives will, however, show |G| as well as |O|. Notice that a representation involving these two components can only be that for a voiced implosive – these are the only segments involving both airstream mechanisms in question. Thus the representations for the voiced implosives in the system outlined above will be:

(5.27)   {O,G}   {|C|;}
           | |
         {|C|;}   {O,G}

         /ɓ/   /ɓ/

In (5.27), the relationships between |O| and the phonatory sub-gesture remain constant with respect to (5.26). It is only in the absence of |O|, then, that the relationship between |G| and the phonatory sub-gesture is crucial, as in (5.25). If |O| is present, only one kind of glottalic airstream mechanism is possible – that for the voiced implosive – and so the presence of |G| is in itself sufficient to characterise this. Similarly, there is no need to propose a dependency relation between |G| and |O| in (5.27), since there is no opposition to be made with any other combination of the two components. We also see that the phonologically less common series of voiced implosives have a more complex representation than the pulmonic stops in (5.26).

5.5.3   Velaric airstream mechanisms

In the use of the velaric airstream mechanism:

a body of air is enclosed by raising the back of the tongue to make contact with the soft palate, and either closing the lips or (more commonly) forming a closure on the teeth or alveolar ridge with the tip (or blade) and sides of the tongue. The air in this chamber is rarefied by the downward and backward movement of the body of the tongue, the back of the tongue maintaining contact with the soft palate. When a more forward part of the closure is released, air rushes into the mouth, and a sound known as a click is produced. This mechanism is always ingressive. (Ladefoged 1971:28)

The airstream mechanism can be used simultaneously with a pulmonic egressive airstream mechanism, and Ladefoged & Traill (1984:2) note the following oppositions in the dental click series of Nama:

(5.28)
ACCOMPANIMENT	SYMBOL		
voiceless unaspirated	/kǀ/	ǀgoa	'put into'
voiceless aspirated	/kǀh/	ǀkho	'play an instrument'
delayed aspiration	/ǀh/	ǀho	'push into'
voiced nasal	/ŋǀ/	ǀno	'measure'
glottal closure	/ǀʔ/	ǀo	'sound'

(Here we replace Ladefoged & Traill's [/] with the IPA symbol for the dental click.) Ladefoged characterises the velaric airstream mechanisms by means of a feature [velaric suction]. This feature is binary at the phonological level, as no oppositions are made between different degrees of the mechanism. In the dependency model, this state of affairs is simply captured by a component which we shall label |K| – a component which will be present if the mechanism is employed, and absent otherwise.

However, a means of distinguishing the various accompaniments to the click mechanism is clearly required. Ladefoged & Traill (1984:9) propose that the Nama clicks can be given the phonological classification in (5.29):

(5.29)

	/kı/	/kıh/	/ıh/	/ŋı/	/ı?/
voiced	+	−	−	+	−
glottal	−	−	−	−	+
nasal	−	−	+	+	+

The value [+ nasal] is assigned to the delayed aspiration series, in that the reason for the delay in the onset of oral airflow is the presence of a nasal airflow. Thus the aspiration associated with the oral airflow only sets in as the nasal airflow begins to decrease, and is thus delayed in comparison with the 'normal' aspirated series. In the clicks with accompanying glottal stop there is also nasal airflow at the release of the click.

Notice too that Ladefoged & Traill (1984:9) assign [+ voice] to the unaspirated click, although it is completely voiceless, in order to distinguish it from its aspirated counterpart, 'so the phonetic specification rules will have to show that, when the value [+ voice] occurs in conjunction with the values [+ click, − nasal], it must be interpreted as an abduction (opening) of the vocal cords'. In terms of the dependency model, the difference between the unaspirated and aspirated clicks must involve not |V|, but |O|, as in the case of the aspirated and unaspirated stops in Icelandic (see §5.4). In other words, the difference between the various voiceless clicks is simply one of relative prominence of |O|, as in (5.30):

(5.30)   {O,K}   {O,K}:{|C|}   {|C|}   {K},{|C|}
          | |
        {|C|}   {O,K}

         /kıh/   /ıh/   /kı/   /ı?/

where the relative prominence of |O| corresponds to degree of aspiration, ranging from unilateral government for /kıh/ to complete absence for /ı?/, produced with a closed glottis. Notice that Ladefoged & Traill's aerodynamic records of Nama show that the oral airflow is higher for the normal aspirated clicks than for those with delayed aspiration. In (5.30), |K| is simply combined with |O|; as in the case of |G|, there is no dependency relation within the initiatory sub-gesture, as the presence of |K| is sufficient to characterise the airstream mechanism involved.

For the characterisation of the nasal clicks, we require the introduction of a component of nasality |n|, a component of the articulatory gesture (see §6.9 for discussion), to give:

(5.31)   {K},{|V;C|}
                :
                :
             {n}
             /ŋ/

where the nasality component is simply associated with the categorial components. We assume that the other segment-types represented by Ladefoged & Traill as [+ nasal] do not require to be specified as containing |n| phonologically.

6   *The articulatory gesture*

In this chapter we consider the representations of the second of the two gestures discussed in §II.3, the articulatory gesture. Here again, we are concerned with two sub-gestures, the locational and the oro-nasal, but, clearly, the bulk of the discussion will deal with what is traditionally referred to as place of articulation for consonants, and with the location of vowels in articulatory space, i.e. with purely locational matters.

It seems appropriate to deal with vowels and consonants in separate sections, although, as we shall see, the representations for the two are not entirely distinct.

6.1   Vowels: the basic vocalic components

In chapter 1 we discussed in some detail the problems associated with systems of phonological representation which characterised vowels by means of binary features (*SPE*; Wang 1968; etc.), with or without the various extensions to the standard *SPE* system, or by means of *n*-ary or scalar features (Contreras 1969; Ladefoged 1971; Saltarelli 1973), and we do not intend to repeat the arguments which led us to propose a set of single-valued vowel components in place of any version of binary or multi-valued distinctive feature theory. Our intention in this section is to explore further the precise nature of these components, and to survey some of the implications of the particular set which we will establish.

We begin by investigating in detail the three vowel components introduced in §1.5. It will be clear by now that these components have the same status within the locational sub-gesture as the basic components of the phonatory and initiatory sub-gestures. The three components established in (1.44) are repeated as (6.1):

(6.1) |i| 'frontness' (or 'acuteness' and 'sharpness')
         |a| 'lowness'   (or 'sonority')
         |u| 'roundness' (or 'gravity' and 'flatness')

In §1.5 we showed that these three components, and the dependency relations between them, were adequate to characterise the data considered there. However, we wish now to consider the question of whether the articulatory and acoustic glosses for each component are appropriate, and whether the set of components is adequate for the description of the phonological systems found in language.

We examine first some proposals which are in some ways similar to ours: those of NATURAL PHONOLOGY (Donegan 1973, 1976, 1978) and PARTICLE PHONOLOGY (Schane 1984a,b). Within the model of natural phonology, three 'cardinal properties' are established: PALATALITY and LABIALITY, which are 'chromatic' properties, optimised by a minimally open, maximally constricted vocal tract, and SONORITY, optimised by a more open vowel tract (Donegan 1973:386). Palatality and labiality, then, represent one of two conflicting qualities, chromaticity, opposed to the other, sonority. The qualities are phonetically incompatible – the more sonorant a vowel, the less chromatic it is, and vice versa. [ɑ], the most sonorant vowel, is achromatic (lacking palatality and labiality), while [i] and [u] have relatively low sonority. Thus, the minimum vowel triangle, containing only /i/, /u/ and /ɑ/, represents the maximal opposition of the three properties.

It will be seen that the three properties bear a strong relationship to the three dependency components in (6.1). However, no formal mechanism for representing vowels, in particular different vowel heights, is provided. The kind of representation used is illustrated in (6.2) (from Donegan 1976:146):

(6.2)

	− chromatic	+ chromatic			
	− palatal − labial (− tense)	+ palatal − labial	+ palatal + labial	− palatal + labial	
		− tense + tense	− tense + tense	− tense + tense	
high	ɨ	ɪ i	ʏ y	ʊ u	
mid	ʌ	ɛ e	ɔ̈ ö	ɔ o	
low	ɑ	a æ		ɒ̆ ɒ	

This implies a non-binary feature of vowel height, rather than a binary feature representation; indeed, Donegan notes (1978:36–7) that the acoustic correlates of sonority are clearly scalar, and that phonological evidence, too, suggests a scalar interpretation. However, as far as the various vowel properties are concerned, the formalism implied by (6.2) seems at odds with the concepts discussed above. The feature notation used obscures the claim of natural phonology that chromaticity and sonority are in an inverse, apparently scalar relationship. The table in (6.2) does not show that as a vowel becomes more sonorant, it becomes less chromatic, and vice versa. As in the Chomsky & Halle system, the notation fails to allow for the possibility of any structural variables other than binary feature-values.

That this failure is indeed a drawback for the natural phonology model is apparent from a consideration of the various 'natural processes' discussed by Donegan (1973). She defines two such processes – bleaching and colouring. Bleaching is manifested as the removal of either palatality or labiality, or both simultaneously, i.e. the removal of either or both of the chromatic properties. So changes such as [y] → [i], [u] → [ɨ] involve bleaching by removal of the labiality colour, and [y] → [u], [i] → [ɨ] involve bleaching by removal of the palatality colour. Colouring is manifested by two distinct processes – palatalisation and labialisation (rounding). Changes such as [i] →[y] or [u] → [y], then, are colouring processes.

Donegan claims that bleaching and colouring have opposite causalities, which together have the tendency to polarise or optimise the properties of individual segments. Thus, more sonorant vowels tend to lose colour and increase sonority, thereby increasing their distinctiveness. This basic causality leads to various conditions on the applicability of each process. Bleaching is more likely to affect low vowels than high vowels, because of the general condition on applicability that the less colour a vowel has, the more likely it is to bleach. Low vowels already have a lower degree of chromaticity than high vowels, and therefore bleaching makes them even less chromatic – a change such as [a] → [ɑ] is rated as highly likely, involving as it does the removal of the palatality colour to give a non-palatal and non-labial (hence achromatic) vowel. This change is therefore more favoured as a bleaching process than, say, the depalatalisation or delabialisation of high vowels. Thus [y] → [u], [y] → [i] and [y] → [ɨ] are less favoured than the corresponding bleachings of the mid vowel in the changes [ö] → [o], [ö] → [e] and [ö] → [ʌ].

Further, bleaching favours 'mixed' vowels rather than pure vowels. Mixed vowels are those containing both colours, while pure vowels are those with just a single colour. Thus, changes such as [y] → [ɨ] and

[y] → [u], involving the removal of one colour from the mixed vowel [y], are favoured over changes such as [u] → [ɨ] and [i] → [ɨ], involving the same bleachings, but this time affecting vowels which have only a single colour, and whose properties are therefore already maximally polarised. This has a perceptual motivation; thus Donegan (1978:47) notes:

If [lip-rounding and tongue-fronting occur simultaneously], they attenuate each other's acoustic effects, so that they are, at least perceptually, less labial than pure labials and less palatal than pure palatals. They are thus 'marked' or non-optimal; they tend to become monochromatic, and they are consequently rarer in the phoneme inventories of the world than pure labials or pure palatals.

But, as noted above, there is no way in which the representations of (6.2) can be said to reflect these notions: bleaching and colouring involve the same kind of formal change, the change in value of one of the features involved.

The proposals for the characterisation of vowels within Schane's model of particle phonology show in some respects an even closer resemblance to the system outlined in §1.5. Schane operates with three ELEMENTARY PARTICLES, *a*, *i* and *u*, which correspond in isolation to the vowels [a], [i] and [u]. In combination, they represent phonological 'traits', as in (6.3):

(6.3) *i* palatality or frontness
       u labiality or rounding
       a aperture or openness

The parallel with the dependency components of (6.1) is clear. As in Donegan's model, the particles form two groups, with *i* and *u* as manifestations of TONALITY being opposed to the APERTURE particle *a*:

(6.4) (palatality) *i* ——— TONALITY ——— *u* (labiality)

                       APERTURE

                       a

Vowels other than [a], [i] and [u] are represented as combinations of the three elementary particles. Thus, (6.5) gives the representations for a typical seven-vowel system:

(6.5) [i] **i**   [u] **u**
       [e] **ai**   [o] **au**
       [ɛ] **aai**   [ɔ] **aau**
            [a] **a**

Three aspects of Schane's system should be noted. Firstly, representations are system-dependent. Thus, while [a] has the representation **a** in the system in (6.5), it would have the representation **aa** in a vowel system containing [ɑ], which would then be represented as **a**. Secondly, vowel height is linked to the number of aperture particles: addition of **a** to a representation produces a more open vowel. Thus, particles are not involved in any hierarchical relation: the only relation holding between them is that of simple combination. Finally, as a result of the lack of any kind of hierarchical relation, properties can be 'intensified' or 'reduced' in one of only two ways, as in (6.6):

(6.6)   *Intensification*: A property x can be increased either by the addition of x or (in particular, where x is already present) by the removal of an opposing property y.

   Reduction: A property x can be diluted either by the removal of x or by the addition of an opposing property y.

We shall consider below various aspects of natural and particle phonology in relation to dependency representations. However, we first want to examine the basic assumptions made by all three of the models under discussion – that vowels should be defined by properties of the kind outlined above. The discussion will be in two parts: firstly, whether there should be such properties, and secondly, if so, what the phonetic correlates of these should be.

As is well known, there is a great deal of evidence to support the view that /i/, /u/ and /ɑ/ are the phonologically least complex vowels. Jakobson (1968:50) shows that the fundamental vocalic triangle contains /i/, /u/, /ɑ/; these are the vowels acquired earliest in language acquisition, and represent also the minimal vowel system of languages of the world. For Jakobson, such a system is 'characterised fundamentally by the presence of phonemes which combine two distinct qualities'. /u/ is narrow compared to /ɑ/, and velar (or rounded) compared to /i/.

There are, in fact, good phonetic factors underlying the status of vowels in the [i], [u] and [ɑ] regions as phonologically basic. These are just the vowels which are QUANTAL (Stevens 1972). Quantal vowels have the property that more or less the same acoustic effect can be produced with a fairly wide range of articulatory configurations. In other words, the degree of articulatory precision required to produce these vowels is less than for other, non-quantal, vowels such as [ɪ], [e], [œ], etc.

This acoustic – and hence perceptual – effect is due to the convergence of certain formant frequencies for each of the vowels in question, resulting in distinct peaks in their spectra. For [i], F_2 and F_3 are both high, for [u], F_1 and F_2 are both low, and for [ɑ], F_2 is low and F_1 is high. Stevens shows that this effect is maintained even though the tongue position is moved, i.e., that the perturbation caused by the position of the tongue in the supralaryngeal tract may be displaced by up to a centimetre without affecting the acoustic signal. These facts indicate the phonetic basis for assuming [i], [u] and [ɑ] to be the most basic phonological vowels.

Such considerations lead Lieberman (1976:101) to propose a phonetic vowel theory in which 'the quantal vowels /i/, /a/ and /u/ delimit the total acoustic vowel space that defines human speech'. He illustrates this with (6.7), in which the first and second formant frequencies of the vowels of Swedish are plotted on a mel scale (derived from Fant 1971):

(6.7)

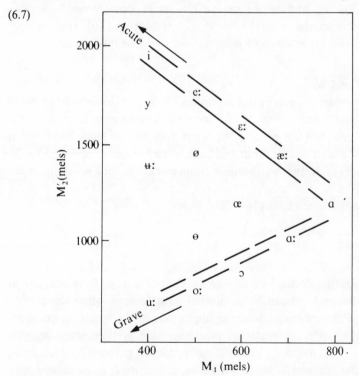

It will be seen from (6.7) that the two axes are labelled 'grave' and 'acute'. However, Lieberman explicitly rejects the binarity assumption, and claims, rather, that these two axes define, in part, the vowel space, and that vowels can be characterised in terms of their *relative* gravity or acuteness.

There are obvious similarities between this 'phonetic' theory and the kind of phonological theory outlined in §1.5, and it is phonetic evidence like this which leads us to believe that the kind of characterisation under discussion here is appropriate and natural. The second aspect of Lieberman's theory 'is quite simple; it is that *quantal* vowels being most useful – easiest to produce while yielding distinct acoustic signals – are the most highly valued vowels of human speech'.

It seems appropriate at this point to investigate further the phonetic properties corresponding to the basic components of the locational sub-gesture. A variety of acoustic and articulatory parameters might be used in the definition of our components. [i], for example, is, in articulatory terms, high, front and unrounded, and in acoustic terms, characterised by a relatively high F_2 and F_3 (i.e. acute, in Jakobson's terms), and a relatively low F_1 (diffuse, as opposed to more open vowels). Similar phonetic characteristics might be derived for [ɑ] and [u], and, indeed, perceptual and other kinds of information might be introduced.

6.1.1 |i| and |u|

Our first problem concerns the definition of the components represented as |i| and |u|, i.e. the 'chromatic' or 'tonality' components, in terms of the Donegan and Schane models. In what follows we shall confine our discussion to high vowels, front and back, rounded and unrounded, i.e. [i], [u], [ɯ] and [y]. In the Jakobsonian framework, the four possibilities are characterised by two 'tonality' features, flat *vs.* plain, and acute *vs.* grave (Jakobson, Fant & Halle 1969:28):

(6.8)   acute   grave
     plain   i   ɯ
     flat   y   u

Flatting is manifested by a downward shift of a set of formants, and at the articulatory level can be associated with (among other things) lip-rounding. For acute segments, the upper side of the spectrum predominates, while for grave segments the lower side predominates: roughly speaking, if F_2 is nearer F_1 than F_3, the segment is grave; if F_2 is nearer F_3 than F_1, the segment is acute. Acute *vs.* grave, then, is associated with cavity variation, and flat *vs.* plain with rounding variation.

The *SPE* system, using articulatorily based features, is that in (6.9):

(6.9)   [−back]   [+back]
     [−round]   i   ɯ
     [+round]   y   u

(where [+ back] characterises retraction of the tongue from the 'neutral' position).

The relationship between the front/back and rounded/unrounded parameters has been examined by Schane (1973). In certain languages one of these two tonality features may be primary. Trubetzkoy (1969:§4.3) notices that three situations are possible. Firstly, tongue position may be primary and lip shape redundant, as in Japanese, in which there are processes which operate before [u o ɑ] (a set of back vowels), but not before [i e] (front vowels). Secondly, lip shape may be primary and tongue position redundant, as in Russian, in which [i] and [ɯ] are allophones of one phoneme, and [u] and [y] of another. Finally, there are languages in which neither can be considered primary, i.e. in Trubetzkoy's terms, the opposition is between front unrounded and back rounded, and is equipollent.

This leads Schane to consider the question of whether backness or roundness (i.e. gravity or flatness) should be considered primary for back rounded vowels. He notices that in redundancy-free feature matrices it is often the case that either backness may be predictable from roundness, or vice versa, and considers a variety of evidence which leads him to propose that frontness is primary for front unrounded vowels, and roundness for back rounded vowels. His examples concern processes such as assimilation in Nupe (from Hyman 1970), in which consonants are palatalised before front vowels and labialised before round vowels, but do not assimilate before /ɑ/, a vowel which is not front and not round. Similarly, he notes that two umlauting processes occur in the history of Icelandic. In *i*-umlaut, back rounded vowels become front under the influence of a following /i/; in *u*-umlaut, front unrounded vowels become rounded (but not back) under the influence of a following /u/. (We return to this in some detail in §6.1.3.) One of Schane's proposals is that instead of [back], the appropriate feature-name is [front], as frontness is primary for vowels such as /i/, /e/ and /æ/.

Such evidence appears to confirm our preliminary characterisation of |i| and |u| in (6.1). The basic articulatory correlate of the perceptual unit |i|, then, is frontness, or palatality, and that of |u| roundness, or labiality. Acoustically, |i| is characterised by acuteness, |u| by gravity, and flatting. These components, of course, are relative to any other components in a particular segment (cf. both Lieberman's and Schane's approaches). A segment with |i| alone will be perceived as fronter and more acute than one in which |i| combines with another component, e.g. |u| (cf. the natural phonology approach).

214 The articulatory gesture

For a language with the vowels /i/, /y/, /u/, then, the dependency representations will be:

(6.10)   {|i|}   {|i,u|}   {|u|}
          /i/   /y/   /u/

Thus the two basic series, in Trubetzkoy's terms, i.e. front unrounded and back rounded, have the simplest representations, while the mixed series, the front rounded, has more complex representations. Further, the natural phonology notion of bleaching and colouring is given a more natural interpretation here. Bleaching, the removal of a colour, is interpreted as the removal of a component (e.g. {|i,u|} → {|i|}), while colouring is characterised as the addition of a component (e.g. {|u|} → {|i,u|}). The status of mixed vowels as less distinctive than pure ones (Donegan 1973:388) is reflected in the representations: |i| and |u| alone are maximally distinctive, containing the maximal possible degree of their respective defining characteristics, whereas the combination |i,u| is shown to be a 'mixture' of the different characteristics, producing a less distinctive vowel.

We consider below (§6.3) the problem of the representation of the back unrounded series of vowels, i.e. those vowels which apparently contain neither the frontness component nor the roundness component.

6.1.2 |a|

The third basic vocalic element, |a|, presents fewer problems. In (6.1) this component was glossed as 'lowness', or 'sonority'. In Jakobson's model low vowels are compact, as opposed to diffuse, i.e. they show a relatively predominant, centrally located formant region. As we have seen, [ɑ] is characterised by high F_1 and low F_2. Associated with compactness is a higher 'phonetic power' than with diffuseness (Jakobson et al. 1969:28). It is this property which leads the natural phonologists to characterise the achromatic vowel property as 'sonority' (open vowels are more sonorous than close ones), and means that the vowel component |a| in our model corresponds with maximal opening on the articulatory level and maximal sonority on the acoustic level.

However, there is clearly a relationship between |a|, as a component within the articulatory gesture, and |V|, as a component of the categorial gesture. Consider the acoustic glosses which we have given the two components: |V| corresponds with maximal periodicity, and |a| with maximal sonority. Vowels, by virtue of their periodicity, are the most sonorous of the categorial segment-types, while open vowels are the most sonorous within the class of vowels. A segment containing |a| alone, then, is the 'optimal' vowel in this respect. On the basis of this, we can view Donegan's 'sonority' axis (cf. Schane's 'aperture' axis in (6.4)) as representing not simply relative preponderance of |a| but, rather, relative preponderance of |V|. The open unrounded vowel, then, might have {|V|} both as the representation of the categorial gesture and of the articulatory gesture. (For a more formal discussion of such representations, see §7.2.)

Although, for expository convenience, we shall not here replace |a| by |V| in articulatory representations, it is interesting to note that a system employing |V| in the articulatory gesture allows a notational distinction between |i| and |u|, corresponding to Donegan's chromatic properties and Schane's tonality particles, and the aperture/sonority component |a|/|V|. This distinction is made in all the models under discussion but is not otherwise formalised in the notation: replacing |a| by |V| shows the difference in type characterised by the various descriptive labels. Indeed, this two-way distinction may underlie the fact that |a| shows many more combinatorial possibilities with |i| and |u| than do the other two components with each other. Thus, in virtually all languages, we find at each height maximally one segment containing both |i| and |u|; in other words, dependency relationships holding between |i| and |u| are not required. |a|, on the other hand, typically displays dependency relationships with both |i| and |u| in vowel systems. (Correspondingly, in Schane's system, *a* is the only particle which can occur more than once in the representation of a vowel.) Within the vowel space, then, it seems that difference in type correlates with increased ability to combine in different ways: components of the same sub-type are resistant to combination.

6.1.3 Old Norse vowel mutation

The appropriateness of the vowel components and of the characterisations we have given them can be illustrated by an examination of the Germanic mutations, whose differential effects (as noted by Schane with respect to Icelandic) are directly associated with the character of the mutating component. Let us consider here only what seems to have happened in Old Norse, particularly Old Icelandic, where mutation is most widely found.

In pre-Norse, a stressed vowel was assimilated to the articulatory position of an [i] or [j] in the following syllable, giving (6.11) (where we consider only the short vowels):

(6.11)   *i/j*-umlaut:

u → y   fylla 'fill' (cf. *fullr* 'full')
         þynnre (comp. of *þunnr* 'thin')
o → ø   nørðri (comp. of *norðr* 'north')
         kømr (pres. sg. of *koma* 'come')
a → ɛ   ketill 'cauldron' (cf. dat. *katli*)
         dreginn (past part. of *draga* 'draw')

Before [u] or [w] in the same circumstances, however, vowels are rounded:

(6.12)   *u/w*-umlaut:

i → y   tryggr 'faithful' (cf. Gothic *triggws*)
e → ø   søkkva 'sink' (class III strong verb – cf. *bresta* 'burst')
         tøgr 'ten'
a → ɔ   hǫggva 'hew'
         ǫrmum (dat. pl. of *armr* 'arm')

(For some discussion see Benediktsson 1959, 1963.) Mutation attributable to an element with the articulatory representation {|i|} involves fronting, or more generally, movement towards the position of [i] (not unrounding); whereas a following {|u|} results in rounding (not backing).

We thus cannot agree with Hockett's claim (1959:595) that:

from the point of view of realism in phonetic change, particularly in assimilations, it is certainly as likely that a back-umlauting of front unrounded vowels should produce unrounded back vowels as it is that a front-umlauting of back rounded vowels should produce front rounded vowels.

The unreality of this 'realism' results in the eccentric analysis of the Germanic mutations offered by Antonsen (1961): see Benediktsson (1963).

In terms of the notation developed here, *i/j*-umlaut involves (6.13):

(6.13)   {|V|}   {V;}
          | → |i| before |
         {~i}   {|i|}

and *u/w* umlaut is:

(6.14)   {|V|}   {V;}
          | → |u| before |
         {~u}   {|u|}

Either an |i| or an |u| is added to the specification of a vowel which previously lacked |i| or |u|, respectively. We have, shift by shift, (6.15):

(6.15)   {|u|} → {|i,u|}   (fylla)
         {u;a} → {i,u;a} (nørðri)
         {|a|} → {a;i}   (ketill)

and (6.16):

(6.16)   {|i|} → {|i,u|}   (tryggr)
         {i;a} → {i,u;a} (søkkva)
         {|a|} → {a;u}   (hǫggva)

(Here again we use ';' to denote (unilateral) government.) Given an input phonetic short-vowel system of the character of (6.17):

(6.17)   {|i|}   {|u|}

              {i;a}   {u;a}

                   {|a|}

i/j-umlaut of [a] gives [ɛ], i.e. {a;i}, and *u/w*-umlaut of [a] gives [ɔ] i.e. {a;u}. That is, they change in accordance with the general convention that they move only one step away from {|a|}, so that |i| is added in (unilaterally) dependent position (cf. our discussion of the English vowel shift in §1.5), though subsequently [e] and [ɛ] do indeed merge. However, an opposition between high mid and low mid front rounded vowels is not established; both *i/j*-umlaut of [o] and *u/w*-umlaut of [e] thus give {i,u,a}, phonologically, rather than {i,u;a}.

The 'asymmetry' of assimilations to [i] and [u] (fronting/raising *vs.* rounding) – let alone the apparently 'dual' character of assimilation to [i] (fronting or raising) – is quite unexpected, and complex to formulate, in terms of representations based on binary (or multi-valued) features, i.e. representations which incorporate the componentially minimal assumption. In these terms we would expect that Hockett's 'realism' would be warranted. The dependency notation, however, provides a transparent characterisation of assimilations to {|i|} and {|u|}.

The non-tonality component |a| triggers only 'incomplete mutation' or 'breaking' of [e], to give a diphthong which undergoes a syllabicity shift (and reduction in complexity of the (new) non-syllabic):

(6.18)   [e] → [eạ] → [i̯a]   hjálpa 'help' (cf. OE *helpan*)
                             hjarta 'heart' (cf. OHG *herza*)

We also find 'breaking' of [e] as an alternative to simple *u*-mutation (under conditions which are uncertain), resulting in an [i̯ɔ] diphthong: *jǫrð* 'earth' (cf. OHG *erda*) – contrast *tøgr* 'ten', from *u*-mutation. Since the rounding in *jǫrð*, etc. can be attributed to the operation of *u*-umlaut (quite regular with [a]), after the syllabicity shift, we can collapse the two 'breakings' as in (6.19):

(6.19)

$$\emptyset \rightarrow \begin{matrix} \{|V|\} \\ | \\ \{|a|\} \end{matrix} / \begin{matrix} \{|V|\} \\ | \\ \{i,a\} \end{matrix} \quad \text{before} \quad \begin{matrix} \{|V|\} \\ | \\ \{\sim i\} \end{matrix}$$

giving the derivations in (6.20):

(6.20)

$$[e] \rightarrow [e\underset{\,}{a}] \rightarrow [\underset{\,}{i}a] \overset{\nearrow}{\underset{\searrow}{}} \begin{matrix} [\underset{\,}{i}\mathfrak{o}] \text{ before } [u] \\ \\ [\underset{\,}{i}a] \text{ before } [a] \end{matrix}$$

$$\qquad \text{breaking} \qquad \begin{matrix} \text{syllabicity} \\ \text{shift} \end{matrix} \qquad u\text{-umlaut}$$

(see Nielsen 1961). For breaking, we can associate the weakness of the influence (incomplete mutation) with the negative character of the trigger.

Neither *u*-umlaut nor *u*-breaking affect [i]; only *u*-umlaut affects [a]: as in *ǫrmum* (dat. pl. of *armr* 'arm'). And, as we have just noted, [e] is affected by either *u*-umlaut or *u*-breaking (in the latter case it is the epenthetic [a] that undergoes *u*-umlaut). If we can regard *u*-breaking as 'incomplete *u*-umlaut', then we can establish a hierarchy of resistance to the influence of {|u|}, such that it affects only {|a|} consistently, {i;a} fully in some instances, incompletely in others, and {|i|} not at all. Again, this hierarchy is reflected in the nature of the representations; the more |i|-like the segment, the greater its resistance to the process.

6.2   Central vowels

The set of vowel components developed so far is adequate for the expression of only a subset of the total set of vowels found in languages; specifically, no combination of |i|, |u| and |a| can account for the articulatory properties of central vowels such as [ə] and [ɨ]. [ə] is not front, not round and not low, and as such, any representation involving only one or more of |i|, |u| and |a|, respectively the components of frontness, roundness and lowness (to use the articulatory glosses of the previous sections), would appear to be unnatural.

This suggests, at least in those instances where [ə] is not a reduction-vowel, the need for a further vowel component – a component with an articulatory gloss CENTRALITY, which we shall represent as |ə|. While we in any case require some component of this sort in order to provide for the phonetic possibilities of language, the data surveyed by Crothers (1978) and Lass (1984b) appear to show that a component with a 'centrality' gloss is indeed phonologically basic, in much the same way as |i|, |u| and |a|, rather than being simply a shorthand notation for ~{i,u,a}.

Consider, for example, vowel systems such as that of Gadsup with a central vowel as one member of a triangular system (Crothers 1978:136; we use here the IPA-type notations proposed by Lass 1984b):

(6.21)   i   u

          ɜ

or that of Quechua:

(6.22)   ɪ   ʊ

          ɐ

with two centralised vowels in the basic system. If we are concerned with the absolute values of the segments involved (as is Lass), rather than with the 'normalisation' strategy of Crothers (who considers both Gadsup and Quechua to be examples of the /i a u/ vowel system-type), then a centrality component will be required as a basic element in the system. Thus the vowels in (6.21) will be represented as (6.23):

(6.23)   {i}   {ə}   {u}

and the Kwakiutl system in (6.24) as (6.25):

(6.24)   i   u

              ə

              ɐ

(6.25)   {i}   {ə}   {a}   {u}

By and large, the principles which we have established concerning representations containing the other three basic components apply to those with |ə|. For example, the Quechua system in (6.22) might have either of the representations in (6.26):

(6.26)   a. {i}   {a}   {u}
          b. {i,ə} {a}   {u,ə}

(6.26a) would be the dependency interpretation of Crothers' normalisation strategy, and would thus characterise only the oppositions involved; (6.26b) would represent a somewhat more 'phonetic' approach, with /ɪ/ /ʊ/ containing |ə| in simple combination with |i| and |u| respectively.

However, representations for /ɪ/ and /ʊ/ incorporating even more phonetic information are possible, as in (6.27):

(6.27)   {i;ə}   {u;ə}

with the centrality component being unilaterally dependent. The choice between the various possibilities in (6.26) and (6.27) depends on the point of view taken with respect to normalisation and phonetic 'responsibility': the notation is flexible enough to allow either strategy to be adopted. Here we note merely that representations such as (6.27) will in any case be required phonetically, while (6.26a) is the minimum required to express the contrasts apparent in the Quechua system; our system of representation must be able to characterise both.

However, although the centrality component is clearly required for the representation of central vowels in systems like (6.21), in which there is a phonemic opposition involved, we should note that in a system in which a schwa-type vowel is non-contrastive, i.e. where it functions as a reduction-vowel, there is no need to invoke |ə| in our phonological characterisation of the system. Specifically, as argued by Anderson & Ewen (1981:21–2), in such systems, in which [ə] is the product of the neutralisation of the other vowel components, it is the vowel which simply lacks these contrastive components: it is non-front, non-round and non-low. In other words, it is the 'minimal vowel'; as such, it is represented by {|V|} alone, and lacks any articulatory specification.

6.3   Back unrounded vowels

It will be noted that no combination of the components developed so far appears at first sight to be available for the characterisation of the set of non-low back unrounded vowels. In fact, a vowel like [ɯ] lacks all four components discussed above, at least if we consider only their articulatory glosses: it is not front, round, low or central.

Back unrounded vowels are comparatively uncommon, perhaps because of their lack of perceptual distinctiveness. Schane (1973:178), too, notices the rarity of the series, and offers the following explanation. For front vowels, lack of rounding is unmarked, and rounding marked, while for rounded vowels, the other basic series, back vowels are unmarked, and front vowels marked. Consequently, marking either 'basic' series produces front rounded vowels. Back unrounded vowels, then, deviate in two respects from the maximally unmarked series.

The characterisation of the back unrounded series in all three models under discussion here diverges in interesting ways from that of other vowel series. Thus, in natural phonology, [ɯ] is treated as colourless or achromatic. As [ɯ] also lacks sonorancy, it also lacks distinctiveness, and is thus disfavoured in phonological systems. Similarly, in particle phonology, [ɯ] is the only 'particleless' vowel – although it should be noted that Schane observes that this does not mean that it is an 'empty' vowel: it still has vocalicness, as do all the other vowels.

In earlier work within dependency phonology, too, back unrounded vowels were treated as the class of vowels not containing |i| or |u|, i.e. as (6.28):

(6.28) $\sim\{i,u\}$

Thus Ewen (1980a:§8.2.1) and Anderson & Ewen (1980b:§4.2) suggest that representations like the following are appropriate for the vowels of the back unrounded series:

(6.29) $\{|\sim\{i,u\}|\}$ $\{|\sim\{i,u\};a|\}$ $\{|\sim\{i,u\}:a|\}$
          /ɯ/   /ɤ/   /ʌ/

While such representations show the relative phonological complexity of this series of vowels as opposed to the other series, they are nevertheless inadequate in a number of respects, discussed by Lass (1984a:277ff). Crucially, in the system outlined above, only /ɯ ɤ ʌ/ are a negative class, 'defined virtually by what they aren't'. All other vowels are positively defined, so that there is a 'notational discontinuity' involved. This clearly arises from the nature of the parameters, together with the fact that dependency components, unlike standard features, are unary: |i|, |u|, and |a| define (articulatorily) orthogonal parameters, and there must inevitably be a point in the universe described by the components which is characterised by their absence. (Notice that this does not appear to hold in the categorial gesture, where |V| and |C| are not wholly orthogonal.) As it does not seem appropriate to treat /ɯ/ as the empty vowel (as noted above, /ə/ has this status in certain systems), we are forced to specify the components which the back unrounded vowels do *not* contain.

Lass proposes a solution to this problem which involves a fairly radical revision of the set of components: |u| is abandoned, and two new components |ɯ| 'velarity' and |ω| 'labiality'/'roundness' are added to the notational system. Essentially, then, we now have components of frontness *and* of backness, with an additive component of roundness, which only appears in combination with one of the other components, to yield representations such as those in (6.30):

(6.30)   {|i|}   {|i,ω|}   {|ɯ|}   {|ɯ,ω|}
          /i/   /y/   /ɯ/   /u/

Notice that Lass explicitly rejects the notion that segmental represent-ations should reflect relative complexity, so that the fact that /ɯ/ contains fewer components than /u/ raises no problems in his approach.

Lass also attacks the normalisation strategy adopted by Crothers with respect to the back unrounded vowels, and taken up by Ewen (1980a). This strategy involves interpreting back unrounded vowels under certain circumstances as being central; and thus means a step away from phonetic accuracy. Thus the vowel system of Naga:

(6.31)   i   ɯ   u
            ε   ə   ɔ
              ä

is treated by Crothers as if it had two non-low central ('interior') vowels; i.e. as if /ɯ/ were the high counterpart of the central vowel /ə/. By treating back unrounded vowels as central (in the absence of a corresponding central vowel in the system), we certainly avoid the notational problems associated with (6.29), but we are clearly reducing the content of part (a) of the natural recurrence assumption (although notice that Maddieson 1984:167 observes that [ɯ] is acoustically, perceptually and auditorily 'quite centralised').

However, this does not force us to follow Lass in abandoning the basic principle underlying the system as presented so far. For while the back unrounded vowels are clearly 'neither |i| nor |u|' from the point of view of the articulatory glosses for the two components, things look rather different when their acoustic and perceptual properties are taken into account. Consider, for example, (6.32), an acoustic formant chart for the cardinal vowels, taken from Catford (1977:187), where the value of F_1 is given on the vertical axis, and that of F_2 on the horizontal. Here the back unrounded vowels are more or less intermediate between their front unrounded and back rounded counterparts. This is suggestive of a representation containing both |i| and |u|, rather than one lacking the two components altogether. However, such a representation is already required for the representation of front rounded vowels, so the simple combination of |i| and |u| for the back unrounded series would be

(6.32)

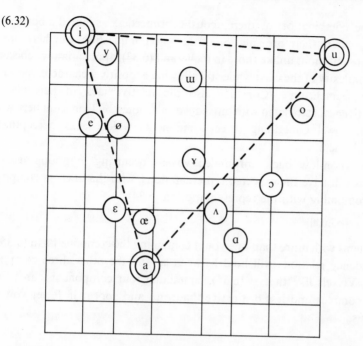

inadequate. Nor does it seem appropriate to suggest that [y] and [ɯ] both contain only |i| and |u|, with a difference in relative prominence, as in the set of representations in (6.33):

(6.33)   {|i|}   {|i;u|}   {|u;i|}   {|u|}
          /i/   /y/   /ɯ/   /u/

Such representations (apart from any considerations of complexity) would suggest that there is an acoustic gradient from {|i|} to {|u|}, which does not seem to be the case, given the apparently divergent status of [ɯ] with respect to notions such as chromaticity and distinctiveness.

Rather, it seems appropriate to utilise the fact that back unrounded vowels are acoustically similar to central vowels – but not in the way proposed earlier. We suggest that back unrounded vowels incorporate the centrality component in their representations, as well as |i| and |u|. /ɯ/, then, will have the representation in (6.34):

(6.34)   {|ə,i,u|}

Notice again that although an inspection of the articulatory glosses of the various components suggests that (6.34) should represent a vowel which is central(ised), front, and round, rather than the back unrounded [ɯ], the combination of their acoustic properties, as noted above, is appropriate to the representation of the vowel in question. Furthermore, the representation, unlike those in (6.30) and (6.33), appropriately reflects the complexity of the class while still allowing a 'positive' characterisation of the segment-type. Consider also the relative lack of perceptual distinctiveness associated with 'mixed' vowels, noted by Donegan: here we have a vowel containing three components which lacks perceptual distinctiveness.

Other non-low back unrounded vowels occurring in phonological systems will have the expected representations, with the lowness component combining with the representation in (6.34):

(6.35)   {|ə,i,u,a|}

In systems with more than one vowel containing the components in (6.35) dependency relations will hold between |a| and the other three components. Vowels like that in (6.35), containing four components, are still more complex and less distinctive than /ɯ/, and appear in fewer vowel systems.

6.4   Vowels: a minimal phonemic set

In the previous sections we were concerned with establishing the set of primes required for the description of vowels. However, what is it that these primes must be able to describe? In other words, which vocalic segment-types occur in phonological systems and thus require distinct representations in the notation?

This problem is discussed by Lass (1984b:§7), although not with respect to notational systems as such. Rather, he is concerned with establishing the number of 'basic' vowel types in phonological description, on the basis of two principles, given as (6.36):

(6.36)   i. *Phonemic Availability Principle*
         Any pair of qualities that contrast phonemically in some language are primitive.

         ii. *Dialect Distinguishability Principle*
         Any pair of qualities capable of consistently signalling a dialect difference within one language, and therefore available as speaker choices, are primitive.

'Primitive' vowel-types are those which cannot be taken as 'counting as a variety/type of' something else, so that, as noted above, [ɯ] and [ɨ] are distinct primitives.

On the basis of these two principles, Lass sets up the grid given here as (6.37), which contains the traditional three dimensions: five degrees of height on the vertical axis and five degrees of backness on the horizontal axis, with lip attitude running 'diagonally':

(6.37)

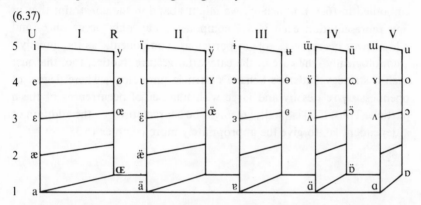

This grid is claimed to show all segment-types occurring in language and meeting the criteria imposed by (6.36). Where there are no known examples of a segment-type meeting the criteria, we find an empty point on the grid.

If (6.37) indeed represents some kind of universal patterning, then it seems reasonable to demand of any notational system that it can distinguish all of the segment-types appearing on it. However, if we attempt to do this with the dependency representations established here, we appear immediately to run into problems. For consider the number of vowel-types in category I: i.e. front unrounded. Here we find /i e ɛ æ a/; i.e. there are four vowels which apparently must be represented as combinations of |i| and |a| alone. However, the notation developed so far allows us only three combinatorial possibilities: {|i;a|}, {|i:a|} and {|a;i|}. But this may not be a serious problem. For consider the 'gaps' in the grid. Nearly all of these are at level 2: indeed only [æ] and [ǣ] appear here. Furthermore, as Lass points out, the contrast [æ]:[a] meets only Principle (ii), but not (i); in other words, [æ] and [a] never contrast phonemically. (Lass does not discuss the status of the [ǣ]:[ä] contrast, although this apparently occurs in many American dialects of English in minimal pairs such as *can* (n.) *vs. con.*) It may well be, then, that (6.37) is too 'fine-grained' for our purposes, at least with respect to the height dimension.

We suggest, then, that it be replaced by a grid with just four heights, lacking the categories [æ] and [ǣ].

Notice that this does not mean that the notation is in principle unable to represent [æ] or [ǣ]: it would be perfectly possible, and, indeed, perhaps desirable, to relax the constraints on the types of representation developed so far in order to be able to incorporate more phonetic detail than is embodied in (6.37). Crucially, we might abandon the constraint that in any representation each vowel component may only occur once, and allow two occurrences of a particular component, as is already – phonologically – the case in the categorial gesture. Notice, too, that just such a strategy underlies Schane's particle phonology, where degree of openness correlates by and large with number of occurrences of the *a* particle. Thus, if [ɛ] is {|i:a|}, [æ] might be characterised by the addition of a dependent |a|, to give the appropriately more complex (6.38):

(6.38)   i:a
           |
           a

We shall not explore the consequences of this here: indeed, we shall not consider any further the question of phonetic representation. Rather, we shall now investigate another problem associated with the grid in (6.37), its shape. Observe that the shape of the grid disguises the traditional triangular interpretation of the vowel space. Specifically, it fails to show that there is a distinction between the high and low vowel areas such that the amount of 'articulatory space' at Lass's heights 2–1 is less than at, say, height 5. (This indeed may be the reason for the lacunae at heights 2–1.) Clearly, this is relevant to the dependency representations developed here in so far as they predict that there will be one vowel, represented as {|a|}, which is the 'optimally' low or sonorant vowel. We suggest, then, that Lass's grid should be adapted in such a way as to incorporate this, and in (6.39) we give a dependency interpretation of this revised grid. Notice that this revision is merely in presentation: it retains the minimum phonemic inventory proposed by Lass (with the exception of [æ] and [ǣ] noted above), and thus incorporates a characterisation of all the segment-types proposed by Lass. These segment-types can all be given a natural representation using the principles established so far. Several points should be noted, however.

Firstly, as noted in §6.1.2, |i| and |u| do not show dependency relations with each other, whereas |a| and |ə| do enter freely into relations, both with

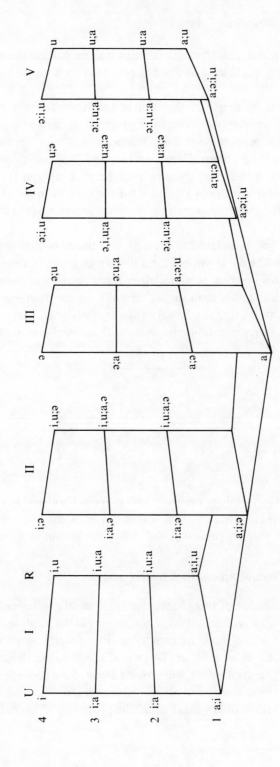

(6.39)

each other, and with |i| and |u|. (Compare again particle phonology, where the tonality particles *i* and *u* are restricted to a single occurrence per segment.)

Secondly, the simple combination of |i,u| denotes a front rounded vowel unless it is unilaterally or mutually governed by |ə|, when, on the basis of the acoustic properties involved, it represents a back unrounded vowel.

Thirdly, the representations {|a;ə;i,u|} and {|a;əːi,u|} do indeed characterise the low back unrounded vowels [ä] and [ɑ], and thus occupy the lowest slots in categories IV and V for the back unrounded vowels. {|a|}, as suggested above, represents the 'optimal' low vowel [ɐ], i.e. a low *central* vowel.

Lastly, {|ə|} is assigned to the high unrounded central vowel [ɨ], rather than to [ə] (the cover symbol for a further unspecified unrounded central vowel). This involves an articulatory interpretation of |ə| involving non-peripherality, rather than simply centrality in the front–back dimension. Schematically, then, any vowel in the non-peripheral area in (6.40) will have |ə| in its representation (together with the back unrounded vowels, as discussed above):

(6.40)

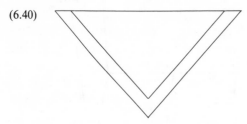

Peripherality in this sense, then, differs from Crothers' interpretation of segment-types, in which front rounded vowels are also treated as non-peripheral. Our assignment of {|ə|} to [ɨ] accords with its status as non-low.

6.5   Place of articulation: feature systems

In the remainder of this chapter we shall mostly be concerned with the problem of the representation of consonants in the locational sub-gesture, an area in which there appears to be little general agreement on some crucial issues, as we shall see. Our contribution to this debate will consist of a set of proposals which will provide a basis for a dependency treatment of place of articulation and associated matters. In what follows we do not intend to review in any great detail the proposals which have been made for feature treatments of place. However, it will be useful to consider some aspects of various approaches, both binary and multi-valued.

In the minimally componential theory of *SPE*, place of articulation is principally defined by the two binary features [anterior] and [coronal]. [+ anterior] sounds are those produced 'with an obstruction that is located in front of the palato-alveolar region of the mouth', and [+coronal] sounds are those 'produced with the blade of the tongue raised from its neutral position' (*SPE*:304). These two features yield the following distinctions among various places of articulation:

(6.41)	labials labio- dentals	dentals alveolars	palato- alveolars	palatals velars uvulars pharyngeals
[anterior]	+	+	−	−
[coronal]	−	+	+	−

Labials are distinguished from labio-dentals by means of the feature [distributed] – labials ([+ distributed]) being 'produced with a constriction that extends for a considerable distance along the direction of the air flow', as opposed to labio-dentals ([− distributed]) (*SPE*:312). We return in §6.8 to the relevance of [distributed] to the making of distinctions among sounds which are [+ anterior, + coronal], i.e. among dentals and alveolars.

As is apparent from (6.41), body of the tongue consonants are all [− anterior, − coronal]. These can be distinguished by the use of the features [high], [low] and [back], i.e. the features also used to distinguish vowels, as in (6.42) (from *SPE*:305):

(6.42)	palatals	velars	uvulars	pharyngeals
[high]	+	+	−	−
[low]	−	−	−	+
[back]	−	+	+	+

We can distinguish various kinds of criticisms of the *SPE* system, of which three are particularly relevant to the following discussion. Firstly, there is evidence which has led various phonologists to propose replacing the binary feature system with a multi-valued one (see §1.7). Secondly, but related to the first point, there have been various suggestions that it is possible to set up hierarchies of strength, such that certain places of articulation can be considered to have a 'stronger' position on the hierarchy than others with respect to their phonological behaviour.

Thirdly, a number of phonologists have suggested, while retaining the binary system (at least in some cases), that certain recurrent classes cannot be adequately characterised by the system given above, and so, on the natural recurrence assumption, have proposed new features to remedy this apparent defect.

In the immediately following sections we return to some detailed discussion of this last area, as it is particularly relevant to the proposals we will make below, while in the remainder of this section we consider the first two types of criticism.

Multi-valued systems have been proposed by, among others, Ladefoged (1971, 1975) and Williamson (1977). Perhaps the most important reason advanced for a multi-valued treatment of place is that 'neither the tongue nor the roof of the mouth can be divided into discrete sections' (Ladefoged 1971:37). Nevertheless, Ladefoged's 'multi-valued' feature [articulatory place] has ten distinct phonetic categories ranging from [bilabial] to [glottal]. No language, according to Ladefoged, makes a phonological opposition amongst more than six types.

Various phonological arguments in favour of a multi-valued interpretation of place are offered by Williamson (1977). They include the fact that nasals are frequently homorganic with following consonants; if a multi-valued feature system is used, only a single variable is required to express this (cf. the problems associated with a binary approach discussed in §1.3). In addition, she notes that rules often involve adjacent places of articulation.

It is not relevant to our concerns here to pursue these arguments in any detail. However, we should note that Williamson interprets the feature [place] as a scalar feature, with 'the central vowel position' being the most neutral, thus having the value 0, and the other values ranging from 6 (bilabial) to −4 (glottal). This assignment of values apparently arises from Williamson's belief that 'the neutral, "unmarked" value of a feature is that which is, other things being equal its most common value in speech' (1977:859). This theoretical viewpoint means that she must find a neutral position for [place] somewhere near the centre of the scale. This is achieved by an appeal to the notion that the tongue position for [ə] is in some sense the neutral position (rather than *SPE*'s [e] (or [ɛ])). It is not clear to us whether there is any phonological evidence to support this claim; Williamson offers one argument whose validity is not obvious, viz.: 'a further reason for regarding the neutral position as central on the scale is that, of the three most common places of articulation for consonants (labial, alveolar/dental, velar), it is the velar one, adjacent to the central one, which most commonly weakens or is lost entirely'. The implication of this with respect to a scalar feature would appear to be that we should expect phonological processes to favour deletion of values towards the centre and reinforcement in some way of values towards the extremes of the scale – as far as we know, this is not the case.

As both Ladefoged and Williamson note, a multi-valued feature of place cannot, in itself, characterise the cross-classificatory properties of different places. Thus, features such as [apicality], [labiality] and [gravity] are proposed for the characterisation of natural recurrent groupings of (not necessarily adjacent) values of the feature [(articulatory) place]. We return to the motivations for each of these features in the following section; however, given the existence of such cross-classificatory prop-erties, it is appropriate to ask whether there is in fact any phonological motivation for a place of articulation feature which is multi-valued. If adjacency of place of articulation is not in general a relevant notion for phonological processes, then an ordered scalar feature such as Williamson's is inappropriate, while the existence of cross-classificatory processes suggests that an *unordered* multi-valued feature is simply not relevant in the phonology.

Finally in this section, let us consider whether there is reason to set up a hierarchy of 'strength' holding between the various places of articulation. Such a hierarchy would, of course, be expected to support the view that there is a scalar relation between the places of articulation (whether or not the hierarchy corresponded to adjacency of place). Proposals of this kind (particularly associated with the work of Foley – see, e.g., 1977:25ff) assume that relations between places of articulation can be set up on the basis of the propensity of each class to undergo certain processes. Thus Foley notes that spirantisation of intervocalic voiced stops occurs in various languages (North German, Danish, Spanish). However, there are restrictions on how this spirantisation can be manifested. Specifically, the only possible combinations are the following:

(6.43) a. g   → ɣ   / V — V (North German)
        b. g   d   → ɣ   ð   / V — V (Danish)
        c. g   d   b → ɣ   ð   β / V — V (Spanish)

Thus, Foley claims, spirantisation may affect only the velars and not the others (a), or only the velars and dentals and not the labials (b), or all three places (c); but no other combination is possible. This he regards as 'a manifestation of an abstract relation among phonological elements, which we call α. The relation α is the relative phonological strength of elements appearing phonetically as velars, dentals, and labials' (1977:28), as in (6.44):

(6.44)   g   d   b
          ——————→
          1   2   3
          relative phonological strength α

Foley cites various pieces of evidence to support this claim. Notice that his 'phonetic manifestation principles' allow the α scale to be realised differently in different languages. Thus, we find (1977:49) the 'particular consistent principle': 'though the phonetic manifestation of phonological elements may vary from language to language, it does not vary within any particular language'. In Germanic, then, Foley claims, the manifestation of the α relation is different from that in Romance languages (which is that given in (6.44)). Since in Germanic dentals strengthen in preference to labials they must be interpreted as stronger, thus giving (6.45) (Foley 1977:50):

(6.45)   g   b   d
          ——————→
          1   2   3
          relative phonological strength α (Germanic)

Because Foley rejects part (b) of the natural recurrence assumption (i.e. that natural recurrent classes must have a phonetic basis), he is not interested in providing a phonetic explanation for these differences, a belief which renders him immune to the kinds of arguments that have been offered against this point of view. It has, however, been claimed in various places that there is little evidence for such positional strength hierarchies, if given a universal phonetic interpretation, in that the evidence as to which positions are stronger than others is so contradictory.

Thus Lass & Anderson (1975:§5.4) show that the 'α relation' is different in different languages, and even within a single language – Hungarian shows strong velars in intervocalic position, but weak velars and labials in initial position. Katamba (1979), too, cites various similar phenomena in Luganda and Aho Bantu languages. Seeing that we adopt the natural recurrence assumption as a whole, the existence of so many (phonetic, in Foley's terms) counterexamples means that we cannot adopt the notion that the places of articulation can be hierarchically ranked on a strength scale. The most that can be claimed, we believe, is that among the three major positions there appears to be some evidence that velars show a greater propensity to weaken than either of the other two. Notice also that Jakobson's universals of language acquisition predict that velars are acquired later than the other two types. As such, then, they would be phonologically more complex than the other major articulation-types.

We assume, then, that there is no conclusive evidence for a hierarchical relation amongst different places of articulation, and we shall not, therefore, attempt to characterise this relation in the dependency representations which we will establish in §6.7.

6.6 Gravity, linguality and apicality

In this section we examine some proposals which have been made with respect to the systems outlined in the previous section. Some involve proposals to remedy deficiencies in the binary system of *SPE*, specifically the introduction of features to characterise recurrent classes not catered for there. Others are put forward by the proponents of a multi-valued feature of place for much the same reason. This is not the appropriate place to investigate these issues in any depth; rather, we intend to look at only those arguments which are relevant to the proposals which we shall make for the characterisation of place in dependency phonology, and then only in the broadest outline. For detailed discussion of the various issues, the reader is referred to the appropriate sources.

6.6.1 Gravity

One of the most important areas in which there have been proposals for the introduction of new features is the characterisation of labials and velars. We can distinguish two main types of arguments – those leading to the proposal for the introduction of an articulatory feature [labial], and those which suggest reincorporating the Jakobsonian 'acoustic' feature [grave].

Arguments for the introduction of [labial] are put forward by S. R. Anderson (1971), Reighard (1972) and Campbell (1974), among others. Anderson, while keeping the rest of the *SPE* framework intact, suggests the introduction of a feature [labial], in addition to [round], which would characterise all 'primary' labial consonants, in view of the existence of apicalised labials in the phonological inventory of languages such as Nzema. The segment /p͡t/ in Nzema, then, would have the features

[+anterior, +coronal, +labial, −round]. Articulatorily, he argues, the postulation of both [labial] and [round] can be defended by the fact that there are two distinct types of labial closure: the rounding type, controlled by the *orbicularis oris* muscle, and the type involved in the production of (unrounded) labials such as [p], [b] and [m], i.e. raising of the lower lip, controlled by the *mentalis* muscle.

The other group of proposals in this area concern the reintroduction of the Jakobsonian feature [grave]. Grave sounds show predominance of the lower side of the spectrum. The arguments for the use of the feature concern primarily the fact that labials and velars form a recurrent class in languages. Thus Hyman (1973) records instances in which velars change into labials historically, and in which front vowels become back before labials and velars. The *SPE* features are not appropriate for the characterisation of this natural class, although in languages which have phonologically only labials, dentals, and velars, the class can be unambiguously defined as [−coronal]. As Lass points out (1976:206ff), this is a 'negatively' defined class: it is not clear why the fact that there is no raising of the blade of the tongue involved in these sounds should make them a natural class. In Trubetzkoy's terms, [−coronal] apparently represents the negative term of a privative opposition, rather than one of the terms of an equipollent opposition. Lack of raising in no way *explains* the fact that this is a natural recurrent class. Even worse, in a language which has phonemic palatals, the set of labials and velars cannot be shown to form a class at all, as palatals are also [−coronal]. The characterisation of the recurrent class involves something like (6.46):

$$(6.46) \quad \left\{ \begin{array}{c} \begin{bmatrix} +\text{ant} \\ -\text{cor} \end{bmatrix} \\[2ex] [+\text{back}] \end{array} \right\}$$

Similar arguments are advanced by other writers, for example Davidsen-Nielsen & Ørum (1978), who suggest that certain assimilation processes in Old English and Danish involve [gravity].

It is not our intention to pursue these arguments any further; we take it that there is sufficient evidence of this sort to indicate the need for a feature, or component, of [gravity]. It will be recalled, indeed, that the component |u| proposed above for the characterisation of vowels was also acoustically glossed as 'gravity', and in §6.7 we will show how this component can be incorporated into the representations characterising place of articulation. We will also show that there is no need for a 'labiality' component as such. In the meantime, however, we turn our attention to another set of proposals arising from the existence of recurrent classes undefined by the Chomsky & Halle feature system.

6.6.2 Linguality

Lass (1976:ch. 7) surveys a range of sixteen processes from the history of English and from Modern English 'involving considerable recurrence and similarity'. These processes involve fronting, high vowel epenthesis, and raising. He suggests that there is a recurrent grouping of segments triggering these processes, consisting of high front vowels, dental, alveolar, palatal and velar consonants, and possibly also high back vowels. This, he argues, is a class that cannot be characterised in the *SPE* system – crucially because dentals (and alveolars) differ from velars, palatals and high vowels in their values for the features [anterior], [coronal], and [high].

Lass's solution to the problem of characterising this natural class is the introduction of a feature [lingual], which he defines as follows (1976:187–8): 'horizontally speaking, all predentals and postvelars are [−ling], and dentals, palatals and velars are [+ling] (as are high vowels . . .)'. Because uvulars are not produced with primary activity of the blade or body of the tongue they are not [+lingual]. High vowels are [+lingual] because they are unique among the vowels in that they alone might be said to have 'homorganic' consonants. He concludes that the various processes can all be characterised as involving an assimilation towards linguality; 'non-lingual vowels become lingual before linguals (or after them), the diphthongizations insert the appropriate [+ling] vowels in environments marked the same way, and so on'.

6.6.3 Apicality

As we noted above, the *SPE* feature [distributed] is used to make certain distinctions in the dental and alveolar region. Thus (*SPE*:312) laminals are [+distributed] (involving a constriction that extends for a consider-able distance along the direction of the air flow) as opposed to apicals, which are [−distributed]. Similarly, retroflex sounds are [−distributed], while non-retroflex sounds are [+distributed]. Thus, [ʃ] [+distributed] can be opposed to retroflex [ʂ] [−distributed], where the constriction is relatively short. Notice, too, that this feature can also be used to distinguish alveolar fricatives, e.g. [s] ([+distributed]), from dental fricatives such as [θ] ([−distributed]).

The feature [distributed] has been criticised on various grounds, notably because it obscures the difference in *place* of articulation between, for example, [s] and [θ]. Further, Ladefoged notes that the claim which Chomsky & Halle make with respect to laminal and apical articulations, i.e. that no language makes an opposition between two apical articulations in the dental/alveolar (i.e. [+anterior, +coronal]) region, is falsified by the nasal series of Malayalam, in which the dental, alveolar, and retroflex nasals are all apical. This leads Ladefoged (1971) to propose a feature [apicality], for which tip of the tongue consonants have the value 0, and blade of the tongue sounds the value 1. Retroflex consonants are characterised as having the value [retroflex] for the [place] feature.

Williamson (1977) proposes an extension of the [apicality] feature to include retroflex sounds, as in (6.47):

(6.47)   1 blade of tongue as articulator   (laminal)
          0 tip of tongue as articulator   (apical)
          −1 underside of tongue as articulator   (retroflex)

The argument against characterising retroflex consonants as one of the values on the [place] feature is that retroflex sounds differ not in the passive articulator (which is often the same as for non-retroflex post-alveolar sounds), but in the active articulator; in the same way as laminal and apical sounds may have the same passive articulator (notice, however, that the difference between laminal and apical sounds appears never to be phonologically contrastive in itself).

Finally, Spencer (1984), in terms of a standard binary feature system (but one in which the *SPE* feature [lateral] is abandoned), proposes that both [apical] and [distributed] are required, with [distributed] being distinctive for continuant sounds: thus, the apical lateral /ɬ/ differs from apical /s/ in being [+distributed].

6.7   The dependency representation of place

Let us see how these various facts about natural recurrent classes and their characterisation can be incorporated into a system of representation using the kinds of components we have postulated in the rest of Part II. We consider first the representations of the three 'basic' places of articulation – labials, dentals/alveolars, and velars.

In §6.1 we noted that the component |u|, used in the characterisation of back vowels, has an acoustic correlate similar to the Jakobsonian feature [grave]; i.e. the more prominent |u| is, the greater is the predominance of the lower part of the spectrum. We assume then that the component |u| forms part of the representation of labials and velars, thus enabling their status as a natural class to be characterised, together with the class discussed by Reighard (1972), i.e. that of labial consonants, [w], and rounded vowels ([w] will have the same representation in the articulatory gesture as [u], differing only in its specification in the categorial gesture). All these segments, then, contain |u| in the articulatory gesture.

Velars can be distinguished from labials by the presence in their representation of a component of LINGUALITY |l|. Segments displaying this component in their representation are produced with the blade or body of the tongue as an active articulator. However, we do not interpret this component as some sort of 'second-order' or 'cover' feature, as does Lass, who claims that [lingual] is 'classificatory' but never distinctive. Rather, we suggest that this component has the same status as any other, giving the following characterisations for the three main places of articulation:

(6.48)   {|u|}   {|l|}   {|l,u|}
          labials   dentals/alveolars   velars

These representations will be adequate for the characterisation of a phonological system utilising only the three-way opposition in (6.48). Thus labials are characterised as containing |u| alone, while dentals/ alveolars contain only the linguality component. Velars, however, contain both components and, as such, can be shown to form natural recurrent classes with both labials and dentals. Further, velars have a more complex representation than the other positional classes. As noted in §6.5, what evidence there is appears to suggest that velars are phonologically more complex than labials and dentals; in this respect, then, the natural recurrence and complexity assumptions are satisfied.

For the moment, we postpone the question of whether |l| is also required in the characterisation of high vowels, as suggested by Lass for [lingual]; it may well be that these vowels redundantly show |l| in their representation, thus allowing the characterisation of the linguality assimilation processes discussed by Lass. However, it seems likely that |l| will have only a classificatory function for high vowels.

A system containing phonemic palatals in addition to the positional types in (6.48) might be expected to have a parallel representation for the palatals, i.e. that in (6.49):

(6.49)   {|l,i|}
         palatals

However, certain difficulties arise with respect to this representation. As is well known, velar consonants typically palatalise under the influence of front vowels, while palatals do not velarise under the influence of back vowels. This appears to parallel the situation with vowels: one of our arguments for glossing |u| as roundness rather than backness concerned the behaviour of vowels in similar environments. Thus the fronting of back rounded vowels under the influence of a front vowel is a natural assimilation process, given as (6.50):

(6.50)   {|u|} → {|i,u|} / — {|i|}

However, the change of, say [k] to [c] preceding [i] can not be shown to be more natural than that of [c] to [k] preceding [u], given the representations proposed here:

(6.51)   a. {|l,u|} → {|l,i|} / — {|i|}
         b. {|l,i|} → {|l,u|} / — {|u|}

Formally, (6.51a) and (6.51b) are equally complex. We might expect, then, that the palatalisation process represented by (6.51a) should, like that in (6.50), involve addition of a component, rather than replacement. This would give {|l,i,u|} as the representation for palatals, allowing a natural formulation of the process characterised as (6.51a). However, it is not clear that the presence of |u| is appropriate – certainly, the expected articulatory properties of |u| would suggest that such a representation would be that of a rounded palatal (although these are more appropriately dealt with as involving secondary articulation: see §6.8.1). Any such interpretation, then, would depend on taking the articulatory scope of |u| in consonants to include the whole tongue body when combined with |l|. Independent motivations for such an assumption are far from well established, however. We offer no definite solution to this problem here.

6.7.1   Apicals and laminals

We turn now to the dental/alveolar region. As we have seen, various kinds of opposition can be made within this area. Consider first of all the 'positional class' of post-alveolars. Ladefoged (1971:40) notes that there is probably no reason to distinguish these consonants phonologically from palatals: all languages which use both these places have stops in one position and affricates in the other. Similarly, Lass (1976:188–9) claims that palato-alveolars are not a true positional class, even phonetically. Rather, as their name suggests, they are palatalised alveolars, i.e. alveolars with a secondary palatal articulation. We consider these sounds, therefore, along with other double and secondary articulations, in the following section.

The distinction between laminal, apical, and retroflex segments, as we noted above, again does not involve different positional classes; rather, the distinction is between different uses of the active articulator. Languages do not appear to make oppositions amongst more than two of these classes; thus Ladefoged (1971:39) notes oppositions between apical dentals and laminal alveolars in Temne, between laminal denti-alveolars and apical alveolars in Isoko, and between laminal denti-alveolars and apical retroflexes in Ewe.

We propose the introduction of a component of APICALITY, |t|, whose characterisation will be similar to that of Williamson's multi-valued feature [apicality]. That is to say, three possible configurations can be represented, as in (6.52):

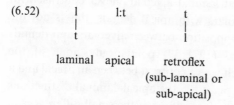

(6.52)

l	l:t	t
laminal	apical	retroflex
		(sub-laminal or
		sub-apical)

It will be noted that retroflexes show |t| in governing position, whereas they have a negative value for Williamson's [apicality] feature. We believe that (6.52) more successfully shows the relation of the tip of the tongue in the segment-types in (6.47) to the role of the blade of the tongue. For the laminals, the blade is more 'important' than the tip, and hence governs; for the apicals the tip is more important and the blade less important; and for retroflexes, *only* the tip and underblade can make actual contact with the passive articulator because of the nature of the configuration of the tongue.

However, as the above indicates, no language makes a three-way phonological opposition amongst these segment-types, although all occur phonetically. The two-way oppositions which are found all involve a distinction between {|l;t|} and {|t;l|} (or perhaps between {l,t} and {|ll|}, depending on the system in the language in question, and/or the nature of the segment-types involved). Thus, as in the case of the glottal opening component in the initiatory gesture, or of the characterisation of vowels above, it is the function of a particular segment-type in the phonological system which determines its representation: the same phonetic type may have different representations in different languages.

Notice that the relative complexity of systems involving phonological oppositions in this area is reflected both by the need to introduce the component |t| in phonological representations, and in the introduction of dependency relations between components.

6.7.2   Dentals and alveolars

The apicality component might also be used to characterise the difference between various other segments which are distinguished by means of the feature [distributed] in the *SPE* model. Thus, apical [s] might be distinguished from laminal [ş] and from sub-laminal (retroflex) [ṣ] by the relative prominence of |t| (while palato-alveolar [ʃ], as noted above, will be treated as an alveolar with secondary palatalisation). However, although the component |t| can distinguish laminals from apicals, and dentals from alveolars, on the assumption that laminal alveolars never contrast with laminal dentals, nor apical alveolars with apical dentals, this is not the ideal way of characterising the opposition between alveolars and dentals in all languages. As Ladefoged (1971:39) points out, 'none of the languages that I have heard myself uses a contrast between an apical and a laminal articulation at the same place . . . the apical–laminal distinctions could be said to function simply as intensifiers of the small differences in the place of articulation'.

It seems preferable, then, to characterise the alveolar/dental distinction directly, i.e. by means of a component concerned with the passive, rather than the active, articulator. This does not mean, however, that the laminal/apical distinction is not required. Clearly, it is necessary to be able to characterise the opposition between retroflexes and non-retroflexes, and it is also needed to specify whether a particular sound – e.g. English /d/ – is *phonetically* laminal or apical. (Notice that Spencer 1984 uses both [apical] and [dental], as well as [distributed], in his feature system.)

The appropriate way of representing the opposition directly is by means of a component of DENTALITY, represented as |d|. This component will be required, in any case, to distinguish labials from labio-dentals, phonetically in most languages but phonologically in, for example, Ewe, which shows an opposition between bilabial and labio-dental fricatives (see Ladefoged 1971:38). This opposition will be represented as:

(6.53)   {|u|}   {|u,d|}
           labials   labio-dentals

A language employing this opposition is shown to have a more complex system than one which does not, because of the presence of |d|. In languages such as English, |d| will be required only in phonetic realisation rules; phonologically, both bilabial stops and labio-dental fricatives will be characterised simply as {|u|}.

The component |d|, then, can also be used to make the distinction between dentals and alveolars in languages where this phonological opposition is required. Thus Temne /t̪/ *vs.* /t/, and English /θ/ *vs.* /s/ might both be characterised as follows:

(6.54)   {|l,d|}   {|l|}
           dentals   alveolars

Again, relative system-complexity is characterised by the need to have |d| in phonological representations.

What we have here, then, is a case of two parameters – dental articulation *vs.* alveolar articulation, and apicality *vs.* laminality – which are phonetically independent and which must therefore both be characterised in our system of representation. The decision on whether to characterise a particular opposition by means of |d| or |t| depends on the phonologist's interpretation of the data in the language in question, but it seems likely that, by and large, the direct representation of the dental /alveolar distinction by the use of |d| is more appropriate. However, there are cases in which both are required. In the Malayalam data given by Ladefoged (1971:40) we find dentals, alveolars and retroflexes, all of which are apical. The high degree of complexity of the Malayalam nasal system, which also has bilabials, palatals and velars, is shown in (6.55):

(6.55)   u   l,d   l   t   l,i   l,u
                       | |
                       t   l
           /m/ /n̪/   /n/   /ɳ/   /ɲ/   /ŋ/

where both |d| and |t| are required, as well as |l|, |i|, and |u|. Notice that |t| will also be present in the phonetic representation of (apical) /n̪/, which will have the characterisation {|l,d,t|}; cf. (apical) alveolar /n/, which has

{|l,t|}. Both |t| and |d| are 'secondary' components in that, unlike |u| and |l|, they cannot occur alone in the articulatory gesture. Rather, the occurrence of |t| is restricted to segments which are specified as {l}, while |d| can only occur with |u| or |l|. If this is a constraint imposed on the system of representation, the characterisation of /ɲ/ in (6.55) as {|d|} is precluded, even though it would be formally unambiguous.

6.7.3   Uvulars and pharyngeals

Chomsky & Halle, as we saw in (6.42), characterise uvulars as [−high, −low, +back] and pharyngeals as [−high, +low, +back]. In other words, uvulars have the same 'body of the tongue' feature-values as [o], and pharyngeals the same as [ɑ].

For pharyngeals, especially, this feature-assignment has been criticised on the grounds that 'the front–back distinction is concerned with the configuration of the *upper surface* of the tongue', while pharyngealisation 'involves an approximation of the rear or *root* of the tongue to the pharyngeal wall' (Sommerstein 1977:102).

This point is also raised by Lass & Anderson (1975:18) with respect to the distinction between uvulars and pharyngeals. They claim that the distinction is not of degree of lowness, as the Chomsky & Halle features would suggest, but of backness, caused by the tongue root retraction associated with pharyngeals. They note further that the vowels cognate to uvulars are not mid vowels, such as [o ɔ], as would be expected from the *SPE* features, but low back vowels. This leads them to characterise uvulars as [+low].

Thus we might argue that uvulars should be characterised as containing both |a|, the 'lowness' component, and |l|, the 'linguality' component, as in (6.56):

(6.56)   {|l,a|}

However, it will be recalled that uvulars are excluded from the set of segments having the positive value for Lass's [lingual] feature, because they do not trigger the linguality assimilation process, and because 'uvulars and pharyngeals, even though the tongue is involved in them, are not made with primary activity of either the blade or body' (1976:188). It is not clear to us, however, that this is the case, at least as far as the uvulars are concerned, given Catford's (1977:160–3) account of these sounds. He distinguishes *dorso-uvulars* (produced with the surface of the tongue) from two types of pharyngeals: *faucal*, produced without use of the tongue, and *linguo-*, produced with retraction of the root of the tongue. A second problem which arises is that uvulars must be considered to be grave, and hence to have the |u| component in their representation.

We are not sure how to evaluate the various possibilities for the representation of uvulars – i.e. which of |l|, |u| and |a| should their representation contain? This hesitancy arises partly from the fact that there is little information on the status of these segments with respect to their behaviour in natural recurrent processes, information which might give more support to the claim which we make here, i.e. that uvulars should be represented as:

(6.57)   {|l,u,a|}
         uvulars

As far as the representation of pharyngeals is concerned, it is clear that |l| can in any case not be used. It may well be, however, that |a| is required (at least phonetically), but the status of |u| is more problematical. Although some phonologists have interpreted pharyngeals as grave (see, for example, Davidsen-Nielsen & Ørum 1978:210, who consider Danish [ʁ], [ɒ], and [ɑ] to be grave and pharyngeal), Ladefoged (1971:102) states that pharyngeal sounds are not grave. As far as |a| is concerned, Ladefoged (1971:80) suggests that [ħ] (a voiceless pharyngeal fricative) and [ɑ] share the features pharyngeal, back and low; notice, too, that Davidsen-Nielsen & Ørum characterise [ɑ] as pharyngeal.

In any case, however, |a| (with or without |u|) is not in itself sufficient for the characterisation of pharyngeals. Rather, it seems that pharyngeals must be characterised more directly (cf. the case of dentality above); that is, we need a component whose presence defines a pharyngeal articulation. This is a proposal which can be found in various distinctive feature treatments.

The relevant phonetic property appears to be width of the pharynx, which in turn is controlled by tongue root retraction (Lindau, Jacobson & Ladefoged 1973). Thus, Williamson (1977) and Lindau (1978) have a multi-valued feature [expanded], whose phonetic correlate is the size of the pharynx. We assume tentatively that pharyngeals are characterised by a component |r| RETRACTED TONGUE ROOT (and consequent pharyngeal narrowing), giving the possible representation in (6.58):

(6.58)   {|r,(u),a|}
         pharyngeals

Again, further evidence is required to determine the appropriate charac-
terisation of pharyngeals at different levels in the phonology. Clearly, {|r|}
alone will be sufficient to distinguish pharyngeals phonologically, but it
may well be that |a| (and perhaps |u|) may function as 'second-order'
components in particular phonological processes.

A similar mechanism is also used in a rather different area, that of vowel
harmony, in a number of languages. Thus Lindau (1978:550) notes that
many Niger-Congo and Nilo-Saharan languages show systems in which
the vowels of the language divide into two sets, the members of each of
which must harmonise within the morpheme. These two sets differ in the
size of the pharynx, as controlled by variations in the positions of the root
of the tongue and the larynx. (6.59) shows the segments occurring in the
Akyem dialect of Akan:

(6.59)   Set 1   Set 2
         i   u   ɩ   ʊ
         e   o   ɛ   ɔ
            a   ʌ

Various features have been proposed for the characterisation of the
difference between the two sets. Thus, Chomsky & Halle (*SPE*:314–15)
have [covered], with [+covered] sounds having a narrower and tensed
pharynx and raised larynx, while Ladefoged (1975:266) has [wide] (i.e.
width of the pharynx). Halle & Stevens (1969) have simply the feature
[advanced tongue root] ([ATR])–cf. Lindau *et al.* (1973)–a proposal
which dates back to Stewart (1967:196ff) and which is now used in
various autosegmental approaches to the type of vowel harmony processes under consideration.

Clearly, the same mechanism is involved in these vowel harmony
processes as in pharyngealisation. In dependency terms, then, the
difference between the two sets participating in vowel harmony processes
might be characterised as:

(6.60)

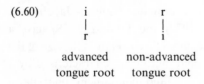

       advanced   non-advanced
     tongue root   tongue root

However, there is a great deal of evidence that in the overwhelming
majority of tongue root harmony systems the advanced set is dominant, so
that the equipollent nature of the representations in (6.60) is inappropri-

ate. It is this asymmetry between the advanced and non-advanced sets which suggests that in a binary framework [advanced tongue root] rather than [retracted tongue root] is the appropriate feature, so that the dominant property has the '+' value for the feature, and in an autosegmental approach is involved in spreading from one vowel to another.

Phonetically, however, the situation is not quite so straightforward. Hall & Hall (1980:207) note that the tongue root can be pulled forward by the *genioglossus* muscle, and retracted by the *glossopharyngeus* muscle, and that a two-way opposition can involve phonetically: (a) advanced tongue root *vs.* retracted tongue root; (b) advanced tongue root *vs.* neutral tongue root; or (c) neutral tongue root *vs.* retracted tongue root.

For [+ATR] dominant systems, then, it is clear that, in common with other single-valued approaches, we require an ADVANCED TONGUE ROOT component, which we shall represent as |α|. In systems like Akan, the dominant set will show |α| in combination with the normal vowel representations, while the recessive set will simply lack the component, as in (6.61):

(6.61)   {|i,α|}   {|i|}
         /i/   /ɪ/

It may be the case that in those few languages in which [−ATR] is dominant, e.g. Nez Perce (see Hall & Hall 1980), |r|, rather than |α|, is the element involved in the harmony process, so that the dominant set shows |r| in its representations, with the more advanced tongue root vowels simply lacking the component.

6.7.4 Laterals

The treatment of laterals is quite straightforward. As in nearly all the systems of representation, we propose a component of LATERALITY, |λ|, which is defined as involving lowering of the side(s) of the tongue. Thus non-lateral alveolar liquids will be distinguished from the corresponding laterals as in (6.62):

(6.62)   {|l|}   {|l,λ|}
           non-lateral   lateral
           alveolar liquid   alveolar

We do not, then, adopt Spencer's (1984) proposal, which is to abandon the feature [lateral], on the grounds that all lateral segments are by definition also [+distributed]: we prefer to characterise the property directly.

We have now allowed for the expression of a large range of the possibilities with respect to place of articulation and the recurrent classes operating within this area. It still remains, however, to consider double and secondary articulations, and the oro-nasal sub-gesture.

6.8   Secondary and double articulation

Phonetically, at least, we can distinguish two types of 'co-articulation': COORDINATE (or DOUBLE) ARTICULATION, and SECONDARY ARTICULATION (Catford 1977:188). In the case of double articulation, the two articulations have the same degree of stricture, while in primary and secondary co-articulation, the secondary articulation is of lower structural rank than the primary articulation (i.e. it has a more open degree of stricture).

6.8.1   Secondary articulation

Ladefoged (1971:62) distinguishes four types of secondary articulations: labialisation, palatalisation, velarisation and pharyngealisation. In *SPE*, palatalisation, velarisation and pharyngealisation are characterised by the assignment of a '+' value for at least one of the tongue-body features ([high], [low] or [back]) to a non-tongue-body consonant (i.e. one which is [+anterior] and/or [+coronal]). The tongue-body features for a secondary articulation are the same as those for the corresponding primary articulation, so that a palatalised alveolar, say [sʲ], differs from palatal [ç] only in the values for [anterior] and [coronal]: [high], [low] and [back] have the same values for both segments. Chomsky & Halle claim that their account shows why palatalisation, velarisation, and pharyngealisation do not occur with tongue-body (i.e. [−anterior, −coronal]) consonants, that it shows that primary and secondary articulations at the same place of articulation have the same tongue-body features, and that the secondary articulations are mutually exclusive. Labialisation is treated as the addition of [+round] to the primary articulation.

Ladefoged (1971) considers consonants with secondary articulations to have added vowel-like characteristics. Thus, these consonants have values for backness and height as well as place of articulation, so that [kʲ], for example, is [velar, front, high]. This notation, unlike that in *SPE*, allows the characterisation of the palatalised velar [kʲ], i.e. a tongue-body consonant with secondary articulation. Labialisation is again handled by the addition of the [+ round] feature value to the place feature; thus [bʷ], with the values [bilabial, + grave, + round], is distinguished from [b] only by the value for [round].

Williamson (1977:857–8) has a rather different solution to the problem of the representation of such segments. She claims that in the production of consonants with secondary articulation, 'the two articulations cannot be described as exactly simultaneous', and proposes that they should be assigned two successive values for the relevant features, i.e. [stricture] and [place], as in (6.63):

(6.63)   [bʷ]   [bʲ]   [bᵚ]   [bˤ]
        stricture   2/0   2/0   2/0   2/0
        place   6/6   6/1   6/−1   6/−3

(where [2 stricture] is stop and [0 stricture] approximant; [6 place] bilabial, [1 place] palatal, [−1 place] velar, and [−3 place] pharyngeal).

Whatever the phonetic merits of such a proposal, its phonological appropriateness seems dubious. There seems to be no particular reason to suggest that what is involved here is phonologically a stop *followed* by an approximant; indeed it would have unfortunate repercussions for the notion that the order of segments within the syllable can be predicted according to a hierarchy of sonority, as syllable-final consonants with secondary articulation would violate this hierarchy in such a proposal. In addition, the representations in (6.63) fail to show that one of the phases of the consonant is primary. We shall see below that Williamson's proposal for the characterisation of double articulations involves a rather similar strategy, but one in which no sequencing is involved; however, the distinction between the two types of articulation (double and secondary) can only be represented by means which are formally quite arbitrary.

In the dependency model, secondary articulations can be given a rather obvious interpretation. Consonants showing secondary articulation are, at least phonologically, single segments, in which the components characterising the place of the secondary articulation are subjoined to those characterising the place of the primary articulation. Thus, palatalis-ation, velarisation and pharyngealisation might be represented as (6.64):

(6.64)   l   l   l
              | | |
             l,i   l,u   r

        palatalised   velarised   pharyngealised
         alveolar   alveolar   alveolar

Palato-alveolars, we argued above (following Lass 1976), are in fact alveolars with secondary palatalisation. As such, then, they will have the representation for the 'palatalised alveolars' in (6.64).

It seems reasonable to suggest that in palatalisation, the dependent |l| can be suppressed phonologically, in that any secondary articulation involving |i| must be palatalisation; contrast this with velarisation, in which |l| cannot be suppressed, as the presence of dependent |u| alone denotes labialisation:

(6.65)   l
            |
            u

        labialised
        consonant

We might then associate the asymmetry between palatalisation in the environment of front vowels and velarisation in the environment of back vowels (see §6.7) with this difference in the nature of the representations of the two phenomena: velarisation requires an extra component in its representation as compared with palatalisation.

As we noted above, it does not seem necessary to introduce a distinct component of labiality in addition to |u|. The distinction between rounded and unrounded labials will thus be represented as in (6.66):

(6.66)   u   u
                        |
                        u

        labial   rounded labial

Other less common secondary articulations such as labio-dentalisation and uvularisation can be characterised in the same manner, i.e. by subjunction of the appropriate representations to that of the primary articulation.

6.8.2   Double articulation

The characterisation of double articulations has proved problematical to proponents of binary feature theories. Jakobson *et al.* (1969:22–3) consider double stops to be 'but special forms of consonant clusters'. Apparently, then, they are to be treated as two segments, a position which runs into the same problems as Williamson's interpretation of secondary articulations, namely that it obscures the fact that the two articulations are simultaneous and function phonologically as a single segment.

Chomsky & Halle (*SPE*: 311) consider the problem of labio-velars (or, more correctly, labial-velars), i.e. the sounds represented as ⟨kp⟩ in various languages, and notice that such sounds have to be characterised either as labials with extreme velarisation or as velars with extreme rounding, utilising the same notational mechanism as for secondary articulations. The choice between the two possibilities for labial-velars depends on phonological, not phonetic, evidence. This viewpoint is defended extensively by S. R. Anderson (1976), who argues that phonetically identical labial-velars may be interpreted as labials (with superimposed velarisation) or as velars (with superimposed labialisation), according to purely phonological considerations. The arguments which he adduces are principally distributional, but he also cites evidence from various phonological processes in which, for example, labial-velar [w] is replaced in some languages by [g] (and hence must be treated as a velar), and in other languages by a labial obstruent (and hence is a labial). This interpretation, however, forces the treatment of one of the articulations of a double articulation as primary, even though there may not be any phonological evidence to support this in a particular case. Ohala (1979), as part of an attack on the emphasis put on structuralist considerations in an approach like Anderson's, cites phonological evidence which shows that the treatment of either the labial or velar slot as primary cannot be maintained. He concludes that the tendency for labial-velars to behave as labials in some environments and as velars in others is due to physical phonetic causes arising from the different nature of the two constrictions. In addition, it can be observed that at the phonetic level we need to be able to specify that the two degrees of stricture are equivalent, and so it seems appropriate to have some mechanism in the phonological framework whereby double articulations can be directly specified.

This interpretation is apparent in the multi-valued frameworks of Ladefoged and Williamson. Ladefoged (1971) has simply two additional values for the feature [place], i.e. [labio-velar] and [labio-alveolar], while Ladefoged (1975) makes use of the feature [labial]. Thus, [k͡p t͡p w ɥ] have the value [velar] for the [place] feature, and are also [+ labial]. Williamson, however, assigns to labial-velars two simultaneous specifications for the feature [place], as in (6.67):

(6.67) | | [k͡p] | [w] |
| --- | --- | --- |
| stricture | 2 | 0 |
| place | $(-1/6)$ | $(-1/6)$ |

Williamson's representations for double articulations, in which the two specifications for [place] are simultaneous, and for secondary articulations, in which the two specifications are successive, differ only (as far as [place] is concerned) in the presence of brackets around the values for the double articulation. It is difficult to see this as anything other than a notational diacritic.

The structural properties available within dependency theory allow a simple representation of double articulations. Such articulations can be very simply characterised as:

(6.68)   {|C|}   {|C|}   {|V;V,C|}
              | | |
          {|l,u|,|u|}   {|ll,|u|}   {|l,i,u|,|u|}
             [k͡p]   [t͡p]   [ɥ]

i.e. as involving simple combination, and sequential non-distinctness, holding between the elements of the locational sub-gesture. Thus, double articulations are interpreted in a very traditional way, in which the notion of the articulations having the same strictural rank is represented by a single categorial specification, together with the fact that neither articulatory specification is dependent on the other.

6.9   The oro-nasal sub-gesture

As will be expected, the oro-nasal sub-gesture contains just one component, a component of NASALITY |n|. Articulatorily, this component involves lowering of the velum, thus allowing air to escape through the nasal cavity. Alveolar nasals will have the articulatory representation in (6.69):

(6.69)   {|l,n|}

It will be noted that we now have two means of characterising nasals uniquely – by the representation {|V;C|} in the categorial gesture, and by the presence of |n| in the articulatory gesture. It may be asked why such a double characterisation is necessary. Clearly, there are two distinct phonetic parameters involved, parameters which determine the behaviour of nasal consonants with respect to natural recurrence. Nasal consonants, by virtue of their acoustic properties, form a natural class with the other sonorant consonants, and as such share certain characteristics in the representations of the categorial gesture. However, they also have to be characterised as forming a natural class with nasalised consonants and nasalised vowels (segments which may have quite different categorial specifications); this recurrence is determined by the presence of a lowered velum, i.e. by the component |n|. Thus (6.70) shows the representations for various nasal(ised) segments:

(6.70)   {|V;C|}   {|V|}   {V,C;V}
              | | |
              | | |
          {|l,i,n|}   {|i,n|}   {|l,n|}
            [ɲ]   [ĩ]   [ž̃]

Notice that there is evidence to suggest that there is at least one language in which |n| shows dependency relations with other components, although usually (as in (6.70)) it only occurs in simple combination. Both Ladefoged (1971:35) and Catford (1977:139) cite the case of Chinantec, in which the minimal set /ha/∼/hã/∼/hã̃/ is found, involving an opposition between two different degrees of nasalisation. The vowels would have the articulatory representations in (6.71):

(6.71)   a   a   n
                | |
                n   a
          /a/   /ã/   /ã̃/

Finally, observe that the status of the nasal stop as the 'prototypical' nasal category is reflected by the fact that only in these segments can the nasality component |n| be omitted phonologically. As we have seen, nasal stops have a double characterisation, and so any segment containing {|V;C|} is, by definition, nasal. For all other nasal segments, nasality must be specified, as the categorial type is shared by other non-nasal segments.

PART III

OVERVIEW

7 Dimensions of phonological representation

In Part III we attempt to draw together various aspects of the preceding discussion, and we also touch on some issues which are relevant to the assessment of any model of phonological representation, but which have not as such been considered so far.

Chapter 8 is devoted to the relationship between representational and other aspects of phonological theory; in this chapter, however, we consider the relationship between segmental and suprasegmental representation, and the nature of the 'segment' itself, together with the nature of the distinction between lexical and utterance phonology. The organisation of the chapter is from small to large: we begin with a discussion of relationships within the gesture, i.e. the smallest structural units within which phonological primitives are organised, and end with suprasegmental structure.

7.1   Intragestural relationships

As we noted in §1.3, the framework of *SPE* is minimally componential in that there is no attempt to organise the phonological primitives into sub-groupings within the segmental feature matrix, nor is there any variety in the type of relationships holding between the primitives in the model; i.e. all segments are characterised by an unordered set of features, each of which can have only the value '+' or '−', at least phonologically. The notion of GESTURE provides the sub-grouping lacking in the *SPE* model (see the discussion in the introduction to Part II); here we want to look in rather more detail at the way in which the incorporation of dependency relations overcomes some of the other problems associated with minimal componentiality.

Within the model developed here the degree of structural variety is much greater than that within any binary or multi-valued feature system, or, indeed, within any single-valued system which does not incorporate

255

hierarchical relations between the features or components. As far as intragestural structure is concerned, segments may differ from each other in the number of components present, in the number of occurrences of individual components (e.g. $\{|V:C|\}$ *vs.* $\{|V:C;V|\}$), and in the structural relations holding between the components (e.g. $\{|i,a|\}$ *vs.* $\{|i;a|\}$ *vs.* $\{|i:a|\}$ *vs.* $\{|a;i|\}$). This greater structural variety allows a correspondingly greater richness in segmental representation, while at the same time constraining the ability of the notation to express a number of non-recurring and, *a fortiori*, non-occurring segment-types.

Thus, as noted in §1.3, the combination [+high, +low] is formally possible in the minimally componential *SPE* notation, though substantively undesirable (because of the non-orthogonal nature of the parameters characterised by the features in question), and has to be excluded by two universal Morpheme Structure Conditions of the type in (7.1):

(7.1)   a.   if: [+high]   b.   if: [+low]
                        ⇓   ⇓
              then: [−low]   then: [−high]

Similar rules are required for other pairs of non-orthogonal features. The need to postulate any universal redundancies such as those characterised by (7.1) must be seen as a deficiency of the notation: the notation predicts the occurrence of segment-types that necessarily cannot occur. The characterisation of phonological structure should in itself ideally be such as to render impossible the representation of any universally non-occurring segment-types.

Consider too the related, though less severe, problems associated with multi-valued feature systems, and, indeed, with Schane's particle phonology. In these models the notation is inherently unable to restrict the number of distinctions that can be made by any multi-valued feature. Thus, a system involving a multi-valued feature [high] in no way characterises the fact that languages with more than four or five distinctive degrees of vowel height are not recorded – [6 high] (or even [42 high]) is formally no more or less complex than [4 high] or [1 high], while in Schane's system, in which vowel height is characterised by the number of instances of the *a* particle, a representation such as (7.2) cannot be excluded:

(7.2)   **aaaaaai**

Even though (7.2) is, apparently appropriately, characterised as more complex than a representation such as **aai**, this does not provide an appropriate metric; thus, in a system containing at least two front mid unrounded vowels, the representation for /ɛː/ (**aai**) would be more complex than that for /eː/ (**ai**), although the motivation for this remains unclear.

As we have seen, the structural properties of the dependency model considerably reduce the number of instances of this problem, or, at the very least, make the expression of increasingly unlikely segment-types increasingly complex.

However, it is unrealistic to expect of any notational system that the expression of apparently universal non-occurrences should be totally excluded. There is clearly a conflict between the desire to keep the expression of such non-occurring segment-types to a minimum and the excessive reductionism (see Lass 1984a:§5.1.1) which may result from this strategy. A reductionist approach such as that of Jakobson involves the expression of phonological oppositions within a notational system which is not required to express all the relevant *phonetic* parameters; consider the acoustic feature [flat], subsuming three articulatory variables which, it is claimed, are never contrastive within a single language. The model resulting from this approach clearly fails to achieve any close match between phonological primitive and phonetic parameter – or even to come near to Schane's (1984b:§4) rather more abstract concept of 'mirroring'. The extent to which the goal of mirroring is reached is measured by 'how accurately the notational system is able to track the nature of the events it describes'. In the case of [flat], too, the model fails to differentiate between an articulatorily variable unit with which the feature is perhaps most commonly associated (lip rounding) and others which are less prevalent.

However, as not all phonetic parameters interact freely in phonological systems and processes, any approach in which relevant phonetic parameters are mirrored on a one-to-one basis by phonological primes will also run into problems of the sort noted above, i.e. a number of non-occurring combinations of primes can be specified within the formalism used. Thus, within the notational system for place of articulation discussed in §6.7, the representations in (7.3) are well-formed, given the constraints on representations within the locational sub-gesture, yet apparently do not occur as phonologically distinctive segment-types in language:

(7.3)   l   u,t

                                   |
                                  u,r
        labialised pharyngealised   apical labial
        (alveolar) stop

It is not that these combinations cannot be excluded by redundancies such
as those which apply to |t| and |d| (see §6.7.2), whereby the presence of the
former in an articulatory gesture presupposes |l|, and that of the latter
either |l| or |u|. These redundancies define hierarchical relationships
between components, rather than simply rendering particular combinations universally impossible (as does (7.1)). However, unsupplemented
by redundancy rules, the notation does provide for a fuller range of
possibilities than appears to be attested.

It seems to us that erring on the side of over-generation of segmental
representations is less reprehensible than excessive reductionism, particularly if such reduction as is invoked in the notation already involves an
intrinsic complexity metric: less prevalent segment-types are more complex to express. Given a commitment to part (b) of the natural recurrence
assumption, the greater degree of phonetic responsibility arising from this
must be more highly valued than the advantages of restricting the number
of phonological primes and thus failing to render the less prevalent more
complex.

We claim, then, that of the various notational systems for the
representation of segments discussed above, that of dependency phonology most successfully meets Schane's goal of mirroring, by steering
between the two extremes of excessive reductionism and over-generation.

7.2   Gestures and the segment

In our discussion so far we have viewed segmental representation as being
essentially the minimal interaction of the representations of the various
gestures and sub-gestures proposed in Part II, as illustrated by the abstract
matrix in (II.13). But we have not as yet discussed the problem of what
exactly constitutes the segment as such, though some relevant considerations were introduced in §§3.6.3–4. It is clear that there are circumstances
in which there is not necessarily a one-to-one relation between one gesture
and another. The existence of phenomena such as these has, of course, led
to the development of various versions of the model of autosegmental
phonology, originating with Goldsmith (1976). In such models, as is
familiar, a number of tiers are postulated for the characterisation of

phenomena in which certain features – i.e. autosegments – have domains which are not coterminous with those of other features. As noted above, however, the notion of tier is not equivalent to that of gesture – separate autosegmental tiers were established only for processes in which a feature behaves autosegmentally (although it has recently been claimed that *all* features may occupy distinct tiers – see Clements 1985). Thus, in a language which shows vowel harmony, such as Hungarian, the harmonising features will be extracted from the rest of the segmental representation and placed on a separate tier, as in (7.4) (see Clements 1976):

(7.4)   O + fItI + I

         + ATR

where (7.4) is the underlying representation for $o + fiti + i$ (from the root *fiti* 'to pick'), or in terms of a single-valued system based on the components of dependency phonology, (7.5):

(7.5) $|i|_w$

   {|V|}   {C}   {|V|}   {C} + {C}   {|V|}   {C}
     | | |
   |a,u| |a,u| |a|

   örömnek 'joy' (dat.)

where $|i|_w$ is a word-level autosegment of frontness (see Ewen & van der Hulst 1985). Notice that one feature of what we have termed the locational sub-gesture occurs on one autosegmental tier, while the other features which would be assigned to this sub-gesture remain on a separate tier. In so far as one might want to recognise autosegmental status as involving a distinct gesture, this remains secondary and language-particular, or at least typologically restricted (see further §7.6).

In autosegmental phonology, too, the question of what constitutes a segment arises, and, in relation to this, we find proposals in various recent versions for a number of different kinds of tiers. Thus in the CV phonology of Clements & Keyser (1983), representations contain (at least) three tiers, as in that for *Jennifer* in (7.6):

(7.6)   σ   σ   σ

        C   V   C   V   C   V   C

        d   ʒ   e   n   ɪ   f   r

We shall not here be concerned with the syllabic tier, whose elements are represented by σ. Rather, we wish to consider the relationship between the other two tiers – the CV TIER and the SEGMENTAL TIER. The segmental tier has a 'vocabulary' consisting of single-column phonetic matrices characterising consonants and vowels in the usual manner (1983:25), i.e. standard feature matrices (although notice that in the framework of Clements 1985, the segmental tier itself has a complex internal structure). The CV tier, on the other hand, has various functions. Firstly, the elements of this tier represent functional positions in the syllable, any segment being dominated by V being interpreted as a syllabic peak, any dominated by C as a non-peak. In addition, they can be interpreted as sub-syllabic units of timing. Perhaps most relevant for our discussion, however, is that the 'useful but ill-defined notion of "phonological segment" can best be reconstructed at this level' (1983:11). Thus, in cases where there is not a one-to-one correspondence between the CV tier and the segmental tier (as in the first C in (7.6)), it is the number of elements on the CV tier, rather than the number of elements on the segmental tier, which determines the number of phonological segments. The affricate in (7.6), then, is interpreted as a single segment, associated with two sequentially distinct feature matrices.

More generally, the CV tier is seen as the SKELETON of phonological representation, in that it is associated not only with the syllabic and segmental tiers, but also, where appropriate, with other autosegmental tiers, such as the nucleus tier, or language-specific tiers required for particular processes.

How is the notion of segment to be defined in dependency phonology? Do we need to incorporate a tier – or perhaps gesture – corresponding to the CV skeleton proposed by Clements & Keyser, or are the elements of dependency phonology in themselves sufficient to characterise the phonological segment?

It seems to us that there is no need to propose a structural tier whose *sole* status is functional, in serving to define the phonological segment, for example. A tier of this sort is only required in the model discussed above because of the failure to assign sufficient internal structure to the 'segmental' tier, i.e. to the tier with phonetic content. Specifically, it is the fact that Clements & Keyser do not separate the categorial features of the segmental tier from the articulatory features which forces them to introduce an extra structural entity. In a model in which appeal is made to a division of the segment into gestures, this problem is overcome. The need to postulate a separate CV tier arises essentially from possible mismatches between categorial and articulatory specifications, i.e. situations in which, for example, one categorial specification corresponds to two articulatory specifications (often giving rise to 'complex segments' – see §7.3). But the representations of the categorial gesture (specifically the phonatory sub-gesture) correspond to the elements of the CV tier in the sense that they too define the distinction between syllabic peak and syllabic non-peak (in terms of the relative prominence of |V|). Moreover, they are available for interpretation as units of timing in exactly the same way, and thus convey the same information about segment status. Due to the independently motivated decision to assign greater structure to the feature matrix (or its dependency equivalent), we do not have to introduce a tier which is purely structural in function.

In this interpretation, then, the CV tier is replaced by the categorial gesture, and the segmental tier by the articulatory gesture. These two gestures can be associated in exactly the same way as the two relevant tiers in the autosegmental model. Thus, a syllable such as *mad* will have the following representations in the two models:

(7.7)   C   V   C   (7.8) {|V;C|}   {|V|}   {|C;V|}
        | | |
        m   a   d   {|u|,n} {|a;i|} {|ll|}

(where the elements on the segmental tier in (7.7) are, of course, merely abbreviations for the appropriate feature matrices, while the dependency representations of the articulatory gesture in (7.8) are in themselves complete).

As noted above, Clements (1985) proposes an extension of the autosegmental model in which all features occupy separate tiers. These feature tiers are further grouped into 'class tiers', consisting of a root tier, a laryngeal tier, a supralaryngeal tier, a place tier and a manner tier. Of these, the root tier is superordinate to the others, with the nodes on this tier being directly related to the CV tier. Thus *mad* will have the partial representation in (7.9). 'This conception resembles a construction of cut and glued paper, such that each fold is a class tier (labelled *aa'*, etc.), the lower edges are feature tiers, and the upper edge is the CV tier' (1985:229). It is claimed by Clements to correspond to a fundamental characteristic of speech production, namely that it is 'componential', in that it involves the 'coordination of simultaneous and partly overlapping gestures'. In (7.9)

(7.9)

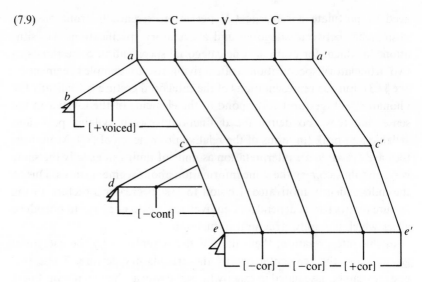

aa' = root tier, bb' = laryngeal tier, cc' = supralaryngeal tier, dd' = manner tier, ee' = place tier

the first node of the root tier is linked by association line to all the features of [m], and so on.

It will be clear that Clements' approach has much in common with the model adopted here, although, in spite of the rather different formalism adopted, the internal structure of the segment which he assumes resembles most closely the 'enriched' theory of Lass (1976) (see §1.3.1). With respect to our current concerns, (7.9) makes no crucially different claims about the relationship between the segmental representations and the CV tier than does (7.7): segmental status is still determined by the CV tier.

The characterisation of elements such as long vowels involves the same mechanism in both the CV and the dependency models. In both cases, a single element on one 'level' is associated with two on the other, so that the representation of [iː] would be:

(7.10)

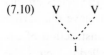

(Here we omit the braces and verticals for the dependency representation.) The interpretation of the symbols in (7.10) differs according to the model under consideration. 'V' is either a structural element on the CV tier or a representation (with 'phonetic' content) within the categorial gesture, while 'i' is either an abbreviation for a feature representation or the representation for the high front articulation within the articulatory gesture, i.e. {|i|}.

The dependency model, then, appears to be able in principle to dispense with the extra structural apparatus required by the CV model. However, we still have to consider the status of complex segments, such as the affricate in (7.6) or the prenasalised consonants discussed in §3.6.3. These items, like long vowels, involve two specifications on the segmental tier and only one on the CV tier, but in dependency phonology appear to differ from long vowels in that they also involve two categorial specifications – in the case of (voiceless) affricates, a stop ({|C|}) followed by a homorganic fricative ({|V:C|}). We turn now to a brief consideration of the representation of complex segments in dependency phonology.

7.3   Complex segments and intrasegmental adjunction

It is not our intention to reiterate here the discussion of §§3.6.3–4. However, it is relevant to our concerns in this chapter to consider the relationship between the categorial and articulatory gestures in the representation of complex segments and other related items such as long vowels and diphthongs.

7.3.1   Complex segments
In §3.6.3 we outlined two possible ways of approaching complex segments such as prenasalised consonants, in which the relationship between linear order and the sonority hierarchy is violated. One approach, that of Ewen (1982), involves a direct translation of the violation of the hierarchy into a characterisation within the categorial gesture in which the normal relation between precedence and dependency is reversed, so that Tiv /mbè/ will be represented (schematically) as in (7.11):

(7.11)

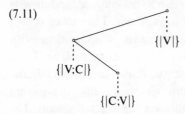

A similar structure is proposed for syllable-initial *sC* clusters, which have also been interpreted as single phonological units by some writers (e.g.

Kohler 1967; Fudge 1969). Arguments are also adduced for treating affricates as involving reversed dependency structures, although in this case on phonological grounds rather than because they display violation of the sonority hierarchy. The notion of complex segment, then, is associated with the structure displayed by all three types, and instantiated by (7.11). It is claimed that the fact that all these cases involve two phonetic – specifically categorial – events functioning as a single phonological unit is reflected by the reversed dependency structure which, it is suggested, is non-committal with respect to the question of whether such phenomena constitute one or two phonological segments.

The alternative approach involves a commitment to the view that the items under discussion form single segments. Here it is the segment itself which is internally complex, involving intrasegmental adjunction of one categorial representation to another. Thus, prenasalised consonants are treated in this view as a sub-class of stops, and hence show |C;V| governing |V;C|, rather than the reverse:

(7.12)

$$\{|C;V|\}$$

$$\{|V;C|\}$$

Similarly, (voiceless) affricates have the structure in (7.13):

(7.13)

$$\{|C|\}$$

$$\{|V:C|\}$$

Whichever approach towards the representation of these phenomena is adopted, the generalisation that the segmental status of any item is determined by its categorial representation can be maintained, and there is again no need to have recourse to a structural CV tier. Thus Ewen (1982) argues that the status of prenasalised consonants is ambivalent with respect to mono- *vs.* multi-segmentality, in that a structure such as (7.11), while involving three separate phonetic 'events', shows immediate adjunction of the first consonant to the syllabic element, while the second consonant is subordinate to the syllabic only via the first consonant. The more 'intimate' relation of the marginal consonant and the syllabic than in the unmarked case, on the one hand, and the presence of three sequential units, on the other, can be associated with the 'intermediate' status of complex segments: we have a gradient between segment and sequence on which complex segments occupy an intermediate position.

If, however, as perhaps in the case of *sC* sequences, we decide on a bisegmental interpretation, the appropriate representation in this approach is that in (7.14):

(7.14)

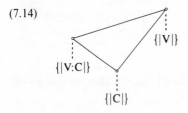

where there is a further (direct) adjunction between the stop and the syllabic: here we have only violation of the sonority hierarchy, but no reduction in length. Thus the fact that prenasalised consonants are typically closer to the length of single segments than *sC* sequences is appropriately represented.

This approach to the representation of complex segments assumes that the appropriate dependency structure arises only after application of the normal dependency assignment rules (see §3.4). Lexically, they are represented simply in linear sequence, with no hierarchical structure. In the alternative view of affricates, where such structures are interpreted as representing a segment with internal structure – i.e. as involving the adjunction of a sub-segment – (7.13) will also be the lexical structure: in this case, exceptionally, the dependency relation is lexical.

But notice that on either view, the generalisation we drew in §7.2 can be maintained. That is, the status of the various complex segments as segments, sequences, or something intermediate is determined entirely by the categorial representation and its relation either to suprasegmental structure or to the articulatory gesture, and there is again no need to make reference to a structural tier for the definition. Also, as noted above, the lack of a one-to-one relationship between the CV tier and the segmental tier in Clements & Keyser's model is reflected, where appropriate, by an association of two categorial representations with a single articulatory representation. Thus prenasalised stops and affricates, the component elements of both of which are necessarily homorganic, will have representations exemplified by those in (7.15):

(7.15)   a.

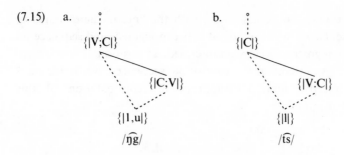

7.3.2   **Long vowels and diphthongs**

In terms of Clements & Keyser's three-tiered theory, the various vowel-types are represented as in (7.16):

(7.16)

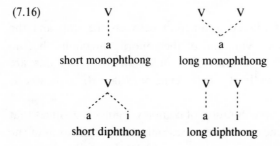

(We ignore here the possibility of the second elements of long monoph-thongs and diphthongs being represented as C, rather than V.) Long monophthongs, then, have a representation in which two elements on the CV tier are associated with a single element on the segmental tier; short diphthongs show the reverse pattern.

As in the case of the consonantal phenomena discussed in the previous section, more than one approach is possible for the dependency represent-ation of the short diphthongs. In §3.6.4 we suggested that their represent-ation involves intrasegmental adjunction:

(7.17)

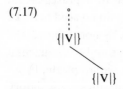

where the structure as a whole is assigned to a single segmental node, as in (7.17). If we take this view, the appropriate articulatory representations will simply be associated on a one-to-one basis with the |V| nodes:

(7.18)

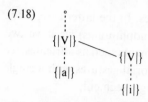

This may be unnecessarily complex, however. It seems more appropriate to treat short diphthongs as involving just a single categorial specification, associated with two distinct articulatory specifications. This would give the following dependency representations for the various vowel-types:

(7.19)

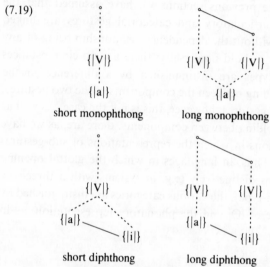

where the dependencies within the articulatory representations for the diphthongs result from lexical redundancies – the elements of the diphthongs are stored simply as sequences in the lexicon, as, for example, in (7.20) (long diphthongs) and (7.21) (short diphthongs):

(7.20) ({C}) {|V|} {|V|} ({C})   (7.21) ({C})   {|V|}   ({C})

    α   {|a|} {|i|} β   α {|a|} {|i|} β

All the phenomena discussed in these two sections, then, allow us to maintain the view that segmental status is determined by the representations of the categorial gesture, without any need to invoke purely functional representations: in the unmarked case, a single categorial specification corresponds to a single segment. One categorial gesture may be associated with two articulatory gestures (short diphthongs), or one articulatory gesture with two categorial gestures. In the latter case, if the two categorial gestures are identical (long monophthongs) we have two segments. However, in the case of complex segments such as affricates, we have (intrasegmental) association of two categorial gestures with a single articulatory gesture – here, then, we have a single segment.

7.4   Intergestural relationships

In the discussion of the previous sections we have assumed that the representations of the articulatory and categorial gestures are linked simply by association, without the dependency relationship being of any relevance. This appears to hold universally: there are no circumstances under which segment-types are distinguished by a difference in the dependency relation holding between the components of the two gestures.

Within the individual gestures, however, this is not the case. As well as dependency relations holding between components, there are, as we have seen (see §5.1.1), situations in which the representations of sub-gestures display such relations. Thus, in languages in which the glottal opening component |O| functions distinctively (e.g. in systems with a three-way opposition in phonation-type), the various categories are distinguished by the relative prominence of |O| and the phonatory representation, as in (5.3) (reproduced as (7.22):

(7.22)   {O}   {O}:{|C|;}   {|C|;}
          | |
        {|C|;}   {O}

          /p/   /b/   /b̰/

The representations of the individual sub-gestures, then, show greater interaction than those of different gestures, in accordance with the particular sub-division of the segmental matrix adopted here.

Although dependency relations do not hold between the articulatory and categorial gestures, there is nevertheless an interesting sense in which the two sets of representations cannot be said to be totally independent. This concerns the 'capacity to split' of the various categorial segment-types. In general, we can say that the less complex the categorial representation, the greater its capacity to split, i.e. the greater the number of articulatory 'realisations' of the segment-type. Consider, for example, a language such as Brahui (Maddieson 1984:421), which shows the phonemic system in (7.23):

(7.23)   p ṭ t k ʔ
         b ḍ d g
         f s x h
         v z ɣ

(We ignore here the affricates, which have a complex internal structure.)

A representation of this system in dependency terms shows the interaction between the categorial and articulatory representations; the class-membership of the categorially simpler types is greater than that of the categorially more complex types:

(7.24)   {|C|}   {|C|}   {|C|}   {|C|}   {|C|}
          ¦   ¦   ¦   ¦
         {|u|}   {l,d}   {|l|}   {l,u}

         {|C;V|}   {|C;V|}   {|C;V|}   {|C;V|}
          ¦   ¦   ¦   ¦
         {|u|}   {l,d}   {|l|}   {l,u}

         {|V;C|}   {|V;C|}   {|V;C|}   {|V;C|}
          ¦   ¦   ¦
         {|u|}   {|l|}   {l,u}

         {V;C;V}   {V;C;V}   {V;C;V}
          ¦   ¦   ¦
         {|u|}   {|l|}   {l,u}

Similarly, there are generally more nasals {|V;C|} in a phonemic system than the more complex class of liquids {|V;V;C|}. Patterns like that in (7.24), in which categorial complexity is in inverse proportion to articulatory class-membership, appear to be typical of language inventories.

As in the various other phenomena discussed here and and in chapter 4, claims of this sort – irrespective of whether they are valid or not – are simply not available to a minimally componential theory: the greater degree of structure afforded by the incorporation of gestures in itself allows questions to be framed, and generalisations offered, which would not otherwise arise.

7.5   The tonological gesture

As already noted, the bigestural structure proposed in Part II is inadequate for the characterisation of tonal phenomena. For these we require the postulation of a third sub-unit, the TONOLOGICAL GESTURE. Elements in this gesture will often fail to show a one-to-one correspondence with elements within the categorial gesture. In other words, tone is typically a non-segmental phenomenon, and it is this, of course, that originally led to the development of models of autosegmental phonology in which the tonal features are placed on a separate autosegmental tier (see Goldsmith 1976).

In autosegmental works on tone, two binary features are often postulated for the tonal tier, such as [high pitch] and [low pitch] (Goldsmith 1976:54), giving representations such as those in (7.25):

(7.25) $\begin{bmatrix} +\text{high pitch} \\ -\text{low pitch} \end{bmatrix}$ $\begin{bmatrix} +\text{high pitch} \\ +\text{low pitch} \end{bmatrix}$ $\begin{bmatrix} -\text{high pitch} \\ +\text{low pitch} \end{bmatrix}$

          high tone   mid tone   low tone

The tonal feature matrix – occupying a distinct autosegmental tier – is simply associated with any other tiers involved in the segmental representation.

How, then, is the tonological gesture associated with the other gestures, and what components do we require to characterise the various tonal possibilities? We consider first the second question, though the two are closely related.

Notice first that Maddieson (1978:318) suggests that languages may contrast up to five levels of tone. If this is indeed correct, then the system proposed by Goldsmith must be extended to account for it – indeed, Wang (1967) suggests that we need three binary features [high], [central], and [mid] for this purpose.

There appear to be various possibilities for translating this claim into dependency phonology. One possibility would be to suggest that there are two components in the tonological gesture, which interact with each other but not with the representations of the other gestures. Recall that two components allow a maximum of five combinations, as in the case of vowel height, so that given two components |a| and |b|, the representations in (7.26) are formally possible:

(7.26)   {|a|}   {|a;b|}   {|a:b|}   {|b;a|}   {|b|}

Maddieson notes that tonal systems are found with anything from two to

five contrasts, and a two-component system would allow the representation of the various systems in the expected way, ranging from a simple
opposition between two components via simple combination and unilateral dependency up to the maximal system in (7.26).

However, associated with this proposal are two closely related problems. Firstly, on what grounds can we defend the postulation of two
components; secondly, what are their correlates?

Tone is, of course, determined by pitch, i.e. by the fundamental
frequency (F_0) determined by the rate of vibration of the vocal cords (we
ignore phenomena such as declination – see Ladd 1984 for discussion: here
we are solely concerned with the general problem of the representation of
tone, rather than with the operation of any tonal rules). Thus a low tone
involves merely a lower F_0 than a higher tone in a particular context in any
language. Tone, then, is the phonological correlate of a single phonetic
parameter: the value of F_0. As such, a feature system like Goldsmith's,
involving as it does two binary features for the characterisation of a single
dimension, encounters the same kinds of problems with respect to non-
orthogonality as Chomsky & Halle's treatment of vowel height by means
of [high] and [low], or, indeed, Goldsmith's features [high pitch] and [low
pitch].

Similar objections might be raised to the dependency treatment
suggested above, where the postulation of two components would at first
sight appear to be a violation of part (b) of the natural recurrence
assumption: there would be no one-to-one relationship between phonetic
parameter and phonological prime.

What happens if only one component is proposed to handle tonal
phenomena? We might then suggest that this component, which we shall
represent for the sake of discussion as |x|, enters into dependency relations
with the elements of some other gesture, presumably the categorial. Thus,
the representation of a set of vowels with three distinctive tone levels
might be as in (7.27):

(7.27)   {|x|}   {|x|}:{|V|}   {|V|}
           | |
       {|V|}   {|x|}

       high tone   mid tone   low tone

But this treatment raises at least three problems. Firstly, we have
abandoned the standpoint that dependency relations hold only between
the sub-gestures *within* gestures, and not between gestures themselves.

Secondly, it is not clear what phonetic grounds there might be for suggesting that high and low tones differ in the dependency relations holding between a tonal component and a component of 'sonority'. In other cases where an analogous treatment has been proposed, such as the relation between |O| and |V| in appropriate systems, the phonetic correlate of the dependency relation is clear: $\{|O|\} \rightrightarrows \{|V|\}$ shows greater glottal opening and less sonority than $\{|V|\} \rightrightarrows \{|O|\}$. Here no such correlate is apparent. Thirdly, only three distinctive tone levels are available, whereas Maddieson's account suggests five are needed.

Thus there are difficulties associated both with a one-component and with a two-component approach to the representation of tone. We might circumvent these problems by taking a third approach, which would involve introducing a non-unary component into the system of representation: specifically, a multi-valued scalar feature of tone, with up to five values. This, though, would mean a quite new type of phonological primitive being introduced into the model, one which would bring with it all the problems associated with multi-valued features that we have exemplified.

We suggest that the two-component approach raises the fewest problems. That is, we consider the various tones to be represented by two components which are simply associated with the representations of other gestures, so that, for example, the vowel /i/ realised with a high tone would be:

(7.28) $\{|h|\}$ tonological

        $\{|V|\}$ categorial

        $\{|i|\}$ articulatory

where |h| for the moment represents high tone. This, we suggest, offers an account of tone which is the most consistent with the model developed in Parts I and II.

However, if we take this two-component view, we must establish the nature of these components. As noted above, the relevant phonetic parameter is F_0, with high values of F_0 presumably being assigned to one of the components, and low values to the other. Notice that a not dissimilar situation holds in the acoustic correlates of the components of the articulatory gesture, where |i| involves, among other things, concentration of formant energy at higher frequencies, and |u| concentration at lower frequencies (see Jakobson *et al.* 1969 on features such as [acute] and [grave]). Indeed, we propose that the appropriate representations for the two tonal components are also |i| and |u|. In other words, we are suggesting that |i| and |u| in the tonological gesture bear the same relation to |i| and |u| in the articulatory gesture as |V| in the categorial gesture does to |a| in the articulatory gesture (recall that we suggested in §6.1.2 that |a| could be replaced by |V|). That is, |i| involves (relatively) 'high frequency' and |u| (relatively) 'low frequency'; whether this is interpreted as high (or low) F_0 or as concentration of energy in the higher (or lower) regions of the spectrum depends on the context – i.e. gesture – in which it occurs.

The dependency representations for, say, /é/ (high tone), /u/ (mid tone) and /à/ (low tone) might be as in (7.29) (where, for illustration, we use |V| rather than |a| in the articulatory gesture):

(7.29)   {|i|}   {|i,u|}   {|u|}   tonological

       {|V|}   {|V|}   {|V|}   categorial

     {|i,V|}   {|u|}   {|V|}   articulatory
     /é/   /u/   /à/

However, we still have to consider the problem of the representation of contour tones. In autosegmental phonology, contour tones are interpreted as sequences of level tones on the relevant tier, so that a falling tone associated with a short /a/ is represented as:

(7.30)   H   L

        a

where H and L are abbreviations for the appropriate feature-matrix (see Goldsmith 1976:§1.2). This treatment seems equally appropriate in the notational system developed here: the tonal representations will occur in simple linear sequence without being hierarchically organised, so that a short /a/ with falling tone (from high to mid) will be:

(7.31)   {|i|}   {|i,u|}

        {|V|}

        {|a|}

       /ā/

7.6   Associations between gestures and segments

In our discussion of suprasegmental structure in chapter 3 we made the assumptions that suprasegmental dependency structures are (a) unlabelled and (b) a projection of infrasegmental representations. We have nothing to add here to our previous discussion of the first assumption; we merely note that our investigation of the suprasegmental level indeed reveals no necessity to have recourse to labels beyond those associated with the sets of gestures on the basis of which suprasegmental structure is erected. The schematic account of the assignment of suprasegmental structure given in §§3.4–5 was intended to illustrate the appropriateness, in the case of English, of the latter assumption. However, we are now in a position to be a little more precise about constraints on associations between gestures and segments.

In the unmarked case, a single bundle of distinct gestures is associated with a single node or subjunction path in the suprasegmental representation. However, we have allowed for a segment to consist of one categorial gesture associated with two articulatory gestures, or vice versa (see §7.3), unless the two categorial gestures are identical, in which case we have two segments. Thus we can define association between gestures and suprasegmental structure in general as: associate a suprasegmental node with each segment defined as above. This holds both in the unmarked case and in the exceptional circumstances just described.

Intergestural associations are also typically one-to-one and thus need not be a property of individual lexical entries. A redundancy-free lexical representation thus consists of independent sequences of gestures. These are then associated by conventions, which must, of course, contain language-particular provisions. For example, a sequence of plosive + fricative categorial gestures is associated in English with a single articulatory gesture. Thus, the entry in (7.32), for *judge*:

(7.32)   {|C;V|}   {V:C;V}   {|V|}   {|C;V|}   {V:C;V}

        {l;i}   {|a;ə|}   {l;i}

is associated as in (7.33) (for the articulatory representation for /ʌ/ see Ewen 1981):

(7.33)   {|C;V|}   {V:C;V}   {|V|}   {|C;V|}   {V:C;V}

        {l;i}   {|a;ə|}   {l;i}

This fails only where an articulatory gesture is thereby left unaccounted for, so that for *adze*, with a sequence of stop + fricative, rather than a phonemic affricate, association is one-to-one:

(7.34)   {|V|}   {C;V}   {V:C;V}
             ¦   ¦   ¦
            {|a|}   {|l|}   {|l|}

More complex patterns of association are typically formed with a tonological gesture, where present. Thus, in Mende (Leben 1971, 1978), a tone sequence such as {u} {i} {u} may be associated with one, two or three categorial gestures, as illustrated in (7.35):

(7.35)

a. *mbâ* 'companion'

{u}   {i}   {u}   {u} {i} {u}
                                            ＼ ¦ ╱
{C}   {|V|}   →   {C}   {|V|}
                                             ¦
α   {|a|}   α   {|a|}

b. *nyàhâ* 'woman'

{u}   {i}   {u}   {u}   {i}   {u}
                                                        ＼   ╱
{C} {C} {|V|} {C} {|V|}   →   {C} {C} {|V|} {C} {|V|}
                                              ¦   ¦
α   β   {|a|}   γ   {|a|}   α   β   {|a|}   γ   {|a|}

c. *nìkílì* 'ground nut'

{u}   {i}   {u}   {u}   {i}   {u}

{C} {|V|} {C} {|V|} {C} {|V|} →   {C} {|V|} {C} {|V|} {C} {|V|}
                                             ¦   ¦   ¦
α   {|i|}   β   {|i|}   γ   {|i|}   α   {|i|}   β   {|i|}   γ   {|i|}

(where {C} segments, as irrelevant, are left unspecified for articulatory properties). Here, association works from left to right until the relevant categorial gestures are exhausted. However, the question of the principles of tonological association – apart from the requirement that association (and dependency) lines do not cross – remains contentious. Given our present interests, all we wish to illustrate here is the capacity of the notation to express the appropriate associations.

It is also possible that some gestural associations may remain unspecified until suprasegmental word structures are erected. Consider in this regard the much-discussed phenomenon of vowel harmony in Khalkha Mongolian. (Here we rely particularly on Goldsmith 1985.) Relevant to this is the notion autosegment (or prosody). We interpret autosegments as language-particular groupings of components which are not assigned to a particular position in the sequence of segments, and we distinguish between basic and derivative autosegments. Basic autosegments are either lexical or grammatical, with lexical autosegments being initially associated with the entire word, grammatical autosegments with a particular word form (e.g. with a particular tense). Both are derivatively assigned to a particular node in the word structure. Derivative autosegments, on the other hand, result from the spread of a particular set of components from one segment to others, as exemplified by pharyngealisation spread in Berber (see §2.2.2) or by nasalisation in many languages.

Khalkha Mongolian, which has backness and roundness harmony, exhibits lexical autosegments. Vowels within a word agree in backness, except that [i] may appear in words that are otherwise back, but not in initial (stressed) position. Similarly, vowels within a word agree in roundness, except that high vowels are immune. More specifically, as Goldsmith observes, this means that although Mongolian has seven surface vowels there is only a three-way vowel contrast in non-stressed (non-initial) syllables: {i} *vs.* {u} *vs.* {a}. {i} surfaces as {|i|} under all circumstances. In a word which is not front, {u} surfaces as {|u|}; in one which is front, {u} surfaces as {|i,u|}. In a word which is not front and not round, {a} surfaces as {|a|}; in one which is front and non-round, it appears as {|i,a|}; in front and round as {i,u,a}; in non-front and round as {u,a}:

(7.36)   [i] {|i|}   ⟵   {i}   {u}   ⟶   {|u|}   [u]

                                                        ↘

                                                {|i,u|}   [y]

                                {a}

                        ↙   ↙   ↘   ↘

                {|i,a|} {i,u,a} {|a|} {|u,a|}

                 [e]   [ø]   [a]   [o]

Stressed (initial) syllables show the three-way contrast, plus the possibility of [y] and [u] in words which are otherwise unrounded, and [i] in words which are otherwise rounded.

We can characterise this situation by saying that all articulatory gestures associated with vowels are either {i}, {u} or {a}, but that each lexical item either has or has not attributed to it an autosegment, where the autosegment is either {u} (rounding), {i} (frontness) or {i,u}. Thus, a word like *xara* 'to look at' has no autosegment:

(7.37) {C}   {|V|}   {C}   {|V|}

      α   {a}   β   {a}

whereas *temeen* 'camel' has {i}:

(7.38) {i}

    {C}   {|V|}   {C}   {|V|}   {|V|}   {C}

    α   {a}   β   {a}   γ

Oroyoo 'let me enter' has {u}:

(7.39) {u}

    {|V|}   {C}   {|V|}   {C}   {|V|}   {|V|}

    {a}   α   {a}   β   {a}

and *ögöyöö* 'let me give' has {i,u}:

(7.40) {i, u}

    {|V|}   {C}   {|V|}   {C}   {|V|}   {|V|}

    {a}   α   {a}   β   {a}

To account for the failure of roundness harmony with high vowels we need to stipulate that as stressed vowels they are incompatible with the {u} autosegment, while in unstressed position they are immune or opaque to it, as in *nüüyee* 'let me move':

(7.41) {i}

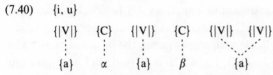

    {C}   {|V|}   {|V|}   {C}   {|V|}   {|V|}

    α   {u}   β   {a}

The first (stressed) vowel rejects the {u} autosegment, but the {i} autosegment is realised as both *-üü-* and *-ee-* (underlying {a}). On the other hand, stressed {i} requires the presence of the {i} autosegment.

Given the central role of stressedness in the formulation of these regularities, it seems appropriate to suggest that the autosegments are associated (derivatively) with the foot-head or word-head node in the lexical structure, which is itself associated with those segments which potentially reject or require particular autosegments. Thus for *nüüyee* we have:

(7.42)

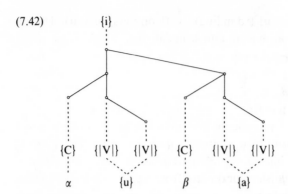

the autosegment being realised in at least any non-|C| segment (see Rialland & Djamouri 1984); whereas, in the case of autosegmental {u}, any {|V|} segment that is {~a} is also immune.

We observe finally here that some elements may remain unassociated until the erection of the utterance (not merely lexical) structure. For instance, Durand (1986b), following Clements & Keyser (1983), argues that in French the final consonant in, e.g., *deux*, [z], is 'floating', i.e. is not associated at the lexical level. If *deux* occurs in appropriate syntactic circumstances before a syllable with empty onset, the [z] is associated with that onset node, as in *deux amis*, i.e. we have liaison. Before a non-null onset, as in *deux turcs*, the 'floating' segment remains unattached and is accordingly suppressed, we assume by a general convention analogous to that proposed in Anderson (1984b), whereby segments that retain negative specifications are deleted.

Typically, then, intergestural associations and those between gestures and suprasegmental structure are non-contrastive, and are determined by general principles. Lexical entries need not contain such information, and phonological specification in the lexicon can thus consist of unassociated sequences of gestures. Indeed, particularly if intergestural associations are stipulated lexically (where they are not 'autosegmental'), even such precedence relations between gestures/segments may become redundant. Linearity is predominantly non-contrastive; it is, for instance, determinate within onset and coda with respect to the sonority hierarchy, supplemented by information concerning language-particular violations of the hierarchy. We do not develop here this alternative conception of the scope of this redundancy: for a preliminary account, however, see Anderson (1986b). Clearly, there exist extensive redundancies among the structural relations (dependency, precedence, association) which characterise the phonological structure of lexical items. As we have seen, suprasegmental dependencies are derivative; what remains to be determined is the trade-off relationship between association and precedence.

7.7   Afterthoughts on lexical *vs.* utterance structure

We have attempted to provide motivations for a phonology which involves several dimensions of organisation, such that in particular we can distinguish different levels of representation. One such dimension is 'derivational': we distinguish a contrastive from a phonetic level. Another involves 'scale' or domain, such as the distinction between infrasegmental and suprasegmental structure. We have suggested, however, that this is also a 'derivational' relationship in so far as suprasegmental structure is a projection of segmental representations. A similar dual relationship holds between lexical and utterance structures: they differ in domain (word *vs.* utterance) and in the non-phonological factors relevant (morphology *vs.* sentence, involving syntactic and informational structure), and utterance structure involves interpretation of the word-trees provided by the lexical phonology.

These organisational suggestions are offered rather tentatively; our main concern has been with establishing the appropriateness of the dependency relation to these various levels – and we return to this in the chapter which follows. Moreover, even if these distinctions in level are the appropriate ones, the precise nature of further similarities and differences between them is as yet unclear.

For example, Anderson (1984b) suggests that whereas for lexical structures in English at least, a limitation to binary (single-modifier) constructions seems to be appropriate, this is not obviously true of utterance structures, such as that in (7.43):

(7.43)

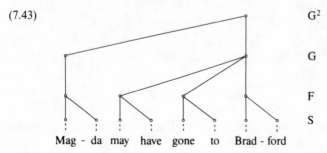

in which the second group has two modifiers, apparently unhierarchised.

The validity of this, however, even in relation to English is uncertain. Another suggestion that seems to us to have some inherent plausibility is the assumption that lexical structures will show less 'nesting' (embedding within F^2 and G^2 structures) than utterance structures. However, it is not certain that this distinction can be made categorical rather than a question of 'likelihood'. Again, we are at the beginning of the serious investigation of such structural properties of utterance representations.

As far as the relationship between word and utterance representations is concerned, we see some promise in an attempt to limit this, as in other inter-level relations in the phonology, to a set of principles of association, perhaps developed along the lines hinted at in §3.5. It seems possible in principle to allow even for variations such as that involved in 'iambic reversal' in terms of alternative associations between the levels, thus avoiding recourse to structure-changing or 'transformational' formulations. The avoidance of such mutations contributes to the 'concreteness' of the descriptions allowed by the notation, in the sense discussed in the chapter which follows, where, as a conclusion to our discussion, we return to this and other consequences of adopting the notational proposals we have made.

8 Conclusions and consequences

We do not provide here (any more than in chapter 7) a detailed account of the conclusions that may be drawn from the preceding discussions. On the one hand, this would in many instances merely repeat concluding statements to other sections, chapters or parts. On the other, the firmness with which different individual conclusions may be drawn is variable, and best assessed in the context of specific discussions. However, we should like to state and elaborate upon some general conclusions. Furthermore, it is also possible at this point to examine some of the consequences of adopting the notation argued for here, consequences which it was inappropriate to introduce in the course of the preceding discussion but whose validity provides significant 'external' support to the argument.

Most notable, it seems to us, are consequences concerning: (a) our view of linguistic representation in general, and (b) non-notational aspects of the phonology, particularly its organisation. Both sets of consequences are associated with our general contention that phonological representations, both suprasegmental and infrasegmental, are more highly structured, and display more structural variables, than the matrix representation of 'classical' feature phonology. They are associated also with our more specific contention that many of these structural properties are most appropriately modelled by representations incorporating the dependency relation.

We have argued that suprasegmental structure, both at the lexical and at the utterance level, involves a fixed hierarchy of constructions which are individually identified by their place in this hierarchy and by the direction of modification associated with them. Direction of modification is characterised in terms of the dependency relation: each construction is headed. Given these properties, suprasegmental structures involve un-labelled dependency trees (or their equivalent). We have tried to show, particularly in chapters 2 and 3, that such structures are appropriate for the formulation of phonotactic constraints and other phonological phenomena. Within the (simplex) segment, unary features or components are grouped into gestures and sub-gestures which have a systematic status with respect to various phonological regularities. Within gestures, components may or may not be present, and may or may not be hierarchised, i.e. be involved in a (non-linear) dependency relation. Intra-gestural representations involve labelled subjunctions. As argued in chapter 1, and particularly in Part II, such characterisations allow both for the division of segments into (natural) classes and for their hierarchisation with respect to parameters such as sonority or vowel height, as well as directly specifying relative markedness in terms of the internal complexity of segment representations.

Typically, as we noted in chapter 7, gestures are simply associated with each other and with a single node in the suprasegmental representation. However, some segments show a further internal complexity, in that there may be associated with a single suprasegmental node a segmental configuration in which one gesture or bundle of gestures (i.e. a potential segment) has another such bundle adjoined to it, as in the case of diphthongs and, possibly, affricates (§7.3). Also, at least derivatively, a particular gesture may be associated with two or more distinct suprasegmental nodes, as in the case of homorganicity (shared articulatory gesture) or in some cases of tonal harmony (shared tonological gesture). Or a particular gesture or autosegment may be associated with a whole configuration of suprasegmental nodes, as in the case of vowel harmony discussed in §7.6. In all these cases participating suprasegmental nodes are linked by dependency. Such conditions on divergences from the 'typical' were discussed in chapter 7.

What has emerged from our study is that the atoms and bundles of atoms of phonological representations are related, apart from simply by association, only by precedence and subordination. No other structural properties need to be invoked, and no non-atomic labels. The structural 'richness' that we argued to be attributable to phonological representations is primarily characterised in terms of a variety of dependency relations. This is of some considerable interest in itself, but it also has interesting consequences for our view of linguistic representations in general, given the plausibility of the STRUCTURAL ANALOGY assumption — which we now proceed to examine (see too Anderson 1985a, ms b).

8.1 Structural analogy

It has long been recognised and agreed that linguistic structure displays distinct levels of organisation, characterised by distinctive properties – though there may be dispute about the number and status of these levels. However, there is also general agreement that some differences in level are more crucial than others, specifically, where the different levels are characterised in terms of disjoint sets of basic elements. Let us call such a distinction a difference in PLANE (see Anderson 1982). Thus syntactic and phonological representations belong to different planes: they are constructed out of different basic elements. Whatever different levels one might want to recognise within the syntax belong to the same plane in so far as they are constituted out of the same set of categories: N, V, etc. Within the phonology, one might wish to recognise (as suggested in §7.7): distinct lexical and utterance levels, characterised by different constraints and different extra-phonological conditions; a distinction between suprasegmental and infrasegmental structure, based on syntagmatic *vs.* paradigmatic orientation with respect to the segment; and, cross-cutting these, levels of abstractness and realisational or derivational levels, such as the phonological *vs.* the phonetic. However, the representations at all these latter (combinations of) levels are homo-planar; they reflect different aspects of the organisation of phonological atoms or components.

We have argued that a variety of structural properties at these phonological levels are appropriately characterised in terms of dependency relations. In chapter 3 we introduced our discussion of dependency in phonology with a brief exposition of the role of the dependency relation in the characterisation of syntactic structure. At that point this was motivated as primarily a matter of expository convenience: dependency grammar first developed and is most familiar in relation to syntactic structure. We now want to approach this 'coincidence' (the relevance of dependency to the two different planes) in a more principled way. Specifically, we can say that the recurrence of dependency in the two planes is a manifestation of structural analogy (SA).

Crudely, SA embodies an assumption that the same structural properties will recur at different levels, including different planes. Differences between levels (apart from, in the case of interplanar differences, distinct sets of basic elements) should follow from well-motivated differences in their principles of organisation, such as 'cyclicity', 'recursivity' and more specific properties. Quite simply, we expect, *ceteris paribus*, different levels to display the same basic structural properties. Conceptual economy demands no less.

The idea of SA has not been explicitly prominent in recent work in linguistics, so far as we are aware. The structural properties of syntax, morphology and phonology have tended to be investigated independently. Only the tradition culminating in glossematics (Hjelmslev 1943) maintained the principle of structural 'isomorphism' between the two planes of expression and content (see Spang-Hansen 1961, for a cautious statement, and Siertsema 1965:207–24, for a rather more expansive one) – Hjelmslev, indeed, provides a detailed typology of the relations shared by the planes. Certainly, SA is implicit in much of the work of Pike and Halliday (see Anderson ms b), as well as in the shared rule formalisms (cyclicity, etc.) characteristic of the Chomskian tradition. And this continues in the recognition of the transmodular status of 'move-α' (Chomsky 1981), and in the 'modularisation' of the phonology (Kiparsky 1982) as well as the syntax. But such manifestations are sporadic and often unprincipled; the concept itself receives little recognition. This neglect is unwarranted. SA provides a principled constraint on the proliferation of ad hoc notations prompted by specific phenomena.

For example, consider again the notation of 'particle phonology' (Schane 1984a,b), which is designed to capture many of the same properties that are provided for by the dependency account of vowels given here. It is not clear to what extent this notation is appropriate elsewhere, even within the phonology; it is proposed in isolation from a consideration of the structural properties appropriate at other levels, or even to other segment-types. Moreover, even within the restricted domain considered by Schane, it is clear that structural properties appropriately characterised by the dependency relation are inadequately expressed in terms of the notation he proposes. For example, syllabicity (or rather non-syllabicity), a relational notion, is represented by a diacritic on particular particles, a diacritic which, in addition, entails sequentiality rather than simultaneity (another relational notion). This is as inappropriate as the [syllabic] feature of *SPE* (see §2.1.2).

Anderson (1985a), like Hjelmslev, argues for detailed analogies between the syntactic and phonological planes. Just as suprasegmental structure can be characterised by unlabelled dependency stemmata showing both adjunction and subjunction, so syntactic structure is characterisable in this way (see §3.1). Just as infrasegmental structure displays labelled adjunctions and subjunctions, so too does word structure, with derivationally related categories having the base subjoined to the derivative category and compounds showing adjunction. Furthermore, lexical suprasegmental structure displays the same hierarchy of constructions as utterance structure, though they differ in domain and in the principles determining their erection.

It is worth noting, too, that SA also extends to morphological structure. We assume here the word-and-paradigm view of morphological structure adopted in Anderson (1980b, 1985a,c) and Colman (1985). Inflectional and derivational categories constitute simple subjunction paths in the word structure, which is associated with morphological structure proper by the rules of the morphology. Morphological structure as such is constituted by unlabelled dependency trees in which affixes are dependent on roots (neither of which therefore need be labelled as such). This is illustrated by the lexical representation in (8.1):

(8.1)

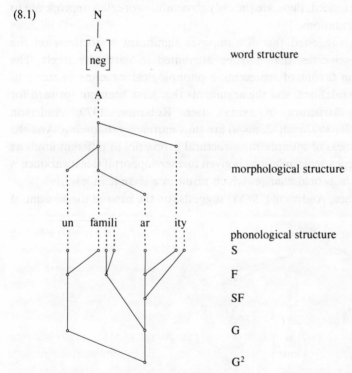

In (8.1) segmental structure is abbreviated by the conventional orthography, and we assume that the internal structure of *famili + ar* is morphological only and not represented in word structure: i.e. it is not synchronically related to the noun *family*. (On the suprasegmental structure, which assumes a group-head status for *un-*, see Booij & Rubach 1984.) Each morphological head is a base for morphological processes.

The planar status of morphological representations is thus rather interesting. The rules which introduce them interpret word structures; and morphological representations themselves, together with segmental specifications, are the basis for the erection of lexical suprasegmental structures. But the morphology does not introduce a distinct set of categories, in that it associates unlabelled trees with the word structure provided by the syntax and the lexicon: it constitutes a 'plane without an alphabet', an 'inter-plane', perhaps.

This is not the place to pursue a concern with morphology. We merely wish to illustrate the compatibility of morphological representations with SA and, specifically, with a characterisation in terms of dependency and precedence; indeed, these are the only structural properties appropriate to such representations.

We have suggested that SA imposes significant restrictions on the structural properties that may be attributed to particular levels. The arguments in favour of representing phonological structure in terms of dependency relations, and the arguments that have been put forward for dependency structure in syntax (see Robinson 1970; Anderson 1971a,b, 1976, 1977a:ch. 2, ms a) are thus mutually reinforcing. And the appropriateness of interpreting structural properties at different levels as involving dependency relations is given further support if this invariance is reflected in historical changes which result in a change in level.

For instance, Anderson (1985a) suggests (on the basis of the account of

(8.2)

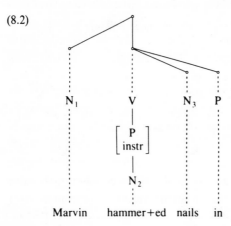

Marvin   hammer+ed   nails   in

word structure delineated in Anderson 1984a) that the development by historical 'conversion', in late Middle English, of the de-nominal verb *hammer* shows just such invariance, an invariance manifesting what we have called the dependency preservation condition (§3.6.2). Such a verb derives historically from a noun, but a noun with a particular semantic function: when one 'hammers' one strikes something 'with', or, by extension, 'as if with', 'a hammer'. Thus, a word structure such as that associated with the V in (8.2) (where inflectional categories are ignored) replaces, or rather comes to exist as an alternative to, the periphrastic construction in (8.3):

(8.3)

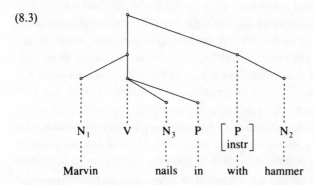

$$
\begin{array}{cccccc}
N_1 & V & N_3 & P & \left[\begin{array}{c} P \\ \text{instr} \end{array}\right] & N_2 \\
\text{Marvin} & & \text{nails} & \text{in} & \text{with} & \text{hammer}
\end{array}
$$

In (8.2) and (8.3) the instances of N_2 share semantic properties and realisation (*hammer*), but the overall syntactic category assignment is determined by the highest node in the subjunction path. Of course, this is not to deny that such derived forms may develop idiosyncratic properties not predictable from the configuration embodied under V in (8.2); such non-compositionality, or 'obscuration', is typical of established forms (see Anderson 1984a:ch. 1). But to the extent that V in (8.2) is (part of) a plausible synchronic word structure for the verb *hammer*, it reflects the dependency relations of its periphrastic template; such invariance supports the ascribing of dependency structure to both levels.

In §3.6.2 we discussed similar examples concerning diachronic shifts from suprasegmental to infrasegmental structure (and see again Anderson 1985a:§7). Again, other things being equal, particular dependency relations are preserved, but possibly at a different level; for example, when diphthongs are monophthongised: /ai/ → /ɛ(ː)/ rather than /e(ː)/, where these are distinct in the language. Such phenomena once more lend independent support to the positing of dependency as a crucial structural property at both levels.

The limits of SA have yet to be determined. It seems clear that the different planes are governed by not entirely identical organisational principles, partly as a result of their different status (phonology is interpretive), and this is partly reflected in different roles for dependency structures. For instance, whereas the syntactic distribution of words is determined by the character of the head of the word structure (*hammer* is a verb in (8.2) but a noun in (8.3)), distribution in the phonology, to the extent that something like the sonority hierarchy is viable as a predictor of syllable structure, is sensitive to the whole of the categorial gesture, not just its governing category. This may be a reflection of the absence of 'synchronically derived segments', as compared with derived words.

Recall too that we have already associated one dimension of distinction in level with whether nodes are distinctly labelled or not: contrast the infrasegmental and the suprasegmental, or word and sentence structure.

However, despite this indeterminacy in limitation of its domain, SA imposes significant restrictions on linguistic representations in so far as it embodies the 'unmarked' assumption. Level-particular structural properties or restrictions, as violations of SA, are particularly vulnerable: the violation needs to be shown to be necessary. SA also, of course, requires that the substantive claims embodied in different notations be identified and evaluated. This we have tried to do in relation to dependency.

8.2   Realisation and neutralisation

As far as the nature of the relationship between different phonological levels is concerned, the most striking consequence of adopting a dependency-based notation is the preference for non-mutative relationships it entails. It is simpler to add specifications than to change them.

Consider this, in the first place, in relation to simple allophony. Old English had two dental fricatives, differing in voice, which were in complementary distribution, where the complementarity involved morphological considerations. We can characterise their respective distributions as in (8.4):

(8.4)   voiceless [θ]:   a. adjacent to a voiceless segment
                        b. in gemination
                        c. initially in a morpheme
                        d. finally in a prefix or word

       voiced [ð]:   e. between voiced segments in other morphological
                          conditions

This is exemplified in (8.5):

(8.5) a. sniþst   'you cut' (pres. sg.)
       b. sceþþan   'injure' (inf.)
       c. þolian   'suffer' (inf.)
          under-þiedan   'subjugate' (inf.)
       d. wiþ-drifan   'expel' (inf.)
       e. æþele   'noble'
          baþian   'bathe' (inf.)

Such segments are also found spelled as ⟨ð⟩; variation between ⟨þ⟩ and ⟨ð⟩ in the spelling has no phonological significance.

[θ] and [ð] thus belong to the same contrastive unit. This unit is contrastively indeterminate with respect to voice, but it does contrast with homorganic plosives (voiced and voiceless) and liquids. It should thus be specified categorially as {V:C;}, i.e. a segment which contains at least a |V| and a |C|, both of which are governors, i.e. a fricative. With plosives there is no (non-governed) |V|; with liquids there is no governing |C|. The specification for the unit is simpler than that of either allophone, i.e. {|V:C|} and {V:C;V}, given the additional component in the voiced variant and the presence of the verticals in the specification for [θ]. And the underlying unit is related to its variants merely by addition: for [θ] the |V| and |C| are further specified as being alone and mutually dependent; with [ð] a further |V| is present and is dependent on the 'original' |V| and |C| components.

It would be more complex to designate the contrastive unit as voiceless and to derive the voiced variant as a mutation, involving not just addition of another |V| but also suppression of the verticals. Such natural recurrent allophonies thus select non-mutative formulations within a dependency framework. Diversificatory *realisation* (structure-building) is preferred to *mutation* (structure-changing), and the 'third value' problem associated with the unsupplemented binary feature notation (Stanley 1967) is avoided.

Likewise, archiphonemic neutralisations can be transparently characterised in terms of specifications from which particular components and/or dependency relations, elsewhere contrastive, are simply absent. Consider again the Old English labial fricatives. We found in §4.6 that, as with the dentals, the voiced and voiceless variants are in complementary distribution. This is shown in (8.6) to be quite parallel with the situation of the dentals illustrated in (8.5):

(8.6)   a. eft   'afterwards'
        b. pyffan   'puff' (inf.)
        c. fell   'ruin'
           befæstan   'fasten' (inf.)
        d. of-sittan   'sit on' (inf.)
        e. æfre   'ever'
           stafas   'staves'

The generalisation embodied in (8.4) can be transferred to the labials. However, in addition, the voiced fricative is also in complementary distribution with the voiced plosive, which does not occur in environment (e) of (8.6), where only [v] is found. Thus, while the labial and dental voiced plosives both occur in initial position, for example, only the dental shows up in environment (e) of (8.4)–(8.6), with the labial unit being realised as a voiced fricative:

(8.7)   a. drīfan   'drive' (inf.)
        b. bīdan   'wait' (inf.)

[v], then, represents not an allophone of a contrastive unit also manifested as [f], but rather the realisation of the neutralisation in environment (e) of the contrast between /f/ and /b/, i.e. an archiphoneme. Assignment of [v] to either the /f/ or the /b/ unit would be arbitrary here. The dependency notations allow us to express this neutralisation in a quite transparent fashion. /f/, /p/ and /b/ are contrastive in Old English, so that the categorial representations in (8.8) are appropriate:

(8.8)   a. /f/   {V:C}
        b. /p/   {|C|}
        c. /b/   {|C;V|}

Neutralisation of the /f/ ≠ /b/ contrast involves non-specification of the relation between the governing |C| and the |V|, which may also govern, as in (a), or be dependent only, as in (c). Thus the archiphoneme is {V,C;} (provided that ';' does not exclude ':'), i.e. an obstruent that is not a voiceless plosive. This obstruent archiphoneme is quite naturally realised as [v] ({V:C;V}), given the voiced environment: we have assimilation to the |V| of this environment; [v] is more |V|-like than both [f] (by voicing) and [b] (by continuancy). Notice that the latter 'assimilation' (/b/ is neutralised to {V,C;} and realised as [v] in a voiced environment) is not naturally expressible in a binary feature notation; its characterisation depends on the claim that both continuancy and voice involve presence of |V|.

We can diagram the various relationships as in (8.9):

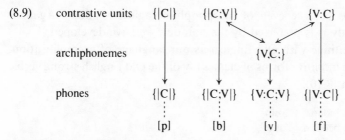

(8.9)   contrastive units   {|C|}   {|C;V|}   {V:C}

        archiphonemes   {V,C;}

        phones   {|C|}   {|C;V|} {V:C;V} {|V:C|}

                        [p]   [b]   [v]   [f]

where the unidirectional arrows indicate realisation and the double-headed arrows indicate neutralisation. The overall behaviour of Old English obstruents is more complex than we have indicated, but these additional factors do not disturb the analysis of the segments and environments discussed here. See in particular Anderson (1985b), where it is argued in more detail in relation to these phenomena that such archiphonemic analyses are appropriate and preferable to 'strict phonemic', and that the relationships are transparently characterised in terms of the dependency notation.

In the present instance, the formulation both of the neutralisation and of the nature of its realisation is not susceptible to specification in terms of binary (or multi-valued) features. It is necessary to specify what a (voiceless) fricative and a voiced plosive have in common, and this archiphoneme is then realised as the segment-type resulting from assimilation to a voiced environment. Both these aspects are quite transparently captured by a dependency representation, in terms of the archiphonemic representation in (8.9) and its relationship to its realisation and context. The addition which gives {V:C;V} from {V,C;} is the minimum one which will increase the preponderance of |V| in the segment.

8.3   Epilogue on concreteness

The realisations discussed in the preceding section all involve addition, increase in specification, rather than mutation. We have argued that such non-mutative 'derivational' relationships are favoured by the dependency notation. In this respect, CONCRETE synchronic derivations are preferred to abstract. Absence of, or at least reduction in, mutation, in the context of a well-defined notation, severely constrains the way in which 'underlying' representations may differ from their realisations. This is discussed in more detail in Anderson (1986a). We conclude the present work with an illustration of how this particular, perhaps unexpected, consequence can be argued to be true even of morphophonological relations. Again a concrete analysis is preferred by the notation we have developed.

Let us continue with Old English as our language of exemplification. Consider the infinitive forms of classes I–V of the Old English strong verbs, illustrated in (8.10):

(8.10)   I   bīdan   'wait'
         II   bēodan   'offer'
         IIIa helpan   'help'
               feohtan   'fight'
         IIIb bindan   'bind'
         IVa   beran   'bear'
         IVb   niman   'take'
         V   metan   'measure'

Each class is associated with a distinct paradigm, specifically a distinctive set of vowel alternations shown by all regular members of the class. However, not only is the articulation of the stem vowel of such verbs predictable within individual classes – for example, class IVa infinitives always have -*e*- (and the variation between *eo* and *e* in IIIa is a reflection of a general Old English phonological variation associated with the character of the following cluster) – but the class of each verb is predictable from the structure of the rhyme of the stem.

The superficial stem rhyme structure for each infinitive in (8.10) is given in (8.11):

(8.11)   I   {|V|}   {|V|} {C}
                    ⟍ ⟋ |
                    {|i|}   α

         II   {|V|}   {|V|}   {C}
                | | |
              {i;a}   {u;a}   α

         IIIa {|V|}   {|C,V;|} {C}
                | | |
              {i;a}   β   α

         IIIb {|V|}   {|V;C|} {C}
                | | |
               {i}   {n}   α

         IVa {|V|}   {|V;V:C|}
                | |
              {i;a}   α

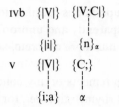

The α and β specifications indicate that the articulatory gestures concerned are irrelevant. All the other specifications are fixed, except that the {|C,V;|} categorial representation for the second segment of the rhyme in IIIa allows for either liquids {|V;C|} or fricatives {|V:C|}; and {C} and {C;} allow for any consonant type and any obstruent, respectively.

The character of the first segment in the rhyme is predictable from the nature of the rest of the rhyme. It is {|i|} if a nasal follows, as in IIIb and IVb. Otherwise, it is {i;a} or its diphthongal variant, except in class I. Only in classes I and II is the second segment a vowel: we can thus say that if in a strong verb the second segment is a vowel other than {u;a}, its specification is shared with the first segment. None of these verbs need be specified lexically for the articulatory gesture of the initial segment of the rhyme: they are simply {|V|}. Nor need the infinitive forms be indexed in the lexicon as to classes, given that the articulatory character of the rhyme-initial segment of the stem is predictable from the rest of the rhyme.

The same holds for these segments throughout the paradigms. Thus, for example, it is only in rhymes consisting of just two segments (i.e. classes IV and v) that we find a long front vowel in the preterite subjunctive and indicative plural and second singular forms. Contrast *mǣton, bǣron*, the preterite indicative plurals of *metan, beran*, with *bidon* (from *bīdan*), *budon* (*bēōdan*), *hulpon* (*helpan*), *fuhton* (*feohtan*) and *bundon* (*bindan*). Only before a single obstruent do we fine -*e*- in the past participle, as in *gemeten* (cf. *geholpen, genumen*, etc.). For a full documentation of this, see Anderson (1986a); and in a feature framework, Anderson (1970) and Lass & Anderson (1975:ch. 1).

The realisation of the first segment in the rhyme of class I–v strong verbs involves the addition of a range of articulatory specifications determined by the rest of the structure of the rhyme. It would be more complex, both in terms of lexical specifications and in the formulation of the appropriate realisation rules, to select some underlying articulatory specification (say that of /e/) which then undergoes mutations in the various phonological and morphological circumstances which are relevant. In terms of the notation, adding is simpler than changing (superfluous specifications are eliminated), and 'archisegments' can be transparently and unproblematically expressed. Again, a non-mutative, and thus more concrete, account is preferred by the dependency notation.

Analyses of this sort fulfil two crucial requirements of any concept of contrast: spurious contrastive units (such as a rhyme-initial /e/, for strong verb stems, for example) are avoided; realisations are maximally concrete (non-mutative). The contrastive core of the various realisations is thereby factored out.

Consider further in this regard the relationship between the infinitive and preterite indicative first and third person singular forms of class ɪ: *bīdan/bād*. How are we to characterise lexically the second segment in such rhymes? It appears as the second part of the long vowel represented by -*ī*- in the one instance, and as the second part of that represented by -*ā*- in the other. This segment contrasts in terms of its categorial gesture with corresponding segments in classes ɪɪɪ–ᴠ: it is a vowel, unlike any other of these non-rhyme-initial segments. However, class ɪɪ is also divocalic (see (8.11)); thus the second rhyme-segment of class ɪ cannot be merely unspecified for articulatory gesture. The second rhyme-segment in class ɪɪ is realised as {u;a} (infinitive -*ēō*-) or {a;u} (preterite indicative first and third singular -*ēā*-) – on this analysis of these diphthongs, see again Anderson (1986a) – as well as by {|u|} in the preterite indicative plural, as in *budon* (where the rhyme-initial segment is lost). An appropriate representation for the second rhyme-segment in class ɪɪ is therefore {u}, the |u| being shared by all its realisations (the past participle is also -*o*-). What then characterises the contrasting segment in class ɪ is that it does not contain |u| (*bīdan* ~ *bād*), and that it involves only one component other than |u|, either |a| or |i| (the {|i|} also turns up in the rest of the paradigm). Its articulatory specification is thus {| ~ u|}, in contrast with the {u} of class ɪɪ.

The derivations given in (8.12) are appropriate:

(8.12)   a. *Class I rhyme*

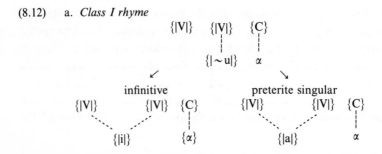

b. *Class II rhyme*

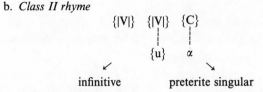

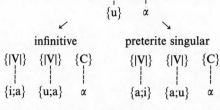

The realisation of |∼u| as {|i|} or {|a|} is morphologically determined, while {u;a} and {a;u} are given by a general condition on Old English diphthongs whereby the second element agrees in height (relative preponderance of |a|) with the first (by diphthong height harmony – Lass & Anderson 1975:ch. 3; Anderson 1986a). {i;a} and {a;i} for the first segment are morphologically determined: these are the infinitive and preterite indicative first and third singular values throughout strong verbs I–V, except before a nasal and before {{|V|},{|∼u|}}, as in class I, where the rhyme-initial segment shares its articulation with the following segment.

References

The following abbreviations are used:

ALH   Acta Linguistica Hafniensia
ARIPUC Annual Report of the Institute of Phonetics, University of Copenhagen
CLS   Papers from the Annual Regional Meeting, Chicago Linguistic Society
FL   Foundations of Language
FLH   Folia Linguistica Historica
IJAL   International Journal of American Linguistics
IULC   Indiana University Linguistics Club
JAOS   Journal of the American Oriental Society
JL   Journal of Linguistics
JPh   Journal of Phonetics
Lg   Language
LI   Linguistic Inquiry
NJL   Nordic Journal of Linguistics
PhY   Phonology Yearbook
SL   Studia Linguistica
YPL   York Papers in Linguistics

Abercrombie, D. 1965. *Studies in phonetics and linguistics.* Oxford: Oxford University Press.

1967. *Elements of general phonetics.* Edinburgh: Edinburgh University Press.

Aitken, A. J. 1962. Vowel length in Modern Scots. Edinburgh: University of Edinburgh, Department of English Language.

1981. The Scottish vowel-length rule. In M. Benskin & M. L. Samuels (eds.) *So meny people longages and tonges,* pp. 131–57. Edinburgh: M. Benskin & M. L. Samuels.

Anderson, J. M. 1969. Syllabic or non-syllabic phonology? *JL* 5: 136–42.

1970. 'Ablaut' in the synchronic phonology of the Old English strong verb. *Indogermanische Forschungen* 75: 166–97.

1971a. Dependency and grammatical functions. *FL* 7: 30–7.

1971b. *The grammar of case: towards a localistic theory.* London: Cambridge University Press.

1971c. A proposal concerning the lexicalisation of complex structures. *SL* 25: 1–8.

1975. Principles of syllabification. *YPL* 5: 7–20.

1976. *On serialization in English syntax. Ludwigsburg Studies in Language and Linguistics* 1.

1977a. *On case grammar.* London: Croom Helm.

1977b. Noch einmal ae. *samcucu. YPL* 7: 67–76.

1979a. Serialisation, dependency and the syntax of possessives in Moru. *SL* 33: 1–25.

1979b. Syntax and the single mother. *JL* 15: 121–38.

1980a. On the internal structure of phonological segments: evidence from English and its history. *FLH* 1: 165–91.

1980b. Towards dependency morphology: the structure of the Basque verb. In Anderson & Ewen (1980a: 227–71).

1982. Analysis and levels of linguistic description. In E. Siciliani, R. Barone & G. Aston (eds.) *La lingua inglese nell'università*, pp. 3–26. Bari: Adriatica Editrice.

1984a. *Case grammar and the lexicon. University of Ulster Occasional Papers in Linguistics and Language Learning* 10.

1984b. Suprasegmental dependencies. *IULC.* Revised version in Durand (1986a: 55–130).

1985a. Structural analogy and dependency phonology. *ALH* 26: 5–44.

1985b. The status of voiced fricatives in Old English. *FLH* 6.

1985c. The case system of Old English: a case for non-modularity. *SL* 39: 1–22.

1986a. Old English ablaut again: the essentially concrete character of dependency phonology. In C. Duncan-Rose, J. Fisiak & T. Vennemann (eds.) *Rhetorica, Phonologica et Syntactica.* London: Croom Helm.

1986b. The English prosody /h/. In D. Kastovsky & A. Szwedek (eds.) *Linguistics across historical and geographical boundaries*, vol. 2, pp. 799–809. Berlin: Mouton de Gruyter.

To appear a. The great kEntish collapse. *Proceedings of the Luick symposium, Vienna 1985.*

To appear b. Gothic obstruents: the limits of reconstruction. In A. G. Ramat, O. Carruba & G. Bernini, eds. *Proceedings of the 7th Conference on Historical Linguistics, Pavia, 1985.* Tübingen: Narr.

ms a (1986). The lexical head hypothesis.

ms b (1986). The tradition of structural analogy.

Anderson, J. M. & C. J. Ewen (eds.) 1980a. *Studies in dependency phonology. Ludwigsburg Studies in Language and Linguistics* 4.

1980b. Introduction: a sketch of dependency phonology. In Anderson & Ewen (1980a: 9–40).

1981. The representation of neutralisation in universal phonology. In Dressler *et al.* (1981: 15–22).

Anderson, J. M., C. J. Ewen & J. Staun 1985. Phonological structure: segmental, suprasegmental and extrasegmental. *PhY* 2: 203–24.

Anderson, J. M. & C. Jones 1974a. Three theses concerning phonological representations. *JL* 10: 1–26.

(eds.) 1974b. *Historical linguistics*, 2 vols. Amsterdam: North-Holland.

1977. *Phonological structure and the history of English*. Amsterdam: North-Holland.

Anderson, S. R. 1971. On the description of 'apicalized' consonants. *LI* 2: 103–7.

1976. Nasal consonants and the internal structure of segments. *Lg* 52: 326–44.

Antonsen, E. 1961. Germanic umlaut anew. *Lg* 37: 215–30.

Archangeli, D. 1984. Underspecification in Yawelmani phonology and morphology. Ph.D. dissertation, MIT.

Árnason, K. 1980. *Quantity in historical phonology: Icelandic and related cases*. Cambridge: Cambridge University Press.

Aronoff, M. & R. T. Oehrle (eds.) 1984. *Language sound structure*. Cambridge, Mass.: MIT Press.

Bartsch, R. & T. Vennemann 1972. *Semantic structures*. Frankfurt: Athenäum.

Basbøll, H. 1974. The phonological syllable with special reference to Danish. *ARIPUC* 8: 39–128.

1977. The structure of the syllable and a proposed hierarchy of distinctive features. In Dressler & Pfeiffer (1977: 143–8).

1985. Review of Maddieson (1984). *PhY* 2: 343–53.

Bell, A. 1978. Syllabic consonants. In Greenberg (1978a: 153–201).

Bell, A. & J. B. Hooper (eds.) 1978a. *Syllables and segments*. Amsterdam: North-Holland.

1978b. Issues and evidence in syllabic phonology. In Bell & Hooper (1978a: 3–22).

Benediktsson, H. 1959. The vowel system of Icelandic: a survey of its history. *Word* 15: 282–312.

1963. Some aspects of Nordic umlaut and breaking. *Lg* 39: 409–31.

Bliss, A. J. 1952–3. Vowel quantity in Middle English borrowings from Anglo-Norman. *Archivum Linguisticum* 4: 121–47; 5: 22–47. Reprinted in Lass (1969: 164–207).

Bloomfield, L. 1926. A set of postulates for the science of language. *Lg* 2: 153–64.

Booij, G. and J. Rubach 1984. Morphological and prosodic domains in Lexical Phonology. *PhY* 1: 1–27.

Botha, R. P. 1971. *Methodological aspects of transformational generative phonology*. The Hague: Mouton.

Brown, G. 1972. *Phonological rules and dialect variation*. London: Cambridge University Press.

1977. *Listening to spoken English*. London: Longman.

Cairns, C. E. 1969. Markedness, neutralization, and universal redundancy. *Lg* 45: 863–85.

Cairns, C. E. & M. Feinstein 1982. Markedness and the theory of syllable structure. *LI* 13: 193–226.

Campbell, L. 1974. Phonological features: problems and proposals. *Lg* 50: 52–65.

Catford, J. C. 1977. *Fundamental problems in phonetics*. Edinburgh: Edinburgh University Press.

Chomsky, N. 1981. *Lectures on government and binding*. Dordrecht: Foris.

Chomsky, N. & M. Halle 1968. *The sound pattern of English*. New York: Harper & Row.

Clements, G. N. 1976. Vowel harmony in nonlinear generative phonology. IULC.
1985. The geometry of phonological features. *PhY* 2: 225–52.
Clements, G. N. & S. J. Keyser 1983. *CV phonology: a generative theory of the syllable.* Cambridge, Mass.: MIT Press.
Colman, F. 1985. Some morphological formatives in Old English. *FLH* 6.
Comrie, B. 1980. Morphology and word order reconstruction: problems and prospects. In Fisiak (1980: 83–96).
Contreras, H. 1969. Simplicity, descriptive adequacy and binary features. *Lg* 45: 1–8.
Crothers, J. 1978. Typology and universals of vowel systems. In Greenberg (1978a: 93–152).
Davidsen-Nielsen, N. & H. Ørum 1978. The feature 'gravity' in Old English and Danish phonology. *ALH* 16: 201–13.
DeArmond, R. 1984. On the development of the verb phrase node in English syntax. In N. F. Blake & C. Jones (eds.) *English historical linguistics: studies in development. CECTAL Conference Papers Series* 3, pp. 205–26. Sheffield: Centre for English Cultural Tradition and Language, University of Sheffield.
Derbyshire, D. & G. K. Pullum 1981. Object-initial languages. *IJAL* 47: 192–214.
Dixon, R. M. W. 1977. *A grammar of Yidiɲ.* Cambridge: Cambridge University Press.
Dogil, G. 1981. Elementary accent systems. In Dressler *et al.* (1981: 89–99).
Donegan (Miller), P. J. 1973. Bleaching and coloring. *CLS* 9: 386–97.
Donegan, P. J. 1976. Raising and lowering. *CLS* 12: 145–60.
1978. On the natural phonology of vowels. Ph.D. thesis, Ohio State University.
Drachman, G. 1977. On the notion 'phonological hierarchy'. In Dressler & Pfeiffer (1977: 85–102).
Dressler, W. U. & O. E. Pfeiffer (eds.) 1977. *Phonologica 1976.* Innsbruck: Innsbrucker Beiträge zur Sprachwissenschaft.
Dressler, W. U., O. E. Pfeiffer & J. R. Rennison (eds.) 1981. *Phonologica 1980.* Innsbruck: Innsbrucker Beiträge zur Sprachwissenschaft.
Durand, J. 1981. Esquisse d'une théorie de la syllabe en phonologie de dépendance. *Modèles Linguistiques* 3: 147–71.
(ed.) 1986a. *Dependency and non-linear phonology.* London: Croom Helm.
1986b. French liaison, floating consonants and other matters in a dependency framework. In Durand (1986a: 161–201).
Escure, G. J. 1977. Hierarchies and phonological weakening. *Lingua* 43: 55–64.
Ewen, C. J. 1977. Aitken's Law and the phonatory gesture in dependency phonology. *Lingua* 41: 307–29.
1978. The phonology of the diminutive in Dutch: a dependency account. *Lingua* 45: 141–73.
1980a. Aspects of phonological structure. Ph.D. thesis, University of Edinburgh.
1980b. Segment or sequence? Problems in the analysis of some consonantal phenomena. In Anderson & Ewen (1980a: 157–204).
1981. Phonological notation and foreign language teaching. In A. R. James &

K. J. P. Westney (eds.) *New linguistic impulses in foreign language teaching*, pp. 99–119. Tübingen: Narr.

1982. The internal structure of complex segments. In van der Hulst & Smith (1982a: Part 2, 27–68).

1986. Segmental and suprasegmental structure. In Durand (1986a: 203–22).

Ewen, C. J. & H. van der Hulst 1985. Single-valued features and the nonlinear analysis of vowel harmony. In H. Bennis & F. H. Beukema (eds.) *Linguistics in the Netherlands 1985*, pp. 39–48. Dordrecht: Foris.

Fallows, D. 1981. Experimental evidence for English syllabification and syllable structure. *JL* 17: 309–18.

Fant, C. G. M. 1971. Distinctive features and phonetic dimensions. In G. E. Perren & J. L. M. Trim (eds.) *Applications of linguistics*, pp. 219–39. London: Cambridge University Press.

Fischer-Jørgensen, E. 1952. On the definition of phoneme categories on a distributional basis. *ALH* 7: 299–319.

Fisiak, J. (ed.) 1980. *Historical morphology*. The Hague: Mouton.

Foley, J. 1977. *Foundations of theoretical phonology*. London: Cambridge University Press.

Fromkin, V. (ed.) 1978. *Tone: a linguistic survey*. New York: Academic Press.

Fudge, E. C. 1969. Syllables. *JL* 5: 253–86.

Fujimura, O. 1975. Syllable as a unit of speech recognition. *IEEE Transactions on Acoustics, Speech, and Signal Processing*. ASSP-23, 1: 82–7.

1981. Elementary gestures and temporal organisation – what does an articulatory constraint mean? In T. Myers, J. Laver & J. M. Anderson (eds.) *The cognitive representation of speech*, pp. 379–88. Amsterdam: North-Holland.

Giegerich, H. 1980. On stress-timing in English phonology. *Lingua* 51: 187–221.

1985. *Metrical phonology and phonological structure*. Cambridge: Cambridge University Press.

1986. Relating to metrical structure. In Durand (1986a: 223–56).

Goldsmith, J. A. 1976. An overview of autosegmental phonology. *Linguistic Analysis* 2: 23–68.

1979. *Autosegmental phonology*. New York: Garland.

1985. Vowel features and umlaut in Khalkha Mongolian, Yaka, Finnish and Hungarian. *PhY* 2: 253–75.

Grammont, M. 1933. *Traité de phonétique*. Paris: Delagrave.

Greenberg, J. B. 1970. Some generalizations concerning glottalic consonants, especially implosives. *IJAL* 36: 123–45.

1978a. *Universals of human language. Vol. 2: Phonology*. Stanford: Stanford University Press.

1978b. Some generalizations concerning initial and final consonant clusters. In Greenberg (1978a: 243–79).

Gussenhoven, C. 1983. Focus, mode and nucleus. *JL* 19: 377–417.

Hall, B. L. & R. M. R. Hall 1980. Nez Perce vowel harmony: an Africanist explanation and some theoretical questions. In R. M. Vago (ed.) *Issues in vowel harmony*, pp. 201–36. Amsterdam: John Benjamins.

Halle, M. & S. J. Keyser 1971. *English stress*. New York: Harper & Row.

Halle, M. & K. Stevens 1969. On the feature 'Advanced Tongue Root'. *MIT Quarterly Progress Report* 94: 209–15.

  1971. A note on laryngeal features. *MIT Quarterly Progress Report* 101: 198–213.

Halliday, M. A. K. 1967. *Intonation and grammar in British English*. The Hague: Mouton.

Hankamer, J. & J. Aissen 1974. The sonority hierarchy. In A. Bruck, R. A. Fox & M. W. La Galy (eds.) *Papers from the parasession on natural phonology*, pp. 131–45. Chicago: Chicago Linguistic Society.

Haugen, E. 1956. The syllable in linguistic description. In M. Halle, H. G. Lunt, H. McLean & C. H. van Schooneveld (eds.) *For Roman Jakobson*, pp. 213–21. The Hague: Mouton.

Hayes, B. 1980. A metrical theory of stress rules. Ph.D. dissertation, MIT.

  1982. Extrametricality and English stress. *LI* 13: 227–76.

  1984. The phonology of rhythm in English. *LI* 15: 33–74.

Hays, D. G. 1964. Dependency theory: a formalism and some observations. *Lg* 40: 511–25.

Herbert, R. K. 1977. Language universals, markedness theory, and natural phonetic processes: the interaction of nasal and oral consonants. Ph.D. thesis, Ohio State University.

Hermans, B. 1985. The relation between aspiration and preaspiration in Icelandic. In H. van der Hulst & N. Smith (eds.) *Advances in nonlinear phonology*, pp. 237–66. Dordrecht: Foris.

Hjelmslev, L. 1943. *Omkring sprogteoriens grundlæggelse*. Copenhagen: Munksgaard. (Transl. F. J. Whitfield as *Prolegomena to a theory of language*. Madison: University of Wisconsin Press, 1961.)

Hoard, J. E. 1971. Aspiration, tenseness and syllabication in English. *Lg* 47: 133–40.

Hockett, C. F. 1947. Peiping phonology. *JAOS* 67: 253–67.

  1950. Peiping morphophonemics. *Lg* 26: 63–85.

  1959. The stressed syllabics of Old English. *Lg* 35: 575–97. Reprinted in Lass (1969: 108–32).

Hooper, J. B. 1972. The syllable in phonological theory. *Lg* 48: 525–40.

  1976. *An introduction to natural generative phonology*. New York: Academic Press.

van der Hulst, H. & N. Smith (eds.) 1982a. *The structure of phonological representations*. 2 parts. Dordrecht: Foris.

  1982b. An overview of autosegmental and metrical phonology. In van der Hulst & Smith (1982a: Part 1, 1–45).

Hyman, L. M. 1970. How concrete is phonology? *Lg* 46: 58–76.

  1973. The feature [grave] in phonological theory. *JPh* 1: 329–37.

  1975. *Phonology: theory and analysis*. New York: Holt, Rinehart & Winston.

  1985. Review of Lass (1984a). *PhY* 2: 355–9.

Jackendoff, R. 1977. *X̄-syntax: a study of phrase structure.* Linguistic Inquiry Monograph 2.

Jakobson, R. 1968. *Child language, aphasia and phonological universals.* The Hague: Mouton.

Jakobson, R., C. G. M. Fant & M. Halle 1969. *Preliminaries to speech analysis.* Cambridge, Mass.: MIT Press.

Jakobson, R. & M. Halle 1956. *Fundamentals of language.* The Hague: Mouton.

Jespersen, O. 1950. *English phonetics.* Revised and translated by Bengt Jürgensen. Copenhagen: Gyldendal.

Kahn, D. 1976. Syllable-based generalizations in English phonology. *IULC.*

Kaisse, E. M. & P. A. Shaw 1985. On the theory of Lexical Phonology. *PhY* 2: 1–30.

Katamba, F. 1979. How hierarchical and universal is consonant strength? *Theoretical Linguistics* 6: 25–40.

Keenan, E. L. 1978. The syntax of subject-final languages. In W. P. Lehmann (ed.) *Syntactic typology,* pp. 267–327. Sussex: The Harvester Press.

Keyser, S. J. & W. O'Neil 1983. Exceptions to high vowel deletion in the Vespasian Psalter and their explanation. In M. Davenport, E. Hansen & H. F. Nielsen (eds.) *Current topics in English historical linguistics,* pp. 137–64. Odense: Odense University Press.

Kim, C.-W. 1970. A theory of aspiration. *Phonetica* 21: 107–16.

Kiparsky, P. 1979. Metrical stress assignment is cyclic. *LI* 10: 421–42.

1981. Remarks on the metrical structure of the syllable. In Dressler *et al.* (1981: 245–56).

1982. From Cyclic Phonology to Lexical Phonology. In van der Hulst & Smith (1982a: Part 1, 131–75).

1985. Some consequences of Lexical Phonology. *PhY* 2: 85–138.

Kohler, K. 1967. Modern English phonology. *Lingua* 19: 145–76.

Kučera, H. 1961. *The phonology of Czech.* The Hague: Mouton.

Kuryłowicz, J. 1971. A problem of Germanic alliteration. In M. Brahmer, S. Helsztyński & J. Krzyżanowski (eds.) *Studies in language and literature in honour of Margaret Schlauch,* pp. 195–201. New York: Russell & Russell.

Ladd, D. R. 1980. *The structure of intonational meaning: evidence from English.* Bloomington: Indiana University Press.

1984. Declination: a review and some hypotheses. *PhY* 1: 53–74.

Ladefoged, P. 1968. *A phonetic study of West African languages.* London: Cambridge University Press.

1971. *Preliminaries to linguistic phonetics.* Chicago: Chicago University Press.

1973. The features of the larynx. *JPh* 1: 73–83.

1975. *A course in phonetics.* New York: Harcourt Brace Jovanovich.

Ladefoged, P. & A. Traill 1984. Linguistic phonetic descriptions of clicks. *Lg* 60: 1–20.

Lass, R. (ed.) 1969. *Approaches to English historical linguistics.* New York: Holt, Rinehart & Winston.

1971. Boundaries as obstruents: Old English voicing assimilation and universal strength hierarchies. *JL* 7: 15–30.

1973. A case for making phonological rules state things that don't happen. *Edinburgh Working Papers in Linguistics* 3: 10–18.

1974. Linguistic orthogenesis? Scots vowel quantity and the English length conspiracy. In Anderson & Jones (1974b: Vol. 2, 311–52).

1975. How intrinsic is content? Markedness, sound change, and 'family universals'. In D. Goyvaerts & G. Pullum (eds.) *Essays on the Sound Pattern of English*, pp. 475–504. Ghent: Story-Scientia.

1976. *English phonology and phonological theory*. London: Cambridge University Press.

1980. *On explaining language change*. London: Cambridge University Press.

1984a. *Phonology*. Cambridge: Cambridge University Press.

1984b. Vowel system universals and typology: prologue to theory. *PhY* 1: 75–111.

Lass, R. & J. M. Anderson 1975. *Old English phonology*. London: Cambridge University Press.

Leben, W. R. 1971. Suprasegmental and segmental representation of tone. *Studies in African Linguistics*, Supp. 2, pp. 183–200.

1978. The representation of tone. In Fromkin (1978: 177–219).

Liberman, M. 1975. The intonational system of English. Ph.D. dissertation, MIT.

Liberman, M. & A. Prince 1977. On stress and linguistic rhythm. *LI* 8: 249–336.

Lieberman, P. 1976. Phonetic features and physiology: a reappraisal. *JPh* 4: 91–112.

Lindau, M. E. 1978. Vowel features. *Lg* 54: 541–63.

Lindau, M. E., L. Jacobson & P. Ladefoged 1973. The feature advanced tongue root. *UCLA Working Papers in Linguistics* 22: 76–92.

Maddieson, I. 1978. Universals of tone. In Greenberg (1978a: 335–65).

1984. *Patterns of sounds*. Cambridge: Cambridge University Press.

Malsch, D. L. & R. Fulcher 1975. Tensing and syllabification in Middle English. *Lg* 51: 303–314.

Marcus, S. 1967. *Algebraic linguistics: analytic models*. New York: Academic Press.

Matthews, P. H. 1981. *Syntax*. Cambridge: Cambridge University Press.

Minkova, D. 1982. The environment for open syllable lengthening in Middle English. *FLH* 3: 29–58.

Nespor, M. & I. Vogel 1982. Prosodic domains of external sandhi rules. In van der Hulst & Smith (1982a: Part 1, 225–55).

Nielsen, K. M. 1961. Scandinavian breaking. *Acta Philologica Scandinavica* 24: 33–45.

Ó Dochartaigh, C. 1978. Lenition and dependency phonology. *Éigse* 17: 457–94.

ms (n.d.). Phonology of the Gaelic liquids.

Ohala, J. J. 1979. Universals of labial velars and de Saussure's chess analogy. *Proceedings of the 9th International Congress of Phonetic Sciences*, Vol. 2, pp. 41–7.

Pétursson, M. 1972. La préaspiration en islandais moderne. *SL* 26: 61–80.

1976. Aspiration et activité glottale. *Phonetica* 33: 169–98.

Pilch, H. 1970. *Altenglische Grammatik*. München: Hueber.

Pope, M. K. 1934. *From Latin to Modern French*. Manchester: Manchester University Press.

Prince, A. 1983. Relating to the grid. *LI* 14: 19–100.

Pulgram, E. 1970. *Syllable, word, nexus, cursus*. The Hague: Mouton.

Pullum, G. K. 1981. Evidence against the 'AUX' node in Luiseño and English. *LI* 12: 435–63.

Reddy, N. 1979. Problems of syllable-division in Telugu. *University of Edinburgh, Department of Linguistics, Work in Progress* 12, pp. 135–40.

Reighard, J. 1972. Labiality and velarity in consonants and vowels. *CLS* 8: 533–43.

Rialland, A. & R. Djamouri 1984. Harmonie vocalique, consonantique et structure de dépendance dans le mot en mongol khalkha. *Bulletin de la Société de Linguistique de Paris* 79: 333–83.

Roach, P. 1982. On the distinction between 'stress-timed' and 'syllable-timed' languages. In D. Crystal (ed.) *Linguistic controversies: essays in linguistic theory and practice in honour of F. R. Palmer*, pp. 73–9. London: Edward Arnold.

Robinson, J. J. 1970. Dependency structures and transformational rules. *Lg* 46: 259–85.

Rudes, B. 1977. Another look at syllable structure. *IULC*.

Saib, J. 1978. Segment organization and the syllable in Tamazight Berber. In Bell & Hooper (1978a: 93–104).

Saltarelli, M. 1973. Orthogonality, naturalness, and the binary feature framework. In B. B. Kachru, R. B. Lees, Y. Malkiel, A. Pietrangeli & S. Saporta (eds.) *Issues in linguistics: papers in honor of Henry and Renée Kahane*, pp. 798–807. Urbana: University of Illinois Press.

Schachter, P. 1969. Natural assimilation rules in Akan. *IJAL* 35: 342–55.

Schane, S. A. 1973. [back] and [round]. In S. R. Anderson & P. Kiparsky (eds.) *A Festschrift for Morris Halle*, pp. 174–84. New York: Holt, Rinehart & Winston.

1979. Rhythm, accent and stress in English words. *LI* 10: 483–502.

1984a. Two English vowel movements: a particle analysis. In Aronoff & Oehrle (1984: 32–51).

1984b. The fundamentals of particle phonology. *PhY* 1: 129–55.

Selkirk, E. O. 1978. The French foot: on the status of French 'mute' *e*. *Studies in French Linguistics* 1: 141–50.

1980. The role of prosodic categories in English word stress. *LI* 11: 563–605.

1982. The syllable. In van der Hulst & Smith (1982a: Part 2, 337–83).

1984. On the major class features and syllable theory. In Aronoff & Oehrle (1984: 107–36).

Siegel, D. 1974. Topics in English morphology. Ph.D. dissertation, MIT.

Siertsema, B. 1965. *A study of glossematics*. The Hague: Martinus Nijhoff.

Sigurd, B. 1965. *Phonotactic structures in Swedish*. Lund: Uniskol.

Sommerstein, A. H. 1977. *Modern phonology*. London: Edward Arnold.

Spang-Hansen, H. 1961. Glossematics. In C. Mohrmann, A. Sommerfelt & J. Whatmough (eds.) *Trends in European and American linguistics 1930–1960*, pp. 128–64. Utrecht: Spectrum.

Spencer, A. 1984. Eliminating the feature [lateral]. *JL* 20: 23–43.

Stanley, R. 1967. Redundancy rules in phonology. *Lg* 43: 393–436.

Stevens, K. 1972. The quantal nature of speech. In E. E. David & P. B. Denes (eds.) *Human communication: a unified view*, pp. 51–66. New York: McGraw Hill.

Stewart, J. M. 1967. Tongue root position in Akan vowel harmony. *Phonetica* 16: 185–204.

Ternes, E. 1973. *The phonemic analysis of Scottish Gaelic.* Hamburg: Helmut Buske Verlag.

Thráinsson, H. 1978. On the phonology of Icelandic preaspiration. *NJL* 1: 3–54.

Trubetzkoy, N. S. 1969. *Principles of phonology.* Berkeley & Los Angeles: University of California Press.

Vaiana Taylor, M. 1974. The great Southern Scots conspiracy: pattern in the development of Northern English. In Anderson & Jones (1974b: Vol. 2, 403–26).

Vennemann, T. 1972. On the theory of syllabic phonology. *Linguistische Berichte* 18: 1–18.

    1974. Topics, subjects and word order: from SXV to SVX via TVX. In Anderson & Jones (1974b: Vol. 1, 339–76).

Vennemann, T. & P. Ladefoged 1973. Phonetic features and phonological features. *Lingua* 32: 61–74.

Vogt, H. 1942. The structure of the Norwegian monosyllable. *Norsk Tidsskrift for Sprogvidenskap* 12: 5–29.

Wang, W. S-Y. 1967. Phonological features of tone. *IJAL* 33: 93–105.

    1968. Vowel features, paired variables, and the English vowel shift. *Lg* 44: 695–708.

Wells, J. C. 1982. *Accents of English*, Vol. 1. Cambridge: Cambridge University Press.

Williamson, K. 1977. Multivalued features for consonants. *Lg* 53: 843–71.

Yamada, N. 1984. On characterizing the English Great Vowel Shift. *Lingua* 62: 43–69.

Zwicky, A. 1972. A note on a phonological hierarchy in English. In R. P. Stockwell & R. K. S. Macaulay (eds.) *Linguistic change and generative theory*, pp. 275–301. Bloomington: Indiana University Press.

Index

achromatic: *see* chromatic
acoustic zero 151–2, 165
acute vs. grave 212–13
addition vs. mutation 289–95
adjunction: *see* subjunction; labelled 128,
   129–36, 266–8, 282, 283–8
advanced tongue root (component) 244–5
'advanced vs. retracted tongue root' 243–5
affricate 106, 132–4, 263–6, 269, 274
Aguacatec 49
Aho Bantu 232
airstream mechanism 186, 199–205
Aitken's Law in Scots and Scottish
   English 62, 159
Akan 244–5
alliteration 98, 165
ambidependency 97, 98–100, 109 (*see
   also* ambisyllabicity)
ambisyllabicity 61–9; and
   morphology 61–4, 68; and the
   foot 64–9, 71, 82–4, 97; pre-stress 72–
   8, 97
Amharic 200
aperture (particle) 209–10, 215
aphasia and acquisition 167
apicality (component) 238–40
Apinayé 131–2, 170
arc 90
archiphoneme 289–91
'archi-segment': *see* addition,
   archiphoneme
articulatory gesture 106, 148–50, 157,
   206–51, 261–2, 267–9, 272–9, 282, 294–5
aspiration 148, 193–9, 203–5; in
   English 55–8, 59, 61, 64, 66, 82–3
assimilation 172, 184, 213, 215–17, 234,
   290–1
association 90, 197–8, 259–62, 265–6,
   273, 274–9, 282; as redundant 278–9
-*ate* in English 77
autosegmental phonology 2, 35–6, 41, 99,
   150, 195, 244, 258–63, 270–1, 273, 275,
   276–8
auxiliary in syntax 88–9, 91–3

basic vs. derivative autosegment 276–8
Berber, 'emphasis' in 53–5, 276
binarity of structure 82–4, 101–2, 108,
   109, 279–80
bleaching 208–9, 214
brace notation 20
Brahui 269
breathy voice: *see* voice
Burera 170
Burmese 185, 191–3, 195
Buryat Mongolian enclisis 79

'capacity to split' 268–9
'cardinal properties' 207
categorial gesture 32, 106, 130, 142–5,
   149–50, 151–205, 261–79, 292–4
category in syntax 86
centrality (component) 218–24
centre (= ultimate head of a string) 88–9
   (*see also* root)
chest pulse 98 (*see also* isochrony) ⸳
Chinantec 251
chromatic 207–9, 212–14
click 199, 203–5
'close contact' 67
cluster of consonants 46–50, 56–8, 59–61,
   195 (*see also* s*C* clusters); weak: *see*
   syllable
co-constituency 85–6
coda 50, 97–100
colour: *see* chromatic
colouring 208–9, 214
complementarity operator: *see* negative
   operator
'complex segments' 133, 165, 261, 263–8
complexity: *see* markedness
component (unary feature) 28–34, 126–9,
   282 (*see also* consonant, vowel);
   articulatory 28–34 (*see also*
   articulatory gesture); multi-gestural 34;
   relativity of 29, 32, 190, 213;
   strength/preponderance of: *see*
   preponderance

componentiality assumption 8–40, 153;
    minimal 11–28, 172–4, 192, 195, 217,
    255–6, 269, 271, 281, 289: elaborated
    minimal 14–19, 167, enriched
    minimal 13–14, 34–40, super-
    elaborated 18–19
compound 57; obscuration of 63, 66
'concreteness' 280, 288–91;
    morphophonological 292–5
consonant 158 (*see also* affricate,
    continuant, fricative, glide, liquid, nasal,
    sonorant, stop); apical 235–6, 238–42;
    dental 236–7, 240–2; 'distributed' 229,
    235–6, 245–6; grave 233–5, 237–8, 243;
    labial 229–35; labial-dental, labial-
    palatal 250; labial-velar 249–50;
    labiodental 229, 241; laminal 239–42;
    lateral 236, 245–6; lingual 235, 237–8,
    241–3, 245, 247–8, 250; palatal 229,
    234, 237–8, 241; pharyngeal 229, 242–
    4; place of articulation 228–51;
    retroflex 235–6, 239–40; uvular 229,
    242–3; velar 229, 231–5, 237–8, 249–50
    (*see also* double articulation, secondary
    articulation)
consonant scale 172 (*see also* sonority
    hierarchy)
consonantisation 175
constituency 41, 45–84, 100–2; and
    phonotactics 99–100; in syntax 85–6,
    87–8: immediate 86
constituentiality assumption 45
constitute 85–6, 89, 92
constricted vs. spread glottis 146, 188
constructional iteration 103–4
continuant (consonant) 155, 158, 163,
    180
continuantisation 183–4
contrast 220, 225, 279, 289–95
'conversion' 286–7
coordinate articulation: *see* double
    articulation
'cover feature'; *see* feature/second order
creak 187, 189–90
creaky voice: *see* voice
CV phonology 259–63, 265
cyclicity 121–2, 283, 284
Czech 159–60, 162

Danish 178–9, 231–2, 234
'de-accentuation' 104, 123–4
declination 271
defricativisation 176
dentality (component) 240–2
'de-oralisation' 141–2

dependency in syntax: *see* syntactic
    dependency
dependency preservation 129, 286–7
diphthong: *see* vowel
diphthong height harmony 295
double articulation 246, 248–50
Dutch 153
Dyirbal 170

ejective 199, 200–3
enclitic 71–2, 79
endocentric vs. exocentric 87
equipollent 173, 213, 234
evaluation metric 168
Ewe 239, 241
extralexical: *see* utterance structure
extrametricality 114–15, 181
extrasegmental 197–9

F^2 103–4, 118, 122, 123, 280
feature 10; binary 8, 11, 19–28, 173–4,
    176, 193, 207–8, 230, 255–6, 290–1;
    'third value' problem with 289;
    hierarchy 178–82; multi-valued 24,
    229–31, 255–7, 291; scalar 24–8, 146,
    173–4, 188, 191, 192, 201, 207–8, 229,
    231–3, 236, 247, 249–50; second
    order 28, 173, 235, 237;
    'tonality' 212–14, 272–3; unary: *see*
    component
'flapping' in English 79
flatting 212–13
'floating' segment 278
foot 61, 64–9, 71–2, 78–9, 81–2;
    boundedness 106; -formation 110–18,
    122–5: and right-to-left iteration 120–1;
    -prominence 106; quantity-
    sensitivity 106 (*see also* F^2, sub-foot,
    superfoot)
formative 52, 62–4, 69–70
French 170, 278; foot 64, 182–3
fricative 153–6, 289–91; voiced 157,
    158, 164–6

G^2 80, 103–4, 123–4, 280; and
    cyclicity 118–19, 121–2
Gadsup 219
Gaelic (Scottish) 162–4, 194, 195, 198
Gallo-Roman 182–3
geminate 197–8
German 51, 231–2
Germanic 153 (*see also* alliteration)
gesture 34–40, 106, 126, 141–50, 255,
    282; deletion of 141–2, 175; phonetic
    evidence for 39–40, 142–3, 144–6

glide   44, 108
glottal opening (component)   186, 189–205, 268
glottal stop   37–8, 190–1, 192
glottal stricture   145–6, 157, 185–91
glottalic (pressure/suction), glottalicness: *see* airstream mechanism, ejective, implosive
glottalisation in English   56–7, 61, 64, 70, 71
glottals and reduction   37–8
Gorgia Toscana   79–80
Gothic   98
'gradual' vs. 'privative' opposition   156 (*see also* scales)
graph   90–1, 128
Greek-letter variables   12–13, 14–15, 18, 20–1, 25, 34, 73; crossed   22–3
grid   41, 45, 82
group: *see* tone group
Gujarati   146, 187, 190, 195

h in English   78
Hausa   187, 189–90
Hawaiian   170
head   80–2, 96–104: convention   89–90, 109; in syntax   87–96: as distinctive   88, 94–5, as lexical   88, obligatory   87, of the sentence   91–3; ultimate: *see* centre, root
homo-planar   283
homorganicity   11–13, 25, 37, 265–6, 282
Hungarian   232, 259
hypermetricality and morphology   69–70 (*see also* extrametricality)

iambic reversal: *see* stress-reversal
Icelandic   148, 177, 186, 194–9, 204, 213, 215–18
ictus   100, 103, 105, 123–5 (*see also* foot-formation); unrealised   120, 123, 125
implosive   199–203
Indonesian   185, 187, 190
information structure   104, 122–3
initiatory sub-gesture   145–8, 149–50, 162, 177, 185–205, 272 (*see also* glottalicness, glottal opening, velaricness)
interlude   50–3, 59–61
'inter-plane'   286
intonation: *see* 'tune–text-association'
intralexical: *see* word
intrasegmental adjunction   129–36, 266–8
Iroquoian   68
isochrony   64, 67
Isoko   239
'isomorphism': *see* structural analogy

Japanese   213; word order   87

Khalkha Mongolian   276–8
Korean   148, 193–4
Kumam   187, 190
Kwakiutl   219

labialisation   208, 213, 216–18, 246–7, 248
labiality (component)   207–18
labio-dentalisation   248
lateral   162–4
laterality (component)   245–6
Latin   182–3
'law of finals'   60
'law of initials'   57, 59, 60, 74
lenition   142–4, 171–7, 289–91
level   283, 286–8
lexical: *see* word
lexical phonology   122
linearity   85–7, 282 (*see also* segment); as redundant   278; partial vs. total order   92
linguality (component)   237–8
linking principle   15, 18
liquid   152–3, 155, 157, 162–4
locational sub-gesture   149–50 (*see also* articulatory gesture)
Luganda   232
Lumasaaba syllabicity   43–5

'Main Stress Rule'   72–4
Malayalam   236, 241–2
Maori   170
Margi   147–8, 187, 190
markedness   14–19, 30, 46–50, 126–7, 160, 165–6, 166–71, 191–2, 203, 209, 210–12, 214, 224, 233, 237, 282; of system   168–9, 186, 193, 240
medial voicing of *s* in English   62–3
Mende   275
metrical phonology   2, 41, 45, 82, 84, 101–2, 178
mid vowel   22–3
Middle English   129, 287; *ne*   79; Open Syllable Lengthening   66–8
minimal componentiality: *see* componentiality
'mirroring'   257–8
modifier   81
modularity   283–8
monophthongisation   129, 287
morpheme   62–4, 69–70
morphological structure   285–8
'move-α'   284
murmur   187, 190, 195
mutation: *see* realisation

Naga 222
Nama 203–5
nasal 152–3, 155, 162–4, 172, 176–7, 241,
 250–1; velaric 203–5; voiceless 177
nasality (component) 250–1
Nasioi 170
natural class 8, 30, 127, 152–3, 158, 166–
 7, 234, 282
natural phonology 28, 34, 207–9, 212,
 214, 215, 224
natural recurrence assumption 8, 40, 46,
 167, 232, 258, 289
natural serialisation 87
naturalness 1, 14–19, 26–7;
 conventions 18–19 (*see also* natural
 recurrence assumption)
negative operator 27, 30, 127
'neutral position' 230–1
neutralisation 182–4, 289–91;
 rules of 47–50
Nez Perce 245
Niger-Congo 244
Nilo-Saharan 244
node: *see* vertex
non-componentiality 9–10
non-constituentiality 41–50, 73–4
Norwegian 179–80, 182
not in English 79
nucleus 97, 100
Nyanga 131
Nyangumata 170

'obscuration' 287
obstruent 151, 158, 173, 290–1
-oid in English 77–8, 114–15
|O|-languages 195–9
Old English 7–8, 234; fricative voicing
 in 51, 183–4, 288–91; high vowel
 deletion in 83–4; homorganic
 lengthening in 37, 161; *i*-umlaut
 in 17–18, 33; short diphthongs 135–6;
 strong verb 292–5; syntax 92
onset 50, 97–100
oro-nasal sub-gesture 149–50, 153
orthogonality 21, 23, 30

palatalisation 208, 213, 215–18, 246–8
palatality (component) 207–18
Pali 173
Papago 170
particle phonology 28, 34, 207, 209–10,
 212–13, 215, 226, 228, 256–7, 284
periodicity 151–2, 192
pharyngealisation 246–7; in Berber 53–
 5, 276
phonation 142–8, 185

phonatory sub-gesture 145–8, 149–50,
 151–84, 188–95, 268, 272
phonemics 9–10
phonological phrase 42
phrasal categories in syntax 89–90
plane 283–8
postaspiration 194–9
postnasalisation 106, 131–3
preaspiration 36, 194–9
precedence: *see* linearity
prenasalisation 13, 106, 131–3, 263–6
preponderance (of a component) 32, 107,
 126–9, 291, 295
'pre-tonic' vs. 'tonic' 80
privative 173, 174, 192, 234
proclitic 79
projectivity: *see* tangling
prominence 81–2, 97–102, 125, 128–9
'proper tree': *see* tangling, tree from a
 point
prosodic: *see* extrasegmental
'prosodic categories' 100–1, 282

'quantal' vowel: *see* vowel
Quechua 219–20

realisation 279, 283, 288–95
recurrence 1, 73, 289 (*see also* natural
 recurrence assumption)
recursivity 283
'reductionism' 257–8
'resonance' vs. 'source' feature 145
retracted tongue root (component) 242–4
'reversed dependency' 97, 132–4, 263–5
rhyme 82, 97–8, 100, 104, 108, 198,
 292–5; complex 102–3, 109–10
rhythm 105–6, 122, 124–5
root 91
Rotokas 170
rounding: *see* labialisation
r-types 159–62, 164, 171

Sanskrit 129
sC cluster 76–8, 98–9, 133, 181, 263–5
scales 19–28, 30, 126–7, 143–5, 146, 155–
 8, 171–82, 207–8, 209–12, 225–8, 282,
 295
Scots 62, 134, 162, 171, 172; breaking
 in 159–61; lengthening and
 vocalisation in 161
Scottish vowel length rule: *see* Aitken's
 law
secondary articulation 163, 246–8
secondary phonation 163–4, 166

segment 36, 141, 149–50, 255–79, 283; 'floating' 278; segment-internal sequence 13, 36, 106, 131–6
Sentani 170
sequence: *see* linearity, segment
sibilant 155, 164–6
'silent stress' 72, 120, 123
simplicity metric 8, 20–1
Sindhi 201
skeleton 260
slack vs. stiff vocal cords 146, 188
sonorance scale 172 (*see also* sonority hierarchy)
sonorant 158, 163
sonorant consonant 152–3, 158, 173; voiceless 185, 191–3, 195, 198
sonorisation 175, 176
sonority 27–8, 59–60, 98, 107–9, 111, 282; component 207–18, 273; hierarchy 97–100, 143–5, 171–82; infringement of 98–100, 133, 165
'source' feature 151
Spanish 231–2; nasal assimilation in 80
SPE (= Chomsky & Halle 1968) 11–23, 25–6, 35, 37, 41–3, 46–50, 72–4, 77, 122, 144, 145, 150, 188, 201, 212–13, 229–30, 233–4, 235–6, 244, 246, 249, 255–6, 284
spirantisation 176
state of glottis 146–8, 185–91, 194 (*see also* glottal opening, glottal stop, etc., voice)
stop: nasalised 131–3; voiced 154–5; voiceless 130, 190–1, 193–4; vs. continuant 155
strength: *see* sonority; of articulatory 'place' 229, 231–3; of component: *see* preponderance
strengthening 172, 176
stress 96–7, 277–8 (*see also* foot); and syllabification 72–8 (*see also* word structure/placement of stress in English)
stressedness: *see* ictus, stress
stress-neutral affixes 62, 64
stress-reversal 105, 280
stress-timed: *see* isochrony
'strident' 164
string 85, 87; simple structured 89
structural analogy 282–8
sub-foot 83–4, 102–3
sub-gesture 146–50; and dependency 186, 188–95
subjunction vs. adjunction 92–6, 109; labelled and unlabelled 95, 126, 282, 284–8
subordination in syntax: *see* syntactic subordination

sub-segment 132
sub-string 85, 91
superfoot 83–4, 102–3, 114, 117–19, 121
suprasegmental structure 50–84, 96–125, 274; as projective 106–7, 123, 130, 274, 279; extralexical: *see* utterance structure; intralexical: *see* word structure
Swedish 179
syllabicity 42–5, 80–2, 96–100, 284; shift 217–18
syllabification 50–3, 58–78, 122–4, 196–7; as non-contrastive 43–5, 68–9; maximalist vs. minimalist 75–8; pre-stress 69
syllable 50–8, 104; maximalisation under stress 68; quantity 71; strength 84, 134–6; weak 72–4, 112–16
syllable structure 107–10, 144, 172; and markedness 17, 49; and sonority 177–82; as interpretative 53, 97–100, 129–30
syntactic dependency 45, 85–96; antisymmetric vs. non-symmetric: *see* linearity/partial vs. total order; trees 90–6
syntactic subordination 88–9

Tagalog 190
tangling 91, 97
Temne 239, 241
tempo 70–1, 79, 106, 122–4, 172
tense 20–7, 32–4, 52, 72, 74, 78; and ambisyllabicity 67; of consonants 66
Thai 147–8
tier 259–63, 265
Tiv 263
tone 35–6, 122–3, 195, 270–3; harmony 282
tone group 79–80, 81–2, 103–4; formation (word structure) 116–20: and cyclicity 121–2; formation (utterance) 122–5
'tone language' 122–3
tonic 81–2, 96–7, 123–5 (*see also* tone group formation)
tonicity: *see* tonic
tonological gesture 150, 270–3, 275, 282
tree from a point 91
'tune–text-association' 80, 122

umlaut: *see* vowel mutation
'underspecification' 192
utterance structure 70–2, 104–6, 122–5, 278, 279–80, 282
uvularisation 248

velar nasal in English   51–3, 61–3, 65–6
velaric (suction), velaricness: *see* airstream
   mechanism, click
velarisation   246–7
vertex   90, 128, 282
vocal cord vibration: *see* voice
vocalisation   176–7
voice   143, 146–8, 154–6, 157–8, 173, 185,
   186, 187, 189–90, 192; breathy   146,
   187, 190, 195; creaky   187, 190, 195;
   'lax' vs. 'tense'   185, 187, 190
voicing   176, 183–4
vowel   151–2, 156, 158; back
   unrounded   220–4, 228; 'basic
   types'   224–8; central   218–20, 228;
   components   28–34, 206–28;
   diphthong   102, 106: short
   diphthong   134–6; front rounded   30,
   214, 228; harmony   244–5, 259, 276–8,
   282; height   20–6, 30–4, 207–8, 209–12,
   225–8, 282, 295; long   102–3, 129, 134,
   262–3, 266–8; mutation   17–18, 215–18;
   peripheral   228; 'quantal'   167, 210–12;
   reduction   78; 'strengthening'   172

vowel shift (English)   16, 20–6, 32–4, 217;
   historical   25–6, 33, 129
VP and word order   92–5

'weak cluster'/weak syllabic: *see* syllable
weakening: *see* lenition
weakening of stops in English   79
Welsh   161–2, 164
Western Desert   170
word   52, 62, 69–70
'word-and-paradigm': *see* morphological
   structure
word structure (non-phonological)   286–8
word structure (phonological)   107–22,
   274–8, 282, 285; placement of stress in
   English   72–8, 110–16; -utterance
   association   122–5, 279; vs. utterance
   structure   104–6, 279–80

X-bar notation (X̄)   86–7, 101

Yidiɲ   170